SCHAUM'S
outlines

German
Grammar

Fourth Edition

Elke Gschossmann-Hendershot

Former Instructor
Rutgers University

Lois M. Feuerle

Former Coordinator of Court Interpreting Services
New York Unified Court System

Schaum's Outline Series

New York Chicago San Francisco
Lisbon London Madrid Mexico City
Milan New Dehli San Juan
Seoul Singapore Sydney Toronto

ELKE GSCHOSSMANN-HENDERSHOT, a native of Germany, received her formal schooling in Regensburg, Germany, and completed her postgraduate work at Rutgers University, New Jersey. She has teaching experience at various levels, from elementary school through college. She designed programs for the Army Language School and served as supervisor for Deutsche Sprachschule. Her most recent teaching assignment was at Rutgers University, New Jersey.

LOIS M. FEUERLE received her B.A. in German from the University of Vermont, her J.D. from the New York University School of Law, and her doctorate in Germanic Languages and Literatures from the University of Kansas. Dr. Feuerle also spent two years at the Christian-Albrechts-Universität in Kiel, Germany, in addition to her studies in Vienna and Salzburg, Austria. She was later Lektorin für Amerikanistik at the Pädagogische Hochschule in Kiel. She has taught German to students of all ages in a variety of contexts, including the University of Kansas Intensive Language Institute in Holzkirchen, Germany, Marshall University, the German Language School of Morris Plains, and Montclair State University. She was later Adjunct Assistant Professor of German and Translation in the Department of Foreign Languages at the New York University School of Continuing Education, where she also administered the Translation Studies Program. She subsequently served as the Coordinator of Court Interpreting Services for the New York State Unified Court System, Office of Court Administration, and then as Coordinator of Court Interpreter Certification, Testing and Training for the Oregon Judicial Department. She has translated numerous books, law review articles, and a wide variety of other legal materials and non-legal materials from German into English. She currently serves on the boards of directors of the National Association of Judiciary Interpreters and Translators (NAJIT) and of the American Translators Association (ATA). She is also the coauthor of the three-book series *Communicating in German: Novice/Intermediate/Advanced* and of the second and third editions of *Schaum's Outline of German Vocabulary*.

Schaum's Outline of
GERMAN GRAMMAR

Copyright © 2010, 1997, 1983, 1975 by The McGraw-Hill Companies, Inc. All rights reserved. Printed in the United States of America. Except as permitted under the Copyright Act of 1976, no part of this publication may be reproduced or distributed in any form or by any means, or stored in a data base or retrieval system, without the prior written permission of the publisher.

4 5 6 7 8 9 0 CUS CUS 0 1 4 3 2

ISBN 978-0-07-161567-9
MHID 0-07-161567-9

Sponsoring Editor: Anya Kozorez
Production Supervisor: Tama L. Harris
Editing Supervisor: Maureen B. Dennehy
Project Supervision: Village Bookworks, Inc.

Library of Congress Cataloging-in-Publication Data

Gschossmann-Hendershot, Elke.
    Schaum's outline of German grammar / Elke Gschossmann-Hendershot,
Lois M. Feuerle. — 4th ed.
        p. cm. — (Schaum's outline series)
    ISBN-13: 978-0-07-161567-9
    ISBN-10: 0-07-161567-9
    1. German language—Grammar—Outlines, syllabi, etc.   I. Feuerle, Lois M.
II. Title. III. Title: German grammar.
    PF3118.G8   2009
    438.2′421—dc22   2009025931

Preface to the Fourth Edition

Much has happened in the German-speaking world in the dozen years since the third edition of *Schaum's Outline of German Grammar* was published in 1997. Although tremors are felt from time to time throughout the world's economies, the Federal Republic of Germany remains a strong economic force. Although memories of the former German Democratic Republic are fading, German continues to be a language of importance in Eastern Europe. Germany has adopted the Euro (EUR) and relinquished its old national currency, the German Mark (DM), and Austria has likewise given up its national currency, the Austrian Schilling (ÖS), in favor of the Euro, giving the so-called Euro Zone a total of 15 participating members as of 2008. However, Switzerland and Liechtenstein, who are not members of the European Union, remain loyal to the Swiss Franc (SFR) as their common currency. But for the student of language, the most significant event of the last decade or so is the introduction of the controversial German Orthographic Reform—*die deutsche Rechtschreibreform*.

On July 1, 1996, the representatives of the four German-speaking countries, Germany, Austria, Switzerland, and Liechtenstein, signed an international agreement to introduce the new spelling by August 1, 1998. After a transition period marked by considerable debate that resulted in minor revisions, the German Orthographic Reform went into effect on August 1, 2006.

The German Orthographic Reform addresses several important issues, the most significant of which is the endeavor to make German orthography reflect the sounds of spoken German more closely. Other issues are capitalization, hyphenation, writing certain words separately or together, and punctuation. It should be reassuring to the student that some authorities estimate that about 90% of the changes mandated by the reform involve the letters **ss** and **ß**. Of course, one will inevitably encounter texts written in accordance with the old rules, since all books, publications, and media published prior to the Orthographic Reform were composed under the old rules.

Although the new spelling rules must be observed in German schools, a number of authors, publishers, and newspapers have chosen to continue to observe some version of the old rules. A simple tip-off as to whether a publication follows the old or the new rules is to find the German word for "that" introducing a subordinate clause. If the German word ends in **ss**, the publication is following the new spelling rules, and if the word is spelled with **ß**, it is adhering to the old rules: **dass** (new) vs. **daß** (old).

Schaum's Outline of German Grammar follows the new rules. For a reference work that presents and illustrates the new rules, consult *Duden, Die Deutsche Rechtschreibung* (ed. 24, vol. 1, Dudenverlag, 2006). This work provides a comprehensive list of 130,000 entries, showing the preferred and acceptable spellings and, importantly, highlighting the differences between the old and the new.

In all other respects, the goal of this new edition of *Schaum's Outline of German Grammar* is the same as previous editions, that is, to be a study aid and reference tool to assist students in the broadest sense of the word to learn, improve, and fine-tune their German.

Lois M. Feuerle

Contents

CHAPTER 1

The Sounds of German: A Key to German Pronunciation

Since German pronunciation is to a large extent phonetic and regular, an understanding of the basic sounds and stress patterns of German will enable the student to pronounce almost all words easily and correctly.

The German Alphabet

The German alphabet has the 26 standard letters found in the English alphabet plus four letters that are specific to German.

Alphabet

LETTER	GERMAN NAME	LETTER	GERMAN NAME	
a	ah	p	peh	
b	beh	q	kuh	
c	tseh	r	err	
d	deh	s	ess	
e	eh	t	teh	
f	eff	u	uh	
g	geh	v	fau	
h	hah	w	veh	
i	ih	x	iks	
j	yot	y	üppsilon	
k	kah	z	tsett	
l	ell	ä	äh	(a-umlaut)
m	emm	ö	öh	(o-umlaut)
n	enn	ü	üh	(u-umlaut)
o	oh	ß	ess-tsett	(scharfes ess)

It is important to learn to pronounce the *German names* of the letters of the alphabet so that you will be able to spell names, addresses, and other essential information when needed during stays in German-speaking countries and over the telephone.

Avoiding Misunderstandings

Sometimes a bad connection makes it particularly difficult to understand the spelling of a word over the telephone. For this reason, the Federal Post Office in Germany has issued an alphabet of code words that make it perfectly clear what letter is intended. The post office spelling chart is as follows.

A	Anton	J	Julius	Sch	Schule
Ä	Ärger	K	Kaufmann	T	Theodor
B	Berta	L	Ludwig	U	Ulrich
C	Cäsar	M	Martha	Ü	Übermut
Ch	Charlotte	N	Nordpol	V	Viktor
D	Dora	O	Otto	W	Wilhelm
E	Emil	Ö	Ökonom	X	Xantippe
F	Friedrich	P	Paula	Y	Ypsilon
G	Gustav	Q	Quelle	Z	Zacharias
H	Heinrich	R	Richard		
I	Ida	S	Samuel		

Remember, There Are Differences

Even though both English and German employ the same basic alphabet, there are, of course, significant differences in the pronunciation of the individual German and English sounds represented by the standard letters. The most obvious of these differences will be noted in the pronunciation key below.

Please bear in mind, however, that the pronunciations given below are only approximations to aid the English-speaking reader. *They are not exact equivalents.* To perfect pronunciation, it is essential to avail oneself of every possible opportunity to hear and use spoken German, e.g., through CDs, DVDs, radio, television, movies, conversations with native speakers, and visits to German-speaking countries.

It might be helpful to remember that precisely those sounds that characterize a German accent in English are the sounds that will require the most work in order for you to overcome *your foreign accent* in German. It might be helpful to imitate those sounds as you practice your German pronunciation.

The Vowels

Vowels in German are either long or short. In our pronunciation key, long vowels are followed by a colon, e.g., [a:], [e:], [i:], [o:], [u:]; short vowels stand alone, e.g., [a], [e], [i], [o], [u]. Note that identical sounds can sometimes be represented by different letters or combinations of letters (i.e., different spellings).

Note that certain sounds are represented orthographically by the umlauts [ä], [ö], [ü]. Both the long and the short umlauts are included in the vowel chart that follows.

VOWEL SOUND	EXAMPLES	APPROXIMATE ENGLISH SOUND
[a]	wann, kalt, rasch, ab	*w**a**nder*
[a:]	ja, Haar, Jahr, kam, sagen	*f**a**ther*
[e]	Bett, Geld, Fenster, sechs, es	*m**e**n*
[e:]	See, Weh, Mehl, dem, Regen	*m**a**y*
[i]	immer, ist, ich, nicht, mit	*in*
[i:]	ihm, mir, wider, wie, Liebe, antik, Musik	*b**ee**t*
[o]	offen, oft, morgen, Ochs	*often*

VOWEL SOUND	EXAMPLES	APPROXIMATE ENGLISH SOUND
[o:]	Boot, ohne, Note, oben, wo	*so*
[u]	Mutter, null, und, Sucht	*foot*
[u:]	Kuh, Stuhl, gut, Fuß, Juni	*moot*
[ä]	Männer, Hände, älter	*men*
[ä:]	Fähre, spät, Käse, Diät	*may*
[ö]	Hölle, Löffel, völlig, können	No close equivalent in English. However, one can approximate this sound by pronouncing the word *further,* but without the first *r*.
[ö:]	schön, böse, Möbel, Höhle, Söhne	No close equivalent in English. To approximate this sound, start to pronounce the [ö], but draw it out longer.
[ü]	müssen, küssen, hübsch, Idylle, Hütte, fünf	No close equivalent in English. To approximate this sound, try to pronounce the [i], but with rounded lips. If you try to say the word **Kissen** with rounded lips, you will come close to the [ü] sound in **küssen**.
[ü:]	Tür, Hüte, Bühne, kühl, Physiker, Lyrik	No close equivalent in English. To approximate this sound, try to pronounce the [i:], but with rounded lips. If you try to pronounce the word **Biene** with your lips rounded, you will come close to the pronunciation of the [ü:] in **Bühne**.

Long Vowels Versus Short Vowels

There are a number of basic rules that help the student in determining whether a vowel is to be pronounced long or short.

(1) A double vowel is *long*.

Haar, Boot, Beet

(2) A vowel followed by a silent **h** (the so-called **Dehnungs-hah**, or *stretching H*) is *long*.

Jahr, ihm, Stuhl, Stühle

(3) A vowel followed by a single consonant is *usually long*. See also note (7).

gut, dem, wen, Mode

(4) An **i** followed by an **e** (that is, **ie**) is *long*.

Liebe, wieder, sieben, die

(5) A vowel followed by a double consonant is *short*.

Bett, kommen, können, hell

(6) A vowel followed by two or more consonants, including the combinations **ch** and **sch**, is usually *short*.

ich, typisch, sicher, Fenster, Sack

(7) A vowel in one-syllable prepositions and other common one-syllable words ending in a single consonant are often *short*.

mit, im, um, es

(8) An **e** not in combination with another vowel, standing at the end of a word, is *short*.

Hase, gebe, bitte, Hilfe

The Diphthongs

A diphthong is a combination of two vowel sounds pronounced with a glide. There are three common diphthongs in German. Note that two of these diphthongs can be spelled in several different ways.

DIPHTHONG	EXAMPLES	APPROXIMATE ENGLISH SOUND
[au]	<u>au</u>f, <u>au</u>s, H<u>au</u>s, Fr<u>au</u>, br<u>au</u>chen	*house*
[ei]	<u>ei</u>n, m<u>ei</u>n, L<u>ei</u>d, M<u>ai</u>, K<u>ai</u>ser, B<u>ay</u>ern, M<u>ey</u>er	*site*
[eu]	F<u>eu</u>er, Fr<u>äu</u>lein, h<u>eu</u>te, H<u>äu</u>ser	*noise*

NOTE: In German, diphthongs are not drawn out as they are in English. They are pronounced short and clipped.

NOTE: The combination **ie** is not a diphthong, but rather a spelling variant of the [i:] sound.

     die, Sie, Lied, Knie, Brief, wieder, Spiegel

See the examples under [i:] above.

The Consonants

Similarities

Many of the German consonants are pronounced more or less as they are in English. Included in this group are **f, h, k, m, n, p, t, x**.

CONSONANT	EXAMPLES
f	**Freitag, Fisch, Neffe, Hanf**
h	**Haus, haben, hastig, gehoben**
k	**kaufen, küssen, Küken, Park**
m	**Montag, immer, dem**
n	**nicht, Biene, bin**
p	**Problem, Mappe, Lampe, schlapp**
t	**Tag, Täter, tat**
x	**Taxi, Axt, boxen**

The consonants **b, d, g** are also pronounced more or less as they are in English when they are at the beginning of a word or a syllable. However, when **b, d, g** appear at the end of a word or syllable, or before **t** or **st**, they are pronounced as **p, t, k**.

	CONSONANTS b, d, g, INITIAL OR MEDIAL POSITION	PRONOUNCED AS p, t, k, FINAL POSITION OR BEFORE t OR st
b	**Bett, Graben, beben**	**Grab, lieb, liebt, liebst, Obst**
d	**Danke, Dorf, wieder, Fremde**	**Bad, fremd, abends, Schmidt**
g	**Tage, lügen, gehen, gegen**	**log, Tag, mag, liegt, liegst**

NOTE: When **g** appears in the suffix **-ig** at the end of a word, the suffix is pronounced like **-ich**.

     hastig, billig, durstig, fertig, zwanzig, neunzig

Differences

The *ich* sound and the *ach* sound

The consonant cluster **ch** can represent two closely related, but different, sounds that are present in German but not in standard English. Both sounds are produced with the tongue and mouth in more or less the same position as for the **k** sound. However, the stream of breath is not cut off as when pronouncing a **k**; rather, it is forced through the narrow opening between the tongue and the roof of the mouth.

Whether the **ch** becomes an **ich** sound or an **ach** sound is determined by the immediately preceding vowel, that is, by the position of the mouth that is required to produce these vowel sounds.

When **ch** follows the vowels **a, o, u** or the diphthong **au**, it is pronounced toward the back of the throat and is very similar to the **ch** in the Scottish word *Loch*.

> **ach, acht, Nacht, doch, Woche, Tochter, Buch, Tuch, Kuchen, besuchen, Frucht, auch, rauchen, gebraucht**

In other environments, that is, after the vowels **e, i, ä, ö, ü**, as well as after the diphthongs **ei (ai, ay, ey)** and **eu (äu)** and the consonants **l, n, r**, the stream of air is forced through a flatter but wider opening between the tongue and the roof of the mouth. The resulting **ich** sound is pronounced more toward the front of the mouth.

> **schlecht, ich, Sicht, lächeln, möchte, Bücher, schleichen, Eiche, euch, räuchern, welcher, München, Kirche, Molch, Männchen**

Other Differences

Other consonants that are pronounced differently in English and German include the letters **l, r, j, w, z, s, v, q, c**.

The Letters [l] and [r]

Although these letters exist in both the English and the German alphabets, they are pronounced very differently in the two languages.

The English **l** is a dark sound that is pronounced rather far back in the mouth. By contrast, the German **l** is pronounced toward the front of the mouth with the tongue flatter and touching the back of the front teeth. This produces a much lighter **l** sound.

Unlike English, German uses either the uvular **r** (the uvula is the small flap of skin hanging from the soft palate at the back of the mouth) or the tongue-trilled **r**. Of the two, the uvular **r**, which is probably more difficult for Americans to pronounce, is the more commonly used **r** in German.

Good listening skills and practice are required to master these sounds.

The Letters [j], [w], and [z]

	GERMAN EXAMPLES	ENGLISH EQUIVALENT
j	**ja, Jahr, Jacke, Juli, Tanja**	*yes*
w	**wild, Winter, Woche, wo**	*vest*
z	**Zimmer, duzen, schwarz, Arzt, Platz**	*cats*

The Letter [s], Alone and in Combination

The pronunciation of the letter **s** depends on its position in the word. If it is in initial position preceding a vowel or stands between two vowels, it is pronounced like an English **z**. In other positions, it is usually pronounced as a soft **s**.

The Letter [s] Alone

	GERMAN EXAMPLES	ENGLISH EQUIVALENT
Initial **s**	**Salz, sehr, Seife, Suppe, sagen, sicher, süß**	*zoo*
s between vowels	**lesen, Käse, Mäuse, Häuser, Eisen**	*zoo*
Final **s**	**Hals, Puls, das, Eis, Gans, Gas, mittags**	*bus*

NOTE: Both **ss** and **ß** are pronounced with a soft **s**, as in English. After the German Orthographic Reform, it continues to be a spelling convention that the **ß** is used after long vowels (**Straße, groß, Fuß**) and diphthongs (**Strauß, äußerst, weiß**) and that **ss** is used after short vowels (**Messer, Tasse, Wasser, küssen**). However, to make German spelling rules more consistent, the Orthographic Reform has *abolished* the old rules requiring the use of **ß** before the letter **t** and at the end of words regardless of the length of the preceding vowel, so that *faßte, ißt, mußt* are now written **fasste, isst, musst**, and *Schloß, Schluß, muß* are now written **Schloss, Schluss, muss**, because the immediately preceding vowels are short. Of course, you should be prepared to encounter these older forms in texts printed prior to the Orthographic Reform and even some printed afterward.

NOTE: The **ß** spelling convention is not followed in Swiss German, which uses **ss** instead.

GERMANY	SWITZERLAND
die Straße	die Strasse
weiß	weiss
der Gruß	der Gruss

Consonant Clusters with [s]

The letter **s** also occurs in combination with other letters.

s COMBINATION	GERMAN EXAMPLES	ENGLISH EQUIVALENT
sch	**schön, wischen, wünschen, Tisch, rasch**	*shine*
sp	**spät, Spiel, sprechen, spazieren, Sprache**	No equivalent—sounds like Yiddish *shpiel*
st	**Stein, Stadt, still, entstehen, studieren**	No equivalent—sounds like Yiddish *shtetl*

The Letter [v]

The letter **v** is normally pronounced like an English **f** in German. In words of foreign origin, however, it is often pronounced as a **v**, unless it is at the end of the word.

	GERMAN EXAMPLES	ENGLISH EQUIVALENT
In German words	**Vater, Vetter, von, viel**	*father*
In foreign words	**Vase, Revolution, Vanille**	*vase*
In final position	**brav, fiktiv, negativ**	*relief*

The Letter [q]

In German as in English, the letter **q** is always followed by **u**. In German, however, this combination is pronounced as if it were written **kv**, like the Yiddish word *kvetch*.

	GERMAN EXAMPLES	ENGLISH EQUIVALENT
In German words	**Qualität, quer, Quartett**	*kvetch*

The Letter [c]

As noted above, the letter **c** in German usually appears in combination with the letter **h** to form the **ich** and **ach** sounds. However, the letter **c** also appears in initial position in certain words of foreign origin used in German.

An initial [**c**] is pronounced as a **ts** if it precedes **e**, **i**, or **ä**. In other cases, it is usually pronounced as a **k**.

	GERMAN EXAMPLES	ENGLISH EQUIVALENT
Before [ä], [e], [i]	Cäsar, Celsius, circa	*cats*
In other environments	Camping, Computer, Courage	*camping*

When the consonant cluster **ch** appears at the beginning of a word of foreign origin, it is pronounced in one of several ways.

	GERMAN EXAMPLES	ENGLISH EQUIVALENT
Consonant cluster **ch** in initial position	Christ, christlich, Chor, Charakter, Chaos	*kitten*
	Champignon, charmant, Chance, Chef, Chauvi	*shine*
	Chemie, chinesisch, Chirurg	No equivalent—a very heavily aspirated version of the **h** in *Hugh*
	Check, checken, Chip	*chip*

Other Consonant Clusters

CONSONANT CLUSTER	GERMAN EXAMPLES	ENGLISH EQUIVALENT
gn	Gnade, Gnom	There is a light **g** sound pronounced just before the **n**.
kn	Knie, knacken, Knochen	There is a light **k** sound pronounced just before the **n**.
ng	singen, Finger, sang, länger, anfangen, jünger	*singer* (not *finger*)
pf	Pfanne, Pfeffer, Pfeife, Pfennig, Pfund, impfen, dumpf	There is a light **p** sound pronounced just before the **f**.
ph	Philosophie, Physiker, Phantasie, Phrase	The **f** sound in *philosophy*
ps	Pseudonym, psychologisch, psychotisch	There is a light **p** sound pronounced just before the **s**.
th	Thomas, Theater, Theologie, Thema, Thron	The **h** is silent, pronounced like English *Thomas.*
tsch	Deutsch, klatschen	*itch*
zw	zwingen, Zwang	*cats* + *v*

The Glottal Stop

The glottal stop is a brief closure of the vocal cords that is used to keep words and syllables from running together. It is used more frequently in German, a language in which words and syllables are pronounced clearly and distinctly, than in English, where there is more of a tendency to link sounds and syllables when they are spoken.

Observe the differences in pronunciation in the following phrases.

a nice house   *an ice house*

You will note that there is a distinct break or glottal stop before the word *ice* in the second phrase. In German, a glottal stop occurs before all words and syllables that begin with a vowel.

jeden *A*bend
Sie kam *u*m *e*lf *U*hr.
Er hat seine *A*rbeit be*e*ndet.
Die Professorin hat meine Frage be*a*ntwortet.

Stress

As a general rule, the stress is on the first syllable in native German words, unless the first syllable is an unstressed prefix, e.g., an inseparable prefix.

In the case of words that have been borrowed from other languages, stress patterns are much less predictable. Often, they follow the rules of the language from which the word has been borrowed.

There are, however, certain suffixes that have predictable stress patterns.

SUFFIX	GERMAN EXAMPLES	STRESS
-tät	**Rarität, Majestät, Aktivität, Elektrizität, Sentimentalität, Universität**	Last syllable
-ik	**Kritik, Musik, Mathematik, Mosaik, Politik, Republik**	Last syllable
-ie	**Chemie, Poesie, Phantasie, Theorie**	Last syllable
-erei	**Malerei, Bücherei, Sklaverei, Zauberei, Konditorei**	Last syllable
-eum	**Museum, Mausoleum, Kolosseum**	Next to last syllable
-ieren	**datieren, servieren, studieren, argumentieren, demokratisieren**	Next to last syllable

Syllabification

The official overarching principle for syllabification after the Orthographic Reform is that when it is necessary to separate multisyllabic words, they should be broken according to the syllables that naturally result when these words are read aloud slowly. Although this might be sound advice for native speakers, it might prove to be less useful for those just learning to speak German.

Fortunately, syllabification in German is relatively simple and highly predictable, and many of the old rules remain unchanged by the Orthographic Reform.

One major exception to the commonsense rule that words are to be broken as they are normally pronounced, is that single vowels standing either at the beginning or at the end of a word are never separated from the remainder of the word, e.g., **Abend**, **Aue**.

Another helpful rule of thumb is that compound words and words with identifiable prefixes and suffixes are broken according to their recognizable components.

Single Consonants and Double Consonants

Words are divided *before single consonants*

     geben   **ge-ben**
     liegen   **lie-gen**
     spazieren   **spa-zie-ren**

and *between double consonants.*

hoffen	hof-fen
Messer	Mes-ser
auffallen	auf-fal-len
donnern	don-nern

Consonant Clusters and Groups of Consonants

Consonant clusters **ch**, **sch**, **ph**, **ß**, as well as **z**, **x**, are regarded as single consonants for purposes of syllabification.

blechen	ble-chen
Mädchen	Mäd-chen
wischen	wi-schen
wünschen	wün-schen
Philosophen	Phi-lo-so-phen
außer	au-ßer
Hexe	He-xe
kreuzen	kreu-zen

In the case of groups of consonants, the last one in the series usually starts a new syllable.

Punkte	Punk-te
Pünktchen	Pünkt-chen (Remember, **ch** is treated as one consonant.)
Schlendrian	Schlend-ri-an
Flüchtling	Flücht-ling

NOTE: Each syllable must contain a vowel or diphthong. However, as mentioned above, words are never divided so that a single vowel stands alone—even when this vowel is pronounced separately. Thus, although the word **Abend** is spoken as two syllables, it would never be divided into two syllables to accommodate a syllable break at the end of a line.

When dividing compound words into syllables, there is always a syllable break between the components of the compound in addition to the syllable breaks that normally occur within each component.

Hausfrau	Haus-frau
Eisenbahn	Ei-sen-bahn
Donnerstag	Don-ners-tag
Mittagessen	Mit-tag-es-sen
Lichtschalter	Licht-schal-ter
Radiergummi	Ra-dier-gum-mi

Under the new rules, the combination **ck** is regarded as a single sound and is treated accordingly.

lecken	le-cken
Becken	Be-cken
anpacken	an-pa-cken
schicken	schi-cken
locken	lo-cken
verschlucken	ver-schlu-cken
frühstücken	früh-stü-cken

The old rule that **st** is never separated no longer applies.

erste	**ers-te**
beste	**bes-te**
hastig	**has-tig**
Liste	**Lis-te**
Liebste	**Liebs-te**

Review

1. Spell your full name using the letters of the German alphabet. If necessary, refer to the chart on page 1.

_____

_____

2. Now spell the name of the town and the state where you live.

_LOUISVILLE   KENTUCKY_____

3. Spell your full name again, this time using the alphabet of code words developed by the German Post Office that appears on page 2.

_____

_____

_____

4. Study the list of words below, and in the order in which they appear, write each word that contains the short [a] sound. If necessary, review the vowel chart on pages 2–3.

Aal, wann, hastig, Vater, Wahnsinn, rasch, Stadt, Städte, Phase, Hand, lang, Bank, Ball, Haar, Hase, Gedanke, Handtasche

1.	WANN	6.	LANG
2.	HASTIG	7.	BANK
3.	RASCH	8.	BALL
4.	STADT	9.	GEDANKE
5.	HAND	10.	HANDTASCHE

5. Study the list of words below, and in the order in which they appear, write each word that contains the long [e:] sound. If necessary, review the vowel chart on pages 2–3.

beten, bitten, Becken, Betten, Kopfweh, Vorlesung, dem, Regenwasser, fehlen, Eltern, Gebrauchtwagen, Mehlwurm, Seemann, mehr, Beet

1.	BETEN	6.	FEHLEN
2.	KOPFWEH	7.	MEHLWURM
3.	VORLESUNG	8.	SEEMANN
4.	DEM	9.	MEHR
5.	REGENWASSER	10.	BEET

6. Study the list of words below, and in the order in which they appear, write each word that contains the long [iː] sound. If necessary, review the vowel chart on pages 2–3.

Dienstag, immer, mir, Tischler, Lieder, ihm, wir, binden, leider, ihnen, Licht, Bier, Sonnenbrille, Briefträger, einmal, hier, antik

1. DIENSTAG DIENSTAG
2. MIR MIR
3. LIEDER LIEDER
4. IHM IHM
5. WIR WIR
6. IHNEN IHNEN
7. BIER BIER
8. BRIEFTRÄGER BRIEFTRÄGER
9. HIER HIER
10. ANTIK ANTIK

7. Study the list of words below, and in the order in which they appear, write each word that contains the short [o] sound. If necessary, review the vowel chart on pages 2–3.

Boot, Spott, schon, morgen, Segelsport, offen, sorgfältig, Bohne, Löffel, Norden, Ofen, Oktett, Stock, Topf, tot, Wochentag, Wohnung

1. SPOTT SPOTT
2. MORGEN MORGEN
3. SEGELSPORT SEGELSPORT
4. OFFEN OFFEN
5. SORGFÄLTIG SORGFÄLTIG
6. NORDEN NORDEN
7. OKTETT OKTETT
8. STOCK STOCK
9. TOPF TOPF
10. WOCHENTAG WOCHENTAG

8. Study the list of words below, and in the order in which they appear, write each word that contains the long [uː] sound. If necessary, review the vowel chart on pages 2–3.

Mutter, kühler, Fuß, Frühjahr, Strumpf, Stuhl, Pullover, lustig, Kuh, gut, Juli, Wurst, Natur, Bluse, Anzug, Mund, Butter, Ruhm, trug

1. FUß FUß
2. STUHL STUHL
3. KUH KUH
4. GUT GUT
5. JULI JULI
6. NATUR NATUR
7. BLUSE BLUSE
8. ANZUG ANZUG
9. RUHM RUHM
10. TRUG TRUG

9. Study the list of words below, and in the order in which they appear, write each word that contains the short [ä] sound. If necessary, review the vowel chart on pages 2–3.

Käse, älter, Eltern, Wände, Haar, Unterwäsche, ändern, anderes, Bett, fern, gefährlich, kalt, sauer, spät, kälter, beschäftigen, Ärzte

1. ÄLTER ÄLTER
2. ELTERN ELTERN
3. WÄNDE WÄNDE
4. UNTERWÄSCHE UNTERWÄSCHE
5. ÄNDERN ÄNDERN
6. BETT BETT
7. FERN FERN
8. KÄLTER KÄLTER
9. BESCHÄFTIGEN BESCHÄFTIGEN
10. ÄRZTE ÄRZTE

10. Study the list of words below, and in the order in which they appear, write each word that contains the long [ö:] sound. If necessary, review the vowel chart on pages 2–3.

blöd, Hölle, Möbel, öffnen, Löwe, Röcke, aushöhlen, Wölfe, öd, offen, völlig, Böhmen, Fön, Föhn, Gesöff, Löcher, Löffel, Öl, Vermögen

1. BLÖD   BLÖB
2. MÖBEL   MÖBEL
3. LÖWE   LÖWE
4. AUSHÖHLEN   AUSHÖHLEN
5. ÖD   ÖD
6. BÖHMEN   BÖHMEN
7. FÖN   FÖN
8. FÖHN   FÖHN
9. ÖL   ÖL
10. VERMÖGEN   VERMÖGEN

11. Study the list of words below, and in the order in which they appear, write each word that contains the short [ü] sound. If necessary, review the vowel chart on pages 2–3.

früh, Müller, müssen, Hüte, müde, Mütter, benützen, übel, Früchte, schüchtern, Züge, beglücken, prüfen, Lücke, Müll, Idyll

1. MÜLLER   MÜLLER
2. MÜSSEN   MÜSSEN
3. MÜTTER   MÜTTER
4. BENÜTZEN   BENÜTZEN
5. FRÜCHTE   FRÜCHTE
6. SCHÜCHTERN   SCHÜCHTERN
7. LÜCKE   LÜCKE
8. MÜLL   MÜLL
9. BEGLÜCKEN   BEGLÜCKEN
10. IDYLL   IDYLL

12. Study the list of words below, and in the order in which they appear, write each word that contains the [ich] sound. If necessary, review the material on the **ich** and **ach** sounds on page 5.

Nacht, sich, nichts, rauchen, schlecht, besichtigen, wöchentlich, Tochter, Nichte, leichter, Frucht, Bauch, noch, Becher, Löcher, Bäuche, Buch

1. SICH   SICH
2. NICHTS   NICHTS
3. SCHLECHT   SCHLECHT
4. BESICHTIGEN   BESICHTIGEN
5. WÖCHENTLICH   WÖCHENTLICH
6. NICHTE   NICHTE
7. LEICHTER   LEICHTER
8. BECHER   BECHER
9. LÖCHER   LÖCHER
10. BÄUCHE   BÄUCHE

13. Study the list of words below, and in the order in which they appear, write each word that contains an [s] that is pronounced like an English **z** sound. If necessary, review the material on the letter **s** on page 6.

heißen, messen, gewesen, Käsekuchen, Eiskaffee, Spaß, Nase, still, also, frischer, als, ansehen, Besuch, Pils, Eisen, sechzehn, so, Stress, Süden, das

1. GEWESEN   GEWESEN
2. KÄSEKUCHEN   KÄSEKUCHEN
3. NASE   NASE
4. ALSO   ALSO
5. ANSEHEN   ANSEHEN
6. BESUCH   BESUCH
7. EISEN   EISEN
8. SECHZEHN   SECHZEHN
9. SO   SO
10. SÜDEN   SÜDEN

14. Study the list of words below, and in the order in which they appear, write each word, underlining the syllable that bears the primary stress. If necessary, review the material on stress on page 8.

Abend, Leute, Musik, sagen, Bäckerei, Phantasie, Suppe, Universität, beenden, studieren

1. _ABEND_ ABEND
2. _LEUTE_ LEUTE
3. _MUSIK_ MUSIK
4. _SAGEN_ SAGEN
5. _BÄCKEREI_ BÄCKEREI

6. _PHANTASIE_ PHANTASIE
7. _SUPPE_ SUPPE
8. _UNIVERSITÄT_ UNIVERSITAT
9. _BEENDEN_ BEENDEN
10. _STUDIEREN_ STUDIEREN

15. Study the list of words and phrases below, and in the order in which they appear, write each word or phrase containing a glottal stop. Mark each glottal stop with a slash. If necessary, review the material on the glottal stop on pages 7–8.

Anrufbeantworter, Postamt, eines Abends, eines Tages, in Aachen, also, Omnibus, was esst ihr?, auf Englisch, garstig, Ebbe und Flut, Verkehrsampel, Großmutter, beenden, der Start, die Eierkuchen

1. _ANRUF/BE/ANTWORTER_
2. _POST/AMT_
3. _EINES/ABENDS_
4. _ABENDS IN/AACHEN_
5. _EINES/TAGES_
   WAS/ESST/IHR

6. _AUF/ENGLISCH_
7. _EBBE/FLUT_
8. _VERKEHRS/AMPEL_
9. _BEENDEN_
10. _DIE EIERKUCHEN_

16. Study the list of words below, and in the order in which they appear, write each word, dividing it into syllables (e.g., **le-sen, brau-chen**). If necessary, review the material on syllabification on pages 8–10.

backen, Würstchen, Omnibus, Programme, Radiergummi, Restaurants, langweilig, Hase, außer, Waschlappen

1. _BA-CKEN_ BACKEN
2. _WÜRST-CHEN_ WÜRSTCHEN
3. _OM-NI-BUS_ OM-NI-BUS
4. _PRO-GRAM-ME_ PRO-GRAM-ME
5. _RADIER-GUM-MI_ RADIER-GUM-MI
   RA-DIER-GUM-MI

6. _RES-TAU-RANTS_ RESTAURANTS
7. _LANG-WEI-LIG_ LANG-WEI-LIG
8. _HA-SE_ HASE
9. _AU-ßER_ AUßER
10. _WASCH-LAP-PEN_ WASCH-LAP-PEN

Nouns and Articles

Capitalization

All German nouns and words used as nouns are capitalized, regardless of their position in the sentence: **der Herr**, **das Haus**, **die Alte**, **der Junge**, **der Reisende**, **die Bekannte**, **das Lesen**, **das Schreiben**, **das Singen**.

Gender

MASCULINE	FEMININE	NEUTER
der	die	das

Unlike in English, where nouns almost always reflect natural gender (that is, the sex of the noun determines its gender, e.g., father, man, and boy are masculine; mother, woman, and girl are feminine; and hand, table, and friendship are neuter), all German nouns have grammatical gender. A noun can be masculine, feminine, or neuter, regardless of its natural gender.

The definite article **der** *the* designates a masculine noun, **die** designates a feminine noun, and **das** a neuter noun.

Nouns that refer specifically to male beings, such as father and uncle, are usually masculine. Those that refer to female beings, such as mother and daughter, are usually feminine. However, nouns referring to things are not always neuter; they can also be masculine or feminine. For this reason, the gender of each noun must be memorized.

Although no definite rules for gender can be given, the following generalizations may be helpful in memorizing the gender of frequently used nouns.

Gender Identification by Noun Groups

Nouns Referring to People

Nouns referring to male beings (people and animals) are usually masculine. Nouns referring to female beings are usually feminine.

MASCULINE		FEMININE	
der Vater	*father*	die Mutter	*mother*
der Mann	*man*	die Frau	*Mrs., Ms., woman*
der Sohn	*son*	die Tochter	*daughter*
der Bruder	*brother*	die Schwester	*sister*
der Herr	*Mr., gentleman*	die Dame	*lady*

MASCULINE		FEMININE	
der Onkel	*uncle*	die Tante	*aunt*
der Sänger	*singer (male)*	die Sängerin	*singer (female)*
der Lehrer	*teacher (male)*	die Lehrerin	*teacher (female)*
der Kater	*cat, tomcat*	die Katze	*cat (female or generic)*
der Hahn	*rooster*	die Henne	*hen*
der Junge	*boy*	BUT **das Mädchen**	*girl*

Nouns referring to young people and young animals are usually neuter. NOTE: All diminutives ending in **-chen** or **-lein** are neuter, regardless of the gender of the stem noun.

NEUTER			
das Mädchen	*girl*	das Kind	*child*
das Fräulein*	*Miss, young woman*	das Kalb	*calf*
das Kätzchen	*kitten*	das Küken	*chick*
das Schwesterlein	*little sister*	das Fohlen	*foal*
das Bübchen	*little boy*	das Lamm	*lamb*
das Tischlein	*little table*	das Ferkel	*piglet*

*The word **Fräulein** has become old-fashioned. These days, it is customary to address adult women as **Frau**, regardless of their age or marital status.

1. Complete each of the following sentences, using the appropriate definite article.

1. __DER__ Lehrer kommt.
2. __DAS__ Kalb ist klein.
3. __DIE__ Dame ist freundlich.
4. __DER__ Mann ist alt.
5. __DAS__ Kaninchen ist weiß.
6. __DIE__ Tante bringt es.
7. __DAS__ Büchlein liegt hier.
8. __DIE__ Katze schläft.
9. __DER__ Sohn schreibt.
10. __DIE__ Tochter ist hübsch.
11. __DER__ Junge ist groß.
12. __DAS__ Küken ist gelb.
13. __DIE__ Lehrerin ist intelligent.
14. __DIE__ Mutter kocht.
15. __DAS__ Kind weint.
16. __DER__ Kater ist schwarz.
17. __DER__ Lehrer sitzt dort.
18. __DIE__ Mädchen ist klein.
19. __DIE__ Henne ist braun.
20. __DIE__ Fräulein sieht uns.

Masculine Nouns

Names of All Days of the Week

NOTE: The gender of the word **Tag** is masculine.

der Montag	*Monday*	der Freitag	*Friday*
der Dienstag	*Tuesday*	der Samstag (Sonnabend)	*Saturday*
der Mittwoch	*Wednesday*	der Sonntag	*Sunday*
der Donnerstag	*Thursday*		

Names of All Calendar Months

der Januar	*January*	der Juli	*July*
der Februar	*February*	der August	*August*
der März	*March*	der September	*September*
der April	*April*	der Oktober	*October*
der Mai	*May*	der November	*November*
der Juni	*June*	der Dezember	*December*

Names of All Seasons

der Frühling	*spring*		der Herbst	*fall*
der Sommer	*summer*		der Winter	*winter*

Names of All Cardinal Directions

der Süden	*south*		der Westen	*west*
der Norden	*north*		der Osten	*east*

2. Complete each of the following sentences, using the appropriate definite article(s).

1. __DER__ Sommer ist eine warme Jahreszeit.
2. __DER__ Süden Deutschlands ist malerisch.
3. __DER__ Juli und __DER__ August sind Sommermonate.
4. __DER__ Frühling kommt bald.
5. _____ Sonntag ist ein Ruhetag.
6. _____ April ist regnerisch.
7. _____ Norden ist flach.
8. _____ Winter ist eine kalte Jahreszeit.
9. _____ Dezember und __DER__ Januar sind Wintermonate.
10. _____ Montag ist der erste Wochentag.

Feminine Nouns

Names of Most Trees

die Tanne	*fir*
die Linde	*linden tree*
BUT **der Ahorn**	*maple*

Names of Most Fruits

die Banane	*banana*
die Pflaume	*plum*
BUT **der Apfel**	*apple*

Names of Most Flowers

die Orchidee	*orchid*
die Lilie	*lily*

3. Complete each of the following sentences, using the appropriate definite article(s).

1. __DIE__ Zitrone und __DIE__ Orange sind sauer.
2. __DIE__ Geranie und __DIE__ Begonie blühen.
3. __DIE__ Birke ist ein Laubbaum.
4. __DIE__ Banane ist süß.
5. __DIE__ Orchidee ist teuer.
6. Wo ist __DER__ Apfel?
7. __DIE__ Lilie ist weiß.
8. __DIE__ Tanne ist ein Nadelbaum.
9. __DIE__ Pflaume ist sauer.
10. __DIE__ Linde ist groß.

Neuter Nouns

Names of Cities

das historische München	*historical Munich*
das übervölkerte Hongkong	*overpopulated Hong Kong*

Names of Most Countries

das neutrale Schweden	*neutral Sweden*
das moderne Deutschland	*modern Germany*

NOTE: The neuter article for cities and countries is used only if the noun is modified. Without a modifier, one simply uses **München**, **Berlin**, **Italien**.

Note, however, that there are exceptions. The names of the following countries are feminine, not neuter.

die Schweiz	*Switzerland*
die Türkei	*Turkey*
die Tschechische Republik	*Czech Republic*

Others are masculine.

der Iran	*Iran*
der Irak	*Iraq*

The names of the following countries are used only in the plural.

die Niederlande	*Netherlands*
die Vereinigten Staaten	*United States*
die USA	*USA*

These exceptions are always used with their articles, whether or not they are modified.

Wir besuchen die Schweiz.	*We are visiting Switzerland.*

4. Complete each of the following sentences, using the appropriate definite article. If an article is not required, place an **X** in the blank.

1. Wir besuchen __DIE__ Türkei.
2. Wo liegt __DER__ Iran?
3. __X__ Köln ist eine alte Stadt.
4. __DIE__ Vereinigten Staaten sind groß.
5. __DAS__ historische Wien ist malerisch.
6. __X__ Schweiz ist neutral.
7. __DIE__ Niederlande sind flach.
8. __DAS__ Deutschland ist modern.
9. Wir besuchen __DAS__ alte Heidelberg.
10. __DIE__ Tschechische Republik liegt im Osten.

Names of Most Metals and Chemical Elements

das Gold	*gold*	**das Helium**	*helium*	
das Kupfer	*copper*	BUT **der Stahl**	*steel*	

5. Complete each of the following sentences, using the appropriate definite article.

1. __DAS__ Aluminium ist ein leichtes Metall. *LITEST*
2. __DAS__ Chlor riecht scharf.
3. Wo wird __DER__ Stahl produziert?
4. __DAS__ Silber glitzert in der Sonne.
5. __DAS__ Radium ist radioaktiv.
6. __DAS__ Neon ist ein Edelgas.
7. __DAS__ Kupfer ist rot.
8. __DAS__ Gold ist teuer.
9. __DAS__ Helium ist leicht.
10. __DAS__ Eisen ist ein Schwermetall.
    IRON   STRONGMETEL

Review

6. Complete each of the following sentences, using the appropriate definite article(s).

1. __DIE__ Fräulein kauft nichts.
2. Wir besuchen __DER__ sonnige Italien.
3. __DER__ Apfel ist grün.
4. __DER__ Sommer ist die schönste Jahreszeit.
5. __DER__ Vater bringt etwas.
6. __DER__ Februar ist der kürzeste Monat.
7. __DER__ Junge spielt.
8. __DER__ Dienstag ist der zweite Wochentag.
9. __DAS__ Gold ist ein Edelmetall.
10. __DER__ Lehrer fährt durch __DIE__ Niederlande.
11. __DIE__ Rose blüht.
12. __DIE__ Mädchen lacht.
13. Wo ist __DIE__ Katze?
14. __DER__ Westen ist reich.
15. __DER__ Januar ist ein Wintermonat.
16. __DIE__ Banane ist gelb.
17. __DIE__ Tanne ist groß.
18. __DIE__ Schweiz ist neutral.
19. __DAS__ historische München ist interessant.
20. __DER__ Mai ist der schönste Monat.

Gender Identification by Word Endings

Masculine Endings

Nouns with the following endings are usually masculine.

-el	-en	-er	-ig	-ich	-ling

der Schlüssel	*key*	der Eimer	*bucket*
der Löffel	*spoon*	der Zucker	*sugar*
der Wagen	*car, wagon*	der Honig	*honey*
der Boden	*floor*	der Pfennig	*penny*
der Teller	*plate*	der Teppich	*rug*
der Arbeiter	*worker*	der Lehrling	*apprentice*

There are important exceptions to this rule.

die Butter	butter	das Wasser	water
die Mutter	mother	das Fenster	window
die Tochter	daughter	das Wetter	weather
die Nummer	number	das Leder	leather
die Mauer	wall	das Kissen	pillow
das Messer	knife	die Gabel	fork
das Zimmer	room	die Kartoffel	potato

7. Complete each of the following sentences, using the appropriate definite article(s).

1. __DER__ Mantel liegt hier.
2. Warum ist __DAS__ Fenster offen?
3. __DER__ Sperling ist ein Vogel.
4. __DIE__ Gabel, __DER__ Löffel und __DAS__ Messer sind aus Stahl.
5. __DER__ Himmel ist blau.
6. __DER__ Käfer fliegt durch __DAS__ Zimmer.
7. __DER__ Rettich schmeckt scharf.
8. __DER__ Essig ist sauer, aber __DER__ Honig ist süß.
9. __DER__ Teppich ist alt.
10. Wo ist __DER__ Teller?
11. __DAS__ Wetter ist schön.
12. __DER__ Wagen ist in der Garage.
13. __DIE__ Lehrling ist jung.
14. Wo ist __DIE__ Butter?
15. __DER__ Zucker ist weiß.
16. __DIE__ Mutter und __DIE__ Tochter sind hübsch.
17. __DAS__ Leder ist weich.
18. Wo ist __DAS__ Kissen?
    WERE

Nouns with the following foreign suffixes are usually masculine.

-and	-ant	-ar	-är	-ast	-ent	-eur	-ier	-ist	-ismus	-or	-us

der Kommandant	*commander*	der Friseur	*hairdresser, barber*
der Kommissar	*commissioner, inspector*	der Offizier	*officer*
der Millionär	*millionaire*	der Optimist	*optimist*
der Enthusiast	*enthusiast*	der Idealismus	*idealism*
der Student	*student*	der Tenor	*tenor*

8. Complete each of the following sentences, using the appropriate definite article.

1. __DER__ Pianist spielt sehr gut.
2. __DER__ Professor ist sehr beliebt.
3. __DER__ Pessimist ist selten glücklich.
4. __DER__ Pastor besucht die kranke Frau.
5. __DER__ Präsident ist noch nicht hier.
6. __DER__ Abiturient studiert nächstes Jahr an der Uni.
7. __DER__ Visionär will die Welt verändern.

8. __DER__ Emigrant ist nach Amerika ausgewandert.
9. __DER__ Jazz-Enthusiast plant eine Reise nach New Orleans.
10. __DER__ Redakteur arbeitet für einen Verlag.

Feminine Endings

Nouns with the following endings are almost always feminine. Nouns ending in **-e** are usually feminine.

-age   -e   -ei   -heit   -keit   -schaft   -ie   -ek   -eke   -ik   -in   -ion   -tät   -ung   -ur

die Courage	courage	die Politik	politics
die Liebe	love	die Musik	music
die Partei	party (political)	die Fabrik	factory
die Krankheit	illness	die Köchin	cook (female)
die Schönheit	beauty	die Nation	nation
die Freundlichkeit	friendliness	die Rarität	rarity
die Freundschaft	friendship	die Universität	university
die Melodie	melody	die Wohnung	apartment
die Familie	family	die Rechnung	bill, invoice
die Diskothek	discotheque	die Diktatur	dictatorship
die Apotheke	pharmacy	die Literatur	literature

There are important exceptions to this rule.

das Auge	eye	der Hase	rabbit, hare
das Ende	end	der Käse	cheese
der Buchstabe	letter (of the alphabet)	der Kunde	customer

Another group of nouns that end in **-e** but are not always feminine are those derived from adjectives and the present and past participles of verbs. Nouns formed in this way normally have both a masculine and a feminine form when they refer to persons, in addition to a neuter form when they refer to a neuter noun or an abstraction.

der Alte	old man	die Alte	old woman
der Kranke	sick person (male)	die Kranke	sick person (female)
der Jugendliche	young person (male)	die Jugendliche	young person (female)
der Angestellte	employee (male)	die Angestellte	employee (female)
der Studierende	student (male)	die Studierende	student (female)

The feminine ending **-in** is often added to a masculine noun to create a feminine form, clearly showing that the individual is female.

der Sänger	singer (male)	die Sängerin	singer (female)
der Lehrer	teacher (male)	die Lehrerin	teacher (female)
der Kommissar	commissar (male)	die Kommissarin	commissar (female)
der Koch	cook (male)	die Köchin	cook (female)

The plural of these feminine nouns is formed by adding **-nen**, e.g., **Sängerinnen**.

9. Complete each of the following sentences, using the appropriate definite article.

1. _DIE_ Pille ist bitter.
2. Er gibt _die_ Hoffnung auf.
3. _DIE_ Kultur dieses Volkes ist primitiv.
4. _DIE_ Universität ist bekannt.
5. _DIE_ Technik ist progressiv.
6. _DIE_ Kopie ist unklar.
7. _DIE_ Krankheit ist gefährlich.
8. _DIE_ Bäckerei ist geschlossen.
9. Er sagt _die_ Wahrheit.
10. _DIE_ Schneiderin macht das Kleid.

11. _DIE_ Fabrik ist im Zentrum.
12. _DIE_ Wohnung ist modern.
13. _DIE_ Familie ist zu Hause.
14. _DIE_ Maschine ist neu.
15. _DIE_ Bibliothek ist neu.
16. Wo ist _die_ Rarität?
17. _DIE_ Köchin kocht.
18. _DIE_ Nation ist stark.
19. _DIE_ Garage ist klein.
20. _DIE_ moderne Musik ist interessant.

Neuter Endings

Nouns with the following endings are usually neuter.

-tum	-ment	-eum	-ium	-um	-ett

das Christentum	*Christianity*	**das Museum**	*museum*
das Instrument	*instrument*	**das Datum**	*date*
das Gymnasium	*secondary school*	**das Duett**	*duet*

Infinitives used as nouns are always neuter.

das Hören	*hearing*	**das Sprechen**	*speaking*
das Sehen	*seeing*	**das Tanzen**	*dancing*

10. Complete each of the following sentences, using the appropriate definite article.

1. _DAS_ Lachen des Kindes ist ansteckend.
2. Wir besuchen _DAS_ Gymnasium.
3. _DAS_ Medikament hat ihm geholfen.
4. Wo ist _DAS_ Heiligtum?
5. _DAS_ Aquarium ist hier.
6. _DAS_ Instrument ist teuer.
7. Wo ist _DAS_ Museum?
8. _DAS_ Datum steht hier.
9. _DAS_ Christentum ist eine Religion.
10. _DAS_ Arbeiten macht müde.

11. Complete each of the following sentences, using the appropriate definite article(s).

1. _DIE_ Explosion zerstört _DAS_ Gymnasium.
2. _DIE_ Gabel, _DAS_ Messer und _DER_ Löffel liegen hier.
3. _DIE_ Straße ist breit.
4. _DER_ Lehrling arbeitet.
5. _DIE_ Konditorei ist geschlossen.
6. _DAS_ Dokument ist gefälscht.
7. _DER_ Honig und _DER_ Zucker sind süß.
8. Wir hören _die_ Melodie.
9. _DIE_ ganze Familie hat _DIE_ Krankheit.

10. _DIE_ Wohnung ist teuer.
11. _DAS_ Lesen und _DAS_ Schreiben lernte er zu Hause.
12. _DER_ Vogel sitzt dort.
13. _DIE_ Rakete umkreist _DIE_ Erde.
14. Warum liegen _DER_ Hammer und _DER_ Nagel hier?
15. _DIE_ Sinfonie ist lang.
16. _DAS_ Zentrum ist modern.
17. _DIE_ Apotheke ist um die Ecke.
18. _DIE_ Fabrik produziert viel.
19. _DER_ Teller ist weiß.
20. _DER_ Schlüssel ist aus Metall.

Words with Different Meanings in Masculine, Feminine, and Neuter Forms

There is a small number of words that have different meanings for masculine, feminine, and neuter forms. Included in this group are the following.

der Gehalt	*content*	**das Gehalt**	*salary*
der Golf	*gulf*	**das Golf**	*golf*
der Leiter	*leader, manager*	**die Leiter**	*ladder*
die Mark	*DM (German currency prior to the introduction of the euro)*	**das Mark**	*marrow*
der See	*lake (inland)*	**die See**	*sea (ocean)*
das Steuer	*steering wheel*	**die Steuer**	*tax*
der Tor	*fool*	**das Tor**	*gate*

There are even a few words that have different meanings for all three genders.

der Band	*volume (book)*
das Band	*ribbon, tape, bond*
die Band	*band (musical group)*

12. Complete each of the following sentences, using the appropriate definite article.

1. _DER_ Golf von Mexiko ist warm.
2. ~~DIE~~ _DER_ Band spielt gut.
3. _DER_ Königssee liegt in Süddeutschland.
4. _DER_ neue Geschäftsleiter ist sympathisch.
5. _DAS_ Golf ist ein Rasenspiel.
6. Wo wird _DIE_ Knochenmark produziert?
7. _DIE_ Deutsche Mark wird aufgewertet.
8. _DAS_ Gehalt ist zu niedrig.
9. _DIE_ Nordsee ist oft stürmisch.
10. _DER_ Mondsee ist in Österreich.
11. _DAS_ Tor war offen.
12. _DER_ Tor tötete den Hund.
13. _DIE_ Leiter ist kaputt.
14. _DIE_ Steuer ist sehr hoch.
15. _DAS_ Haarband ist gelb.

Compound Nouns

Formation

German is well-known for its ability to form compound nouns composed of two or more words. This can be of great help to the student of German, since knowing the meaning of the individual components often makes it possible to understand the meaning of a compound noun that has not been encountered previously.

Often, two singular nouns are joined to form one compound noun.

das Hotel, das Zimmer	das Hotelzimmer	*hotel room*
der Motor, das Boot	das Motorboot	*motorboat*
der Winter, der Mantel	der Wintermantel	*winter coat*
der Zahn, die Bürste	die Zahnbürste	*toothbrush*
das Wasser, die Farbe	die Wasserfarbe	*watercolor*
das Auto, die Bahn	die Autobahn	*freeway*

Another group of compound nouns is formed by joining a plural and singular noun.

die Tannen, der Baum	der Tannenbaum	*fir tree*
die Kranken, der Wagen	der Krankenwagen	*ambulance*
die Kinder, das Zimmer	das Kinderzimmer	*children's room*
die Tage, das Buch	das Tagebuch	*diary*
die Straßen, die Lampe	die Straßenlampe	*streetlamp*
die Blumen, die Vase	die Blumenvase	*vase*

Some compound nouns are formed from two singular nouns connected by **-s** or **-es**.

der Staat, das Examen	das Staatsexamen	*state exam*
der Sport, der Mann	der Sportsmann	*sportsman*
der Geburtstag, der Kuchen	der Geburtstagskuchen	*birthday cake*
das Mitglied, die Karte	die Mitgliedskarte	*membership card*
der Liebling, die Melodie	die Lieblingsmelodie	*favorite melody*
die Universität, der Professor	der Universitätsprofessor	*university professor*

Other compound nouns are formed by joining a verb and a noun.

schreiben, der Block	der Schreibblock	*(writing) pad*
schreiben, die Maschine	die Schreibmaschine	*typewriter*
schreiben, der Tisch	der Schreibtisch	*desk*
lesen, die Brille	die Lesebrille	*reading glasses*
lesen, der Stoff	der Lesestoff	*reading material*
lesen, die Liste	die Leseliste	*reading list*

Note that in these verb-noun formations, the verb preceding the noun drops its final **-en** or **-n**.

Still other compound nouns are formed by joining an adjective and a noun.

rot, der Kohl	der Rotkohl	*red cabbage*
blau, der Stift	der Blaustift	*blue pencil*
dumm, der Kopf	der Dummkopf	*fool*
nah, der Verkehr	der Nahverkehr	*local traffic*
frisch, das Gemüse	das Frischgemüse	*fresh vegetables*
hoch, das Haus	das Hochhaus	*high-rise*

Gender of Compound Nouns

The last component of the compound noun determines the gender of the noun.

der Stahl, <u>die Industrie</u>	die Stahl<u>industrie</u>	*steel industry*
die Suppen, <u>der Löffel</u>	der Suppen<u>löffel</u>	*soupspoon*
der Lehrer, die Hand, <u>das Buch</u>	das Lehrerhand<u>buch</u>	*teacher's guide*

13. Form the compound noun from each pair of nouns on the right, giving the appropriate definite article before the noun.

1. <u>DER GEBURTSTAGSKUCHEN</u> ist süß. Geburtstag, Kuchen
2. <u>DER WINTERMANTEL</u> ist warm. Winter, Mantel
3. <u>DER AUTOBUS</u> kommt. Auto, Bus
4. <u>DAS HOTELZIMMER</u> ist modern. Hotel, Zimmer
5. <u>DER SPORTMANN</u> hat Courage. Sport, Mann
6. <u>DIE BLUMENVASE</u> ist alt. Blume, Vase
7. <u>DAS KINDERZIMMER</u> ist klein. Kind, Zimmer
8. <u>DER KRANKEWAGEN</u> kommt. Kranke, Wagen
9. <u>DIE STRASSENLAMPE</u> ist hell. Straße, Lampe
10. <u>DIE UNIVERSITÄTSPROFESSORIN</u> ist intelligent. Universität, Professorin
11. <u>DAS TAGEBUCH</u> liegt hier. Tag, Buch
12. <u>DIE MITGLIEDSKARTE</u> ist klein. Mitglied, Karte
13. <u>DIE WASSERFARBE</u> ist dunkel. Wasser, Farbe
14. <u>DAS STAATSEXAMEN</u> ist schwer. Staat, Examen
15. <u>DIE ZAHNBÜRSTE</u> ist dort. Zahn, Bürste
16. <u>DER ROTSTIFT</u> liegt auf dem Schreibtisch. rot, Stift
17. <u>DIE RUNDFAHRT</u> war sehr interessant. rund, Fahrt

Nouns Used Only in the Singular

Certain German nouns are used only in the singular. This group includes the names of materials and substances, certain general and abstract nouns, and nouns formed from the infinitive of a verb, as well as collective nouns and other words that, by definition, cannot be plural. The following nouns are normally used only in the singular.

das Gold	*gold*	**die Liebe**	*love*
das Eisen	*iron*	**der Mut**	*courage*
die Milch	*milk*	**die Ehrlichkeit**	*honesty*
die Butter	*butter*	**die Aufrichtigkeit**	*sincerity*
der Honig	*honey*	**das Lesen**	*reading*
das Gute	*good*	**das Singen**	*singing*
das Böse	*evil*	**das Vieh**	*cattle*
die Hitze	*heat*	**die Polizei**	*police*
die Kälte	*cold*	**das Obst**	*fruit*
die Musik	*music*	**das Fleisch**	*meat*

Note that plurals can be created by using compound forms.

Obstsorten   *kinds of fruit*

Note also that collective nouns are used with singular verbs.

Das Vieh ist auf der Weide.   *The livestock is in the pasture.*

14. Form a sentence from each of the following groups of words.

MODEL   Polizei / sein / hier _____ Die Polizei ist hier. _____

1. Obst / sein / frisch _____ DAS OBST IST FRI _____
2. Musik / sein / modern _____ DIE MUSIK IST MODERN _____
3. Fleisch / sein / frisch _____ DAS FLEISCH IST FRISCH _____
4. Butter / sein / teuer _____ DIE BUTTER IST TEUER _____
5. Honig / sein / süß _____ DER HONIG IST SÜSS _____
6. Milch / sein / sauer _____ DIE MILCH IST SAUER _____
7. Vieh / sein / hungrig _____ DAS VIEH IST HUNGRIG _____
8. Gold / sein / kostbar _____ DAS GOID IST KOSTBAR _____

Plural Forms of Nouns

Almost all English nouns form their plurals by adding *-s* or *-es* to their singular forms, such as *cat ~ cats* and *glass ~ glasses*. Only a few English nouns have irregular plural forms, such as *mouse ~ mice* and *woman ~ women*. In German, nouns rarely form their plural forms by adding **-s**. Some plural forms are identical to the singular; others take only an umlaut. Many other nouns are made plural by adding various endings, with or without an umlaut. Regardless of the gender of the noun, the nominative plural form of the definite article is always **die**. Although there are no definite rules, there are basic patterns for the formation of plural noun forms.

Note that the abbreviations below are the ones normally used in standard German dictionaries to indicate the plural forms of nouns.

GROUP NUMBER	ABBREVIATION	DESCRIPTION	EXAMPLES SINGULAR	PLURAL
Group Ia	-	No change	das Fenster der Onkel	die Fenster die Onkel
Group Ib	̈	Umlaut only	der Vogel die Mutter	die Vögel die Mütter
Group IIa	-e	-e ending	der Arm das Jahr	die Arme die Jahre
Group IIb	̈e	-e ending + umlaut	der Stuhl die Nacht	die Stühle die Nächte
Group IIIa	-er	-er ending	das Bild das Kind	die Bilder die Kinder
Group IIIb	̈er	-er ending + umlaut	der Mann das Buch	die Männer die Bücher
Group IVa	-n	-n ending	der Name die Farbe	die Namen die Farben
Group IVb	-en	-en ending	der Herr die Frau	die Herren die Frauen
Group V	-s	-s ending	das Auto das Restaurant	die Autos die Restaurants

Group I

The nominative plurals of nouns in Group I either are identical to the singular or add an umlaut in the plural. They do not take a plural ending.

Masculine and neuter nouns ending in **-el**, **-en**, **-er** belong to Group I, as do neuter nouns ending in **-sel** and nouns with the diminutive endings **-chen** and **-lein**. Two very common feminine nouns belong to this group, **die Mutter** and **die Tochter** (see below).

Masculine Nouns

Singular		Plural
der Bruder	*brother*	die Brüder
der Dichter	*poet*	die Dichter
der Finger	*finger*	die Finger
der Koffer	*suitcase*	die Koffer
der Lehrer	*teacher*	die Lehrer
der Schüler	*student*	die Schüler
der Teller	*plate*	die Teller
der Vater	*father*	die Väter
der Braten	*roast*	die Braten
der Wagen	*car, wagon*	die Wagen
der Apfel	*apple*	die Äpfel
der Löffel	*spoon*	die Löffel
der Mantel	*coat*	die Mäntel
der Onkel	*uncle*	die Onkel
der Schlüssel	*key*	die Schlüssel
der Morgen	*morning*	die Morgen

Neuter Nouns

Singular		Plural
das Rätsel	*puzzle*	die Rätsel
das Fenster	*window*	die Fenster
das Messer	*knife*	die Messer
das Theater	*theater*	die Theater
das Zimmer	*room*	die Zimmer
das Segel	*sail*	die Segel
das Becken	*basin*	die Becken
das Kissen	*pillow*	die Kissen
das Fräulein	*Miss*	die Fräulein
das Mädchen	*girl*	die Mädchen

Feminine Nouns

Singular		Plural
die Mutter	*mother*	die Mütter
die Tochter	*daughter*	die Töchter

15. Rewrite each of the following sentences, changing the noun to plural and making all necessary changes.

1. Das Kissen ist weich.   ~~DAS OBST IST FRISCH~~ DIE KISSEN SIND WEICH
2. Der Onkel kommt.   ~~DIE MUSIK IST MODERN~~ DIE ONKEL KOMMEN
3. Die Tochter ist klein.   ~~DAS~~ DIE TÖCHTER SIND KLEIN
4. Das Zimmer ist kalt.   DIE ZIMMER SIND KALT
5. Der Bruder raucht.   DIE BRÜDER RAUCHEN
6. Der Mantel ist neu.   DIE MÄNTEL SIND NEU
7. Das Fenster ist geschlossen.   DIE FENSTER SIND GESCHLOSSEN

8. Der Apfel ist rot.   DIE ÄPFEL SIND ROT
9. Der Lehrer ist alt.   DIE LEHRER SIND ALT
10. Der Koffer ist aus Leder.   DIE KOFFER SIND AUS LEDER
11. Das Messer ist rostig.   DIE MESSER SIND ROSTIG
12. Das Segel ist weiß.   DIE SEGEL SIND WEISS
13. Der Teller steht dort.   DIE STEHEN TELLER STEHEN DORT
14. Der Schlüssel ist alt.   DIE SCHLÜSSEL SIND ALT
15. Das Mädchen ist hübsch.   DIE MÄDCHEN SIND HÜBSCH
16. Die Mutter wartet.   DIE MUTTER WARTEN
17. Der Wagen steht hier.   DIE WAGEN STEHEN HIER
18. Das Theater ist modern.   DIE THEATER SIND MODERN
19. Der Löffel ist teuer.   DIE LÖFFEL SIND TEUER
20. Der Schüler lernt.   DIE SCHÜLER LERNEN

Group II

These nouns add **-e** to the singular to form the plural. Some nouns also add an umlaut. Group II nouns may be masculine, feminine, or neuter. Many of these nouns have only one syllable.

Masculine Nouns

Singular		Plural
der Arm	arm	die Arme
der Berg	mountain	die Berge
der Besuch	visit	die Besuche
der Brief	letter	die Briefe
der Freund	friend	die Freunde
der Hund	dog	die Hunde
der König	king	die Könige
der Krieg	war	die Kriege
der Monat	month	die Monate
der Schuh	shoe	die Schuhe
der Sohn	son	die Söhne
der Stuhl	chair	die Stühle
der Tag	day	die Tage
der Tisch	table	die Tische
der Zug	train	die Züge

Neuter Nouns

das Boot	boat	die Boote
das Brot	bread	die Brote
das Gedicht	poem	die Gedichte
das Heft	notebook	die Hefte
das Jahr	year	die Jahre
das Papier	paper	die Papiere
das Tier	animal	die Tiere

Feminine Nouns

die Frucht	fruit	die Früchte
die Hand	hand	die Hände
die Nacht	night	die Nächte
die Stadt	city, town	die Städte
die Wurst	sausage	die Würste

16. Rewrite each of the following sentences, changing the noun to plural and making all necessary changes.

1. Die Wurst schmeckt gut.   *DIE WÜRSTE SCHMECKT GUT*
2. Der Monat ist lang.   *DIE ~~DER~~ MONATE ~~IST~~ SIND LANG*
3. Die Hand ist nass.   *DIE HÄNDE ~~IST~~ SIND NASS*
4. Das Gedicht ist kurz.   *DIE ~~DAS~~ GEDICHTE SIND KURZ*
5. Der Hund ist braun.   *DIE ~~DER~~ HUNDE SIND BRAUN*
6. Der Zug kommt an.   *DIE ~~DER~~ ~~Z~~ZÜGE KOMMT AN*
7. Der Tisch ist aus Holz.   *DIE ~~DER~~ TISCH SIND AUS HOLZ*
8. Die Stadt ist modern.   *DIE STÄDTE SIND MODERN*
9. Der Berg ist hoch.   *DIE ~~DER~~ BERGE SIND HOCH*
10. Das Tier ist verletzt.   *DIE TIERE SIND VERLETZT*
11. Der Krieg ist brutal.   *DIE KRIEGE SIND BRUTAL*
12. Der Sohn ist groß.   *DIE SÖHNE SIND GROSS*
13. Der Brief ist interessant.   *DIE BRIEF ~~IST~~ SIND INTERESSANT*
14. Der Schuh ist aus Leder.   *DIE SCHUH SIND AUS LEDER*
15. Der Tag ist kurz.   *DIE TAGE SIND KURZ*
16. Der Freund lacht.   *DIE FREUNDE LACHT*
17. Die Nacht ist kalt.   *DIE NÄCHTE SIND KALT*
18. Das Jahr geht vorüber.   *DIE JAHRE GEHEN VORÜBER ~~GEHE~~*

Group III

These nouns add **-er** to the singular to form the plural. All nouns containing **a, o, u, au** in the stem also add an umlaut. Most of these nouns are neuter, although some are masculine; none is feminine.

Masculine Nouns

Singular		Plural
der Geist	*spirit*	die Geister
der Gott	*god*	die Götter
der Irrtum	*mistake*	die Irrtümer
der Mann	*man*	die Männer
der Wald	*forest*	die Wälder
der Wurm	*worm*	die Würmer

Neuter Nouns

das Bild	*picture*	die Bilder
das Blatt	*leaf*	die Blätter
das Buch	*book*	die Bücher
das Ei	*egg*	die Eier
das Glas	*glass*	die Gläser
das Haus	*house*	die Häuser
das Kind	*child*	die Kinder
das Kleid	*dress*	die Kleider
das Land	*country*	die Länder
das Lied	*song*	die Lieder
das Volk	*people*	die Völker

17. Rewrite each of the following sentences, changing the noun to plural and making all necessary changes.

1. Der Wurm ist lang.   DIE WÜRMER SIND LANG
2. Das Buch ist interessant.   DIE BÜCHER SIND INTERESSANT
3. Das Ei schmeckt gut.   DIE EIR SIE SCHMECKTEN GUT
4. Das Land ist neutral.   DIE LÄNDER SIND NEUTRAL
5. Das Glas ist kalt.   DIE GLÄSER SIND KALT
6. Das Blatt ist grün.   DIE BLÄTTER SIND GRÜN
7. Der Mann raucht.   DIE MÄNNER RAUCHT
8. Das Haus ist teuer.   DIE HÄUSER SIND TEUER
9. Das Kleid passt nicht.   DIE KLEIDER PASST NICHT
10. Das Kind weint.   DIE KINDER WEINEN
11. Das Volk ist hungrig.   DIE VÖLKER SIND HUNGRIG
12. Das Bild ist billig.   DIE BILDER SIND BILLIG
13. Das Lied ist melodisch.   DIE LIEDER SIND MELODISCH
14. Der Gott ist alt.   DIE GÖTTER SIND ALT

Group IV

These nouns add **-n** or **-en** to the singular to form the plural. Nouns belonging to this group never add an umlaut. Most of these nouns are feminine. Feminine nouns ending in **-in** add **-nen** in the plural, e.g., **die Lehrerin ~ die Lehrerinnen**.

Masculine Nouns

Singular		Plural
der Hase	*rabbit*	die Hasen
der Junge	*boy*	die Jungen
der Name	*name*	die Namen
der Held	*hero*	die Helden
der Herr	*Mr., gentleman*	die Herren
der Mensch	*human being*	die Menschen
der Präsident	*president*	die Präsidenten

Neuter Nouns

das Auge	*eye*	die Augen
das Herz	*heart*	die Herzen
das Ohr	*ear*	die Ohren

Feminine Nouns

die Blume	*flower*	die Blumen
die Dame	*lady*	die Damen
die Katze	*cat*	die Katzen
die Minute	*minute*	die Minuten
die Schule	*school*	die Schulen
die Straße	*street*	die Straßen
die Stunde	*hour*	die Stunden
die Tante	*aunt*	die Tanten
die Tasse	*cup*	die Tassen
die Woche	*week*	die Wochen
die Schwester	*sister*	die Schwestern
die Antwort	*answer*	die Antworten

Singular		Plural
die Fabrik	factory	die Fabriken
die Frau	woman	die Frauen
die Nation	nation	die Nationen
die Tür	door	die Türen
die Universität	university	die Universitäten
die Wohnung	apartment	die Wohnungen
die Zeitung	newspaper	die Zeitungen
die Freundin	girlfriend	die Freundinnen
die Studentin	female student	die Studentinnen
die Schauspielerin	actress	die Schauspielerinnen

18. Rewrite each of the following sentences, changing the noun to plural and making all necessary changes.

1. Der Herr ist alt. — *DIE HERREN SIND ALT*
2. Die Dame ist freundlich. — *DIE DAMEN SIND FREUNDLICH*
3. Die Katze ist schwarz. — *DIE KATZEN SIND SCHWARZ*
4. Die Nation ist progressiv. — *DIE NATIONEN SIND PROGRESSIV*
5. Der Junge ist hier. — *DIE JUNGEN SIND HIER*
6. Die Studentin lernt. — *DIE STUDENTINNEN LEREN*
7. Die Tür ist offen. — *DIE TÜREN SIND OFFEN*
8. Die Straße ist breit. — *DIE STRASSEN SIND BREIT*
9. Der Student ist arm. — *DIE STUDENTEN SIND ARM*
10. Die Freundin ist krank. — *DIE FREUNDINEN SIND KRANK*
11. Der Hase ist weiß. — *DIE HASEN SIND WEISS*
12. Die Blume blüht. — *DIE BLUMEN BLÜHEN*
13. Die Fabrik ist grau.
14. Die Tasse ist gelb.
15. Die Wohnung ist kalt.
16. Der Präsident ist alt.
17. Der Name ist lang.
18. Die Antwort ist falsch.
19. Der Held ist stark.
20. Die Zeitung liegt hier.

Group V

These nouns add **-s** to the singular to form the plural. This group consists mainly of nouns of foreign origin, particularly those ending in vowels. However, it also includes German words that end in a vowel, as well as abbreviations.

Masculine Nouns

Singular		Plural
der Job	job	die Jobs
der Park	park	die Parks
der Vati	daddy	die Vatis
der VW	VW	die VWs
der Azubi	trainee	die Azubis*

*Azubi is short for **der Auszubildende** (literally, *the one to be trained*).

Neuter Nouns

Singular		Plural
das Auto	car	die Autos
das Baby	baby	die Babys
das Foto	photo	die Fotos
das Hobby	hobby	die Hobbys
das Hotel	hotel	die Hotels
das Kino	movie theater	die Kinos
das Radio	radio	die Radios
das Sofa	sofa	die Sofas

Feminine Nouns

die Bar	bar	die Bars
die Kamera	camera	die Kameras
die Lobby	lobby	die Lobbys
die Mutti	mommy	die Muttis
die Party	party	die Partys
die Talk-Show	talk show	die Talk-Shows

19. Rewrite each of the following sentences, changing the noun to plural and making all necessary changes.

1. Die Kamera ist teuer. _____
2. Die Bar ist geschlossen. _____
3. Das Radio ist kaputt. _____
4. Das Hotel ist teuer. _____
5. Das Sofa ist weich. _____
6. Der Park ist groß. _____
7. Der Job ist interessant. _____
8. Das Foto ist alt. _____

Irregular Plural Nouns

Masculine Nouns

Singular		Plural
der Bus	bus	die Busse

Neuter Nouns

das Drama	drama	die Dramen
das Gymnasium	secondary school	die Gymnasien
das Museum	museum	die Museen
das Zentrum	center	die Zentren

Feminine Nouns

die Firma	firm, company	die Firmen

NOTE: A few nouns that have the same singular form have two plural forms, each with a different meaning.

die Bank	bench	die Bänke
die Bank	bank	die Banken
das Wort	word	die Wörter (disconnected words in a list)
das Wort	word	die Worte (connected words in a sentence)

Singular		Plural
die Mutter	*mother*	**die Mütter**
die Mutter	*nut*	**die Muttern** (technical)

Some German nouns are used only in the plural.

die Eltern	*parents*
die Ferien	*vacation*
die Geschwister	*brothers and sisters; siblings*
die Leute	*people*

20. Rewrite each of the following sentences, changing the noun to plural and making all necessary changes.

1. Die Firma ist bekannt. _____
2. Ist das Wort auf der Liste? _____
3. Die Bank ist im Park. _____
4. Das Drama ist interessant. _____
5. Das Museum ist modern. _____
6. Der Bus kommt. _____
7. Die Bank ist geschlossen. _____
8. Das Zentrum ist groß. _____

REMEMBER: *When learning new nouns in German, it is necessary to memorize both the gender of the noun and its plural form.*

das Abendessen	*evening meal*	**die Abendessen**
der Bleistift	*pencil*	**die Bleistifte**
das Antibiotikum	*antibiotic*	**die Antibiotika**

Review

21. Rewrite each of the following sentences, changing the noun to singular when possible and making all necessary changes. If the noun does not have a singular form, place an **X** in the blank.

1. Die Teller sind weiß. _____
2. Die Lehrerinnen sind hübsch. _____
3. Die Gläser sind leer. _____
4. Die Mäntel hängen hier. _____
5. Die Zimmer sind warm. _____
6. Die Studenten lernen. _____
7. Die Geschäfte sind geschlossen. _____
8. Die Nächte sind lang. _____
9. Die Helden sind bekannt. _____
10. Die Bars sind billig. _____
11. Die Gymnasien sind progressiv. _____
12. Die Sofas sind rot. _____
13. Die Mütter sind freundlich. _____
14. Die Segel sind weiß. _____
15. Die Städte sind übervölkert. _____
16. Die Radios sind kaputt. _____
17. Die Zeitungen sind alt. _____

18. Die Männer sind krank.   _____
19. Die Hände sind schmutzig.   _____
20. Die Theater sind modern.   _____
21. Die Eltern sind zu Hause.   _____
22. Die Leute sind im Zentrum.   _____

22. Rewrite each of the following sentences, changing the noun to plural when possible and making all necessary changes. If the noun does not have a plural form, place an **X** in the blank.

1. Das Vieh ist im Stall.   _____
2. Der Schuh ist schwarz.   _____
3. Die Freundin ist nett.   _____
4. Das Fleisch ist teuer.   _____
5. Der Apfel ist sauer.   _____
6. Der Schlüssel ist rostig.   _____
7. Das Mädchen ist freundlich.   _____
8. Der Bus ist rot.   _____
9. Die Mutter schreibt.   _____
10. Die Wurst ist lecker.   _____
11. Das Auto ist neu.   _____
12. Der Brief ist lang.   _____
13. Die Hand ist nass.   _____
14. Das Zimmer ist groß.   _____
15. Das Tier ist wild.   _____
16. Das Glas ist teuer.   _____
17. Das Buch ist interessant.   _____
18. Die Straße ist eng.   _____
19. Der Freund ist reich.   _____
20. Das Lied ist kurz.   _____

Cases of Nouns

German has four cases. These cases signal how nouns (and pronouns, too) are used within a sentence, clause, or phrase. The cases are the following.

Nominative
Accusative
Dative
Genitive

The grammatical functions reflected by these four cases correspond more or less to the subject, direct object, indirect object, and possessive cases in English usage. Similarities and differences between German and English usage will be pointed out as each case is discussed.

Most German nouns do not change their endings for the various cases. However, the articles and/or adjectives preceding the nouns do change their forms to reflect the case. Thus, it is often necessary to look to the article and/or adjective in order to be able to identify the case of a noun.

As in English, there are two types of articles in German: the *definite article* and the *indefinite article*.

DEFINITE ARTICLE	INDEFINITE ARTICLE
der, das, die	ein, ein, eine

The *definite article* (**der**, **das**, **die**) is used to refer to a *particular* or *specific* person, place, or thing.

> ***Der* Arzt hat montags Sprechstunde.**   *The doctor has office hours on Mondays.*

Here we are speaking of a particular doctor.

The *indefinite article* (**ein**, **ein**, **eine**) is used to refer to an *unspecified* person, place, or thing.

> ***Ein* Arzt hat viele Patienten.**   *A doctor has many patients.*

In this case we are not referring to a particular doctor.

As noted at the beginning of this chapter, it is the definite article (**der**, **das**, **die**) that most clearly indicates the *gender* of a noun. Due to the changes in the endings of the definite article, the definite article is also most useful in identifying the *case* of a noun. The group of words that take the same grammatical endings as the definite article are referred to as "**der**" words.

dieser	*this*	**mancher**	*many (a)*
jeder	*each, every*	**solcher**	*such*
jener	*that*	**welcher**	*which*

Similarly, the group of words that take the same grammatical endings as the indefinite article (**ein**, **ein**, **eine**) are referred to as "**ein**" words.

mein	*my*	**ihr**	*her* or *their*
dein	*your* (familiar singular)	**unser**	*our*
sein	*his* or *its*	**euer**	*your* (familiar plural)
		Ihr	*your* (formal)

These "**ein**" words are also referred to as *possessive adjectives,* since their function is to describe the nouns they modify by indicating possession or ownership.

Note that **kein** *no, not any* is also an "**ein**" word.

The case endings for the "**der**" words and the "**ein**" words follow slightly different patterns. These patterns are presented for each case, followed by an overview of all cases presented, in the review charts on pages 50–51.

NOTE: The possessive adjective **euer** *usually contracts* by dropping the last (and unstressed) **e** of the stem when an adjective ending is added.

> **eu(e)re Kinder** > **eure Kinder**
> **eu(e)re Hunde** > **eure Hunde**

However, the possessive adjective **unser** usually does not contract but rather retains its unstressed **e**, even when it is followed by an adjective ending, particularly in written German.

> **uns(e)re Kinder** > **unsere Kinder**
> **uns(e)re Hunde** > **unsere Hunde**

(For additional exercises on the uses of the possessive adjectives, see Chapter 5.)

Nominative Case

Singular and Plural

The nominative forms of the definite and indefinite articles and of the "**der**" and "**ein**" words are as follows.

	SINGULAR			PLURAL
	MASCULINE	**NEUTER**	**FEMININE**	**ALL GENDERS**
Definite article "**der**" words	**der**	**das**	**die**	**die**
	dieser	**dieses**	**diese**	**diese**
	jener	**jenes**	**jene**	**jene**
	welcher	**welches**	**welche**	**welche**
Indefinite article "**ein**" words	**ein**	**ein**	**eine**	(no plural)
	mein	**mein**	**meine**	**meine**
	ihr	**ihr**	**ihre**	**ihre**
	unser	**unser**	**unsere**	**unsere**
Negative article	**kein**	**kein**	**keine**	**keine**

The nominative case is used in German in several ways.

As the Subject of the Verb

Der Mann spielt Golf.	*The man is playing golf.*
Die Freundin kommt.	*The girlfriend is coming.*
Das Auto ist neu.	*The car is new.*
Die Kinder weinen.	*The children are crying.*
Dieser Apfel ist sauer.	*This apple is sour.*
Diese Stadt ist bekannt.	*This city is well-known.*
Dieses Zimmer ist groß.	*This room is large.*
Diese Bücher sind interessant.	*These books are interesting.*
Ein Hund bellt.	*A dog is barking.*
Eine Kopie ist hier.	*A copy is here.*
Ein Mädchen singt.	*A girl is singing.*
Mein Bruder ist krank.	*My brother is ill.*
Meine Katze ist weiß.	*My cat is white.*
Mein Messer ist rostig.	*My knife is rusty.*
Meine Eltern sind dort.	*My parents are there.*
Kein Wagen ist billig.	*No car is inexpensive.*
Keine Fabrik ist sauber.	*No factory is clean.*
Kein Hotel ist so modern.	*No hotel is as modern.*
Keine Museen sind geschlossen.	*No museums are closed.*

As a Predicate Nominative

A predicate nominative is a noun (or pronoun) that follows a linking verb and refers back to and is equated with the subject of the sentence or clause. Common linking verbs include the following.

sein	*to be*
werden	*to become*
bleiben	*to remain*
heißen	*to be called*
scheinen	*to appear*

Martin ist *unser Freund*.	*Martin is our friend.*
Die Frau ist *seine Mutter*.	*The woman is his mother.*
Gisela wird *keine Lehrerin*.	*Gisela will not become a teacher.*
Dr. Meyer bleibt *unser Hausarzt*.	*Dr. Meyer remains our family doctor.*
Der Hund heißt *Waldi*.	*The dog is named Waldi.*
Das scheint mir *eine gute Idee*.	*That seems a good idea to me.*

As a Noun of Direct Address

Bitte, nehmen Sie es, *Frau Breu*!　　*Please take it, Mrs. Breu.*
Herr Müller, kommen Sie?　　*Mr. Müller, are you coming?*
Guten Tag, *mein Freund*!　　*Good day, my friend!*

23. Complete each of the following sentences with **der**, **das**, or **die**.

1. _____ Universität ist alt.
2. _____ Mann schreibt.
3. Ist _____ Mädchen krank?
4. _____ Junge studiert.
5. _____ Wohnung ist kalt.

6. _____ Wetter ist schön.
7. Warum schreit _____ Kind?
8. _____ Frau ist hübsch.
9. _____ Lehrer ist jung.
10. _____ Vogel singt.

24. Complete each of the following sentences with **dieser**, **dieses**, or **diese**.

1. _____ Universität ist alt.
2. _____ Mann schreibt.
3. Ist _____ Mädchen krank?
4. _____ Junge studiert.
5. _____ Wohnung ist kalt.

6. _____ Wetter ist schön.
7. Warum schreit _____ Kind?
8. _____ Frau ist hübsch.
9. _____ Lehrer ist jung.
10. _____ Vogel singt.

25. Rewrite each of the following sentences, changing the noun to plural and making all necessary changes.

1. Dieses Land ist reich.　　_____
2. Welcher Mann kommt?　　_____
3. Jenes Haus ist alt.　　_____
4. Wo ist die Zeitung?　　_____
5. Welche Studentin ist hübsch?　　_____
6. Jene Frau ist krank.　　_____
7. Dort liegt der Apfel.　　_____
8. Dieses Mädchen lernt.　　_____
9. Diese Stadt ist modern.　　_____
10. Wo ist das Buch?　　_____

26. Complete each of the following sentences with **ein**, **ein**, or **eine**.

1. Dort ist _____ Junge.
2. _____ Gabel ist aus Silber.
3. Das ist _____ Käfer.
4. _____ Mädchen kommt.
5. Dort steht _____ Museum.

6. Ist das _____ Lilie?
7. Dort liegt _____ Pille.
8. _____ Wohnung ist teuer.
9. Das ist _____ Pfennig.
10. Dort liegt _____ Apfel.

27. Complete each of the following sentences with **kein**, **kein**, or **keine**.

1. Dort ist _____ Junge.
2. _____ Gabel ist aus Silber.
3. Das ist _____ Käfer.
4. _____ Mädchen kommt.
5. Dort steht _____ Museum.

6. Ist das _____ Lilie?
7. Dort liegt _____ Pille.
8. _____ Wohnung ist teuer.
9. Das ist _____ Pfennig.
10. Dort liegt _____ Apfel.

28. Supply the appropriate ending for the possessive adjective in each of the following sentences. If the adjective does not require an ending, place an **X** in the blank.

1. Sein____ Freundin ist hier.
2. Wo ist euer____ Haus?
3. Mein____ Vater ist alt.
4. Ihr____ Tochter lacht.
5. Dein____ Auto ist teuer.

6. Wo ist Ihr____ Hotel?
7. Hier ist sein____ Mantel.
8. Unser____ Kind ist klein.
9. Wo ist mein____ Mutter?
10. Unser____ Kopie liegt dort.

29. Rewrite each of the following sentences, changing the definite article to the possessive **sein**.

1. Ist das die Firma? _____
2. Der Job ist schwer. _____
3. Das Glas ist leer. _____
4. Der Hund bellt. _____
5. Wo ist die Frau? _____
6. Das Auto ist neu. _____
7. Der Bus kommt. _____
8. Das Drama ist lang. _____
9. Wo ist der Junge? _____
10. Die Freundin ist hübsch. _____

30. Rewrite each of the following sentences, changing the noun to plural and making all necessary changes.

1. Meine Freundin lacht. _____
2. Ihr Bruder ist krank. _____
3. Wo ist sein Lehrer? _____
4. Dein Messer liegt dort. _____
5. Wo ist unser Schlüssel? _____
6. Ist das euer Haus? _____
7. Wo ist Ihre Zeitung? _____
8. Dort ist mein Onkel. _____
9. Ist das dein Kind? _____
10. Wo ist eure Lehrerin? _____

31. Supply the appropriate ending for each adjective in the following sentences. If the adjective does not require an ending, place an **X** in the blank.

1. Dies____ Frau ist ihr____ Mutter.
2. Das ist doch kein____ Hund!
3. Solch____ Menschen sind beliebt.
4. Wann kommt euer____ Vater?
5. Jen____ Museum ist bekannt.

6. Dies____ Männer sind wichtig.
7. Welch____ Junge ist dein____ Bruder?
8. Er wird kein____ Doktor.
9. Ist das dein____ Pille?
10. Unser____ Eltern sind dort.

Accusative Case

Singular and Plural

The accusative forms of the definite and indefinite articles and of the "**der**" and "**ein**" words are as follows.

	SINGULAR			PLURAL
	MASCULINE	**NEUTER**	**FEMININE**	**ALL GENDERS**
Definite article	**den**	**das**	**die**	**die**
"**der**" words	**diesen**	**dieses**	**diese**	**diese**
	welchen	**welches**	**welche**	**welche**
Indefinite article	**einen**	**ein**	**eine**	(no plural)
"**ein**" words	**meinen**	**mein**	**meine**	**meine**
	ihren	**ihr**	**ihre**	**ihre**
Negative article	**keinen**	**kein**	**keine**	**keine**

The accusative case is used in German in several ways.

As the Direct Object of the Verb

Wir kaufen *den Wagen*.	*We are buying the car.*
Ich nehme *die Zeitung*.	*I take the newspaper.*
Kennst du *das Drama*?	*Do you know the drama?*
Ich habe *die Bücher*.	*I have the books.*
Wir kennen *ihren Bruder*.	*We know her brother.*
Sie braucht *ihre Tasche*.	*She needs her purse.*
Sie verkaufen *ihr Auto*.	*They are selling their car.*
Sie hat *ihre Karten*.	*She has her tickets.*
Er hat *keinen Hund*.	*He doesn't have a dog.*
Sie hat *keine Zeit*.	*She has no time.*
Ich habe *kein Geld*.	*I have no money.*
Er kauft *keine Schuhe*.	*He is not buying shoes.*

With Expressions of Definite Time and Duration of Time

Er bleibt *eine Woche* in Bonn.	*He is staying one week in Bonn.*
Sie besucht mich *jeden Tag*.	*She visits me every day.*
Sie fährt *jedes Jahr* nach Deutschland.	*She goes to Germany every year.*

The accusative form of **der** is used when dating a letter.

> **Köln,** *den* **13. 8. 2012**

With Prepositions

The accusative case is used with certain prepositions, which are discussed in Chapter 3.

32. Complete each of the following sentences, using the appropriate form of **der, das, die**.

1. Kaufst du _____ Mantel?
2. Wir besuchen _____ Museum.
3. Kennst du _____ Frau?
4. Ich nehme _____ Banane.
5. Brauchst du _____ Buch?
6. Er kennt _____ Mädchen.
7. Hast du _____ Zeitung?
8. Ich esse _____ Apfel.
9. Wir kaufen _____ Haus.
10. Sie sehen _____ Mann.

33. Complete each of the following sentences, using the appropriate form of **dieser**, **dieses**, **diese**.

1. Kaufst du _____ Mantel?
2. Wir besuchen _____ Museum.
3. Kennst du _____ Frau?
4. Ich nehme _____ Banane.
5. Brauchst du _____ Buch?
6. Er kennt _____ Mädchen.
7. Hast du _____ Zeitung?
8. Ich esse _____ Apfel.
9. Wir kaufen _____ Haus.
10. Sie sehen _____ Mann.

34. Rewrite each of the following sentences, changing the noun to plural and making all necessary changes.

1. Wir kennen den Dichter. _____
2. Ich bekomme den Brief. _____
3. Er kauft die Wurst. _____
4. Ich sehe das Tier. _____
5. Sie treffen den Freund. _____
6. Wir besuchen die Stadt. _____
7. Ich kenne den Berg. _____
8. Er schreibt das Gedicht. _____
9. Ich kaufe die Blume. _____
10. Wir singen das Lied. _____

35. Complete each of the following sentences, using the appropriate form of **ein**, **ein**, **eine**.

1. Ich habe _____ Koffer.
2. Er besucht _____ Universität.
3. Wir kaufen _____ Bild.
4. Ich nehme _____ Ei.
5. Wir besuchen _____ Freund.
6. Er bringt _____ Vase.
7. Sie brauchen _____ Tisch.
8. Wir haben _____ Hund.
9. Schreibst du _____ Gedicht?
10. Hast du _____ Freundin?

36. Complete each of the following sentences, using the appropriate form of **kein**.

1. Ich habe _____ Koffer.
2. Er besucht _____ Universität.
3. Wir kaufen _____ Bild.
4. Ich nehme _____ Ei.
5. Wir besuchen _____ Freund.
6. Er bringt _____ Vase.
7. Sie brauchen _____ Tisch.
8. Wir haben _____ Hund.
9. Schreibst du _____ Gedicht?
10. Hast du _____ Freundin?

37. Rewrite each of the following sentences, changing the definite article to the possessive adjective **unser**.

1. Kaufst du das Auto? _____
2. Ich sehe die Katze. _____
3. Wir besuchen das Kind. _____
4. Er ruft den Lehrer. _____
5. Ich nehme den Schlüssel. _____
6. Wir kennen die Lehrerin. _____

38. Supply the appropriate ending for the possessive adjective in each of the following sentences. If the adjective does not require an ending, place an **X** in the blank.

1. Er nimmt mein___ Wagen.
2. Er besucht sein___ Mutter.
3. Besuchst du ihr___ Bruder?
4. Braucht ihr euer___ Zimmer?
5. Ich kenne ihr___ Schwester.
6. Habt ihr eur___ Zeitung?
7. Er kennt unser___ Stadt.
8. Sie verkaufen ihr___ Haus.
9. Ich brauche mein___ Auto.
10. Kennst du sein___ Tante?

39. Rewrite each of the following sentences, changing the noun to plural and making all necessary changes.

1. Hat er mein Bild? _____
2. Brauchst du dein Buch? _____
3. Seht ihr unsere Freundin? _____
4. Ich nehme seine Zeitung. _____
5. Hast du deinen Mantel? _____
6. Wir kennen ihr Kind. _____
7. Ich habe ihren Schuh. _____
8. Verkaufst du unseren Wagen? _____
9. Sie brauchen ihren Freund. _____
10. Treffen Sie Ihren Lehrer? _____

Noun Endings in the Accusative Case

Singular

The accusative singular of most German nouns is identical to the nominative singular. There is, however, a small group of masculine nouns that add an **-n** or **-en** ending to the noun in the accusative singular (as well as in the dative and genitive singular). These nouns are often referred to as *weak nouns* or *n-nouns*.

Although many of these nouns must simply be memorized, it is helpful to remember that masculine nouns formed from adjectives and participles (e.g., **der Junge**, **der Alte**, **der Bekannte**, **der Reisende**, **der Verwandte**) fall into this category, as well as masculine nouns ending in **-ent** and **-ist** (e.g., **der Student**, **der Tourist**).

Examples of other masculine nouns that belong to this group follow.

Nominative Singular		Accusative Singular
der Hase	*rabbit*	**den Hasen**
der Held	*hero*	**den Helden**
der Herr	*gentleman*	**den Herrn**
der Junge	*boy*	**den Jungen**
der Mensch	*human being*	**den Menschen**
der Präsident	*president*	**den Präsidenten**
der Student	*student*	**den Studenten**

Wir treffen *den Studenten*.	*We are meeting the student.*
Kennst du *einen Helden*?	*Do you know a hero?*
Wir haben *euren Nachbarn* gesehen.	*We saw your neighbor.*

40. Supply the appropriate endings in each of the following sentences.

1. Sie liebt d___ Student___.
2. Wir sehen kein___ Mensch___.
3. Ich kenne d___ Präsident___.
4. Er ruft mein___ Junge___.
5. Ich kaufe kein___ Hase___.
6. Wer sieht jen___ Herr___?
7. Kennst du unser___ Präsident___?
8. Sie treffen kein___ Held___.
9. Welch___ Hase___ kaufst du?
10. Sie haben ein___ Junge___.

Review

41. Supply the appropriate ending(s) in each of the following sentences. If no ending is required, place an **X** in the blank.

1. Sein___ Frau fährt jed___ Montag nach Köln.
2. Wann verkauft ihr euer___ Haus?
3. Er füttert d___ Hase___.
4. Welch___ Junge___ kennst du?
5. Dies___ Herr___ schreibt ein___ Brief.
6. Unser___ Mutter kauft kein___ Mantel.
7. Jen___ Student___ besucht sein___ Freundin.
8. D___ Kind hat mein___ Bücher.
9. Ihr___ Freundin bleibt ein___ Tag hier.
10. Welch___ Mann hat Ihr___ Auto?
11. Mein___ Bruder kauft dies___ Bild.
12. Mein___ Schwester kennt d___ Präsident___.
13. Besucht ihr eur___ Kinder jed___ Tag?
14. Unser___ Junge___ kann solch___ Romane lesen.
15. Dies___ Katze trinkt kein___ Milch.
16. Welch___ Museen besucht er?
17. Manch___ Eltern sind streng.
18. Kennen Sie dies___ Herr___?
19. Welch___ Kleider kauft jen___ Mädchen?
20. München, d___ 6. 5. 2011.

Dative Case

Singular and Plural

The dative forms of the definite and indefinite articles and of the "**der**" and "**ein**" words are as follows.

	SINGULAR			PLURAL
	MASCULINE	**NEUTER**	**FEMININE**	**ALL GENDERS**
Definite article	**dem**	**dem**	**der**	**den**
"der" words	**diesem**	**diesem**	**dieser**	**diesen**
	jenem	**jenem**	**jener**	**jenen**
Indefinite article	**einem**	**einem**	**einer**	(no plural)
"ein" words	**meinem**	**meinem**	**meiner**	**meinen**
	ihrem	**ihrem**	**ihrer**	**ihren**
Negative article	**keinem**	**keinem**	**keiner**	**keinen**

The dative case is used in German in several ways.

As the Indirect Object of the Verb

In English, this relationship is often expressed by the prepositions *to* and *for*. The person or animal to whom something is given, shown, or told is in the dative case.

Ich hole *dem Hund* das Futter.	*I am getting the food for the dog.*
Er kauft *der Frau* die Karte.	*He is buying the ticket for the woman.*
Wir zeigen *dem Kind* das Boot.	*We are showing the boat to the child.*
Wir geben *einem Mann* Geld.	*We are giving money to a man.*
Ich schicke *meiner Freundin* nichts.	*I am sending nothing to my girlfriend.*
Sie kauft *unserem Kind* Schokolade.	*She is buying chocolate for our child.*

The following verbs are frequently used with both a direct and an indirect object, that is, with an accusative and a dative object.

bringen	*to bring, take*	**Er bringt *seiner Freundin* Blumen.** *He brings flowers to his girlfriend.*
geben	*to give*	**Wir geben *der Katze* Milch.** *We are giving milk to the cat.*
holen	*to get*	**Ich hole *meinem Bruder* den Schlüssel.** *I am getting the key for my brother.*
kaufen	*to buy*	**Sie kauft *ihrer Mutter* ein Auto.** *She is buying a car for her mother.*
schicken	*to send*	**Sonja schickt *ihrer Tante* ein Geschenk.** *Sonja is sending a gift to her aunt.*
sagen	*to say, tell*	**Sie sagt *ihrem Mann* die Wahrheit.** *She is telling her husband the truth.*
zeigen	*to show*	**Er zeigt *dem Mädchen* das Museum.** *He is showing the museum to the girl.*

With Dative Verbs

A number of German verbs take only dative objects. The following commonly used verbs are always used with the dative case.

antworten	*to answer*	**Ich antworte *dem Herrn*.** *I answer the gentleman.*
danken	*to thank (for)*	**Wir danken *unserem Lehrer*.** *We thank our teacher.*
helfen	*to help*	**Ich helfe *dem Kind*.** *I am helping the child.*
gehören	*to belong*	**Dieses Buch gehört *ihrem Sohn*.** *This book belongs to her son.*
gefallen	*to like, be pleasing*	**Jener Hut gefällt *seiner Frau*.** *His wife likes that hat.*
folgen	*to follow*	**Der Hund folgt *mir* nach Hause.** *The dog follows me home.*

NOTE: The verb **glauben** is used with the dative when its object is a person. The accusative is used when its object is a thing.

Ich glaube *dem Kind*.   *I believe the child.*
Ich glaube *die Geschichte*.   *I believe the story.*

NOTE: Many impersonal constructions also require the dative case.

Es geht *mir* gut.   *I'm fine / doing well.*
Es geht *mir* besser.   *I'm feeling better.*
Es tut *mir* leid.   *I'm sorry.*
Es gefällt *mir* nicht.   *I don't like it.* (literally, *It doesn't please me.*)
Es schmeckt *mir* gut.   *It tastes good to me.*

With Prepositions

The dative case is used with certain prepositions, which are presented in Chapter 3.

42. Complete each of the following sentences, using the appropriate form of **der**, **das**, **die**.

1. Er holt _____ Lehrer Kaffee.
2. Ich schreibe _____ Freundin.
3. Wir helfen _____ Mann.
4. Dankst du _____ Kind?
5. Ich schicke _____ Studentin Geld.
6. Er sagt _____ Mädchen alles.
7. Wir kaufen _____ Onkel das Buch.
8. Es gehört _____ Dame.
9. Ich glaube _____ Frau.
10. Ich gebe _____ Katze Wasser.

43. Complete each of the following sentences, using the appropriate form of **jener**.

1. Er holt _____ Lehrer Kaffee.
2. Ich schreibe _____ Freundin.
3. Wir helfen _____ Mann.
4. Dankst du _____ Kind?
5. Ich schicke _____ Studentin Geld.
6. Er sagt _____ Mädchen alles.
7. Wir kaufen _____ Onkel das Buch.
8. Es gehört _____ Dame.
9. Ich glaube _____ Frau.
10. Ich gebe _____ Katze Wasser.

44. Complete each of the following sentences, using the appropriate form of **ein**.

1. Wir danken _____ Frau.
2. Ich kaufe _____ Studentin das Buch.
3. Wir helfen _____ Tier.
4. Sie geben es _____ Dame.
5. Wir glauben _____ Mann.
6. Ich helfe _____ Familie.
7. Es gehört _____ Dichter.
8. Ich schreibe _____ Freund.
9. Sie schickt es _____ Kind.
10. Er antwortet _____ Mädchen.

45. Complete each of the following sentences, using the appropriate form of **kein**.

1. Wir danken _____ Frau.
2. Ich kaufe _____ Studentin das Buch.
3. Wir helfen _____ Tier.
4. Sie geben es _____ Dame.
5. Wir glauben _____ Mann.
6. Ich helfe _____ Familie.
7. Es gehört _____ Dichter.
8. Ich schreibe _____ Freund.
9. Sie schickt es _____ Kind.
10. Er antwortet _____ Mädchen.

46. Supply the appropriate ending for the possessive adjective in each of the following sentences.

1. Er gibt sein___ Frau Blumen.
2. Ich sage mein___ Onkel nichts.
3. Wir danken unser___ Mutter.
4. Sie hilft ihr___ Mann.
5. Es gehört dein___ Freund.
6. Zeigst du ihr___ Tante den Brief?
7. Ich glaube ihr___ Bruder.
8. Holen Sie Ihr___ Sohn Milch?
9. Zeigt ihr eur___ Tochter das Geschenk?
10. Es gehört unser___ Vater.

47. Complete each of the following sentences, using the dative form of the word on the right.

1. Ich zeige _____ Lehrer dieses Buch.   kein
2. Wir geben _____ Vater ein Geschenk.   unser
3. Es gehört _____ Studentin.   dies____
4. Sie gefällt _____ Bruder.   mein
5. Ich kaufe _____ Mutter etwas.   euer
6. Wir schreiben _____ Tante eine Karte.   unser
7. Er sagt _____ Mann die Neuigkeit.   jen____
8. Ich bringe _____ Kind ein Bonbon.   jed____
9. Er holt _____ Freundin Limonade.   sein
10. Helfen Sie _____ Frau?   Ihr

Noun Endings in the Dative Case

Singular

The dative singular of most German nouns is identical to the nominative singular. The same nouns that add an **-n** or **-en** ending in the accusative singular add the **-n** or **-en** in the dative singular. (See page 40.)

Ich gebe *dem Herrn* die Zeitung.	*I am giving the newspaper to the gentleman.*
Wir bringen *dem Studenten* ein Buch.	*We are bringing a book to the student.*
Er gibt *dem Touristen* eine Landkarte.	*He gives the tourist a map.*

NOTE: Masculine and neuter nouns of one syllable may take an optional **-e** ending in the dative singular. Although this ending was once a grammatical requirement, it has become much less common. Today, the **-e** ending sounds old-fashioned and is limited to certain common idiomatic phrases and extremely formal and poetic utterances.

Idiomatic phrases retaining the **-e** ending include the following.

zu Hause	*at home*
nach Hause	*(go/come) home*
auf dem Lande	*in the country*
am Tage	*during the day*

48. Supply the appropriate endings in each of the following sentences.

1. Wir danken d___ Held___.   5. Er zeigt es sein___ Junge___.
2. Es gehört jen___ Student___.   6. Ich gebe ein___ Hase___ die Karotte.
3. Sie glaubt unser___ Präsident___.   7. Wir helfen kein___ Mensch___.
4. Es gefällt dies___ Herr___.   8. Welch___ Junge___ gehört das Auto?

Plural

The dative plural noun always adds **-n** to the nominative plural form, unless the nominative form already ends in **-n**.

Ich schicke *den Kindern* Geschenke.	*I am sending presents to the children.*
Wir geben *den Mädchen* nichts.	*We are giving nothing to the girls.*

Nouns ending in **-s** in the nominative plural retain the **-s** in the dative plural and do not add **-n**.

Er zeigt *den Babys* das Tier.	*He is showing the animal to the babies.*

49. Rewrite each of the following sentences, changing the dative noun to plural and making all necessary changes.

1. Schreibst du deiner Freundin? _____
2. Er hilft jenem Kind. _____
3. Es gefällt seinem Lehrer. _____
4. Sie zeigt es ihrem Bruder. _____
5. Er antwortet dem Mann. _____
6. Ich hole dem Baby Milch. _____
7. Es gehört diesem Jungen. _____
8. Wir glauben der Frau. _____
9. Sie dankt ihrem Freund. _____
10. Es gehört eurem Studenten. _____

50. Complete each of the following sentences, using the dative form of the word on the right.

1. Ich helfe _____ Frauen.   jen___
2. Ich danke _____ Vater.   mein
3. Sie hilft _____ Kindern.   unser
4. Wir kaufen es _____ Mann.   ihr
5. Gehört es _____ Freundinnen?   dein
6. Er dankt _____ Frau.   dies___
7. _____ Kind gefällt es?   welch___
8. Sie antwortet _____ Herrn.   kein
9. Ich bringe es _____ Baby.   ein
10. Wir schicken _____ Studenten Geld.   jed___

Review

51. Supply the appropriate ending(s) in each of the following sentences. If no ending is required, place an **X** in the blank.

1. Unser___ Junge hilft sein___ Freund.
2. Wer hat mein___ Tante d___ Wohnung gezeigt?
3. Man kann solch___ Leuten nicht helfen.
4. Wer glaubt dies___ Frau?
5. Jen___ Auto gefällt mein___ Tochter.
6. Welch___ Kellnerin holt dies___ Gast d___ Braten?
7. Warum hast du jed___ Kind dies___ Buch gekauft?
8. Wir danken unser___ Eltern.
9. D___ Enkel holt sein___ Großvater d___ Pfeife.
10. Kein___ Mensch hat d___ Invalidin geholfen.
11. Warum schreibt er sein___ Geschwister___ kein___ Brief?
12. Jen___ Hund gehört ihr___ Bruder.
13. Antwortet ihr eur___ Freundinnen___?
14. Wann sagst du dein___ Mann d___ Wahrheit?
15. Wer hat d___ Kinder___ mein___ Puppe gegeben?

Genitive Case

Singular and Plural

The genitive forms of the definite and indefinite articles and of the "**der**" and "**ein**" words are as follows.

	SINGULAR			PLURAL
	MASCULINE	NEUTER	FEMININE	ALL GENDERS
Definite article "**der**" words	des dieses jenes	des dieses jenes	der dieser jener	der dieser jener
Indefinite article "**ein**" words	eines meines ihres	eines meines ihres	einer meiner ihrer	(no plural) meiner ihrer
Negative article	keines	keines	keiner	keiner

The genitive case is used in German in several ways.

To Show Possession or Relationships Between Two Nouns

In English, these concepts are expressed by the preposition *of* or by *'s*. The apostrophe is not normally used in German. (See the exception below.)

Dort liegt das Buch *des Lehrers*.	*There lies the teacher's book.*
Wo ist das Auto *der Frau*?	*Where is the woman's car?*
Der Griff *des Messers* ist rostig.	*The handle of the knife is rusty.*
Das ist die Frau *meines Sohnes*.	*That is my son's wife.*
Wo ist die Tasche *meiner Tochter*?	*Where is my daughter's purse?*
Hier ist ein Foto *unseres Hauses*.	*Here is a picture of our house.*
***Frau Schnabels* Mann ist hier.**	*Mrs. Schnabel's husband is here.*
Die Eltern *dieser Kinder* sind hier.	*The parents of these children are here.*

NOTE: In German, the genitive noun generally follows the noun that it modifies, whereas in English, the possessive noun usually precedes the noun it modifies.

der Wagen *meines Onkels*	*my uncle's car*
das Buch *des Mädchens*	*the girl's book*
die Bluse *meiner Tante*	*my aunt's blouse*

However, when a proper name is put into the genitive in German, it usually precedes the noun it modifies.

***Uwes* Wagen**	*Uwe's car*
***Mariannes* Buch**	*Marianne's book*

With Expressions of Indefinite Time

In English, these are expressed by *one day, some day* (*night, evening*, etc.).

***Eines Tages* wird sie ihren Freund sehen.**	*Some day she'll see her friend.*
***Eines Morgens* kam er zu Besuch.**	*One morning he came for a visit.*

By way of analogy, the feminine noun **Nacht** also adds **-s** in such time expressions.

***Eines Nachts* war er wieder gesund.**	*One night he was well again.*

With Prepositions

The genitive case is used with certain prepositions, which are presented in Chapter 3.

With Genitive Verbs

A very small number of verbs take a genitive object. These constructions often sound rather formal and somewhat archaic.

Wir gedenken *unserer gefallenen Soldaten.*	*We remember our fallen soldiers.*
Er rühmt sich *seines Talentes.*	*He brags about his talent.*

Noun Endings in the Genitive Case

Singular

Masculine and Neuter

-s or -es *Endings*

Most masculine and neuter nouns add an **-s**, or in some cases an **-es**, to form the genitive. Note that no apostrophe is used. An **-s** is added if the masculine or neuter noun has more than one syllable, e.g., **meines Bruders, dieses Zimmers**.

While it was once obligatory to add the **-es** to the genitive of most one-syllable masculine and neuter nouns, over the years both the **-s** and the **-es** endings have become acceptable in most cases, e.g., **Buchs** or **Buches**. This also holds true for certain masculine and neuter two-syllable words when the final syllable is accented, as in the following words.

der Besuch	*visit*	**des Besuchs** OR **des Besuches**
das Gedicht	*poem*	**des Gedichts** OR **des Gedichtes**

However, masculine and neuter words that end in **-s**, **-ss**, or **ß** must take the **-es** ending in the genitive singular.

das Glas	*glass*	**des Glases**
der Hass	*hate*	**des Hasses**
der Maß	*measure*	**des Maßes**

-n or -en *Endings*

Those nouns that take **-n** or **-en** in the accusative and dative singular (the so-called weak nouns) also add **-n** or **-en** in the genitive singular.

Die Frau *des Präsidenten* ist krank.	*The wife of the president is ill.*

-ns or -ens *Endings*

Some nouns add **-ens** to form the genitive singular, e.g., **des Herzens**, **des Namens**, **des Friedens**.

***Traurigen Herzens* zog er in den Krieg.**	*With a heavy heart he went to war.*

Feminine

No ending is added to feminine nouns in the genitive case.

Der Rand *der Tasse* ist angeschlagen.	*The rim of the cup was chipped.*

Proper Names

An **-s** is added to proper names in the genitive case.

***Luises* Bruder spielt Fußball.**	*Louise's brother plays soccer.*
***Frau Bauers* Hut war teuer.**	*Mrs. Bauer's hat was expensive.*

When a masculine name ends in a sibilant (an **s** sound), the genitive can be formed by adding **-ens** or an apostrophe.

> **Maxens Geburtstag ist am 11. Mai.**   *Max's birthday is May 11.*
> **Max' Geburtstag ist am 11. Mai.**

However, a **von** construction is preferred in such cases.

> **Der Geburtstag *von Max* ist am 11. Mai.**   *Max's birthday is May 11.*

Plural

The genitive plural noun form is identical to the nominative plural noun form.

> **Die Kleider *der Frauen* waren modisch.**   *The women's clothing was stylish.*

52. Complete each of the following sentences, using the appropriate form of **der**, **das**, **die** and the appropriate noun ending. If the noun does not take an ending, place an **X** in the blank.

1. Die Fabrik _____ Familie____ ist groß.
2. Das Auto _____ Doktor____ ist kaputt.
3. Die Farbe _____ Wagen____ ist schön.
4. Der Bau _____ Haus____ beginnt bald.
5. Der Mantel _____ Frau____ ist aus Leder.
6. Der Preis _____ Bild____ ist zu hoch.
7. Die Buchstabierung _____ Name____ ist schwer.
8. Der Vater _____ Junge____ ist hier.
9. Der Titel _____ Gedicht____ ist kurz.
10. Die Freundin _____ Student____ wartet.

53. Complete each of the following sentences, using the appropriate form of **dieser** and the appropriate noun ending. If the noun does not take an ending, place an **X** in the blank.

1. Die Fabrik _____ Familie____ ist groß.
2. Das Auto _____ Doktor____ ist kaputt.
3. Die Farbe _____ Wagen____ ist schön.
4. Der Bau _____ Haus____ beginnt bald.
5. Der Mantel _____ Frau____ ist aus Leder.
6. Der Preis _____ Bild____ ist zu hoch.
7. Die Buchstabierung _____ Name____ ist schwer.
8. Der Vater _____ Junge____ ist hier.
9. Der Titel _____ Gedicht____ ist kurz.
10. Die Freundin _____ Student____ wartet.

54. Complete each of the following sentences, using the appropriate form of **ein** and the appropriate noun ending. If the noun does not take an ending, place an **X** in the blank.

1. Das Leben _____ Held____ ist interessant.
2. Es ist die Geschichte _____ Junge____.
3. Ich höre das Lachen _____ Kind____.
4. Das ist die Wohnung _____ Student____.
5. Die Frau _____ Arbeiter____ ist krank.
6. Die Mutter _____ Mädchen____ ist hier.
7. Die Politik _____ Nation____ ist wichtig.

8. Ich esse die Hälfte _____ Apfel___.
9. Wo ist das Bild _____ Herr___?
10. Ich höre den Motor _____ Maschine___.

55. Complete each of the following sentences, using the appropriate genitive form of the word on the right and the appropriate noun ending. If the noun does not take an ending, place an **X** in the blank.

1. Das ist das Buch _____ Lehrer___.   sein
2. Ich nehme den Wagen _____ Mutter___.   mein
3. Wo ist die Frau _____ Präsident___?   unser
4. Dort ist das Zimmer _____ Junge___.   euer
5. Das Leben _____ Vater___ ist schwer.   ihr
6. Wo ist der Mantel _____ Tante___?   dein
7. Wir sehen das Gymnasium _____ Tochter___.   ihr
8. Dort hängt das Foto _____ Kind___.   mein
9. Die Freundin _____ Sohn___ kommt.   sein
10. Wo ist die Katze _____ Großmutter___?   Ihr

56. Rewrite each of the following sentences, changing the genitive noun to plural and making all necessary changes.

1. Die Kinder jener Frau sind krank.   _____
2. Die Sitze seines Autos sind bequem.   _____
3. Das sind die Fotos unserer Tochter.   _____
4. Die Bücher jenes Studenten liegen hier.   _____
5. Wann beginnt der Bau eures Hauses?   _____
6. Die Museen dieser Stadt sind modern.   _____
7. Die Kleider meiner Freundin sind neu.   _____
8. Der Wagen des Herrn steht dort.   _____
9. Die Betonung des Namens ist schwer.   _____
10. Die Gemälde jenes Museums sind bekannt.   _____

Substitute for the Genitive Case

In colloquial German, the preposition **von** with the dative case is frequently used instead of the genitive construction.

Das Kleid *meiner Tochter* war teuer.   *My daughter's dress was expensive.*
Das Kleid *von meiner Tochter* war teuer.

Das Auto *meines Bruders* ist kaputt.   *My brother's car is broken.*
Das Auto *von meinem Bruder* ist kaputt.

57. Rewrite each of the following sentences, substituting the **von**-plus-dative construction for the genitive and making all necessary changes.

1. Die Schneide dieses Messers ist scharf.

   _____

2. Die Dokumente unseres Präsidenten sind im Museum.

   _____

3. Wir haben die Hälfte des Gedichtes gelesen.

   _____

4. Hier ist ein Bild meiner Freunde.

_____

5. Der Preis des Autos ist zu hoch.

_____

58. Rewrite each of the following sentences, substituting the genitive for the **von**-plus-dative construction.

1. Das Wasser von jenem See ist eiskalt.

_____

2. Der Hund von Peter bellt.

_____

3. Die Ohren von solchen Hasen sind sehr lang.

_____

4. Die Mutter von dem Mädchen steht dort.

_____

5. Die Produkte von dieser Fabrik sind teuer.

_____

Review

59. Supply the appropriate endings in each of the following sentences. If no ending is required, place an **X** in the blank.

1. Wo ist d___ Wohnung dein___ Tante___?
2. Das ist d___ Geschäft sein___ Eltern___.
3. D___ Götter jen___ Volk___ waren nicht gütig.
4. Ein___ Nachmittag___ besuchten sie uns.
5. Ist d___ Krankheit eur___ Bruder___ ansteckend?
6. D___ Blätter dies___ Baum___ sind schon abgefallen.
7. Frau Schneider___ Mann ist schon angekommen.
8. D___ Titel dies___ Roman___ ist zu lang.
9. D___ Freunde mein___ Tochter___ sind hier.
10. D___ Mutter jen___ Junge___ ist krank.
11. D___ Hand d___ Frau___ ist kalt.
12. Wo ist d___ Foto dein___ Haus___?
13. D___ Kinder ihr___ Freundin___ sind hier.
14. Ich kenne d___ Professor jen___ Student___.
15. Sie kauft d___ Wagen mein___ Großvater___.

Review of Case Endings for the "der" Words
(der, dieser, jeder, jener, mancher, solcher, welcher)

	SINGULAR			PLURAL
	MASCULINE	NEUTER	FEMININE	ALL GENDERS
Nominative	-er	-(e)s	-e	-e
Accusative	-en	-(e)s	-e	-e
Dative	-em	-em	-er	-en
Genitive	-es	-es	-er	-er

Review of Case Endings for the "ein" Words
(ein, kein, mein, dein, sein, ihr, unser, euer, Ihr)

	SINGULAR			PLURAL
	MASCULINE	NEUTER	FEMININE	ALL GENDERS
Nominative	—	—	-e	-e
Accusative	-en	—	-e	-e
Dative	-em	-em	-er	-en
Genitive	-es	-es	-er	-er

Special Uses of the Definite Article

With General or Abstract Nouns

Die Katze **ist ein Haustier.**   *A cat is a domestic animal.*
Die Liebe **ist eine Himmelsmacht.**   *Love is a heavenly power.*
Das Leben **ist kurz.**   *Life is short.*

60. Complete each of the following sentences, using the appropriate form of the definite article.

1. _____ Panther ist eine Wildkatze.
2. _____ Technik ist progressiv.
3. _____ Leben ist kompliziert.
4. _____ Gravitation ist eine Kraft.
5. _____ Chemie ist eine Wissenschaft.
6. _____ Mensch ist sterblich.
7. _____ Hund ist ein Haustier.
8. _____ Schule ist wichtig.

With Names of Streets, Lakes, Mountains, and Countries

Die Theatinerstraße **ist in München.**   *Theatiner Street is in Munich.*
Der Bodensee **ist tief.**   *Lake Constance is deep.*
Der Tafelberg **ist in Südafrika.**   *Table Mountain is in South Africa.*

The definite article is required with names of countries that are masculine, feminine, or plural. (For the gender of countries, see Neuter Nouns, page 17.)

Der Iran **ist im Osten.**   *Iran is in the east.*
Die Schweiz **ist neutral.**   *Switzerland is neutral.*
Die Vereinigten Staaten **sind groß.**   *The United States is large.*
Die USA **sind weit weg.**   *The USA is far away.*

The definite article is not used with countries that are neuter, unless the name of the country is modified.

Deutschland **produziert viel.**   *Germany produces much.*
Das moderne Deutschland **ist progressiv.** *Modern Germany is progressive.*

61. Complete each of the following sentences, using the appropriate form of the definite article. If the definite article is not required, place an **X** in the blank.

1. _____ Vesuv ist ein Vulkan.
2. Wo ist _____ Bergstraße?
3. _____ Niederlande sind im Norden.
4. Hier liegt _____ Türkei.
5. _____ Tegernsee ist klein.
6. _____ Irak ist im Osten.
7. Wie hoch ist _____ Montblanc?
8. _____ historische Italien ist bekannt.
9. Dort ist _____ Alpenstraße.
10. _____ Vereinigten Staaten sind reich.
11. _____ Afrika ist groß.
12. _____ heutige Deutschland ist modern.

With Weights, Measures, and Expressions of Time

The accusative case of the definite article is used in German with expressions of weight, measure, and time. In English, the indefinite article is used in the sense of *per*.

Das kostet 2 Euro *das Pfund*.	*That costs 2 euros a pound.*
Es kostet 50 Eurocent *das Meter*.	*It costs 50 euro cents a meter.*
Er kommt einmal *die Woche*.	*He comes once a week.*
Wir bezahlen zweimal *den Monat*.	*We pay twice a month.*

62. Complete each of the following sentences, using the appropriate form of the definite article.

1. Er kommt einmal _____ Jahr.
2. Es kostet 20 Eurocent _____ Pfund.
3. Ich sehe Peter einmal _____ Woche.
4. Sie schreit zweimal _____ Sekunde.
5. Das kostet 3 Euro _____ Meter.
6. Es klingelt fünfmal _____ Stunde.

With Parts of the Body or Articles of Clothing

The definite article is used in German to refer to parts of the body or articles of clothing, unless there is doubt as to the identity of the possessor. In English, the possessive is used.

Er zieht sich *den Mantel* an.	*He is putting on his coat.*
Ich wasche mir *das Gesicht*.	*I am washing my face.*

63. Complete each of the following sentences, using the appropriate form of the definite article.

1. Er zieht sich _____ Hose an.
2. Sie waschen sich _____ Hände.
3. Wir putzen uns _____ Schuhe.
4. Ich ziehe mir _____ Mantel an.
5. Wäschst du dir _____ Gesicht?
6. Sie setzt sich _____ Hut auf.
7. Ich wasche mir _____ Kopf.
8. Putzt du dir _____ Zähne?

Review

64. Complete each of the following sentences, using the appropriate form of the definite article.

1. Ich fahre 100 Kilometer _____ Stunde.
2. Er wäscht sich _____ Hände.
3. _____ Vogesenstraße ist dort.
4. Das kostet 50 Euro _____ Pfund.
5. _____ Zugspitze ist in Deutschland.
6. _____ Ammersee ist malerisch.
7. Sie besucht uns zweimal _____ Monat.
8. _____ Vierwaldstättersee ist in der Schweiz.
9. Er putzt sich _____ Zähne.
10. _____ Niederlande sind flach.
11. Sie kommt einmal _____ Woche.
12. _____ Schweiz ist reich.
13. _____ Leben ist schön.
14. _____ Biologie ist wichtig.
15. _____ industrielle Österreich ist modern.
16. Wo ist _____ Schwanseestraße?
17. Wir ziehen uns _____ Schuhe an.
18. _____ Hauptstraße ist breit.

Omission of the Indefinite or Definite Article

The indefinite or definite article is omitted in the following cases.

Before a Predicate Nominative Indicating Nationality or Profession

Sie ist *Russin*.	*She is a Russian.*
Er wird *Zahnarzt*.	*He will be a dentist.*

However, if the predicate nominative is modified, the article is expressed.

Er ist *ein bekannter Pianist*.	*He is a well-known pianist.*
Er ist *der beste Lehrer*.	*He is the best teacher.*

With Certain Set Phrases

Sie hat *Fieber*.	*She has a fever.*
Ich habe *Kopfweh*.	*I have a headache.*
Hast du *Zahnweh*? (*Halsweh*, etc.)	*Do you have a toothache? (a sore throat, etc.)*

After the Conjunction als, Meaning "as a(n)"

Er arbeitet dort als *Ingenieur*.	*He works there as an engineer.*
Sie ist als *Studentin* in Bonn.	*She is in Bonn as a student.*

65. Express each of the following sentences in German.

1. I have a fever. _____
2. He is a teacher. _____
3. She is a good teacher. _____
4. Does he have a toothache? _____
5. He is in Berlin as a student. _____

6. He is a professor.   _____
7. She will become a pianist. _____
8. I have a sore throat.   _____

Review

66. Supply the appropriate endings in each of the following sentences. If no ending is required, place an **X** in the blank.

1. D___ Tochter mein___ Freund___ hat dies___ Brief geschrieben.
2. Ein___ Tag___ kaufte er sein___ Frau___ ein___ Pelzmantel.
3. D___ Eltern dies___ Mädchen___ sind dort.
4. Unser___ Sohn ist dies___ Woche hier.
5. Welch___ Blumen hat d___ Junge sein___ Mutter___ gekauft?
6. Solch___ Tiere fressen kein___ Blätter.
7. Mein___ Freundinnen geben unser___ Eltern___ kein___ Geschenk.
8. D___ Wagen jen___ Herr___ ist teuer.
9. Sie gibt ihr___ Sohn jed___ Tag ein___ Apfel.
10. Welch___ Auto gehört d___ Frau d___ Lehrer___?

67. Rewrite each of the following sentences, changing each noun to plural and making all necessary changes.

1. Wir haben kein Foto.   _____
2. Wo ist sein Bruder?   _____
3. Wer hat jenes Bild genommen?   _____
4. Welches Lied soll ich singen?   _____
5. Wer hilft dem Baby?   _____
6. Das gefällt dem Mädchen.   _____
7. Meine Freundin kommt.   _____
8. Unser Auto ist rot.   _____
9. Wann kommt Ihre Tochter?   _____
10. Das Kind unseres Lehrers ist hier. _____
11. Wo ist unser Hotel?   _____
12. Manches Land ist arm.   _____
13. Wo ist das Museum?   _____
14. Das Buch des Studenten liegt hier. _____
15. Wird diese Geschichte eurem   _____
    Freund gefallen?

68. Complete each of the following sentences, using the appropriate form of the article. If an article is not required, place an **X** in the blank.

1. _____ Deutschland ist modern.
2. Sie ist _____ Engländerin.
3. Hast du _____ Kopfweh?
4. Äpfel kosten 2 Euro _____ Pfund.
5. _____ Bergstraße ist im Zentrum.
6. _____ Tschechische Republik ist im Osten.
7. Er ist _____ reicher Amerikaner.
8. _____ Königssee ist malerisch.
9. Ich wasche mir _____ Hände.
10. _____ Löwe ist eine Wildkatze.
11. Er zieht sich _____ Mantel an.
12. Ich bin einmal _____ Woche hier.
13. _____ Vesuv ist bekannt.
14. _____ heutige China ist übervölkert.
15. Sie ist _____ beste Sängerin.
16. Sie arbeitet als _____ Sekretärin.

Prepositions

Prepositions are words that, in combination with a noun (or pronoun), show position, direction, time, or manner (such as *under* the table, *to* the store, *in* April, *without* a word).

In German as in English, the noun (or pronoun) following a preposition is in a case other than the nominative. In English, all prepositions are followed by the same case (such as with *him*, without *him*, behind *him*, for *him*, by *him*, on *him*). In German, however, prepositions can be followed by the accusative, the dative, or the genitive case. In addition, certain prepositions can be followed by either the accusative or the dative case, depending on whether they are used with verbs that indicate motion or change of position, or with verbs that indicate location or position.

Consequently, when learning the prepositions in German, it is necessary to learn which case each particular preposition requires.

It is also important to bear in mind that the use of prepositions within a language is highly idiomatic, and thus prepositional usage in German does not necessarily correspond to prepositional usage in English.

Prepositions Governing the Accusative Case

The following prepositions are always followed by the accusative case.

bis	für	um
durch	gegen	wider
entlang	ohne	

bis *by, until, up to*

Bis can be used alone or in combination with another preposition. When used alone, it is followed by the accusative case; when **bis** is followed by another preposition, the second preposition determines the case that follows.

Wir müssen *bis* nächsten Montag fertig sein.	*We must / have to be finished* by *next Monday.*
Die Soldaten kämpften *bis auf* den letzten Mann.	*The soldiers fought to the last man.*
Ich laufe mit dir *bis zur* Ecke.	*I'll walk with you* up to *the corner.*

durch *through, by*

Durch is used in passive constructions (see Chapter 7, page 224) to express the means by which something is done.

Er läuft *durch* das Haus.	*He is running* through *the house.*
Wir gehen *durch* die Zimmer.	*We are walking* through *the rooms.*
Er wurde *durch* einen Schuss getötet.	*He was killed* by *a shot.*

entlang *along*

Entlang *follows* an accusative object (the more common usage), but if it *precedes* its object, it takes the dative.

Wir gehen die Straße *entlang*.	*We are walking* along *the street.*
***Entlang* der Straße stehen alte Häuser.**	*Along the street stand old houses.*

für *for*

Warum kaufte er nichts *für* seinen Freund?	*Why didn't he buy anything* for *his friend?*
Sie arbeitet *für* meine Eltern.	*She is working* for *my parents.*
Ich kaufte die Bluse *für* zehn Euro.	*I bought the blouse* for *10 euros.*

gegen *against, toward, about*

Ich habe nichts *gegen* den Lehrer.	*I don't have anything* against *the teacher.*
Er kämpfte *gegen* den Weltmeister.	*He fought* against *the world champion.*
Haben Sie etwas *gegen* Kopfschmerzen?	*Do you have something* for *headaches?*

ohne *without*

***Ohne* seine Frau geht er nicht.**	*He is not going* without *his wife.*
Wir können *ohne* unsere Kinder nicht kommen.	*We can't come* without *our children.*

um *around*

Warum fährst du *um* das Haus?	*Why are you driving* around *the house?*
Die Familie sitzt *um* den Tisch.	*The family is sitting* around *the table.*

wider *against, contrary to*

Wider is used in elevated style and in certain idiomatic expressions.

***Wider* alle Erwartungen hat der Kandidat den Wahlkampf gewonnen.**	*Contrary to all expectations, the candidate won the election.*
Er handelte *wider* das Gesetz.	*He acted* contrary to *the law.*

Contractions of Prepositions Governing the Accusative

durchs	fürs	ums

When followed by the definite article **das**, the prepositions **durch**, **für**, **um** often contract to form **durchs**, **fürs**, **ums**, particularly in spoken German, but also in written German. If, however, the definite article functions as a demonstrative, that is, if it acts as a word that specifies or singles out the person, place, or thing referred to (see Chapter 5, page 92), or if the noun is followed by a clause describing it, these contractions cannot be used.

durch + das = durchs

Er läuft *durchs* Geschäft.	*He is running* through *the store.*

für + das = fürs

Ich bringe es *fürs* Baby.	*I am bringing it* for *the baby.*

um + das = ums

Wir stehen *ums* Auto.	*We are standing* around *the car.*

1. Complete each of the following sentences, using the appropriate accusative preposition.

    1. Der Ball fliegt _____ die Luft.
    2. Das Auto fährt die Straße _____.
    3. Sie laufen _____ die Ecke.
    4. Er stößt den Stuhl _____ die Wand.
    5. Ich muss _____ meine Freundin gehen, weil sie krank ist.
    6. Die Arbeit muss _____ nächste Woche fertig sein.
    7. Ich kaufe es _____ meinen Vater, weil er Geburtstag hat.
    8. Bringst du es _____ deinen Lehrer?
    9. Sie wandern _____ die Museen dieser Stadt.
    10. Der Blinde kann _____ seinen Hund nicht gehen.

2. Supply the appropriate ending or contraction in each of the following sentences.

    1. Das Fahrrad fährt gegen ein___ Baum.
    2. Ich schaue durch___ Teleskop.
    3. Wir fahren ein___ Fluss entlang.
    4. Kaufst du es für dein___ Großmutter?
    5. Wir sind um unser___ Garten gelaufen.
    6. Ohne mein___ Töchter kann ich nicht kommen.
    7. Warum stehen die Leute um___ Auto?
    8. Das Haus wurde durch ein___ Bombe zerstört.
    9. Warum läufst du gegen d___ Wand?
    10. Habt ihr etwas für___ Kind mitgebracht?
    11. Wir fahren um___ Museum.
    12. Ich komme ohne mein___ Freundin.
    13. Er wurde durch ein___ Explosion getötet.
    14. Wer macht es für d___ Lehrer?
    15. Wider all___ Erwartungen hat unser Team gewonnen.
    16. Warum geht ihr durch___ Kaufhaus?
    17. Die Kinder tanzen um ein___ Lindenbaum.
    18. Er geht d___ Straße entlang.
    19. Sie kämpfen gegen d___ Diktatur.
    20. Ich kaufe es für mein___ Schwester.

3. Complete each of the following sentences, using the appropriate form of the word on the right.

    1. Ich komme ohne _____ Frau.   mein
    2. Sie bauen einen Zaun um _____ Garten.   ihr
    3. Wir haben den Brief für _____ Großmutter.   unser
    4. Kurt wurde nicht durch _____ Schuss getötet.   sein
    5. Geht nicht _____ Berg entlang!   jen___
    6. Viele waren gegen _____ Revolution.   dies___
    7. Sie kaufte es für _____ Jungen.   ihr
    8. Der Wagen rollte gegen _____ Auto.   euer

Prepositions Governing the Dative Case

The following prepositions are always followed by the dative case.

aus	gegenüber	seit
außer	mit	von
bei	nach	zu

aus *out of, from* (point of origin; denotes coming from place of birth or domicile),
of (usually without an article)

Das Mädchen kommt *aus* dem Hotel.	*The girl is coming out of the hotel.*
Kommen Sie auch *aus* Deutschland?	*Do you also come from Germany?*
Das Messer ist *aus* Stahl.	*The knife is* (made) *of steel.*

außer *except (for), besides*

Außer meiner Mutter waren wir alle da.	Except for *my mother, we were all there.*
Außer diesem Volkswagen besitze ich nichts.	*I own nothing* besides *this Volkswagen.*

bei *with* (at the home of), *near, at*

Ich bleibe *bei* meinen Großeltern.	*I am staying* with *my grandparents.*
Wohnst du *bei* der Schule?	*Do you live near school?*
Ich treffe dich *bei* der Universität.	*I'll meet you at the university.*

gegenüber *across (from)* (usually follows its dative object)

Wir wohnen dem Park *gegenüber*.	*We live across from the park.*
Er sitzt seinen Eltern *gegenüber*.	*He sits across from his parents.*

mit *with, by (means of)*

Er arbeitet *mit* einem Hammer.	*He is working with a hammer.*
Ich reise *mit* diesen Leuten.	*I am traveling with these people.*
Sie kommt *mit* dem Zug.	*She is coming by train.*

nach *after, according to* (with this meaning, the preposition usually follows the noun),
to (when used with neuter geographical names, no article is expressed (see Chapter 2, page 17))

Nach dem Abendessen gehen wir aus.	*We are going out after dinner.*
Der Geschichte *nach* wurde er 100 Jahre alt.	*According to the story, he lived to be 100 years old.*
Der Flug *nach* Kanada war lang.	*The flight to Canada was long.*
BUT Sie reist *nach* den USA.	*She is traveling to the USA.*

seit *since, for* (with time expressions)

Seit seiner Kindheit wohnt er in Ulm.	*He has been living in Ulm since his childhood.*
Ich habe die Krankheit *seit* einem Jahr.	*I have had the illness for one year.*

von *from, by, of, about*

Er weiß nichts *von* seinen Töchtern.	*He knows nothing about his daughters.*
Die Uhr ist *von* meiner Schwester.	*The watch is from my sister.*

Das Geschenk kommt *von* meiner Großmutter.	*The present is from my grandmother.*
Ist das ein Drama *von* Goethe?	*Is that a drama by Goethe?*

von *from* (coming from a certain direction or place, as opposed to one's origin)

Das Flugzeug kommt *von* Frankfurt.	*The airplane is coming from Frankfurt.*

von *by* (used in the passive construction (see Chapter 7, page 224) to express the personal agent)

Das Essen wurde *von* meiner Mutter gekocht.	*The dinner was cooked by my mother.*

zu *to* (direction toward people or places if no geographical name is used)

Wir gehen *zu* einem neuen Zahnarzt.	*We are going to a new dentist.*
Wir gehen *zu* der großen Buchmesse.	*We are going to the big book fair.*

Contractions of Prepositions Governing the Dative

beim	**zum**
vom	**zur**

The prepositions **bei**, **von**, **zu** contract with the dative singular definite articles **dem** and **der**, unless these articles function as demonstratives or the noun is followed by a descriptive clause.

The following prepositions contract with the dative definite article, unless the article is stressed.

bei + dem = beim

Ich bin *beim* Doktor.	*I am at the doctor's office.*

von + dem = vom

Kommt er schon *vom* Kino?	*Is he already coming from the movies?*

zu + dem = zum

Wir gehen *zum* Museum.	*We are going to the museum.*

zu + der = zur

Warum fährt er *zur* Schule?	*Why is he driving to school?*

4. Complete each of the following sentences, using the appropriate preposition(s) or prepositional contraction(s).

1. Ich fahre _____ dem Auto _____ Hamburg.
2. Ich wohne _____ meinen Schwestern.
3. Er geht _____ Lehrer.
4. Wir wohnen _____ einem Jahr hier.
5. Die Universität ist dem Park _____.
6. _____ dem Frühstück gehe ich _____ Schule.
7. Dieser Brief kommt _____ meiner Freundin.
8. Gehst du _____ deinem Bruder ins Kino?
9. Der Zug kommt _____ Augsburg.
10. Das Fenster wurde _____ unserem Jungen zerschlagen.

5. Supply the appropriate form, ending, or contraction in each of the following sentences. If no ending or contraction is required, place an **X** in the blank.

1. Der Arzt kommt aus d___ Schlafzimmer.
2. Nach d___ Schule besuche ich dich.
3. Ich kenne sie seit jen___ Tag.
4. Bist du zu___ Doktor gegangen?
5. Sie wurde von kein___ Menschen gefragt.
6. Dies___ Park gegenüber wohnt unser Onkel.
7. Er steht bei___ Hotel.
8. Wann fahren wir nach _____ Österreich?
9. Kommt sie schon von d___ Universität?
10. D___ Sage nach wurde er König.
11. Seit ein___ Monat ist sie in der Schweiz.
12. Außer jen___ Herrn war niemand da.
13. Ich fahre mit mein___ Freunden nach _____ Bremen.
14. Sie ist seit ihr___ Abreise dort.
15. Sie bekam von jed___ Kind eine Orchidee.
16. Ich bleibe bei mein___ Geschwistern.
17. Sie kommt von___ Garten.
18. Sie wurde von dies___ Hund gebissen.
19. Arbeitest du bei dies___ Firma?
20. Das Paket kommt von mein___ Eltern.

6. Complete each of the following sentences, using the appropriate form of the word on the right.

1. Er läuft zu _____ Tante.   sein
2. Sie werden von _____ Mädchen gefragt.   ein
3. Er ist bei _____ Kaufhaus.   jen___
4. Ich wohne seit _____ Jahr hier.   ein
5. _____ Geschichte nach ist er reich.   dies___
6. Sie sprechen mit _____ Lehrer.   unser
7. Kommt ihr von _____ Haus?   euer
8. Er wohnt _____ Park gegenüber.   der
9. Nach _____ Vorlesung essen wir.   die
10. Sie kommt aus _____ Museum.   das
11. Ich wohne seit _____ Kindheit hier.   mein
12. Er kam aus _____ Hotelzimmer.   sein
13. Sie sitzt _____ Brüdern gegenüber.   ihr
14. Was machst du mit _____ Mitgliedskarte?   dein

Prepositions Governing Either the Accusative or the Dative Case

Another group of German prepositions can be used with either the accusative or the dative case. For this reason, they are often referred to as *two-way* or *either-or* prepositions.

an	**in**	**unter**
auf	**neben**	**vor**
hinter	**über**	**zwischen**

Whether these prepositions are followed by the accusative or by the dative is determined by how they are used within the sentence.

The accusative case is used when the verb in combination with the preposition expresses *change of position* or *movement toward a place*. These prepositions answer the question "**wohin?**" (literally, "where to?"). (See Chapter 9, page 242.)

The dative case is used when the verb in combination with the preposition expresses *position, location*, or *motion within a fixed location*. These prepositions answer the question "**wo?**" ("where?" or "in what place?"). (See Chapter 9, page 242.)

an (accusative) *to, onto*

Der Hund läuft *an die* Tür.	*The dog runs to the door.*
Sie hängt das Bild *an die* Wand.	*She is hanging the picture on the wall.*

an (dative) *at*

Der Hund steht *an der* Tür.	*The dog is standing at the door.*
Das Bild hängt *an der* Wand.	*The picture is hanging on the wall.*

auf (accusative) *on, on top of, onto, upon*

Er legt das Messer *auf den* Tisch.	*He puts the knife on the table.*
Wir fahren *aufs* Land.	*We are going to the country.*

auf (dative) *on, in*

Das Messer liegt *auf dem* Tisch.	*The knife is lying on the table.*
Wir wohnen *auf dem* Land(e).	*We live in the country.*

hinter (accusative) *behind*

Die Kinder gehen *hinter das* Haus.	*The children go behind the house.*
Er stellt die Schuhe *hinter die* Tür.	*He puts the shoes behind the door.*

hinter (dative) *behind*

Die Kinder spielen *hinter dem* Haus.	*The children are playing behind the house.*
Die Schuhe stehen *hinter der* Tür.	*The shoes are (standing) behind the door.*

in (accusative) *in, into, to*

Die Kinder gehen *in die* Schule.	*The children go to school.*
Er springt *in den* Fluss.	*He jumps into the river.*
Fliegst du *in die* Türkei?	*Are you flying to Turkey?*

in (dative) *in*

Die Kinder sind *in der* Schule.	*The children are in school.*
Er schwimmt *in dem* Fluss.	*He swims in the river.*
Wohnst du *in der* Türkei?	*Are you living in Turkey?*

neben (accusative) *beside, next to*

Luise stellt den Stuhl *neben das* Fenster.	*Louise places the chair next to the window.*
Setze dich *neben diesen* Herrn.	*Sit down beside this gentleman.*

neben (dative) *beside, next to*

Der Stuhl steht *neben dem* Fenster.	*The chair is (standing) next to the window.*
Ich sitze *neben diesem* Herrn.	*I am sitting beside this gentleman.*

über (accusative) *over, above, across*

Ich hänge die Lampe *über den* Tisch.	*I am hanging the lamp over (above) the table.*
Der Junge klettert *über den* Zaun.	*The boy climbs over the fence.*
Das Kind läuft *über die* Straße.	*The child runs across the street.*

über (dative) *over, above*

Die Lampe hängt *über dem* Tisch.	*The lamp is hanging over (above) the table.*
Das Handtuch hängt *über dem* Zaun.	*The towel is hanging over the fence.*
Die Ampel hängt *über der* Straße.	*The traffic light is hanging over the street.*

unter (accusative) *under, below, among*

Der Ball rollte *unter den* Sessel.	*The ball rolled under the easy chair.*
Die Katze verschwindet *unter das* Bett.	*The cat disappears under the bed.*

unter (dative) *under, below, beneath*

Der Ball ist *unter dem* Sessel.	*The ball is under the easy chair.*
Die Katze liegt *unter dem* Bett.	*The cat is lying under the bed.*

vor (accusative) *in front of, before*

Ich habe mich *vor den* Fernseher gesetzt.	*I sat down in front of the TV.*
Der Zeitungsausträger legte die Zeitung *vor die* Tür.	*The newspaper carrier laid the newspaper in front of the door.*

vor (dative) *in front of, before*

Ich sitze jeden Abend *vor dem* Fernseher.	*I sit in front of the TV every evening.*
Die Zeitung lag *vor der* Tür.	*The newspaper lay in front of the door.*

zwischen (accusative) *between*

Sie hat den Brief *zwischen das* Buch und die Zeitung gelegt.	*She placed the letter between the book and the newspaper.*

zwischen (dative) *between*

Der Brief liegt *zwischen dem* Buch und der Zeitung.	*The letter is lying between the book and the newspaper.*

Contractions of the Two-Way Prepositions

ans	ins	übers
am	im	unters
aufs	hinters	vors

The prepositions **an**, **auf**, **in**, **hinter**, **über**, **unter**, **vor** usually contract with the dative singular definite article **dem** and the accusative singular definite article **das**, unless these articles function as demonstratives or the noun is followed by a descriptive clause.

an + das = ans

    Sie geht *ans* Fenster.   *She goes to the window.*

an + dem = am

    Er stand *am* Bett.   *He stood at the bed.*

auf + das = aufs

    Er setzt sich *aufs* Sofa.   *He sits down on the sofa.*

in + das = ins

    Geht ihr *ins* Kino?   *Are you going to the movies?*

in + dem = im

    Sitzt sie *im* Garten?   *Is she sitting in the garden?*

hinter + das = hinters

    Wir gehen *hinters* Haus.   *We go behind the house.*

über + das = übers

    Es fliegt *übers* Nest.   *It flies over the nest.*

unter + das = unters

    Leg es nicht *unters* Bett!   *Don't put it under the bed.*

vor + das = vors

    Stell dich *vors* Mädchen!   *Stand in front of the girl.*

Combinations with Verbs of Direction

The following verbs imply direction. When they are used in combination with any of the preceding prepositions, they require the accusative case.

legen *to lay, put, place*

    Ich *lege* die Zeitung *aufs* Sofa.   *I am putting the newspaper on the sofa.*

setzen *to place, set, sit down*

    Er *setzte* sich *neben die* Frau.   *He sat down beside the young woman.*

stellen *to put, place, set*

    Stell den Stuhl *hinter den* Tisch!   *Place the chair behind the table.*

Combinations with Verbs of Location

The following verbs imply location. When they are used in combination with any of the preceding prepositions, they require the dative case.

liegen *to lie, rest*

    Warum *liegst* du *unter deinem* Bett?   *Why are you lying under your bed?*

sitzen *to sit*

> **Du** *sitzt auf ihrem* **Mantel.**   *You are sitting on her coat.*

stehen *to stand*

> **Warum** *steht* **er** *neben meinem* **Bruder?**   *Why is he standing next to my brother?*

7. Complete each of the following sentences, using the appropriate form of the word on the right. Use a contraction whenever possible.

1. Wir sitzen schon in _____ Auto.   das
2. Er geht über _____ Straße.   die
3. Stell die Schuhe unter _____ Bett!   das
4. Wir sitzen vor _____ Kindern.   unser
5. Wer kommt in _____ August?   der
6. Sie wohnt in _____ Schweiz.   die
7. An _____ Mittwoch fliege ich ab.   der
8. Geh in _____ Haus!   das
9. Schwimmt ihr immer in _____ Fluss?   dieser
10. Wann fährst du in _____ Türkei?   die
11. In _____ Sommer haben wir Ferien.   der
12. Er besuchte uns vor _____ Monat.   ein
13. Warum gehst du an _____ Küchenfenster?   das
14. Ich legte den Löffel neben _____ Teller.   dein
15. Er steht zwischen _____ Brüdern.   sein
16. Sie steht hinter _____ Fabrik.   jene
17. An _____ Abend bin ich müde.   der
18. Dürfen wir in _____ Theater?   das
19. Stell dich neben _____ Eltern!   dein
20. Sein Kopf ist unter _____ Kissen.   das
21. Warst du schon in _____ Irak?   der
22. Setz dich nicht auf _____ Koffer!   mein
23. Es liegt zwischen _____ Zeitungen.   ihr
24. In _____ Mai wird es wieder warm.   der
25. Warum geht er hinter _____ Museum?   das
26. Er legte es auf _____ Tisch.   der
27. Ich bin in _____ Kaufhaus.   ein
28. Es liegt unter _____ Bett.   euer
29. Sie sitzt auf _____ Mantel.   mein
30. Setz dich hinter _____ Freundin!   dein
31. Das Haus ist neben _____ Park.   jener
32. Stell es vor _____ Garage!   unser
33. Setzt euch in _____ Auto!   das
34. Wir sind in _____ Vereinigten Staaten.   die
35. Bist du in _____ Küche?   die

Da-Compounds with Accusative and Dative Prepositions

Da-compounds are used in place of preposition-plus-pronoun constructions to refer back to inanimate objects or abstract ideas that have been discussed in a previous sentence. The **da**-form is used regardless of whether the noun it replaces is masculine, feminine, or neuter, or singular or plural. If the preposition used in the **da**-compound starts with a vowel, **-r-** is inserted between **da** and the preposition (**darin**, **darüber**, **darauf**). NOTE: **Da**-compounds are never used to refer to people. (See Chapter 4, page 78.)

Bist du *gegen den Plan?*	*Are you against the plan?*
Ja, ich bin *dagegen.*	*Yes, I am against it.*
Denkst du *an die Ferien?*	*Are you thinking about your vacation?*
Nein, ich denke nicht *daran.*	*No, I am not thinking about it.*
Was macht ihr *mit den Bleistiften?*	*What are you doing with the pencils?*
Wir schreiben *damit.*	*We are writing with them.*
Steht sie *neben dem Bild?*	*Is she standing next to the picture?*
Ja, sie steht *daneben.*	*Yes, she is standing next to it.*

All accusative, dative, and accusative/dative prepositions can be prefixed by **da(r)-**, with the exception of **entlang**, **ohne**, **außer**, **gegenüber**, **seit**, which are never used to create **da**-compounds.

8. Complete each of the following answers, using the appropriate **da**-compound.

1. Sitzt ihr schon im Bus? Ja, wir sitzen schon _____.
2. Spielst du mit der Puppe? Ja, ich spiele _____.
3. Stellt ihr euch neben die Bank? Ja, wir stellen uns _____.
4. Bist du schon bei der Arbeit? Ja, ich bin schon _____.
5. Legt ihr euch unter die Bäume? Ja, wir legen uns _____.
6. Ist er hinter dem Geschäft? Ja, er ist _____.
7. Glaubst du an seine Schuld? Ja, ich glaube _____.
8. Setzt ihr euch aufs Sofa? Ja, wir setzen uns _____.
9. Unterhaltet ihr euch über den Roman? Ja, wir unterhalten uns _____.
10. Brauchst du Mehl zum Backen? Ja, ich brauche es _____.
11. Geht ihr nach der Arbeit spazieren? Ja, wir gehen _____ spazieren.
12. Hast du ihm von unserer Reise erzählt? Ja, ich habe ihm _____ erzählt.

When dar- Is Not Used

hinein, herein

When the preposition **in** expresses direction rather than location, it is not prefixed by **dar-** but has the following distinct forms.

Motion Away from the Speaker

Gehst du schon *ins Haus?*	*Are you already going into the house?*
Ja, ich gehe schon *hinein.*	*Yes, I am already going in (into it).*

Motion Toward the Speaker

Kommt sie *ins Wohnzimmer?*	*Is she coming into the living room?*
Ja, sie kommt *herein.*	*Yes, she is coming in (into it).*

hinaus, heraus

Similarly, the dative preposition **aus** has distinct forms.

Motion Away from the Speaker

Steigt er *aus dem Fenster?*	*Is he climbing out of the window?*
Ja, er steigt *hinaus.*	*Yes, he is climbing out (of it).*

Motion Toward the Speaker

Kommt sie *aus der Garage?*	*Is she coming out of the garage?*
Ja, sie kommt *heraus.*	*Yes, she is coming out (of it).*

9. Complete each of the following answers with **hinein, herein, hinaus,** or **heraus**.

1. Kommt sie ins Zimmer? Ja, sie kommt _____.
2. Geht sie aus der Küche? Ja, sie geht _____.
3. Läufst du ins Esszimmer? Ja, ich laufe _____.
4. Kommt er ins Haus? Ja, er kommt _____.
5. Kommen sie aus dem Museum? Ja, sie kommen _____.
6. Kommt sie ins Hotel? Ja, sie kommt _____.
7. Geht sie in die Kirche? Ja, sie geht _____.
8. Gehen sie aus dem Haus? Ja, sie gehen _____.
9. Wandern sie in den Wald? Ja, sie wandern _____.
10. Läuft sie aus der Fabrik? Ja, sie läuft _____.

Wo-Compounds with Accusative and Dative Prepositions

In German, the interrogative **was** (referring to things) is usually avoided after an accusative or dative preposition. Instead, **wo-** is prefixed to the preposition. If the preposition starts with a vowel, **wor-** is used.

***Womit** kann ich helfen?*	*What can I help you with?*
***Wovon** soll er denn leben?*	*What is he supposed to live off?*
***Worüber** sprecht ihr?*	*What are you talking about?*
***Worauf** wartest du?*	*What are you waiting for?*

These **wo**-compounds are used only in questions referring to things or ideas. *They cannot be used when referring to people.*

Wo- can be prefixed to accusative, dative, and accusative/dative prepositions, with the exception of **entlang, ohne, außer, gegenüber, seit, hinter, neben, zwischen**.

10. Complete each of the following questions, using the appropriate **wo**-compound, based on the cue provided in the answer.

1. _____ fährt er nach Köln? Mit dem Auto.
2. _____ sitzen sie? Auf dem Kissen.
3. _____ schwimmt sie? Im See.
4. _____ denkst du? An die Prüfung.
5. _____ kommt er? Aus dem Hotel.
6. _____ erzählt ihr? Von der Reise.
7. _____ handelt es sich? Um Geld.
8. _____ sprechen sie? Über Chemie.
9. _____ hat er Angst? Vor der Bombe.
10. _____ brauchst du den Bleistift? Zum Schreiben.
11. _____ liegt er? Auf dem Bett.
12. _____ ist er? Bei der Arbeit.
13. _____ ist sie? Gegen die Reise.
14. _____ schreibt er? Mit dem Kugelschreiber.
15. _____ interessierst du dich? Für Musik.

Prepositions Governing the Genitive Case

The most commonly occurring genitive prepositions are the following.

(an)statt	**während**
trotz	**wegen**

(an)statt *instead of*

(An)statt seiner Schwester ist seine Tante gekommen.	*His aunt came* instead of *his sister.*

trotz *in spite of, despite*

Er kam *trotz* seiner Krankheit zur Schule.	*He came to school* in spite of *his illness.*

während *during*

Während unserer Ferien fahren wir nach Spanien.	*We are going to Spain* during *our vacation.*
Während des Tag(e)s kann ich nicht schlafen.	During *the day I cannot sleep.*

wegen *because of*

Wir konnten *wegen* ihrer Verspätung nicht gleich abfahren.	*We could not depart immediately* because of *her delay.*

NOTE: In colloquial usage, the dative rather than the genitive is often heard with **(an)statt**, **trotz**, **wegen**, particularly when these prepositions are followed by a pronoun.

Other useful genitive prepositions include the following.

außerhalb	**diesseits**
innerhalb	**jenseits**
oberhalb	**um … willen**
unterhalb	

außerhalb *outside of*

Die Kinder spielen *außerhalb* des Gartens.	*The children are playing* outside of *the garden.*

innerhalb *inside of, within*

Innerhalb dieser Mauern stehen die Ruinen.	Inside of *these walls are the ruins.*
Er beendet sein Studium *innerhalb* eines Jahres.	*He is finishing his studies* within *a year.*

oberhalb *on the upper side of, above*

Wir wohnen *oberhalb* jenes Dorfes.	*We live* above *that village.*

unterhalb *on the lower side, below*

> *Unterhalb* unseres Hauses ist ein See.   Below *our house is a lake.*

diesseits *on this side of*

> Die Stadt ist *diesseits* der Berge.   *The city is* on this side of *the mountains.*

jenseits *on the other side of*

> Der Park ist *jenseits* dieses Sees.   *The park is* on the other side of *this lake.*

um ... willen *for the sake of*

> *Um* seiner Mutter *willen* hat er abgesagt.   *He canceled* for the sake of *his mother.*

11. Supply the appropriate ending in each of the following sentences.

1. Wir wohnen außerhalb d___ Stadt.
2. Er ist während d___ Nacht angekommen.
3. Innerhalb ein___ Monats ist er wieder gesund.
4. Trotz d___ Kälte kommt er mit.
5. Liegt das Haus innerhalb dies___ Dorf(e)s?
6. Ich bleibe diesseits d___ Grenze.
7. Ich habe es um mein___ Brüder willen getan.
8. Was liegt jenseits dies___ Berge?
9. Statt ein___ Autos hat er ein Pferd gekauft.
10. Er blieb wegen jen___ Warnung zu Hause.
11. Das Haus steht oberhalb d___ Kirche.
12. Während d___ Sommers gehen wir oft baden.
13. Unterhalb d___ Wald(e)s liegt eine Wiese.
14. Wegen mein___ Erkältung darf ich nicht ausgehen.
15. Statt ein___ Zeitung habe ich diese Zeitschrift gekauft.
16. Während d___ Ferien bin ich in Kanada.
17. Wir sind diesseits d___ Berg(e)s.
18. Ich arbeite trotz d___ Hitze im Garten.
19. Der See ist außerhalb d___ Parks.
20. Er kommt wegen sein___ Krankheit nicht.

Word Order in Prepositional Phrases

As illustrated in the examples above, most German prepositions precede their objects. However, as also noted above (**entlang, gegenüber**), a few prepositions more commonly, or even must, follow their objects. For example, **wegen** can either precede or follow its object.

> *Wegen des schlechten Wetters* blieb ich   Because of the bad weather *I stayed home.*
>   zu Hause.
> *Des schlechten Wetters wegen* blieb ich
>   zu Hause.

Other prepositions, however, require that certain special features be kept in mind when they follow their object.

When **nach** is used in the sense of *according to*, it follows its object.

Der Geschichte nach **war er der Sohn
  eines Königs.**   According to the story, *he was the son of a king.*

When **durch** is used in connection with a period of time, it follows its object. NOTE: The longer form
hindurch is often used in this sense.

Die Kranke schlief *die Nacht (hin)durch.*   *The sick woman slept* through the night.

When **entlang** follows its object, it takes the accusative case. However, when it precedes its object, it
takes either the dative or the genitive.

Den Fluss entlang **sind viele kleine Dörfer.**   Along the river *are many small villages.*
Entlang dem Fluss **sind viele reizende
  kleine Dörfer.**   Along the river *are many charming small villages.*

When the preposition **gegenüber** is used with a noun, it usually follows its object. However, it *always*
follows its object when its object is a personal pronoun.

Er wohnt dem Bahnhof *gegenüber.*   He lives across from *the train station.*
Er wohnt *gegenüber* **dem Bahnhof.**   He lives across from *the train station.*
Er sitzt mir *gegenüber.*   He is sitting across from *me.*

The object + preposition construction is found in a number of standard idiomatic phrases.

Meiner Meinung nach **ist er ein Narr.**   In my opinion *he is a fool.*
Meiner Ansicht nach **ist das ganz falsch.**   In my opinion *that is totally wrong.*
Tu es *deiner Mutter wegen.*   *Do it* for your mother's sake.
Um Himmels willen **tu es nicht.**   For heaven's sake *don't do it.*

12. Complete each of the following sentences, using the appropriate form of the word on the right.

   1. _____ Meinung nach soll man das Rauchen verbieten.   sein
   2. Um _____ Kindes willen mussten sie ihre Lebensweise ändern.   das
   3. Wegen _____ kalten Wetters wollte er nach Süden fahren.   das
   4. Lisa und Loisl gingen _____ Straße entlang.   die
   5. Ich wohnte _____ Post gegenüber.   die
   6. Meine Schwester arbeitete _____ ganzen Sommer durch.   der
   7. Entlang _____ Mauer sah man viele Blumen.   die
   8. _____ Geschichte nach ist er nach Amerika ausgewandert.   die
   9. _____ schlechten Wetters wegen konnten wir euch nicht besuchen.   das
   10. Gegenüber _____ Bahnhof steht die Bank.   der

Review

13. Supply the appropriate ending, preposition, or contraction in each of the following sentences. If no
    ending, preposition, or contraction is required, place an **X** in the blank.

   1. Warum schaust du hinter d___ Tür?
   2. Wir fahren _____ Herbst _____ Deutschland.
   3. Ich fahre zu mein___ Eltern.
   4. Innerhalb ein___ Stunde hatte er kein Kopfweh mehr.
   5. Die Tasse steht in jen___ Küchenschrank.
   6. Er hatte wegen d___ Glatteises den Unfall.
   7. Sie lief in ihr___ Schlafzimmer.
   8. Der Bus fährt unter d___ Brücke.

9. Das Auto fährt um d___ Stadt.
10. Sitzt du gern in d___ Sonne?
11. Wir fahren d___ Nordsee entlang.
12. Nach d___ Essen gehen wir spazieren.
13. Während d___ Krieges waren viele Leute arm.
14. Liegt das Buch schon auf mein___ Schreibtisch?
15. Er wohnt bei sein___ Schulfreund.
16. Hast du soviel für jed___ Bild bezahlt?
17. Sie soll a___ Mittwoch ankommen.
18. Wohnt ihr auch in dies___ Straße?
19. Ich hänge das Bild an d___ Wand.
20. Wir unterhalten uns mit d___ Krankenpfleger.
21. Hat er etwas für sein___ Kinder gekauft?
22. Warum bist du gegen unser___ Freunde?
23. Er wollte trotz sein___ Alters bergsteigen.
24. Sie tanzten um d___ Goldene Lamm.
25. Sie sind ohne ihr___ Sohn _____ Bonn geflogen.

14. Complete each of the following questions, using the appropriate **wo**-compound, based on the cue provided in the answer.

1. _____ liegt das Geld? In der Schachtel.
2. _____ brauchst du es? Zum Lesen.
3. _____ fährt er weg? Mit dem Zug.
4. _____ bist du? Gegen den Plan.
5. _____ unterhaltet ihr euch? Über seine Erfindungen.
6. _____ wartest du? Auf den Bus.
7. _____ fiel das Kind? Vom Pferd.
8. _____ hast du Angst? Vor dem Hund.

15. Complete each of the following answers, using the appropriate **da**-compound.

1. Liegt die Wäsche im Korb? Ja, sie liegt _____.
2. Ist das Ei neben dem Teller? Ja, es ist _____.
3. Steht ihr vor der Kamera? Ja, wir stehen _____.
4. Setzt du dich aufs Sofa? Ja, ich setze mich _____.
5. Liegt der Brief unter der Zeitung? Ja, er liegt _____.

CHAPTER 4

Pronouns

Personal Pronouns

Nominative Case.

SINGULAR		PLURAL	
ich	*I*	wir	*we*
du	*you* (informal)	ihr	*you* (informal)
er	*he, it*	sie	*they*
es	*it*		
sie	*she, it*		
		Sie	*you* (formal)

First Person

The first person (**ich**, **wir**) is used to indicate the speaker, writer, or narrator.

Second Person

The second person is used to indicate the person or persons addressed or spoken to. In German, there are three personal pronouns for *you*: a familiar singular (**du**), a familiar plural (**ihr**), and a formal form of address (**Sie**). The singular familiar pronoun **du** is used when addressing family members, close friends, children below the age of about 16, and pets and other animals, and in prayer. The familiar plural **ihr** is used when addressing two or more members of these groups.

The familiar forms are also increasingly used among members of groups of equals, such as students, athletes, blue-collar workers, members of certain trades and occupations, soldiers, and criminals.

In situations where people are on a first-name basis, it is customary to use the pronoun **du**.

The German pronoun of formal address **Sie** is used for acquaintances and other adults with whom the speaker is not on intimate terms, including anyone whom the speaker would address by last name or title. The **Sie** form is used for both the singular and the plural. **Sie** takes the same verb ending as the third-person plural pronoun, **sie** *they*. All forms of the pronoun **Sie** and its possessive adjective are always capitalized. However, the reflexive pronoun **sich** is not capitalized.

Karin, kannst *du* mir helfen?	*Karin, can* you *help me?*
Kinder, habt *ihr* Zeit?	*Children, do* you *have time?*
Frau Stifter, kommen *Sie* auch?	*Ms. Stifter, are* you *coming too?*
Haben *Sie sich* erkältet?	*Did* you *catch* (yourself) *a cold?*

In correspondence of any kind, it is optional whether or not to capitalize the personal pronouns **du** and **ihr** in all their forms (as well as their corresponding possessive adjectives).

Liebe Inge, ich freue mich schon auf *Deinen* Besuch. Wie nett, dass *Deine* Kinder mitkommen können. Wir werden viel mit *Euch* unternehmen, während *Ihr* bei uns seid.

OR

Liebe Inge, ich freue mich schon auf *deinen* Besuch. Wie nett dass *deine* Kinder mitkommen können. Wir werden viel mit *euch* unternehmen, während *ihr* bei uns seid.

Third Person

The third person indicates the person or persons spoken about or referred to. The gender of a third-person pronoun is determined by its antecedent, that is, by the gender of the word the pronoun refers back to. Masculine, feminine, and neuter nouns are replaced by the masculine, feminine, and neuter pronouns corresponding to their grammatical genders. When the pronouns **er, sie, es** refer to inanimate objects, they are translated by the English word *it*. When they refer to male or female beings, **er** and **sie** are translated as *he* and *she*.

The third-person plural pronoun **sie** *they* refers to both things and people. The third-person plural does not distinguish between masculine, feminine, and neuter.

Wo ist der Wagen?	*Where is the car?*
Er **ist in der Garage.**	*It is in the garage.*
Wo ist der Junge?	*Where is the boy?*
Er **ist im Haus.**	*He is in the house.*
Dort ist die Kirche.	*There is the church.*
Sie **ist sehr alt.**	*It is very old.*
Wann kommt Mutter?	*When is Mother coming?*
Sie **kommt bald.**	*She is coming soon.*
Wo sind die Bücher?	*Where are the books?*
Sie **sind auf dem Schreibtisch.**	*They are on the desk.*
Wann kommen die Gäste?	*When are the guests coming?*
Sie **kommen um 20 Uhr.**	*They are coming at 8 o'clock.*

The neuter noun **das Mädchen** is replaced by the personal pronoun **es**, unless the girl's name is stated. Then it is replaced by **sie**.

Wer ist das Mädchen?	*Who is that girl?*
Es **ist Roberts Schwester.**	*She is Robert's sister.*
Gabi ist nicht hier.	*Gabi is not here.*
Sie **ist in der Stadt.**	*She is in the city.*

The neuter noun **das Fräulein** is always replaced by **sie**.

Welches Fräulein hat dir geholfen?	*Which woman helped you?*
Dort steht *sie.*	*She's standing there.*

NOTE: **Fräulein,** as a form of address for unmarried women, has been replaced by **Frau**, which is now used as the normal form of address for both married and unmarried women.

1. Complete each of the following sentences, using the appropriate personal pronoun.

    1. Paul war in Deutschland. Jetzt spricht _____ gut Deutsch.
    2. Petra, wohin hast _____ das Geld gelegt?
    3. Meine Herren, was brauchen _____ noch?
    4. Wo liegt die Zeitung? Dort liegt _____.

5. Rex, _____ bist ein guter Hund.
6. Liebe Kinder, hoffentlich habt _____ Eure Ferien gut verbracht.
7. Das Mädchen blutet. _____ hat sich verletzt.
8. Wo ist Frau Horstmann? _____ ist am Bodensee.
9. Toni und Georg, wo seid _____ denn?
10. Meine Kinder sind nicht hier. _____ sind in England.
11. Die Katze schläft. _____ ist müde.
12. Inge ist krank. _____ ist im Krankenhaus.
13. Frau Steinhagel, kommen _____ heute Abend mit?
14. Die Blätter sind abgefallen. _____ liegen unter dem Baum.
15. Wo ist das Messer? Hier ist _____.
16. Gudrun and Ute, was habt _____ gemacht?
17. Meine Eltern machen Urlaub. _____ sind in der Schweiz.
18. Günther, hast _____ den Wagen?

Accusative Case

SINGULAR		PLURAL	
mich	*me*	uns	*us*
dich	*you* (informal)	euch	*you* (informal)
ihn	*him, it*	sie	*them*
es	*it*		
sie	*her, it*		
		Sie	*you* (formal)

The accusative personal pronouns are used as the direct object of a verb or as the object of a preposition requiring the accusative case.

Er hat *mich* besucht.	He visited me.
Er liebt *dich*.	He loves you.
Wir gehen ohne *ihn*.	We are going without him.
Liebst du *sie*?	Do you love her?
Wir haben *sie* gesehen.	We saw them.
Ich respektiere *Sie*.	I respect you.

The third-person singular and plural pronouns may refer to either people or things.

Kennst du nicht Herrn Krull?	Don't you know Mr. Krull?
Doch, ich kenne *ihn*.	Of course, I know him.
Hast du die Tasche?	Do you have the bag?
Ja, ich habe *sie*.	Yes, I have it.

2. Complete each of the following answers, using the appropriate personal pronouns.

1. Schreibt Karl den Brief? Ja, _____ schreibt _____.
2. Trifft Marlene ihre Freundinnen? Ja, _____ trifft _____.
3. Seht ihr Helga? Ja, _____ sehen _____.
4. Kocht Mutter das Abendessen? Ja, _____ kocht _____.
5. Will Ute die Blumen pflücken? Ja, _____ will _____ pflücken.
6. Kennt Konrad seine Großeltern? Ja, _____ kennt _____.

7. Siehst du den Beamten? Ja, _____ sehe _____.
8. Erinnerten sich die Kinder an ihre Tante? Ja, _____ erinnerten sich an _____.
9. Kennst du das Mädchen? Ja, _____ kenne _____.
10. Kauft ihr den Mantel? Ja, _____ kaufen _____.
11. Triffst du mich? Ja, _____ treffe _____.
12. Liebt Peter seine Freundin? Ja, _____ liebt _____.
13. Esst ihr den Kuchen? Ja, _____ essen _____.
14. Nimmst du das Auto? Ja, _____ nehme _____.

3. Rewrite each of the following sentences, substituting a personal pronoun for the italicized phrase.

1. Renate braucht *das Buch.*   _____
2. Wir kaufen *den Apparat.*   _____
3. Ich setzte mich neben *die Dame.*   _____
4. Wir essen *die Bananen.*   _____
5. Ich darf *den Roman* lesen.   _____
6. Wer hat *den Hasen* gefüttert?   _____

4. Answer each of the following questions, using a complete sentence beginning with **Ja**.

1. Hat er mich erkannt?   _____
2. Schreibt er euch?   _____
3. Hast du es für mich gekauft? _____
4. Geht er ohne euch?   _____
5. Könnt ihr uns dort besuchen? _____

Dative Case

SINGULAR		PLURAL	
mir	*me*	uns	*us*
dir	*you* (informal)	euch	*you* (informal)
ihm	*him, it*	ihnen	*them*
ihm	*it*		
ihr	*her, it*		
		Ihnen	*you* (formal)

The dative personal pronouns are used as the indirect object of a verb or as the object of a preposition requiring the dative case. NOTE: The accusative and dative forms **uns**, **euch** are identical.

Kaufst du *ihr* etwas?   *Are you buying* her *something?*
Ich sage *Ihnen* die Wahrheit. *I'm telling* you *the truth.*
Warum ist er neben *dir*?   *Why is he beside* you?

5. Rewrite each of the following sentences, substituting a personal pronoun for the italicized phrase.

1. Er gab es *seiner Freundin.*   _____
2. Wir helfen *unserem Lehrer.*   _____
3. Gibst du *dem Hund* das Futter? _____

4. Wir unterhielten uns mit *der Dame*. _____
5. Er erzählte von *dem Bekannten*. _____
6. Wohnst du bei *deinen Verwandten*? _____
7. Ich schrieb *meinen Freunden* _____
   Ansichtskarten.
8. Sie holte *dem Mädchen* Medizin. _____
9. Es gehört *meinen Eltern*. _____
10. Sie bringen *der Kranken* Essen. _____
11. Es gefällt *meinem Onkel*. _____
12. Ich kaufe *Ihrer Mutter* etwas. _____
13. Er kommt von *seinem Freund*. _____
14. Wir stehen hinter *dem Mann*. _____

6. Answer each of the following questions, using a complete sentence beginning with **Ja**.

1. Hat er dir etwas gebracht? _____
2. Zeigst du uns die Stadt? _____
3. Sagt ihr uns die Wahrheit? _____
4. Hat er dir geholfen? _____
5. Bringst du mir etwas mit? _____
6. Hat er dir dafür gedankt? _____
7. Hat sie euch geholfen? _____
8. Kaufen Sie ihm etwas? _____
9. Gefällt dir das Bild? _____
10. Kauft ihr mir den Wagen? _____

Position of Pronoun Objects

With Both a Noun Object and a Pronoun Object

When a sentence contains both a noun object and a pronoun object, *the pronoun object precedes the noun object*, regardless of the cases of the noun and the pronoun.

Er hat *mir* das Problem erklärt.	*He explained the problem to me.*
Er hat *es* seinem Vater erklärt.	*He explained it to his father.*
Er hat *sie* seinem Vater vorgestellt.	*He introduced her to his father.*
Er hat *ihm* seine Freundin vorgestellt.	*He introduced his girlfriend to him.*

7. Rewrite each of the following sentences, substituting a personal pronoun for the italicized phrase and making changes in word order as necessary.

1. Er gab seiner Mutter *das Geld*. _____
2. Ich habe *meiner Freundin* ein Paket geschickt. _____
3. Sie zeigte ihrem Kind *die Tiere*. _____
4. Sie erzählen *ihren Freunden* die Neuigkeit. _____
5. Sie bringen den Kranken *Blumen*. _____
6. Er kauft seiner Tante *die Orchidee*. _____
7. Ich schreibe *dem Lehrer* eine Karte. _____
8. Sie glaubt *dem Jungen* die Geschichte. _____
9. Ich gebe der Dame *die Karte*. _____
10. Wir kaufen *den Kindern* Geschenke. _____

With Two Pronoun Objects

When a sentence contains two pronoun objects, *the accusative pronoun always precedes the dative pronoun.*

Er hat *es* mir erklärt.	*He explained* it *to me.*
Er hat *sie* ihm vorgestellt.	*He introduced* her *to him.*
Hat er *es* dir geschrieben?	*Did he write* it *to you?*
Ich habe *ihn* ihm geschenkt. (der Ring)	*I gave* it *to him as a present.*
Ich habe *es* ihm geschenkt. (das Armband)	*I gave* it *to him as a present.*

8. Rewrite each of the following sentences, changing each noun object to a pronoun and making changes in word order as necessary.

1. Wir bringen dem Verletzten Wasser. _____
2. Ich hole meinem Freund den Fußball. _____
3. Wir erzählten den Kindern die Geschichte. _____
4. Er gibt dem Kind den Hund. _____
5. Er hat seiner Freundin die Geschichte geglaubt. _____
6. Johann zeigte den Ausländern das Rathaus. _____
7. Der Professor erklärte den Studenten die Theorie. _____
8. Ich kaufe meinen Eltern die Maschine. _____
9. Er schreibt seinem Lehrer die Neuigkeit. _____
10. Dieter holt dem Hund das Wasser. _____

9. Answer each of the following questions, using a complete sentence beginning with **Ja**. Change the noun object to a pronoun and make all necessary changes.

1. Hat er dir die Theaterkarten geschenkt? _____
2. Hast du ihnen die Aufnahme gezeigt? _____
3. Hat er euch die Bücher gekauft? _____
4. Bringst du mir den Kaffee? _____
5. Hat sie euch den Wagen gegeben? _____

Pronouns in Relation to the Subject

Following the Subject

If the subject (either a noun or a pronoun) is in first position in the sentence, the pronoun object (or objects) follows the subject. The subject and the object (or objects) are separated only by the verb.

Jörg kennt *ihn.*	Jörg *knows* him.
Ich zeige *dir* nichts.	I'm *not showing* you *anything.*
Max hat *ihn* gesehen.	Max *saw* him.
Sie bringen es *uns.*	They *are bringing it* to us.

Following or Preceding the Subject

If the subject is a noun and is not in first position in the sentence or clause, the pronoun object (or objects) may either precede or follow the subject.

Kennt *ihn* Jörg? OR **Kennt Jörg *ihn*?**	*Does Jörg know* him?
Kauft *dir* Ute etwas?	*Is Ute buying* you *something?*
OR **Kauft Ute *dir* etwas?**	

However, if the subject is a pronoun, the pronoun object must always follow the subject.

Kennt er *ihn*?	*Does he know* him?
Kauft sie *dir* etwas?	*Is she buying* you *something?*
Gibt er *es uns*?	*Is he giving* it to us?

10. Rewrite each of the following sentences, substituting a personal pronoun for the italicized phrase. Place the pronoun object before the subject when possible.

1. Hilft Ellen *ihren Brüdern*?

   _____

2. Ich glaube, dass Maria *das Kleid* gekauft hat.

   _____

3. Wir wissen nicht, ob er *die Kirche* besichtigt hat.

   _____

4. Ich habe Zeit, weil Norma *unseren Onkel* abholt.

   _____

5. Morgen kauft Susi *ihrer Freundin* den Pullover.

   _____

11. Rewrite each of the following sentences, substituting a personal pronoun for the italicized phrase. Place the pronoun object after the subject.

1. Jeden Tag holt Pia *ihrem Vater* die Zeitung.

   _____

2. Ich weiß, wann Peter *Frau Müller* geholfen hat.

   _____

3. Bringt Gabriele *das Programm*?

   _____

4. Hat er *das Geld* genommen?

   _____

5. Weißt du, wo Dieter *die Leute* getroffen hat?

   _____

Pronouns in Idiomatic Verb + Preposition Combinations (Phrasal Verbs)

Pronouns following prepositions in idiomatic expressions with verbs may be in either the accusative or the dative case. As expected, accusative prepositions are followed by accusative pronouns and dative prepositions are followed by dative pronouns. However, the cases following the *either-or* prepositions must be learned, since the movement/lack of movement distinction is not applicable to these idiomatic verb constructions.

Accusative Case

Many verb phrases containing the prepositions **an**, **auf**, **über** are followed by the accusative case.

denken an	*to think of*	**Ich denke oft an *dich*.**
lachen über	*to laugh about*	**Wir lachten über *ihn*.**
sprechen über	*to talk about (in detail)*	**Sprecht ihr über *sie*?**
warten auf	*to wait for*	**Warten Sie auf *uns*?**

Dative Case

The dative case is required after verb phrases containing the prepositions **von, zu, nach, vor**.

Angst haben vor	*to be afraid of*	**Er hat keine Angst vor *Ihnen*.**
einladen zu	*to invite to*	**Wir laden ihn zu *uns* ein.**
fragen nach	*to ask about*	**Hat er nach *mir* gefragt?**
hören von	*to hear from*	**Hast du von *ihr* gehört?**
sprechen von	*to talk of*	**Wir haben von *ihm* gesprochen.**
wissen von	*to know about*	**Was weißt du von *ihnen*?**

12. Rewrite each of the following sentences, substituting a personal pronoun for the noun phrase.

1. Er lachte über die Geschichte. _____
2. Wir sprechen von den Leuten. _____
3. Er fragt nach meiner Schwester. _____
4. Was weißt du von dem Herrn? _____
5. Er denkt an seine Frau. _____
6. Warten Sie auf den Professor? _____
7. Warum hast du Angst vor dem Hund? _____
8. Wir sprechen über seinen Onkel. _____
9. Ich habe von meinem Bruder gehört. _____
10. Er lädt sie zu seinen Eltern ein. _____

13. Complete each of the following sentences, using the appropriate accusative or dative pronoun.

1. Sie haben von _____ (du) gesprochen.
2. Wer hat Angst vor _____ (er)?
3. Was weiß er von _____ (wir)?
4. Wir haben über _____ (sie) gelacht.
5. Haben Sie über _____ (wir) gesprochen?
6. Hast du etwas von _____ (er) gehört?
7. Er fragt immer nach _____ (du).
8. Er wartete auf _____ (du).
9. Ladet ihr mich zu _____ (ihr) ein?
10. Denkst du auch an _____ (ich)?
11. Wer lacht über _____ (wir)?
12. Wir sprechen von _____ (du).
13. Ich spreche über _____ (sie).
14. Er wartet auf _____ (Sie).

Da-compounds

When third-person pronouns are used with prepositions, they refer only to people.

Sprecht ihr von Klaus?	*Are you talking about Klaus?*
Ja, wir sprechen *von ihm*.	*Yes, we are talking about him.*
Wartet er auf seine Frau?	*Is he waiting for his wife?*
Ja, er wartet *auf sie*.	*Yes, he is waiting for her.*
Bist du bei deinen Eltern?	*Are you with your parents?*
Ja, ich bin *bei ihnen*.	*Yes, I am with them.*

When a third-person pronoun is required to refer to an object, concept, or idea, a **da**-compound is formed from a preposition prefixed by **da(r)-**. (See Chapter 3, pages 64–65.)

Sprecht ihr von dem Plan?	*Are you talking about the plan?*
Ja, wir sprechen *davon*.	*Yes, we are talking about it.*
Wartest du auf den Brief?	*Are you waiting for the letter?*
Ja, ich warte *darauf*.	*Yes, I am waiting for it.*

14. Answer each of the following questions, using a complete sentence beginning with **Ja**. Substitute the appropriate **da**-compound or personal pronoun for the noun phrase.

1. Denkst du an deine Reise? _____
2. Liegst du unter dem Auto? _____
3. Wartest du auf Anna? _____
4. Sprecht ihr über die Oper? _____
5. Sprichst du von Marlene? _____
6. Fährst du mit dem Zug? _____
7. Stehst du vor den Bildern? _____
8. Wartest du auf das Paket? _____
9. Steht ihr neben euren Eltern? _____
10. Denkt er an seine Frau? _____
11. Fragt sie nach deiner Schwester? _____
12. Sitzen Sie hinter dem Herrn? _____
13. Arbeitest du mit dem Hammer? _____
14. Fahrt ihr mit euren Freunden? _____
15. Weißt du etwas von dem Plan? _____
16. Hast du Angst vor dem Lehrer? _____

Reflexive Pronouns

Reflexive pronouns are used when the action of the verb is both executed by and performed upon the subject. (For a complete review of reflexive verbs, see Chapter 7.)

Accusative Case

SINGULAR		PLURAL	
mich	*myself*	**uns**	*ourselves*
dich	*yourself* (informal)	**euch**	*yourselves* (informal)
sich	*himself, herself, itself*	**sich**	*themselves*
		sich	*yourself, yourselves* (formal)

The accusative reflexive pronouns are identical to the accusative personal pronouns, except in the third-person singular and plural. The reflexive pronoun for the formal **Sie** is **sich**. Note that this form is not capitalized.

15. Complete each of the following sentences, using the appropriate reflexive pronoun.

1. Ich verletzte _____ beim Skilaufen.
2. Er rasiert _____ jeden Tag.
3. Wir müssen _____ waschen.
4. Stellt _____ vor!
5. Fürchten Sie _____ vor dem Hund?
6. Helga kann _____ nicht daran erinnern.
7. Warum hast du _____ verspätet?
8. Freust du _____ auf Weihnachten?
9. Ich lege _____ aufs Bett.
10. Die Kinder ziehen _____ um.

Dative Case

SINGULAR		PLURAL	
mir	*myself*	uns	*ourselves*
dir	*yourself* (informal)	euch	*yourselves* (informal)
sich	*himself, herself, itself*	sich	*themselves*
		sich	*yourself, yourselves* (formal)

The dative reflexive pronouns are identical to the dative personal pronouns, except in the third-person singular and plural. Here, as in the accusative, the reflexive pronoun is **sich**, and the reflexive form for the formal **Sie** is also **sich**, which is not capitalized.

16. Complete each of the following sentences, using the appropriate reflexive pronoun.

1. Kauft ihr _____ das Pferd?
2. Ich habe _____ das Bier bestellt.
3. Er hat _____ weh getan.
4. Nimm _____ etwas!
5. Ich wasche _____ das Gesicht.
6. Kannst du _____ das vorstellen?
7. Die Kinder kauften _____ Schokolade.
8. Ich nehme _____ das Buch.
9. Kaufst du _____ das Auto?
10. Holen wir _____ die Möbel!

Position

Reflexive pronouns are placed as close to the subject as possible. The reflexive pronoun follows a pronoun subject, but never comes between a pronoun subject and the verb.

Er kauft *sich* einen Anzug.　　*He is buying himself a suit.*
Erinnerst du *dich* an ihn?　　*Do you remember him?*

If the subject is a noun and is not the first element in a declarative sentence (see Chapter 10, page 248), the reflexive pronoun may either precede or follow it.

Gestern hat *sich* Erika verletzt.　　*Yesterday, Erika got hurt.*
OR **Gestern hat Erika *sich* verletzt.**

17. Answer each of the following questions, using a complete sentence. Start your answer with the phrase on the right and place the reflexive pronoun in the same position as in the original question.

1. Wann haben sich die Kinder weh getan?　　heute Morgen
_____

2. Worauf freut sich Max?　　auf die Ferien
_____

3. Warum hat sich der Beamte verspätet?　　wegen des Unfalls
_____

4. Wann hat Vater sich das Auto gekauft?　　vor einer Stunde
_____

5. Woran erinnert sich dein Freund? _____   an seine Ferien

6. Wann putzt Barbara sich die Zähne? _____   am Abend

7. Was kauft sich Herr Obermeyer? _____   ein Motorrad

8. Wann rasiert sich Vater? _____   am Morgen

Possessive Pronouns

mein-	*mine*	**unser-**	*ours*
dein-	*yours* (informal)	**eur-**	*yours* (informal)
sein- **ihr-**	*his, its* *hers*	**ihr-**	*theirs*
		Ihr-	*yours* (formal)

The possessive pronoun takes the endings of **dieser**, **dieses**, **diese** in all cases. The gender of the possessive pronoun is determined by the gender of the noun it replaces.

Possessive Used as an Adjective

Wann triffst du *deinen* Freund?
When are you meeting your friend?

Das ist *sein* Mantel.
That is his coat.

Eure Kinder sind hier.
Your children are here.

Possessive Used as a Pronoun

Ich treffe *meinen* um zwei Uhr.
I am meeting mine at two o'clock.

Meiner hängt im Schrank.
Mine is hanging in the closet.

Wo sind *unsere*?
Where are ours?

18. Complete each of the following sentences, using the appropriate form of a possessive pronoun.

   1. Ich habe meine Bücher. Hast du _____?
   2. Wir sprechen von unserer Reise. Sprecht ihr von _____?
   3. Habt ihr schon eure Freunde gesehen? Wir haben _____ noch nicht gesehen.
   4. Er hat sein Geld bekommen. Ich habe _____ noch nicht bekommen.
   5. Er schreibt seinen Freunden. Schreibst du _____?
   6. Das ist nicht meine Schwester, sondern _____ (*his*).
   7. Ich habe nicht deinen Mann gesehen, sondern _____ (*hers*).
   8. Er wohnt nicht in seinem Haus, sondern in _____ (*ours*).
   9. Ich war nicht bei deinen Eltern, sondern bei _____ (*mine*).
   10. Ich schreibe nicht mit seinem Bleistift, sondern mit _____ (*hers*).

Demonstrative Pronouns

	SINGULAR			PLURAL
	MASCULINE	NEUTER	FEMININE	ALL GENDERS
Nominative	der	das	die	die
	dieser	dieses	diese	diese
Accusative	den	das	die	die
	diesen	dieses	diese	diese
Dative	dem	dem	der	*denen*
	diesem	diesem	dieser	*diesen*

The demonstrative pronouns (**der, das, die** or **dieser, dieses, diese**) are used in place of the personal pronouns (**er, es, sie**) when the pronoun is to be given special emphasis. They follow the same pattern of case endings as the definite article, except for the dative plural form, which is **denen** instead of **den** (see page 50). The gender and number of a demonstrative pronoun is determined by the noun it refers back to, and its case is determined by the pronoun's function in the sentence.

In spoken German, the demonstrative pronouns receive greater vocal stress than the personal pronouns or the definite articles, and they are frequently expanded by the addition of **hier** *this one / these,* **da, dort** *that one / those* to more clearly specify the object referred to.

Ich kaufe *den hier.*	*I'll buy this one.*
Wem gehört *dieser dort?*	*To whom does that one belong?*
Geben Sie mir *diese da!*	*Give me those.*
Bleib bei *denen hier!*	*Stay with these.*

19. Complete each of the following sentences, using the appropriate form of the demonstrative pronoun **der**. Follow the model.

    MODEL   Der Mantel hier ist wärmer als ___der dort (da)___ .

    1. Der Film hier ist länger als _____.
    2. In dem Parkhaus dort sind mehr Autos als in _____.
    3. Die Frau hier ist jünger als _____.
    4. Er kam aus dem Haus da, nicht aus _____.
    5. Ich kaufe die Maschine dort, nicht _____.
    6. Wir sprechen von den Leuten hier, nicht von _____.

20. Complete each of the following sentences, using the appropriate form of the demonstrative pronoun **dieser**.

    1. Diese Brücke hier ist breiter als _____.
    2. Wir fahren mit diesem Auto dort, nicht mit _____.
    3. Er kauft nicht diese Bücher hier, sondern _____.
    4. Dieser Ring da ist teurer als _____.
    5. Ich möchte dieses Kleid dort, nicht _____.

Indefinite Pronouns

The indefinite pronouns refer to persons, things, and concepts that are not precisely defined.

Singular

The following indefinite pronouns refer back to *persons*. They are used only in the singular nominative, accusative, and dative.

jeder
jemand
niemand
man (nominative only)

jeder *everyone*

Jeder **muss mitmachen.**	*Everyone has to participate.*
Ich habe *jeden* **gefragt.**	*I asked everyone.*
Er bekommt von *jedem* **etwas.**	*He gets something from everyone.*

Note that the accusative and dative forms take the same endings as the definite article **der**, **das**, **die**. The neuter form can be used to refer back to things.

jemand *someone*

Ist *jemand* **da?**	*Is anyone there?*
Er hat *jemand(en)* **gehört.**	*He heard someone.*
Ich rede gerade mit *jemand(em).*	*I'm talking with someone at the moment.*

Note that the accusative and dative forms can take the same endings as the masculine definite article. However, these endings can also be omitted. The genitive is used rarely, but when it is used, it precedes the noun.

jemand(e)s **Hilfe**	*someone's help*

niemand *no one*

Niemand **war zu Hause.**	*No one was home.*
Ich kenne *niemand(en)* **hier.**	*I know no one here.*
Sie hat mit *niemand(em)* **geredet.**	*She spoke with no one.*

Note that like **jemand**, **niemand** can take the same endings as the masculine definite article in the accusative and dative. However, these endings can also be omitted. The genitive is used rarely, but when it is used, it precedes the noun.

niemand(e)s **Hilfe**	*no one's help*

man *one, you, we, they, people*

Man **kann nicht alles wissen.**	*One can't know everything.*
Er sieht *einen* **nicht, wenn er sich beeilt.**	*He doesn't see you when he's in a hurry.*
Er redet nicht mit *einem.*	*He doesn't talk to people.*

The indefinite pronoun **man** occurs only in the nominative case. It is used with a verb in the third-person singular. If the accusative or dative case is called for, the form **einen** or **einem** is used, respectively. There is no genitive form of **man**; the possessive adjective **sein** is used instead.

The following indefinite pronouns refer only to *things*. They do not take any endings.

alles	**viel**
etwas	**wenig**
nichts	

alles *everything*

> **Ich habe *alles* gegessen.**   *I ate everything.*

etwas *something*

> **Ja, er hat *etwas* gesagt.**   *Yes, he said something.*

NOTE: The shortened form **was** is often used colloquially.

> **Ich habe *was* gesehen.**   *I saw something.*

nichts *nothing*

> **Sie hat uns *nichts* gebracht.**   *She brought us nothing.*

viel *much*

> **Wir haben *viel* gelernt.**   *We learned much.*

wenig *little*

> **Er weiß *wenig*.**   *He knows little.*

Plural

The following indefinite pronouns may refer to *things* or to *persons*. They take the plural endings of the definite article.

alle	**mehrere**
andere	**viele**
einige	**wenige**
manche	

alle *everyone, all*

> **Es gehört *allen*.**   *It belongs to everyone.*

andere *others, other ones*

> **Wir haben auch *andere*.**   *We also have others.*

einige *some, several*

> **Einige haben ihn im Park getroffen.**   *Some met him in the park.*

manche *many*

> **Manche bleiben gern hier.**   *Many like to stay here.*

mehrere *several*

> **Ich habe *mehrere* davon gekauft.**   *I bought several of them.*

viele *many*

> **Er hat mit *vielen* gespielt.**   *He played with many.*

wenige *few*

> ***Wenige* haben das Problem verstanden.**   *Few understood the problem.*

21. Complete each of the following sentences, using the appropriate form(s) of the indefinite pronoun(s).

1. Ich habe _____ (*no one*) gesehen.
2. Er hat _____ (*something*) gesagt.
3. _____ (*Few*) haben ihn besucht.
4. Er hat sich mit _____ (*some*) unterhalten.
5. _____ (*Everyone*) war zu Hause.
6. Sie kann _____ (*nothing*).
7. _____ (*One*) sollte ihm danken.
8. _____ (*Many*) haben es gewusst.
9. Ich kenne _____ (*everyone*).
10. Sie gibt _____ (*one*) _____ (*nothing*).
11. Er weiß _____ (*much*).
12. Wir haben _____ (*little*) gesehen.
13. _____ (*Someone*) ist gekommen.
14. Ich habe dann _____ (*other ones*) gesucht.
15. Hast du _____ (*several*) gekauft?
16. _____ (*Many*) haben Talent.
17. Habt ihr _____ (*everything*) gemacht?
18. _____ (*People*) hat ihn gern.

Relative Pronouns

	SINGULAR			PLURAL
	MASCULINE	NEUTER	FEMININE	ALL GENDERS
Nominative	der	das	die	die
Accusative	den	das	die	die
Dative	dem	dem	der	denen
Genitive	dessen	dessen	deren	deren

A relative pronoun both refers back to a previously mentioned noun or pronoun (often referred to as its *antecedent*) and introduces a dependent relative clause that modifies this antecedent. The most frequently used relative pronoun in German is a form of **der**, **das**, **die**.

A relative pronoun must have the same number and gender as its antecedent. However, the grammatical case of a relative pronoun is determined by its function within the relative clause. Thus, if the relative pronoun is the subject of the relative clause, it must be in the nominative case; if it is the direct object of the relative clause, it will usually be in the accusative case, and so forth. (See Cases of Nouns in Chapter 2, page 33.) The endings of the relative pronouns are the same as those for the definite articles, except for the dative plural **denen** and the genitive singular and plural forms **dessen** and **deren**.

Since the relative clause is a dependent (also called *subordinate*) clause, the conjugated verb moves to final position in the clause. (See Chapter 10, page 256). In this position, separable prefixes remain joined to the verb. The relative clause is set off from the main clause by a comma (or commas).

The relative pronoun **welcher, welches, welche** is used relatively infrequently. It is used primarily in written German and usually either to clarify meanings or for stylistic considerations, such as to avoid repetitions of identical forms.

Nominative Case

SINGULAR			PLURAL
MASCULINE	NEUTER	FEMININE	ALL GENDERS
der	das	die	die
welcher	welches	welche	welche

The relative pronoun in each of the following examples is in the nominative case because it functions as the subject of the relative clause.

Kennst du den Mann, *der* dort steht?	Do you know the man who is standing there?
Otto kommt von der Lehrerin, *die* ihm das Problem erklärt hat.	Otto is coming from the teacher who explained the problem to him.
Das Mädchen, *das* dort steht, ist seine Schwester.	The girl who is standing there is his sister.
Siehst du die Vögel, *die* dort auf dem Baum sitzen?	Do you see the birds that are sitting there on the tree?

In the following sentence, the appropriate form of the relative pronoun **welch-** is preferred to avoid repetition of **die**.

Die Dame, *welche* (*die*) die Brosche gekauft hat, ist sehr reich.	The lady who bought the brooch is very rich.

22. Complete each of the following sentences, using the appropriate form of the nominative relative pronoun **der**.

1. Wo ist das Buch, _____ dir gehört?
2. Der Junge, _____ dort steht, ist mein Bruder.
3. Wo sind die Bilder, _____ uns so gefallen?
4. Die Frau, _____ bei uns wohnt, ist keine Sängerin.
5. Wie heißt der Dichter, _____ dieses Gedicht geschrieben hat?
6. Kennst du das Mädchen, _____ dort sitzt?
7. Dort ist die Lehrerin, _____ uns geholfen hat.
8. Wir fahren mit dem Zug, _____ jetzt ankommt.

Accusative Case

SINGULAR			PLURAL
MASCULINE	NEUTER	FEMININE	ALL GENDERS
den	das	die	die
welchen	welches	welche	welche

The forms of the accusative relative pronouns are identical to the nominative forms, except in the masculine singular. The accusative case of the relative pronoun is used when it functions as the direct object of the verb or as the object of an accusative preposition. No contractions are possible.

Der Anzug, *den* **du trägst, ist altmodisch.**	*The suit that you are wearing is old-fashioned.*
Die Geschichte, *die* **wir gelesen haben, war sehr lang.**	*The story that we read was very long.*
Das Haus, in *das* **wir ziehen, ist hundert Jahre alt.**	*The house into which we are moving is one hundred years old.*
Das sind die Freunde, für *die* **ich es gekauft habe.**	*Those are the friends for whom I bought it.*

23. Complete each of the following sentences, using the appropriate accusative form of the relative pronoun **der**.

1. Wo sitzt der Junge, _____ du kennengelernt hast?
2. Die Frau, neben _____ ich mich gesetzt habe, ist Schauspielerin.
3. Der Mantel, _____ er angezogen hat, gehört mir.
4. Das Mädchen, auf _____ er wartete, ist meine Freundin.
5. Die Hunde, _____ ich füttern soll, sind ja wild.
6. Die Bluse, _____ du trägst, ist sehr hübsch.
7. Hier ist das Paket, _____ er mir geschickt hat.
8. Wir kennen den Lehrer, für _____ sie es macht.

24. Combine each of the following pairs of sentences, using the appropriate nominative or accusative form of the relative pronoun. Follow the model.

MODEL   Wie heißt das Mädchen? Wir haben es kennengelernt.

Wie heißt das Mädchen, das wir kennengelernt haben?

1. Liest du das Buch? Er hat es gebracht.

   _____

2. Brauchst du die Zeitung? Sie liegt auf dem Tisch.

   _____

3. Kennst du den Herrn? Wir haben ihn getroffen.

   _____

4. Heute kam der Junge. Er hatte uns damals geholfen.

   _____

5. Kennst du die Leute? Sie gehen dort spazieren.

   _____

6. Wo sind die Blumen? Ich habe sie gekauft.

   _____

Dative Case

SINGULAR			PLURAL
MASCULINE	**NEUTER**	**FEMININE**	**ALL GENDERS**
dem	dem	der	*denen*
welchem	welchem	welcher	welchen

The dative relative pronoun is used when it functions as the indirect object of the verb of the dependent clause or as the object of a verb or preposition requiring the dative case. The dative plural relative pronoun differs from the definite article. It adds **-en** to become **denen**. No contractions are possible.

Dort liegt der Hund, vor *dem* ich Angst habe.	*There lies the dog that I am afraid of.*
Heute besucht mich meine Freundin, von *der* ich dir erzählt habe.	*My girlfriend, about whom I told you, is visiting me today.*
Das Mädchen, *dem* ich die Kette gegeben hatte, hat sie verloren.	*The girl to whom I had given the necklace lost it.*
Die Studenten, neben *denen* er sitzt, sind sehr intelligent.	*The students next to whom he is sitting are very intelligent.*

25. Complete each of the following sentences, using the appropriate dative form of the relative pronoun **der**.

1. Das Buch, nach _____ er fragte, gehört mir.
2. Der Deutsche, mit _____ er spricht, kommt aus Berlin.
3. Die Leute, _____ ich helfen wollte, sind weggefahren.
4. Das Haus, in _____ wir wohnen, ist modern.
5. Dort ist die Reisende, _____ ich den Weg gezeigt habe.
6. Die Dame, _____ ich es gebe, ist sehr intelligent.
7. Die Straßen, nach _____ er fragt, sind im Zentrum.
8. Das Hotel, aus _____ er kommt, ist sehr alt.

26. Combine each of the following pairs of sentences, using the appropriate dative form of the relative pronoun **welcher**.

1. Dort sitzt der Tourist. Du sollst ihm das Essen bringen.

   _____

2. Kennst du meine Geschwister? Ich wohne bei ihnen.

   _____

3. Die Leiter ist kaputt. Er steht darauf.

   _____

4. Hier ist das Auto. Wir fahren damit spazieren.

   _____

5. Der Stuhl ist alt. Du sitzt darauf.

   _____

Genitive Case

SINGULAR			PLURAL
MASCULINE	NEUTER	FEMININE	ALL GENDERS
dessen	dessen	deren	deren

All the forms of the genitive relative pronouns differ from those of the definite article. The relative pronoun **welcher** has no genitive forms.

Ich treffe meinen Freund, *dessen* Auto ich brauche.	*I'll meet my friend whose car I need.*
Dort ist die Dame, *deren* Geld ich gefunden habe.	*There is the lady whose money I found.*
Das Haus, *dessen* Baustil mir gefällt, wurde 1910 gebaut.	*The house, the style of which I like, was built in 1910.*
Die Kinder, *deren* Katze verletzt wurde, laufen zum Tierarzt.	*The children whose cat was injured are running to the veterinarian.*

27. Complete each of the following sentences, using the appropriate genitive form of the relative pronoun.

1. Die Frau, _____ Auto kaputt ist, sucht einen Mechaniker.
2. Der Dichter, _____ Roman wir gelesen haben, hält einen Vortrag.
3. Hier kommt das Kind, _____ Eltern ich gut kenne.
4. Die Künstler, _____ Werke wir besichtigen, sind weltbekannt.
5. Die Studentin, _____ Buch ich gefunden habe, ist nett.
6. Die Museen, _____ Sammlungen ich kenne, sind reich.
7. Dort ist der Junge, _____ Vater uns geholfen hat.
8. Wo ist das Mädchen, _____ Fahrrad dort liegt?

Indefinite Relative Pronouns

Wer, was

The indefinite relative pronouns **wer** *whoever* and **was** *whatever* are used when there is no antecedent.

The case of **wer** is determined by its function in the relative clause that it introduces. **Wer** takes the same endings as the **der** form of the relative pronoun. It is always singular.

Nominative	wer
Accusative	wen
Dative	wem
Genitive	wessen

Was does not change its form according to how it is used in the relative clause.

When **wer** or **was** is used in combination with the adverbs **auch**, **immer**, **auch immer**, the already indefinite character of the indefinite pronoun is intensified.

Wer **mitgehen will, muss um fünf Uhr hier sein.**	*Whoever wants to come along has to be here at five o'clock.*
Was **auch immer passiert, ich habe keine Angst.**	*Whatever happens, I am not afraid.*

28. Complete each of the following sentences, using the appropriate form of the indefinite relative pronoun.

1. _____ mir hilft, wird belohnt.
2. _____ er sagt, ist die Wahrheit.
3. _____ das Geld genommen hat, soll es zurückgeben.
4. _____ er auch will, bekommt er.
5. _____ das Problem löst, bekommt den Preis.

The relative pronoun **was** *that, which* must be used if the antecedent is an indefinite pronoun referring to things (**alles**, **nichts**, **etwas**, etc.).

Er erzählte mir etwas, *was* **ich schon wusste.**	*He told me something that I knew already.*

Was is also used when the antecedent is an entire clause.

Er hatte das Geld gewonnen, *was* **mich sehr freute.**	*He had won the money, which made me very happy.*

Wo

When the antecedent is the name of a country, city, or place, **wo** *where, in which* is substituted for the relative pronoun.

Er besucht London, *wo* er viele Freunde hat.   *He is visiting London, where he has many friends.*

29. Complete each of the following sentences, using the appropriate form of the indefinite relative pronoun or pronoun substitute.

    1. Er hat nichts, _____ großen Wert hat.
    2. Wir sind in Bayern, _____ es viele Barockkirchen gibt.
    3. Wir fahren in die Alpen, _____ man gut skifahren kann.
    4. Er ist sehr krank, _____ mir große Sorgen macht.
    5. Alles, _____ ich habe, hat Inge mir geschenkt.
    6. Er weiß etwas, _____ sehr wichtig ist.
    7. Wir landen in Frankfurt, _____ es den internationalen Flughafen gibt.
    8. Er ist der beste Sportler, _____ mich sehr freut.

Wo-compounds in Relative Clauses

When a relative pronoun refers back to a thing or idea and is preceded by a preposition, it may be replaced by a **wo**-compound.

Das Paket, *worauf* (*auf das*) er wartet, soll   *The package for which he is waiting is supposed*
   heute ankommen.   *to arrive today.*

30. Rewrite each of the following sentences, substituting the appropriate **wo**-compound for the preposition + relative pronoun.

    1. Der Stuhl, auf dem du sitzt, ist eine Rarität.
    _____

    2. Wir besuchen das Haus, in dem Goethe geboren wurde.
    _____

    3. Ist das das Spielzeug, mit dem sie sich so amüsiert?
    _____

    4. Dort ist die Kirche, nach der er fragte.
    _____

    5. Sind das die Bücher, für die du dich interessierst?
    _____

    6. Wo ist der Brief, auf den er wartet?
    _____

    7. Das Problem, über das ihr sprecht, ist schwer.
    _____

    8. Wo ist die Ruine, von der er erzählt?
    _____

Review

31. Complete each of the following sentences, using the appropriate form of the relative pronouns **der**, **wer**, **was**, or the pronoun substitute **wo**.

1. Sie gab uns alles, _____ sie hatte.
2. Wo ist der Brief, _____ ich mitnehmen soll?
3. _____ er auch ist, er muss warten.
4. Dort ist der Klub, zu _____ ich gehöre.
5. Die Kinder, _____ Eltern noch nicht gekommen sind, warten noch.
6. Willst du das Auto, _____ dort steht?
7. Ist das das Flugzeug, mit _____ du geflogen bist?
8. Ich habe den Apparat, _____ er vergessen hat.
9. Wir besuchen München, _____ das Bier so gut ist.
10. Der Koffer, _____ dort steht, gehört seiner Freundin.
11. Wo ist das Buch, _____ er vergessen hat?
12. Es gab nichts, _____ er nicht machen konnte.
13. Der Komponist, _____ Oper uns so gut gefallen hat, ist tot.
14. _____ alles weiß, braucht keine Angst zu haben.
15. Kennst du das Gedicht, _____ wir lernen mussten.
16. Die Kranken, _____ dort sitzen, brauchen viel Ruhe.
17. Wir fliegen nach Holland, _____ zur Zeit die Tulpen blühen.
18. Die Kinder, _____ ich die Geschenke brachte, danken mir.
19. Kennst du die Leute, _____ Auto ich parken musste?
20. Ich sehe etwas, _____ ich kaufen will.
21. Wo ist die Kirche, _____ er besuchte?
22. Die Tasche, _____ ich kaufte, ist aus Leder.
23. Der Mann, neben _____ er steht, ist bekannt.
24. Alles _____ du brauchst ist hier.
25. Dort ist der Deutsche, _____ ich den Weg zeigte.

CHAPTER 5

Adjectives and Adverbs

Demonstrative Adjectives

Der, das, die

Demonstrative adjectives are used to point out or give special emphasis to the nouns they modify. In German, the definite article **der**, **das**, **die** can also function as a demonstrative adjective, corresponding to the English *this/these* and *that/those*. The demonstrative adjective, like the definite article, agrees with the noun it modifies in gender, number, and case. Thus the demonstrative adjective has the same endings as the definite article. (See Chapter 2, page 50.) When used as demonstrative adjectives, the various forms of **der**, **das**, **die** are stressed in spoken German.

When **hier** is used with the demonstrative adjective, it corresponds to the English *this/these*. When **da** or **dort** is used, it corresponds to *that/those*. The words **hier**, **da**, **dort** follow the noun that is modified by the demonstrative adjective.

Die Jacke *hier* ist teuer.	*This jacket is expensive.*
Sie kam aus *dem* Haus *dort*.	*She came out of that house.*
Helfen Sie *dem* Jungen *da*!	*Help that boy!*

1. Complete each of the following sentences, using the appropriate form of the demonstrative adjective.

1. Ich kaufe _____ Auto hier.
2. Wie viel kostet _____ Teppich da?
3. Sie wohnten in _____ Straße dort.
4. Warum kaufst du nicht _____ Mantel hier?
5. Er will aus _____ Glas da trinken.
6. _____ Schuhe hier sind bequem.
7. Wie findest du _____ Wein hier?
8. Er ist gegen _____ Baum dort gefahren.
9. Ich wohne bei _____ Leuten da.
10. Kennt ihr _____ Studentin dort?

Dieser, dieses, diese

Another demonstrative adjective is **dieser**. Like **der**, **das**, **die**, it agrees with the noun it modifies in gender, number, and case. Any form of **dieser** can be made to correspond to the English *this/these* by adding **hier**. **Da** and **dort** make it correspond to *that/those*. Note that these patterns are primarily for use in spoken rather than written German. **Dieser** takes the same endings as the definite article.

Willst du *diesen* Pullover *hier*?   *Do you want this sweater?*
Ich fahre mit *diesem* Bus *dort*.   *I am taking that bus.*
***Diese* Häuser *da* sind sehr alt.**   *Those houses are very old.*

2. Form a sentence from each of the following groups of words, using the appropriate form of the demonstrative adjective **dieser**.

   1. Mantel / dort / gehören / mir   _____
   2. Wir / holen / etwas / für / Mädchen / hier   _____
   3. Ich / helfen / Mann / da   _____
   4. Es / liegen / unter / Bücher / da   _____
   5. Mit / Wagen / hier / fahren / wir / nicht   _____
   6. Ursula / haben / Kamera / da   _____
   7. Ich / schlafen / nicht / in / Bett / da   _____
   8. Kennen / du / Mann / dort / ?   _____
   9. Frauen / hier / kaufen / nichts   _____
   10. Er / kaufen / Blumen / hier   _____

Descriptive Adjectives

Descriptive adjectives are words that describe or provide additional information about the qualities of people and things, such as *thin, green, good*. In German as well as English, descriptive adjectives can be used in various ways.

Predicate Adjectives

When an adjective follows a noun or pronoun subject and is preceded by a form of **sein**, **werden**, **bleiben**, it is used as a predicate adjective.

   Der Kaffee war *bitter*.   *The coffee was bitter.*
   Seine Haare werden schon *grau*.   *His hair is already getting gray.*

The predicate adjective never takes an ending.
   Some common German adjectives follow.

alt	*old*	**gesund**	*healthy*
amerikanisch	*American*	**glücklich**	*happy*
arm	*poor*	**groß**	*big, tall*
bequem	*comfortable*	**gut**	*good*
billig	*inexpensive*	**hässlich**	*ugly*
bitter	*bitter*	**heiß**	*hot*
blond	*blond*	**hübsch**	*pretty*
böse	*bad*	**intelligent**	*intelligent*
deutsch	*German*	**interessant**	*interesting*
dick	*heavy, thick*	**jung**	*young*
dunkel	*dark*	**kalt**	*cold*
dünn	*skinny, thin*	**klein**	*small, short*
eng	*narrow*	**klug**	*clever, smart*
faul	*lazy*	**krank**	*ill*
fleißig	*industrious*	**kurz**	*short*
fremd	*strange*	**lang**	*long*
frisch	*fresh*	**langsam**	*slow*

leer	*empty*	**scharf**	*sharp, pungent*
leicht	*easy*	**schmutzig**	*dirty*
nah	*near*	**schnell**	*fast*
nett	*nice*	**schwach**	*weak*
neu	*new*	**süß**	*sweet*
reich	*rich*	**teuer**	*expensive*
sauber	*clean*	**voll**	*full*
sauer	*sour*	**weit**	*far*

3. Complete each of the following sentences, using a predicate adjective that means the opposite of the one after **sondern**.

1. Das Wetter ist nicht _____, sondern kalt.
2. Der Tee ist nicht _____, sondern bitter.
3. Der Schüler ist nicht _____, sondern fleißig.
4. Die Straße ist nicht _____, sondern kurz.
5. Meine Tochter ist nicht _____, sondern gesund.
6. Sein Bruder ist nicht _____, sondern arm.
7. Ihre Hände sind nicht _____, sondern sauber.
8. Diese Aufgabe ist nicht _____, sondern schwer.
9. Sein Mädchen ist nicht _____, sondern hübsch.
10. Dieser Mantel war nicht _____, sondern teuer.
11. Sie ist nicht _____, sondern dünn.
12. Er ist nicht _____, sondern schnell.
13. Es ist nicht _____, sondern gut.
14. Es ist nicht _____, sondern neu.
15. Sie ist nicht _____, sondern groß.

Attributive Adjectives Preceded by the Definite Article or Other "der" Words

When an adjective precedes a noun, it is used as an attributive adjective. An attributive adjective in German always takes an ending. The adjective ending is determined by the number (singular or plural), gender (masculine, feminine, or neuter), and the case (its grammatical function in the sentence, clause, or prepositional phrase) of the noun it modifies. Another key factor determining the ending of the adjective is the presence or absence of a "**der**" or "**ein**" word.

The following words take the same endings as the definite article and are referred to as "**der**" words.

dieser	*this*
jeder	*each, every* (used only in the singular)
jener	*that*
mancher	*many (a)*
solcher	*such* (usually occurs only in the plural)
welcher	*which*
alle	*all* (used only in the plural)

An adjective preceded by the definite article or a "**der**" word requires a specific set of endings.

Nominative Singular (Following "der" Words)

When an attributive adjective modifies a noun in the nominative singular and is preceded by the definite article or a "**der**" word, it takes the following endings.

MASCULINE	NEUTER	FEMININE
der billige Koffer	das hübsche Mädchen	die alte Tasche

Der alte **Tisch ist kaputt.**	*The old table is broken.*
Das kleine **Kind schreit.**	*The small child is screaming.*
Die nette **Frau hilft uns.**	*The nice woman is helping us.*
Dieser deutsche **Wagen ist schnell.**	*This German car is fast.*
Jene große **Maschine ist teuer.**	*That large machine is expensive.*
Welches leere **Glas gehört dir?**	*Which empty glass belongs to you?*

If the noun is modified by two or more attributive adjectives in succession, they all take the same ending.

Wo ist die *kleine, schwarze* **Katze?**	*Where is the small black cat?*

4. Complete each of the following sentences, using the appropriate endings.

1. Dies___ breit___ Fluss ist die Donau.
2. Wo ist d___ neu___, blau___ Kleid?
3. Welch___ deutsch___ Lied ist das?
4. Wann ist d___ hübsch___ Studentin wieder zu Hause?
5. Wie viel kostet dies___ warm___ Mantel?
6. Welch___ bekannt___, amerikanisch___ Dichter hat den Roman geschrieben?
7. Manch___ fremd___ Student hat Heimweh.
8. Dies___ alt___ Schlüssel ist rostig.

5. Complete each of the following sentences, using the appropriate forms of the words on the right.

1. _____ Stadt ist das? — welch, deutsch
2. _____ Kind weint. — jenes, klein
3. _____ Gymnasium ist modern. — jedes, neu
4. Wo ist _____ Lehrerin? — die, jung
5. Wie viel kostet _____ Wagen? — dieser, amerikanisch
6. Wie heißt _____ Student? — jener, blond
7. Wo ist _____ Buch? — das, dünn, rot
8. Was macht _____ Mensch? — jeder, gesund
9. Dort steht _____ Glas. — das, leer
10. Wie viel kostet _____ Lampe? — jene, groß
11. Wann kommt _____ Professor? — der, interessant
12. _____ Limonade schmeckt gut. — diese, kalt

6. Form a sentence from each of the following groups of words, using the appropriate forms of the "**der**" words and adjectives.

1. Jen / französisch / Dichter / ist / weltbekannt _____
2. Der / rot / Bus / wartet _____
3. Manch / deutsch / Drama / ist / lang _____
4. Wie viel / kostet / jen / schnell / Auto / ? _____
5. Jed / modern / Museum / braucht / Geld _____
6. Welch / alt / Maschine / ist / kaputt / ? _____
7. Wo / ist / die / weiß / Katze / ? _____
8. Wo / steht / die / frisch / Milch / ? _____

Accusative Singular (Following "der" Words)

When an attributive adjective modifies a noun in the accusative singular and is preceded by the definite article or a "**der**" word, it takes the following endings.

MASCULINE	NEUTER	FEMININE
den klein*en* Schlüssel	das voll*e* Glas	die reich*e* Sängerin

Ich kenne *den deutschen* Studenten.	*I know the German student.*
Er kauft *das schnelle* Auto.	*He is buying the fast car.*
Sie läuft in *die alte* Fabrik.	*She is running into the old factory.*
Brauchst du *diesen langen* Stock?	*Do you need this long stick?*
Welche billige Uhr hat er?	*Which cheap watch does he have?*
Wir nehmen *jenes dünne* Papier.	*We are taking that thin paper.*

NOTE: The accusative singular adjective endings are identical to the nominative singular endings for neuter and feminine nouns; the accusative singular masculine ending, however, is different.

7. Complete each of the following sentences, using the appropriate endings.

1. Setzt euch auf dies___ bequem___ Sofa!
2. Er bleibt d___ ganz___ Woche in Bonn.
3. Wir sammeln für jen___ krank___ Jungen.
4. Er hat manch___ interessant___ Gedicht geschrieben.
5. Hast du d___ weiß___ Kater gesehen?
6. Wer hat dir jen___ wunderbar___, blau___ Orchidee gekauft?
7. Welch___ neu___ Handschuh hast du verloren?
8. Er kämpft gegen d___ bekannt___ Weltmeister.

8. Complete each of the following sentences, using the appropriate forms of the words on the right.

1. Wir gehen _____ Straße entlang.	die, lang
2. Ich besuche _____ Gymnasium.	jenes, modern
3. Wir laufen um _____ Park.	dieser, groß
4. _____ Roman liest du?	welcher, interessant
5. Ich brauche _____ Messer.	das, scharf
6. Leg es auf _____ Platte!	die, klein
7. Kennst du _____ _____ Mädchen?	jenes, fremd, jung
8. Ich kaufe es für _____ Kind.	jedes, krank
9. Wir nehmen _____ Wagen.	der, schmutzig
10. Setz dich neben _____ Ofen!	jener, heiß
11. Sie stellte sich hinter _____ _____ Mann.	der, groß, blond
12. Er kennt _____ Helden.	jener, klug

9. Form a sentence from each of the following groups of words, using the appropriate forms of the "**der**" words and adjectives.

1. Er / restaurierte / manch / historisch / Haus

   _____

2. Wer / hat / der / alt / Lederkoffer / ?

   _____

3. Bring / dies / schmutzig / Glas / in / die / Küche / !

_____

4. Wir / kaufen / jen / schnell / Motorboot

_____

5. Welch / rot / Apfel / möchtest / du / ?

_____

6. Wir / wandern / durch / die / klein / Stadt

_____

7. Sie / bringt / Blumen / für / das / krank / Kind

_____

8. Ich / brauche / jed / neu / deutsch / Briefmarke

_____

Dative Singular (Following "der" Words)

When an attributive adjective modifies a noun in the dative singular and is preceded by the definite article or a "**der**" word, it takes the following endings.

MASCULINE	NEUTER	FEMININE
dem alt**en** Herrn	dem neu**en** Haus	der krank**en** Mutter

Wir helfen *diesem kranken* Herrn.   *We are helping this ill gentleman.*
Welchem kleinen Kind gibst du das Spielzeug?   *To which small child are you giving the toy?*
Er wohnt bei *jener netten* Familie.   *He is staying with that nice family.*

10. Complete each of the following sentences, using the appropriate endings.

1. Ich habe mich mit d___ scharf___ Messer geschnitten.
2. Er kam aus jen___ eng___ Straße.
3. Sie hat uns von dies___ hoh___ Baum erzählt.
4. Er dankt d___ klein___, freundlich___ Mädchen.
5. Ich gebe jed___ klug___ Studentin ein Buch.
6. Warum sitzt du in d___ kalt___ Zimmer?
7. Ich helfe dies___ krank___ Frau.
8. Wir wohnen d___ groß___ Park gegenüber.

11. Complete each of the following sentences, using the appropriate forms of the words on the right.

1. Sie kam aus _____ Hotel.	jenes, international
2. Wir gehen zu _____ Vorlesung.	jede, interessant
3. Wohnst du bei _____ Familie?	diese, nett
4. Sie sitzt auf _____ Boden.	der, schmutzig
5. Schreib nicht mit _____ Bleistift!	jener, kurz
6. Sie sitzen in _____	der, groß,
_____ Wagen.	amerikanisch
7. Aus _____ Land kommt er?	welches, fremd
8. Er spricht mit _____ Studentin.	die, hübsch
9. Sie erzählt von _____ Mann.	jener, reich
10. Der Ballon gefällt _____ Kind.	das, klein
11. Ich gebe _____ Patientin eine Pille.	jede, krank
12. Sie sitzt auf _____ Teppich.	der, hässlich

12. Form a sentence from each of the following groups of words, using the appropriate forms of the "**der**" words and adjectives.

1. Wir / schlafen / in / der / modern / Schlafwagen

   _____

2. Mit / welch / neu / Handy / soll / ich / telefonieren / ?

   _____

3. Er / wohnt / bei / jen / nett / Dame

   _____

4. Der / Ball / liegt / unter / der / blau / Sessel

   _____

5. Trink / nicht / aus / jen / rot / Glas / !

   _____

6. Wir / gehen / bei / dies / kalt / Wetter / nicht / aus

   _____

7. Wer / sitzt / auf / die / alt / rostig / Bank / ?

   _____

8. Wir / bekamen / von / manch / amerikanisch / Studenten / Post

   _____

Genitive Singular (Following "der" Words)

When an attributive adjective modifies a noun in the genitive singular and is preceded by the definite article or a "**der**" word, it takes the following endings.

MASCULINE	NEUTER	FEMININE
des jung*en* Lehrers	des bös*en* Kindes	der dick*en* Katze

Er wohnt jenseits *dieses hohen* Berges.	*He lives on the other side of this high mountain.*
Dort ist die Mutter *des kleinen* Kindes.	*There is the mother of the small child.*
Wir wohnen außerhalb *jener großen* Stadt.	*We live outside of that large city.*

13. Complete each of the following sentences, using the appropriate endings.

1. Wo ist die Tochter dies____ arm____ Mannes?
2. Dort steht das Haus d____ reich____ Familie.
3. Ich kenne die Melodie jen____ deutsch____ Liedes.
4. Die Zimmer dies____ neu____ Hauses sind groß.
5. Wir waren während jen____ kalt____ Nacht zu Hause.
6. Jenseits dies____ klein____ Dorfes ist die Grenze.
7. Sie kommen um d____ interessant____ Professors willen.
8. Wir sind innerhalb jen____ alt____ Stadt.

14. Complete each of the following sentences, using the appropriate forms of the words on the right.

1. Der Preis _____ Mantels ist zu hoch.	der, blau
2. Sie sind innerhalb _____ Gartens.	jener, exotisch
3. Die Frau _____ Technikers ist hier.	der, deutsch
4. Die Farbe _____ Kleides ist hässlich.	dieses, billig
5. Er kommt um _____ Frau willen.	die, krank
6. Die Kissen _____ Sofas sind weich.	dieses, bequem
7. Die Studenten _____ Universität sind hier.	jene, bekannt

   8. Die Straßen _____ Stadt sind eng.   diese, klein
   9. Der Mann _____ Sängerin ist dort.   die, dick
  10. Das ist die Mutter _____ Babys.   das, gesund
  11. Sie wohnt diesseits _____ Sees.   jener, groß
  12. Dort ist der Besitzer _____ Sammlung.   jene, interessant

15. Form a sentence from each of the following groups of words, using the appropriate forms of the "**der**" words and adjectives.

   1. Wo / ist / der / Besitzer / dies / schmutzig / Mantel / ?

      _____

   2. Die / Gedichte / manch / deutsch / Dichter / sind / kompliziert

      _____

   3. Die / Mutter / jen / krank / Kind / ist / hier

      _____

   4. Der / Park / ist / jenseits / das / groß / Monument

      _____

   5. Trotz / dies / stark / Explosion / gab / es / kein / Verwundete

      _____

   6. Die / Straßen / jen / alt / Stadt / sind / eng

      _____

   7. Die / Zimmer / die / neu / Wohnung / sind / modern

      _____

Plural of All Cases and Genders (Following "der" Words)

When an attributive adjective modifies a plural noun and is preceded by a plural form of the definite article or a "**der**" word, the adjective ending is **-en** for all cases. The plural form of **jeder** is **alle**. The plural form of **manche** is not followed by adjectives ending in **-en**. (For a discussion of plurals, see Attributive Adjectives Not Preceded by "**der**" or "**ein**" Words (Unpreceded), page 108.)

Nominative	die deutsch*en* Zeitungen
Accusative	die alt*en* Männer
Dative	den gesund*en* Kindern
Genitive	der hoh*en* Berge

Diese frischen Eier kosten viel.	*These fresh eggs are expensive.*
Ich habe *alle leeren* **Flaschen.**	*I have all empty bottles.*
Mit *solchen neuen Autos* **kann man schnell fahren.**	*One can drive fast with such new cars.*
Das Leben *jener alten Leute* **ist traurig.**	*The life of those old people is sad.*

16. Rewrite each of the following sentences, changing the noun(s) to plural and making all necessary changes.

   1. Welche deutsche Stadt hat er besucht?

      _____

   2. Ohne dieses warme Kleid fahre ich nicht.

      _____

   3. Wir steigen auf jenen bekannten Berg.

      _____

   4. Es gehört jener interessanten, jungen Frau.

      _____

5. Er schenkt etwas in jedes leere Glas.

   _____

6. Ich liege unter dem schattigen Baum.

   _____

7. Er erzählt dem kleinen Mädchen eine Geschichte.

   _____

8. Ich komme um des kranken Lehrers willen.

   _____

9. Jeder gesunde Patient darf nach Hause.

   _____

10. Sie hat den grünen Apfel.

   _____

Special Adjective Forms

A few adjectives omit certain letters when they take an attributive adjective ending. Adjectives ending in **-el** always drop the **e** in the final syllable when an ending is added.

Das Zimmer ist *dunkel*.	*The room is dark.*
Wir sind in dem *dunklen* **Zimmer.**	*We are in the dark room.*

Adjectives ending in **-euer** or **-auer** can drop or retain the **e** when the attributive adjective ending is added.

Das Haus ist *teuer*.	*The house is expensive.*
Ich ziehe in jenes *teure* (*teuere*) **Haus.**	*I am moving into that expensive house.*
Die Orange ist *sauer*.	*The orange is sour.*
Wer kauft diese *sauren* (*saueren*) **Orangen?**	*Who is buying these sour oranges?*

But note that other adjectives such as **bitter** retain the **e**.

Der Kaffee ist *bitter*.	*The coffee is bitter.*
Warum trinkst du den *bitteren* **Kaffee?**	*Why are you drinking the bitter coffee?*

The adjective **hoch** drops the **c** when an attributive adjective ending is added.

Der Turm ist *hoch*.	*The tower is high.*
Er steigt auf jenen *hohen* **Turm.**	*He is climbing that high tower.*

A small number of descriptive adjectives do not take any adjective endings at all, whether they are preceded by a "**der**" word or an "**ein**" word or are unpreceded. Included in this group are certain foreign loanwords ending in **-a**.

Das *rosa* **Kleid schmeichelte sie sehr.**	*The pink dress flattered her very much.*
Er ist ein *prima* **Kerl.**	*He's a first-rate fellow.*
Lila **Blumen sind schön.**	*Lavender flowers are beautiful.*

Another group of adjectives that do not take adjective endings are those formed from city names plus the suffix **-er**.

Sie wohnt an der *Kieler* **Förde.**	*She lives on the Kiel Fjord.*
Ich traf ihn am *Münchner* **Hauptbahnhof.**	*I met him at the Munich main train station.*
Er besuchte die *Frankfurter* **Buchmesse.**	*He visited the Frankfurt Book Fair.*

NOTE: This is one of the rare situations in which a German adjective is capitalized.

17. Complete each of the following sentences, using the appropriate forms of the word(s) on the right.

1. Was machst du in _____ Haus?   das, dunkel
2. Sie nehmen _____ Pille.   die, bitter
3. Er kauft _____ Mantel.   jener, teuer
4. Wir wohnen jenseits _____ Bergs.   dieser, hoch
5. Wo ist _____ Wäsche?   die, sauber
6. Trink nicht _____ Milch!   die, sauer
7. Wo ist _____ Zimmer?   das, sauber
8. Warum kaufst du _____ Spielzeug?   dieses, teuer
9. Wo sind _____ Äpfel?   der, sauer
10. Wie heißt _____ Berg?   dieser, hoch
11. Ich esse gern _____ Lebkuchen.   Nürnberg
12. Wir besuchen die _____ Messe.   Frankfurt
13. Das ist _____ Bier.   Dortmund
14. Er trinkt eine _____ Weiße.   Berlin
15. Wie hoch ist der _____ Dom?   Köln

Review: Attributive Adjectives Preceded by "der" Words

There are only two different endings for adjectives following the definite article or a "**der**" word: **-e** or **-en**. The **-en** ending predominates, except for the three nominative singular forms and the accusative feminine and neuter singular forms.

	SINGULAR			PLURAL
	MASCULINE	NEUTER	FEMININE	ALL GENDERS
Nominative	-e	-e	-e	-en
Accusative	-en	-e	-e	-en
Dative	-en	-en	-en	-en
Genitive	-en	-en	-en	-en

18. Complete each of the following sentences, using the appropriate endings.

1. Hast du d___ deutsch___ Zeitungen auf jen___ rund___ Tisch gelegt?
2. Dies___ gelb___ Mantel habe ich in d___ neu___ Geschäft gekauft.
3. In d___ eng___ Straßen dies___ alt___ Stadt gibt es viel Verkehr.
4. Wer ist d___ dick___ Dame neben d___ schlank___ Herrn?
5. Wegen dies___ schlecht___ Wetters bleibe ich zu Hause.
6. D___ amerikanisch___ Studentin kam aus jen___ modern___, weiß___ Haus.
7. All___ dunkl___ Straßen werden i___ nächst___ Monat beleuchtet.
8. Mit solch___ schmutzig___ Händen kannst du d___ neu___ Buch nicht anfassen.
9. D___ freundlich___ Kellnerin hat gleich jed___ leer___ Glas mit Bier gefüllt.
10. Hat jen___ deutsch___ Dichter auch dies___ traurig___ Gedicht geschrieben?

19. Complete each of the following sentences, using the appropriate forms of the words on the right.

1. _____ Mädchen wohnt   dieses, deutsch;
   bei _____ Familie.   jene, nett
2. _____ Männer kaufen   alle, elegant;
   _____ Mäntel.   diese, kurz

3. _____ Student braucht   jener, blond;
_____ Buch.   dieses, teuer

4. _____ Frau hilft   die, hübsch;
_____ Herrn.   der, dick

5. _____ Besitzer   der, neu;
_____ Wagens ist hier.   der, teuer

6. Wir waschen _____ Hände   die, schmutzig;
_____ Kindes.   das, klein

7. _____ Tourist kauft   jener, amerikanisch;
_____ Kamera.   diese, billig

8. _____ Hund liegt   der, schwarz;
unter _____ Tisch.   der, rund

9. _____ Leute essen   die, jung;
auf _____ Terrasse.   die, dunkel

10. _____ Dame kauft   die, hungrig;
_____ Kuchen.   der, groß

Attributive Adjectives Preceded by the Indefinite Article or Other "ein" Words

The negative article **kein** and all the possessive adjectives are called "**ein**" words, because they take the same endings as the indefinite article. (See page 34 and Possessive Adjectives, pages 118–119.)

Adjectives preceded by the indefinite article or an "**ein**" word require a different set of endings.

Nominative Singular (Following "ein" Words)

When an attributive adjective modifies a noun in the nominative singular and is preceded by the indefinite article or an "**ein**" word, it takes the following endings.

MASCULINE	NEUTER	FEMININE
ein blau*er* Huf	ein bequem*es* Sofa	eine lang*e* Reise

Ein alter Herr wartet.   *An old gentleman is waiting.*
Ein kleines Kind kommt.   *A small child is coming.*
Das ist *eine billige* Tasche.   *That is a cheap purse.*
Wo ist *dein neuer* Freund?   *Where is your new friend?*
Hier ist *unser altes* Radio.   *Here is our old radio.*
Dort ist *seine hübsche* Freundin.   *There is his pretty girlfriend.*

20. Complete each of the following sentences, using the appropriate endings. If an ending is not required, place an **X** in the blank.

    1. Wo ist mein____ weiß____ Hase?
    2. Ihr____ alt____, amerikanisch____ Freundin kommt.
    3. Dein____ hell____ Bluse ist doch schmutzig.
    4. Er ist kein____ gut____ Freund.
    5. Wann besucht euch eur____ reich____ Tante?
    6. Der Löwe ist ein____ wild____ Tier.
    7. Nur ein____ rot____ Apfel liegt im Korb.
    8. Das ist kein____ hübsch____ Melodie.
    9. Das ist ein____ schön____, weiß____ Lilie.
    10. Mein____ deutsch____ Buch liegt dort.
    11. Wo ist dein____ alt____ Onkel?

12. Es ist sein____ neu____ Auto.
13. Das ist unser____ teuer____ Schmuck.
14. Wo ist mein____ weich____ Kissen?
15. Das ist kein____ sauer____ Milch.
16. Dort kommt ein____ französisch____ Tourist.

21. Rewrite each of the following sentences, changing the definite article to the indefinite article and making all necessary changes.

1. Wo ist das weiche Kissen? _____
2. Der alte Freund ist hier. _____
3. Wann schläft das wilde Tier? _____
4. Die neue Maschine steht dort. _____
5. Hier ist der schmutzige Teller. _____
6. Wo ist das kleine Buch? _____
7. Hier liegt die deutsche Zeitung. _____
8. Wie viel kostet das schnelle Auto? _____

22. Form a sentence from each of the following groups of words, using the appropriate forms of the "**ein**" words and adjectives.

1. Mein / alt / Radio / ist / kaputt _____
2. Wo / wohnt / dein / nett / Freundin / ? _____
3. Wie viel / kostet / Ihr / neu / Wagen / ? _____
4. Wann / kommt / sein / reich / Onkel / ? _____
5. Das / ist / kein / eng / Straße _____
6. Ist / unser / deutsch / Foto / interessant / ? _____
7. Wo / ist / euer / schmutzig / Wäsche / ? _____
8. Hier / ist / ihr / alt / Wein _____

Accusative Singular (Following "ein" Words)

When an attributive adjective modifies a noun in the accusative singular and is preceded by the indefinite article or an "**ein**" word, it takes the following endings.

MASCULINE	NEUTER	FEMININE
einen alt*en* Mann	ein süß*es* Getränk	eine blau*e* Jacke

Er schreibt *einen langen* Brief.	*He is writing a long letter.*
Habt ihr *kein scharfes* Messer?	*Don't you have a sharp knife?*
Wir besuchen *unsere gute* Freundin.	*We are visiting our good friend.*

Note that the accusative singular adjective endings are identical to the nominative singular endings, except for the masculine.

23. Complete each of the following sentences, using the appropriate endings. If an ending is not required, place an **X** in the blank.

1. Möchtest du kein____ heiß____ Tee?
2. Setz dich auf unser____ weich____ Sofa!
3. Wir kaufen kein____ teur____ Kamera für unser____ klein____ Tochter.
4. Er geht durch sein____ schmutzig____ Fabrik.
5. Sucht ihr eur____ klein____, schwarz____ Hund?

6. Warum besucht sie nicht ihr___ krank___ Großmutter?
7. Wer braucht ein___ groß___, modern___ Wagen?
8. Ich suche ein___ rot___ Auto.
9. Er hat kein___ hübsch___ Freundin.
10. Wir treffen unser___ neu___ Lehrerin.
11. Nehmt euer___ alt___ Bild!
12. Wir gehen ohne mein___ klein___ Kind.

24. Rewrite each of the following sentences, changing the definite article to the indefinite article and making all necessary changes.

1. Er kauft den hässlichen Teppich. _____
2. Wann bekommst du den neuen Mantel? _____
3. Wir besuchen die historische Stadt. _____
4. Siehst du das rote Auto? _____
5. Ich kaufe es für das kranke Kind. _____
6. Er geht durch den langen Tunnel. _____
7. Der Bus fuhr gegen die alte Mauer. _____
8. Ich möchte das weiße Bonbon. _____

25. Form a sentence from each of the following groups of words, using the appropriate forms of the "**ein**" words and adjectives.

1. Sie / geht / in / ihr / dunkel / Wohnung _____
2. Wir / verkaufen / unser / blau / Sofa _____
3. Haben / Sie / ein / billig / Zimmer / ? _____
4. Ich / habe / ein / bequem / Stuhl _____
5. Braucht / er / sein / neu / Kamera / ? _____
6. Wir / gehen / durch / ein / lang / Tunnel _____
7. Ich / schreibe / ein / kurz / Brief _____
8. Kennst / du / kein / hübsch / Studentin / ? _____

Dative Singular (Following "ein" Words)

When an attributive adjective modifies a noun in the dative singular and is preceded by the indefinite article or an "**ein**" word, it takes the following endings.

MASCULINE	NEUTER	FEMININE
einem scharf*en* Messer	einem dunkl*en* Zimmer	einer rot*en* Blume

Das Buch liegt auf *einem runden* Tisch.   The book is lying on a round table.
Wir wohnen in *keinem alten* Haus.   We are not living in an old house.
Er erzählt von *seiner langen* Reise.   He is talking about his long trip.

26. Complete each of the following sentences, using the appropriate endings.

1. Sie schrieb ihr___ lieb___ Mann eine Karte.
2. Warum sitzt du in dein___ klein___, kalt___ Zimmer?
3. Außer unser___ reich___ Tante kam niemand.
4. Wir fahren mit ein___ schnell___ Wagen.
5. Ich trinke aus ein___ neu___, weiß___ Tasse.
6. Seit sein___ traurig___ Kindheit ist er melancholisch.

7. Es gehört ihr___ alt___ Onkel.
8. Ich helfe mein___ klein___ Schwester.
9. Ich bleibe bei mein___ krank___ Mutter.
10. Sie wurde von ein___ wild___ Hund gebissen.
11. Er arbeitet bei kein___ groß___ Firma.
12. Sie geht zu ihr___ weiß___ Auto.

27. Rewrite each of the following sentences, changing the definite article to the indefinite article and making all necessary changes.

1. Er sitzt auf dem harten Stuhl. _____
2. Sie wohnt in dem modernen Haus. _____
3. Ich bin bei der netten Frau. _____
4. Sie spielt mit dem süßen Baby. _____
5. Wir stehen neben dem großen Mann. _____
6. Ich liege auf dem weichen Bett. _____
7. Hilfst du dem fremden Mann? _____
8. Sie kommt von der langen Reise zurück. _____

28. Form a sentence from each of the following groups of words, using the appropriate forms of the "**ein**" words and adjectives.

1. Er / kam / mit / ein / interessant / Freund
_____

2. Wir / kennen / uns / seit / unser / glücklich / Kindheit
_____

3. Er / schnitt / das / Brot / mit / sein / scharf / Messer
_____

4. Warum / sitzt / du / auf / ein / unbequem / Stuhl / ?
_____

5. Die / Katze / liegt / auf / mein / schwarz / Mantel
_____

6. Sie / kommt / aus / ihr / dunkel / Zimmer
_____

7. Was / steht / in / sein / lang / Brief / ?
_____

8. Sie / sitzt / in / mein / neu / Auto
_____

Genitive Singular (Following "ein" Words)

When an attributive adjective modifies a noun in the genitive singular and is preceded by the indefinite article or an "**ein**" word, it takes the following endings.

MASCULINE	NEUTER	FEMININE
eines nett*en* Mannes	eines bitter*en* Getränks	einer alt*en* Dame

Er liegt im Schatten *eines hohen* Baumes.   *He is lying in the shade of a tall tree.*

Wann beginnt der Bau *eures neuen* Hauses?   *When does the construction of your new house start?*

Hier ist das Zentrum *unserer kleinen* Stadt.   *Here is the center of our small town.*

29. Complete each of the following sentences, using the appropriate forms of the words on the right.

1. Er ist während _____ Nacht   ein, dunkel
   verunglückt.
2. Die Farbe _____ Autos ist hässlich.   mein, alt
3. Wegen _____ Krankheit kann er nicht   sein, schlimm
   kommen.
4. Sie ist die Tochter _____ Arztes.   ein, amerikanisch
5. Trotz _____ Arbeit macht sie Urlaub.   ihr, wichtig
6. Sie tat es um _____ Jungen willen.   euer, krank
7. Wie hoch war der Preis _____   dein, neu
   Waschmaschine?
8. Statt _____ Radios kaufte ich eine   ein, teuer
   Kamera.

30. Rewrite each of the following sentences, changing the genitive definite article to the indefinite article and making all necessary changes.

1. Das ist die Frau des bekannten Dichters.

   _____

2. Es ist die Geschichte des fremden Volkes.

   _____

3. Der Preis des antiken Perserteppichs ist hoch.

   _____

4. Ich singe die Melodie des deutschen Liedes.

   _____

5. Der Direktor der großen Fabrik kommt.

   _____

31. Form a sentence from each of the following groups of words, using the appropriate forms of the "**ein**" words and adjectives.

1. Trotz / mein / lang / Reise / war / ich / nicht / müde

   _____

2. Die / Farbe / dein / neu / Pullover / ist / hübsch

   _____

3. Sie / ist / die / Frau / ein / amerikanisch / Präsident

   _____

4. Hier / ist / das / Foto / sein / bekannt / Bruder

   _____

5. Wo / ist / das / Haus / Ihr / reich / Onkel / ?

   _____

6. Wir / konnten / wegen / sein / lang / Verspätung / nicht / essen

   _____

7. Der / Bus / ist / jenseits / ein / hoch / Turm

   _____

Plural of All Cases and Genders (Preceded by "ein" Words)

When an attributive adjective modifies a plural noun and is preceded by a plural form of an "**ein**" word, the adjective ending is **-en** for all cases. NOTE: There is no plural form of the indefinite article **ein**.

Nominative	keine leer*en* Gläser
Accusative	keine leer*en* Gläser
Dative	keinen leer*en* Gläsern
Genitive	keiner leer*en* Gläser

Ihre deutschen Freundinnen fliegen ab.	*Her German friends are departing. (by plane)*
Hast du *keine amerikanischen* Freunde?	*Don't you have American friends?*
Wir trinken aus *keinen schmutzigen* Tassen.	*We don't drink out of dirty cups.*
Die Lehrerin *unserer kleinen* Kinder ist hier.	*The teacher of our small children is here.*

32. Rewrite each of the following sentences, changing the noun to plural and making all necessary changes.

1. Er hat keinen teuren Ring gekauft. _____
2. Er glaubt seinem kleinen Sohn. _____
3. Ich telefonierte mit meiner deutschen Freundin. _____
4. Unsere neue Nähmaschine war teuer. _____
5. Wer hat meinen roten Bleistift? _____
6. Wegen seines faulen Bruders darf er nicht kommen. _____
7. Wir trinken kein kaltes Getränk. _____
8. Wo ist ihre warme Jacke? _____
9. Willst du deinen alten Lehrer besuchen? _____
10. Wo ist euer progressives Gymnasium? _____

Review: Attributive Adjectives Preceded by "ein" Words

The **-en** adjective ending predominates after the indefinite article or an "**ein**" word. As is the case with adjectives following "**der**" words, the exceptions to the **-en** endings occur in the three nominative singular forms and the accusative feminine and neuter singular forms.

Compare the two sets of endings below.

Following "der" Words

	SINGULAR			PLURAL
	MASCULINE	NEUTER	FEMININE	ALL GENDERS
Nominative	-e	-e	-e	-en
Accusative	-en	-e	-e	-en
Dative	-en	-en	-en	-en
Genitive	-en	-en	-en	-en

Following "ein" Words

	SINGULAR			PLURAL
	MASCULINE	NEUTER	FEMININE	ALL GENDERS
Nominative	-er	-es	-e	-en
Accusative	-en	-es	-e	-en
Dative	-en	-en	-en	-en
Genitive	-en	-en	-en	-en

33. Complete each of the following sentences, using the appropriate endings. If an ending is not required, place an **X** in the blank.

1. Mein___ amerikanisch___ Freund hat dies___ herrlich___ Sinfonie komponiert.
2. In unser___ neu___ Wohnung ist auch ein___ elektrisch___ Ofen.
3. D___ kaputt___ Maschine wurde mit ein___ leicht___ Metall repariert.
4. Sie war wegen ihr___ exotisch___ Schönheit bekannt, nicht wegen ihr___ groß___ Talents.
5. In d___ eng___ Straßen d___ historisch___ Innenstadt können kein___ groß___ Wagen fahren.
6. Ein___ melancholisch___ Melodie kam aus d___ offen___ Fenster.
7. Er brachte mir ein___ rot___ Rose in jen___ klein___ Glasvase.
8. D___ nagelneu___ Auto fuhr gegen unser___ rostig___ Gartentür.
9. Er hat kein___ einzig___ Geschenk von sein___ bekannt___ Geschwistern bekommen.
10. Mit dies___ schmutzig___ Schuhen könnt ihr nicht in d___ sauber___ Küche kommen.
11. Machen dein___ reich___ Eltern schon wieder ein___ lang___ Reise?
12. In jen___ rund___ Korb sind d___ frisch___ Eier.

34. Complete each of the following sentences, using the appropriate forms of the words on the right.

1. Er gibt _____ Studentin _____ Job. — die, jung; ein, interessant
2. _____ Onkel liegt auf _____ Sofa. — mein, krank; unser, gut
3. Sie fährt mit _____ Volkswagen durch _____ Stadt. — ihr, klein; die, leer
4. Wo hat _____ Tante _____ Bild gekauft? — dein, reich; dieses, teuer
5. Wegen _____ Vorlesung konnte ich _____ Freunde nicht treffen. — jene, lang; ihr, neu
6. Wo ist _____ Foto _____ Sängers? — das, neu; der, bekannt
7. _____ Gäste trinken _____ Kaffee. — mein, amerikanisch; kein, bitter
8. Er fährt _____ Auto in _____ Garage. — sein, kaputt; die, dunkel
9. Sie macht mit _____ Geschwistern _____ Reise. — ihr, nett; eine, kurz
10. _____ Leute sitzen in _____ Wohnung. — die, arm; ihr, kalt

Attributive Adjectives Not Preceded by "der" or "ein" Words (Unpreceded)

When an attributive adjective is not preceded by a "**der**" or "**ein**" word, the adjective requires an ending to indicate the number, gender, and case of the noun it modifies. This set of adjective endings coincides with the endings of the definite article except in the genitive masculine and neuter singular.

NOTE: When an attributive adjective follows the uninflected form of certain adjectives (that is, *forms of the adjective that have no endings showing gender, number, and case*), the adjective takes the same endings as the unpreceded adjective. When used as adjectives, **viel** and **wenig** usually take no endings in the singular; in the plural, however, they take the regular adjective endings. *The uninflected forms of* **manch**, **solch**, *and* **welch** *are rarely encountered in colloquial usage and sound old-fashioned and/or poetic.*

viel	much, a lot	manch	many a
wenig	little	solch	such (a)
		welch	what

Sie hat noch *viel* amerikanisches Geld. — She still has a lot of American money.
Er isst sehr *wenig* frisches Obst. — He eats very little fresh fruit.
***Manch* (ein) armer Seemann fand ein nasses Grab.** — Many a poor seaman found a watery grave.
***Solch* schönes Wetter!** — Such nice weather!
***Welch* liebes Kind!** — What a dear child!

35. Complete each of the following sentences, using the appropriate German form for the adjective on the right.

1. _____ schönes Wetter! — *what*
2. Er hat _____ amerikanisches Geld. — *much*
3. Wir haben _____ guten Wein. — *little*
4. Er trank _____ kaltes Bier. — *much*
5. _____ gute Idee! — *such*
6. Sie hat _____ musikalisches Talent. — *much*
7. Ich habe _____ großen Hunger. — *such*
8. _____ neuer Schnee ist gefallen. — *little*

Nominative Singular Unpreceded (Not Following "der" or "ein" Words)

When an attributive adjective modifies a noun in the nominative singular and is preceded by neither a "**der**" nor an "**ein**" word, it takes the following endings.

MASCULINE	NEUTER	FEMININE
schwarz*er* Kaffee	schön*es* Wetter	frisch*e* Milch

***Alter* Wein ist teuer.** — Old wine is expensive.
Das ist *mexikanisches* Geld. — That is Mexican money.
***Frische* Luft ist gesund.** — Fresh air is healthy.
Hier ist *viel moderne* Kunst. — Here is a lot of modern art.

The nominative adjective endings are frequently used in forms of address.

***Lieber* Onkel Franz!** — Dear Uncle Franz,
***Liebe* Tante!** — Dear Aunt,
Du *armes* Kind! — You poor child!

36. Complete each of the following sentences, using the appropriate form(s) of the word(s) on the right.

1. Du _____ Mädchen! — *arm*
2. Das ist _____ Arznei! — *bitter*
3. _____ Tante Anni! — *lieb*
4. Dort liegt _____ Wäsche. — *viel, schmutzig*
5. _____ Großvater! — *lieb*
6. Dort liegt _____ Geld. — *wenig, japanisch*
7. _____ Wein ist teuer. — *gut, alt*
8. Du _____ Kind! — *gut*
9. Hier ist Ursulas _____ Kleid. — *neu*

10. Zuvic _____ Bier ist schlecht für den Magen.   kalt
11. _____ Onkel Herbert!   lieb
12. Du _____ Hund!   arm
13. Das ist _____ Bier.   teuer
14. Sie ist _____ Berlinerin.   typisch

37. Form a sentence from each of the following groups of words, making all necessary changes.

1. Welch / interessant / Gedicht / !   _____
2. Das / ist / teuer / Leder   _____
3. Frisch / Butter / schmeckt / gut   _____
4. Modern / Musik / ist / schnell   _____
5. Ist / das / billig / Schmuck / ?   _____
6. Kalt / Limonade / ist / erfrischend   _____
7. Du / süß / Baby / !   _____

Accusative Singular Unpreceded (Not Following "der" or "ein" Words)

When an attributive adjective modifies a noun in the accusative singular and is preceded by neither a "**der**" nor an "**ein**" word, it takes the following endings.

MASCULINE	NEUTER	FEMININE
weiß*en* Flieder	gelb*es* Papier	bitter*e* Schokolade

Trinkt ihr *viel schwarzen* Kaffee?   *Do you drink a lot of black coffee?*
Ich brauche *wenig amerikanisches* Geld.   *I need little American money.*
Er bestellt *kalte* Milch.   *He orders cold milk.*
Wir trinken *heißen* Tee.   *We drink hot tea.*
Er isst *viel weißes* Brot.   *He eats a lot of white bread.*
Hast du *saubere* Wäsche?   *Do you have clean laundry?*

Salutations are in the accusative case.

Guten Morgen! *Guten* Tag! *Guten* Abend!   *Good morning! Hello! Good evening!*
Gute Nacht!   *Good night!*

38. Complete each of the following sentences, using the appropriate form(s) of the word(s) on the right.

1. Ich trinke _____ Limonade.   viel, sauer
2. Wir essen _____ Brot.   wenig, schwarz
3. _____ Abend! _____ Nacht! _____ Tag!   gut, gut, gut
4. Er hat _____ Hoffnung.   groß
5. Was hast du gegen _____ Zucker?   weiß
6. Ich trinke _____ Tee.   wenig, süß
7. Hattet ihr _____ Wetter?   schön
8. Sie bestellt _____ Kaffee.   schwarz
9. Ich kaufe _____ Papier.   dünn
10. _____ Butter esse ich gern.   frisch, holländisch
11. Wo finde ich _____ Käse?   pikant, französisch
12. Wir geben uns _____ Mühe.   groß
13. Er hat _____ Geld.   viel, amerikanisch
14. Ich brauche _____ Wasser.   viel, heiß

39. Form a sentence from each of the following groups of words, making all necessary changes.

1. Was / hast / du / gegen / klassisch / Musik / ? _____
2. Leg / es / in / kalt / Wasser / ! _____
3. Ich / esse / frisch / Brot _____
4. Wir / brauchen / japanisch / Geld _____
5. Er / hat / groß / Hunger _____
6. Warum / trinkst / du / kalt / Kaffee / ? _____
7. Sie / nimmt / braun / Zucker _____
8. Sie / hat / viel / teuer / Schmuck _____

Dative Singular Unpreceded (Not Following "der" or "ein" Words)

When an attributive adjective modifies a noun in the dative singular and is preceded by neither a "**der**" nor an "**ein**" word, it takes the following endings.

MASCULINE	NEUTER	FEMININE
rostfrei*em* Stahl	kalt*em* Wasser	heiß*er* Milch

Bei *starkem* Wind gehen wir nicht segeln.	*We don't go sailing in strong wind.*
Nach *langem* Leiden ist sie gestorben.	*She passed away after long suffering.*
Ich bin in *großer* Not.	*I am in great need.*
Außer *viel heißem* Tee trinkt er nichts.	*He drinks nothing except a lot of hot tea.*
Sie helfen *manch armem* Kind.	*They help many a poor child.*

40. Complete each of the following sentences, using the appropriate form(s) of the word(s) on the right.

1. Das Auto fährt mit _____ Geschwindigkeit.   groß
2. Nach _____ Zeit kam er wieder.   lang
3. Sie kommt aus _____ Familie.   gut
4. Ich trinke Tee mit _____ Milch.   viel, warm
5. Er lebte auf _____ Fuß.   groß
6. Bei _____ Wetter gehen wir aus.   schön, sonnig
7. Es ist aus _____ Stahl.   rostfrei
8. Ich mache es mit _____ Freude.   groß
9. Es ist aus _____ Gold.   wenig, weiß
10. Er wäscht sich mit _____ Wasser.   viel, heiß
11. Bei _____ Wetter bleiben wir drinnen.   bitter, kalt
12. Der Turm ist aus _____ Metall.   hart

41. Form a sentence from each of the following groups of words, making all necessary changes.

1. Bei / schlecht / Wetter / fliege / ich / nicht _____
2. Wer / schreibt / mit / grün / Kreide / ? _____
3. Nach / kurz / Zeit / wurde / es / still _____
4. Das / Messer / ist / aus / rostfrei / Stahl _____
5. Warum / schwimmst / du / in / eiskalt / Wasser / ? _____
6. Der / Dieb / kam / bei / helllicht / Tag _____
7. Ich / kenne / ihn / seit / lang / Zeit _____
8. Er / trank / nichts / außer / viel / stark / Kaffee _____

Genitive Singular Unpreceded (Not Following "der" or "ein" Words)

When an attributive adjective modifies a noun in the genitive singular and is preceded by neither a "**der**" nor an "**ein**" word, it takes the following endings.

MASCULINE	NEUTER	FEMININE
star**ken** Windes	schlecht**en** Wetters	gut**er** Qualität

Trotz *starken* Regens ging er spazieren. He took a walk despite heavy rain.
Schweren Herzens nahm er Abschied. He took leave with a heavy heart.
Sie war wegen viel *anstrengender* Arbeit She was tired because of much taxing work.
   müde.

42. Complete each of the following sentences, using the appropriate form of the word on the right.

1. Er ist Kenner _____ Kunst.   klassisch
2. Wegen _____ Nebels konnte er uns nicht finden.   dicht
3. Trotz _____ Hilfe war sie einsam.   freundlich
4. _____ Herzens reiste sie ab.   traurig
5. Die Lagerung _____ Weines ist riskant.   alt
6. Es ist eine Geschichte _____ Liebe.   wahr
7. Trotz _____ Krankheit war sie lebensfroh. lang
8. Er hat eine Menge _____ Materials gekauft. neu
9. Trotz _____ Mühe kann sie es nicht.   groß
10. Innerhalb _____ Zeit kam sie heraus.   kurz

43. Form a sentence from each of the following groups of words, making all necessary changes.

1. Trotz / bitter / Kälte / spielten / die / Kinder / im / Schnee   _____
2. Er / ist / Liebhaber / modern / Musik   _____
3. Der / Preis / gut / alt / Wein / ist / hoch   _____
4. Wegen / schlecht / Wetter / hat / er / Verspätung   _____
5. Trotz / gut / Ausbildung / fand / er / keine / Stelle   _____
6. Trotz / nett / Hilfe / kam / sie / nicht / vorwärts   _____

Review

44. Complete each of the following sentences, using the appropriate ending(s).

1. Wir haben nun wieder schön___, sonnig___ Wetter.
2. Bei grün___ Licht darf man fahren.
3. Ich werde dich in nächst___ Zeit besuchen.
4. Billig___ Wein schmeckt mir nicht.
5. Persönlich___ Freiheit ist für den modernen Menschen sehr wichtig.
6. Lieb___ Maria! Lieb___ Johann!
7. Der Schrank ist aus teur___ Holz.
8. Weiß___ Papier, bitte!
9. Hast du etwas gegen warm___ Bier?
10. Trotz groß___ Müdigkeit kann sie nicht schlafen.
11. Ihm gefällt wenig modern___ Musik.

12. Trinkst du viel stark___ Kaffee?
13. Gut___ Nacht! Gut___ Tag! Gut___ Abend!
14. Es ist eine gelbe Schachtel mit braun___ Deckel.

Plural Unpreceded (Not Following "der" or "ein" Words)

When an attributive adjective modifies a plural noun and is preceded by neither a "**der**" nor an "**ein**" word, it has the same endings as the plural definite article. If one of the following indefinite adjectives precedes the attributive adjective, they both have the endings of the plural definite article.

andere	*other*	**mehrere**	*several*	
einige	*some, several*	**viele**	*many*	
manche	*many*	**wenige**	*few*	

***Mehrere* Leute waren krank.**	*Several people were ill.*
***Viele* Metalle sind teuer.**	*Many metals are expensive.*

45. Complete each of the following sentences, using the appropriate German form for the English word on the right.

1. Dort sind _____ Studenten.   *some*
2. _____ Leute machen das nicht.   *other*
3. _____ Kinder hatten Angst.   *several*
4. Dort stehen _____ Menschen.   *many*
5. _____ Hunde sind wild.   *few*
6. _____ Bücher sind interessant.   *many*

Nominative and Accusative Plural of All Genders Unpreceded (Not Following "der" or "ein" Words)

A plural attributive adjective, whether it follows an indefinite adjective or not, takes the following endings in the nominative and accusative plural, when it is preceded by neither a "**der**" nor an "**ein**" word.

Nominative	**große Hunde**
Accusative	**große Hunde**

***Alte* Perserteppiche sind teuer.**	*Old Persian rugs are expensive.*
Ich fahre gern durch *historische* Städte.	*I like to travel through historical cities.*
***Mehrere alte* Leute warten dort.**	*Several old people are waiting there.*
Ich habe *viele deutsche* Briefmarken.	*I have many German stamps.*

46. Complete each of the following sentences, using the appropriate form(s) of the word(s) on the right.

1. Unser Esszimmer hat _____ Wände.   gelb
2. Sie hat _____ Freunde.   viele, gut
3. Wir besuchen _____ Museen.   einige, bekannt
4. Ich esse gern _____ Eier.   braun
5. Jetzt sind _____ Wolken am Himmel.   einige, grau
6. _____ Lastwagen bringen _____ Äpfel.   mehrere, groß; frisch
7. Sie kauft noch _____ Kleider.   andere, neu
8. _____ Menschen sind oft traurig.   alt
9. Ich brauche _____ Sachen.   wenige, teuer

Dative Plural of All Genders Unpreceded (Not Following "der" or "ein" Words)

When an attributive adjective modifies a dative plural noun and is preceded by neither a "**der**" nor an "**ein**" word, it takes the following ending.

Dative   **hoh*en* Bäumen**

Sie wird mit *roten* Rosen empfangen.	*She is welcomed with red roses.*
Sie spricht mit *einigen alten* Freunden.	*She is talking with several old friends.*
Ich sitze auf *mehreren weichen* Kissen.	*I am sitting on several soft pillows.*

47. Complete each of the following sentences, using the appropriate form(s) of the word(s) on the right.

1. Er fand die Antwort in _____ Büchern.	alt
2. Das Buch hat _____ Lesern nicht gefallen.	einige, deutsch
3. Ich wohne jetzt bei _____ Leuten.	nett
4. Sie unterhält sich mit _____ Studenten.	einige, amerikanisch
5. Sie waren in _____ Käfigen.	mehrere, klein
6. Wir sitzen neben _____ Männern.	dick
7. Sie hilft _____ Studentinnen.	viele, intelligent
8. Es liegt unter _____ Zeitungen.	andere, alt

Genitive Plural of All Genders Unpreceded (Not Following "der" or "ein" Words)

When an attributive adjective modifies a genitive plural noun and is preceded by neither a "**der**" nor an "**ein**" word, it takes the following ending.

Genitive   **klein*er* Kinder**

Trotz *guter* Freunde war sie einsam.	*Despite good friends she was lonely.*
Der Preis *mehrerer amerikanischer* Wagen ist hoch.	*The price of several American cars is high.*
Die Qualität *vieler billiger* Sachen ist schlecht.	*The quality of many cheap things is poor.*

48. Complete each of the following sentences, using the appropriate form(s) of the word(s) on the right.

1. Die Blätter _____ Bäume sind abgefallen.	einige, hoch
2. Das Aussterben _____ Tiere ist ein Problem.	mehrere, wild
3. Der Wert _____ Münzen steigt.	alt
4. Innerhalb _____ Städte gibt es historische Funde.	viele, alt
5. Die Häuser _____ Leute sind wie Paläste.	einige, reich
6. Die Götter _____ Völker sind furchterregend.	manche, primitiv
7. Das Dorf liegt jenseits _____ Berge.	hoch

8. Das Leben _____ Studenten ist schwer.   arm
9. Die Farben _____ Blätter sind schön.   herbstlich
10. Die Titel _____ Romane sind   einige, modern
   interessant.

Review: Unpreceded Attributive Adjectives (That Follow Neither "der" nor "ein" Words)

Following is a summary of the endings of attributive adjectives that are preceded by neither a "**der**" nor an "**ein**" word.

	SINGULAR			PLURAL
	MASCULINE	NEUTER	FEMININE	ALL GENDERS
Nominative	-er	-es	-e	-e
Accusative	-en	-es	-e	-e
Dative	-em	-em	-er	-en
Genitive	-en	-en	-er	-er

49. Complete each of the following sentences, using the appropriate ending(s).

1. Trotz schnell____ Hilfe wurde sie nicht gerettet.
2. Ich kenne mehrer____ bekannt____ Schauspieler.
3. Das Messer ist aus rostfrei____ Stahl.
4. Lieb____ Vater! Lieb____ Frau Binder! Lieb____ Großmutter!
5. Krank____ Leute brauchen frisch____ Luft.
6. Gut____ Morgen! Gut____ Tag! Gut____ Nacht!
7. Er will es mit rot____ Farbe anmalen.
8. Es sind hoh____ Berge.
9. Wir sind schon seit lang____ Zeit gut____ Freunde.
10. Warum trinkst du kalt____ Wasser?
11. Er erzählt von alt____ Ruinen.
12. Ich brauche stark____, schwarz____ Kaffee.
13. Bei schlecht____ Wetter spiele ich nicht Golf.
14. Der Preis französisch____ Weines ist sehr hoch.
15. Ich kaufte viel____ halbreif____ Bananen.
16. Einig____ deutsch____ Studenten fuhren nach England.
17. Sie fragte nach weiß____ Brot.
18. Die Sprachkenntnisse viel____ ausländisch____ Arbeiter sind beeindruckend.
19. Mit schnell____ Autos muss man aufpassen.
20. Er schickte rot____ Rosen.

Adjectival Constructions: Adjectives Derived from Verbs

Present Participles Used as Adjectives

In both English and German, the present participle can be used as an attributive adjective. In English, the present participle ends in *-ing*. In German the present participle is formed by the infinitive plus **-d**: **lachend** *laughing,* **singend** *singing.* When used attributively, the appropriate adjective endings are added in German.

Das *weinende* Kind tut mir leid.	*I feel sorry for the crying child.*
Er ist in der *brennenden* Fabrik.	*He is in the burning factory.*
Wie heißt der *regierende* König?	*What is the name of the reigning king?*

50. Complete each of the following sentences, using the appropriate form of the word on the right.

1. Wirf die Nudeln ins _____ Wasser!   kochend
2. Hört ihr den _____ Hund?   bellend
3. Viel Glück im _____ Jahr!   kommend
4. Wo ist das _____ Baby?   weinend
5. Der _____ Holländer ist eine Oper.   Fliegend
6. Ich brauche ein Zimmer mit _____ Wasser.   fließend
7. Sie hilft der _____ Frau.   sterbend
8. Er ist im _____ Haus.   brennend
9. Er sieht die _____ Katze.   leidend
10. Wir suchen jene _____ Frau.   schreiend

Past Participles Used as Adjectives

The past participles of both weak and strong verbs can be used as adjectives. (See Chapter 7 on the formation of past participles.) When used attributively, adjective endings are added to the **-(e)t** suffix of weak verbs and to the **-(e)n** suffix of strong verbs.

Gib das *gestohlene* Geld zurück!	*Return the stolen money.*
Ich nehme ein *weichgekochtes* Ei.	*I'll take a soft-boiled egg.*
Wir stehen vor der *geschlossenen* Tür.	*We are standing in front of the closed door.*

51. Complete each of the following sentences, using the appropriate form of the word on the right.

1. Wo ist die _____ Suppe?   gekocht
2. Sie ist am _____ Fenster.   geöffnet
3. Wo ist der _____ Brief?   geschrieben
4. Er steht auf dem _____ Wasser.   gefroren
5. Dort steht der _____ Wagen.   repariert
6. Wo sind die _____ Blumen?   geschnitten
7. Wir sind in den _____ Staaten.   Vereinigt
8. Ich rieche die _____ Wurst.   angebrannt
9. Hast du die _____ Rechnung?   bezahlt
10. Wo ist die _____ Tasse?   zerbrochen

Adjectives Used as Nouns

In German, many adjectives can also function as nouns. When used in this way, the adjective is capitalized and usually given a definite or indefinite article that corresponds to natural gender. The endings of nouns created in this way follow the same patterns as the adjective endings given above; that is, the ending taken by an adjectival noun is determined by its gender, number, and case, as well as by whether it follows a "**der**" word or an "**ein**" word, or is unpreceded.

der/die Kranke	*the sick person* (masculine/feminine)
ein Kranker/eine Kranke	*a sick person* (masculine/feminine)
Kranke	*sick persons*

The use of adjectival nouns is much more widespread in German than in English, where it is usually confined to a general, plural sense, such as *the rich* should help *the poor*; *the strong* often do not help *the weak*. In German, however, an adjectival noun can be used to refer to a specific individual or group of individuals, as well as to a more generalized group. Many adjectival nouns are created from simple, descriptive adjectives.

Ein *Toter* lag auf der Straße.   *A dead (man) lay in the street.*
Eine *Tote* lag auf der Straße.   *A dead (woman) lay in the street.*

Sie erzählte von dem *Alten*.   *She was telling about the old one (man).*
Sie erzählte von der *Alten*.   *She was telling about the old one (woman).*

Wer hilft der *Kleinen*?   *Who is helping the little one (female)?*

Die *Kranken* sind im Krankenhaus.   *The sick people/persons are in the hospital.*

52. Complete each of the following sentences, using the appropriate form of the word on the right.

1. Er spricht mit der _____.   Klein___
2. Wo ist die _____?   Blond___
3. Der _____ ist besser.   Schnell___
4. Die _____ warten.   Alt___
5. Der Akzent des _____ ist melodisch.   Fremd___
6. Er bekommt es von den _____.   Reich___
7. Sie bringt es für jene _____.   Arm___
8. Wir helfen einem _____.   Krank___
9. Die _____ singt.   Hübsch___
10. Wo sind die _____?   Glücklich___

Adjectival nouns are also created from adjectives that have been derived from the present and past participles of verbs. The endings taken by these adjectival nouns are determined by their gender, number, and case, as well as by whether they follow a "**der**" word or an "**ein**" word, or are unpreceded.

der/die Reisende	*traveler*
der/die Genesende	*convalescent*
der/die Studierende	*student*
der/die Auszubildende	*trainee, apprentice*
der/die Bekannte	*acquaintance*
der/die Verletzte	*injured/wounded person*
der/die Verwandte	*relative*
der/die Verlobte	*fiancé, fiancée*
der/die Gefangene	*prisoner*
der/die Verschollene	*missing person*

Das ist *mein Verwandter*.   *That is my relative (male).*
Wir fragen *den Beamten*.   *We are asking the official (male).*
Die *Angestellten* waren unzufrieden. *The employees were dissatisfied.*

NOTE: The word **der Beamte** *civil servant, official* follows this pattern in the masculine; the feminine form, however, is **die Beamtin**, by analogy with words such as **Ärztin**, **Lehrerin**, **Künstlerin**, **Leserin**, **Schweizerin**.

Der/die Deutsche is the only noun of nationality that takes an adjectival ending.

Ist das *eine Deutsche*?   *Is that a German (woman)?*
Der Deutsche lacht.   *The German (man) is laughing.*
Er spricht mit *einer Deutschen*.   *He is talking with a German (woman).*

53. Complete each of the following sentences, using the appropriate ending.

1. Warum ist der Gefangen____ nicht hier?
2. Er spricht zum Beamt____.
3. Meine Verlobt____ ist hier.
4. Ich sehe viele Reisend____ im Zug.
5. Dort steht ein Deutsch____.
6. Meine Verwandt____ ist krank.
7. Dort ist das Auto meiner Bekannt____.
8. Die Deutsch____ spricht schnell.
9. Der Beamt____ ist nett.
10. Ich besuche meinen Verwandt____.
11. Es liegt unter der Illustriert____.
12. Ist das deine Bekannt____?
13. Der Reisend____ sitzt im Bus.
14. Dort ist eine Gefangen____.
15. Unsere Bekannt____ kommen.
16. Wir besuchen die armen Genesend____.

Neuter Adjectives Used as Nouns (Following etwas, nichts, viel, wenig)

Adjectives following **etwas** *something*, **nichts** *nothing*, **viel** *much*, **wenig** *little* are neuter and are capitalized.

Weißt du etwas *Interessantes*?	*Do you know something interesting?*
Ich habe nichts *Neues* gehört.	*I haven't heard anything new.*
Er macht viel *Gutes*.	*He does much good.*

54. Complete each of the following sentences, using the appropriate German form for the English word on the right.

1. Ich kaufe nichts _____.   *cheap*
2. Wir erfahren wenig _____.   *new*
3. Ich esse gern etwas _____.   *sweet*
4. Ich las nichts _____.   *interesting*
5. Sie kocht etwas _____.   *good*
6. Er schreibt nichts _____.   *personal*
7. Sie bringt etwas _____.   *old*
8. Ich habe viel _____.   *modern*
9. Er trinkt etwas _____.   *cold*
10. Sie hat wenig _____ erfahren.   *important*

Possessive Adjectives

Possessive adjectives are used to denote ownership or possession. The German possessive adjectives are as follows.

SINGULAR		PLURAL	
mein	*my*	**unser**	*our*
dein	*your* (familiar)	**euer**	*your* (familiar)
sein	*his*	**ihr**	*their*
sein	*its*		
ihr	*her*		
Ihr	*your* (formal)	**Ihr**	*your* (formal)

NOTE: The possessive adjective **Ihr** *your*, which is used to refer to a person or persons for whom formal address is appropriate, is always capitalized. However, **dein** and **euer** are capitalized only when written as a form of address in a letter or other correspondence, and capitalization in correspondence is now only optional.

Lieber Hans, vielen Dank für *Deinen* Brief.　　*Dear Hans, thank you very much for your letter.*

The possessive adjectives are "**ein**" words and thus take the same set of endings as the indefinite article (see Chapter 2, page 51). These endings are determined by the gender, number, and case of the noun that the possessive adjective modifies. The choice of which possessive adjective to use in a given situation, however, is determined by who or what possesses the noun in question.

Wo ist *ihr* Bruder?　　*Where is her brother?*

The ending of the possessive adjective **ihr** *her* is masculine, singular, nominative, because the word **Bruder** *as used in this sentence* is masculine, singular, nominative. The choice of the third-person feminine, singular possessive **ihr** is determined by whose brother it is.

Ist das *seine* Mutter?　　*Is that his mother?*

Here, the ending of the possessive adjective **seine** *his* is feminine, singular, nominative, because the word **Mutter** is feminine, singular, nominative. In this case, the third-person masculine, singular possessive adjective **sein** is used, because it is a male whose mother is referred to.

Note also that although the possessive **unser** is sometimes contracted to **unsr-** when the adjective endings are added to the stem, this occurs primarily in colloquial speech and literary writings. In normal usage, **unser** is not contracted.

Unsere (*Unsre*) Nachbarn sind hier.　　*Our neighbors are here.*

The possessive **euer**, however, is normally contracted to **eur-** when an adjective ending is added.

Wo ist *eure* Schwester?　　*Where is your sister?*

55. Complete each of the following sentences, using the appropriate form of the possessive adjective.

　　1. _____ (*His*) Mutter ist krank.
　　2. _____ (*Our*) Bücher liegen dort.
　　3. _____ (*Her*) Bruder ist klug.
　　4. Das ist _____ (*my*) Kätzchen.
　　5. Wo ist _____ (*your*, familiar singular) Freund?
　　6. Herr Walter, _____ (*your*) Wagen steht dort.
　　7. _____ (*Their*) Eltern sind reich.
　　8. Wo sind _____ (*your*, familiar plural) Schuhe?
　　9. _____ (*Our*) Haus ist sehr alt.
　10. Herr und Frau Müller, _____ (*your*) Tochter steht dort.

56. Complete each of the following sentences, using the appropriate form of the possessive adjective on the right.

　　1. Er läuft durch _____ Garten.　　　unser
　　2. Sie kennt _____ Freundin.　　　mein
　　3. Hast du _____ Buch?　　　dein
　　4. Ich habe _____ Mäntel.　　　euer
　　5. Gehen Sie ohne _____ Frau?　　　Ihr
　　6. Das ist für _____ Onkel.　　　ihr
　　7. Kaufst du _____ Haus?　　　sein
　　8. Kennen Sie _____ Großmutter?　　　mein
　　9. Er setzt sich in _____ Auto.　　　unser
　10. Ich nehme _____ Kamera.　　　euer

57. Complete each of the following sentences, using the appropriate ending.

1. Er kommt von sein____ Freundin.
2. Ich wohne bei ihr____ Tante.
3. Sie kommen aus unser____ Haus.
4. Ich gehe mit mein____ Eltern.
5. Sie steht hinter dein____ Wagen.
6. Wir gehen zu eur____ Lehrer.
7. Es liegt unter Ihr____ Zeitung.
8. Außer sein____ Freundinnen war niemand da.
9. Sie ist in mein____ Zimmer.
10. Er ist bei sein____ Professor.

58. Complete each of the following sentences, using the appropriate genitive form of the possessive adjective on the right.

1. Die Farbe _____ Autos ist hässlich.   sein
2. Die Haare _____ Mutter sind grau.   ihr
3. Die Frau _____ Lehrers ist hier.   unser
4. Während _____ Ferien fahre ich nach Berlin. mein
5. Trotz _____ Alters spielt sie Tennis.   ihr
6. Warst du wegen _____ Bruders dort?   dein
7. Wo ist die Brille _____ Vaters?   euer
8. Wo wohnt die Tochter _____ Schwester?   Ihr
9. Der Fluss ist jenseits _____ Gartens.   unser
10. Die Geschwister _____ Eltern sind dort.   ihr

59. Complete each of the following sentences, using the appropriate form of the possessive adjective.

1. Wer hat _____ (*his*) Frau gesehen?
2. Dort steht _____ (*my*) Lehrer.
3. Gerda, _____ (*your*) Freunde warten.
4. _____ (*Her*) Geschwister kommen auch.
5. Wo sind _____ (*our*) Bücher?
6. Dort ist das Haus _____ (*of her*) Tante.
7. Er spielt mit _____ (*his*) Bruder.
8. Was bringt ihr für _____ (*your*) Kinder?
9. Herr Fischer, wer ist in _____ (*your*) Haus?
10. Kinder, sind das _____ (*your*) Hunde?
11. _____ (*My*) Familie wohnt hier.
12. Wo ist das Auto _____ (*of his*) Eltern?

Comparison of Adjectives and Adverbs

In German as in English, adjectives have three degrees of comparison.

Positive	klein	*small, short*
Comparative	kleiner	*smaller, shorter*
Superlative	kleinst-	*smallest, shortest*
	am kleinsten	*the smallest*

The comparative of an adjective is formed by adding **-er** to the base form of the adjective. Many common one-syllable adjectives take an umlaut in the comparative and the superlative.

| **Helga ist *kleiner* als Gisela.** | *Helga is shorter than Gisela.* |
| **Hans ist *älter* als Loisl.** | *Hans is older than Loisl.* |

The superlative is formed by adding **-st** to the adjective. Note that **-est** is added to adjectives ending in **-d, -t, -s, -ß, -st, -x, -z, -sch**. The superlative form always requires an ending, e.g., **der *längste* Tag, die *schönste* Frau**.

| **Gertrud ist *am kleinsten*.** | *Gertrud is the shortest.* |
| **Die Geschichte ist *am interessantesten*.** | *The story is the most interesting.* |

The superlative form **am _____(e)sten** is used as a predicate adjective.

Unlike in English, in German it is not possible to create compound comparative or superlative forms by adding the German equivalent of the words *more* or *most* to an adjective or adverb. Compare the German and English comparatives and superlatives below.

modern	*modern*
moderner	*more modern*
am modernsten	*most modern*

Unlike in English, an uninflected German adjective (that is, an adjective in its base form without any grammatical endings) can be used as an adverb without making any changes to it. In English, the suffix *-ly* is usually added to an adjective in order to make it an adverb.

The comparative and superlative of the adverb is formed in the same way as the comparative and superlative of the adjective, that is, by adding **-er** and **am _____(e)sten** to the adverb.

Er fährt *schnell*.	*He drives fast.*
Er fährt *schneller*.	*He drives faster.*
Er fährt *am schnellsten*.	*He drives fastest.*

Sie singt *schön*.	*She sings beautifully.*
Sie singt *schöner*.	*She sings more beautifully.*
Sie singt *am schönsten*.	*She sings most beautifully.*

As a general rule, there are no comparative or superlative forms for those adverbs that have not been derived from adjectives, such as **heute, zuerst, gerade, dort, nicht, doch, sehr, nur, deinetwegen**.

Vowel Change in Monosyllabic Adjectives

The stem vowels of the following monosyllabic adjectives add an umlaut in the comparative and superlative. Remember, only **a, o**, and **u** take an umlaut in German.

Adjective/Adverb		**Comparative**	**Superlative**	
alt	*old*	**älter**	**ältest-**	**am ältesten**
arm	*poor*	**ärmer**	**ärmst-**	**am ärmsten**
hart	*hard*	**härter**	**härtest-**	**am härtesten**
jung	*young*	**jünger**	**jüngst-**	**am jüngsten**
kalt	*cold*	**kälter**	**kältest-**	**am kältesten**
klug	*smart*	**klüger**	**klügst-**	**am klügsten**
krank	*sick*	**kränker**	**kränkst-**	**am kränksten**
kurz	*short*	**kürzer**	**kürzest-**	**am kürzesten**
lang	*long*	**länger**	**längst-**	**am längsten**
oft	*often*	**öfter**	**öftest-**	**am öftesten**
scharf	*sharp*	**schärfer**	**schärfst-**	**am schärfsten**
schwach	*weak*	**schwächer**	**schwächst-**	**am schwächsten**
stark	*strong*	**stärker**	**stärkst-**	**am stärksten**
warm	*warm*	**wärmer**	**wärmst-**	**am wärmsten**

Irregular Adjectives

Adjectives ending in **-el** always drop the **e** in the comparative; certain adjectives ending in **-er** may drop the **e**.

Adjective/Adverb		Comparative	Superlative	
dunkel	*dark*	dunkler	dunkelst-	am dunkelsten
teuer	*expensive*	teurer	teuerst-	am teuersten

The adjective **hoch** drops the **c** in the comparative.

hoch	*high*	höher	höchst-	am höchsten

The adjective **nah** adds a **c** in the superlative.

nah	*near*	näher	nächst-	am nächsten

Other irregular adjectives and adverbs are as follows.

gern	*(to) like (to)*	lieber	liebst-	am liebsten
groß	*big, tall*	größer	größt-	am größten
gut	*good*	besser	best-	am besten
viel	*much*	mehr	meist-	am meisten

60. Complete each of the following groups of sentences, using the comparative and superlative forms of the adjective used in the first sentence. Follow the model.

   MODEL   Die Bluse ist billig. Das Hemd ist __billiger__. Der Schal ist __am billigsten__.

   1. Der Bleistift ist lang. Das Lineal ist _____. Der Stock ist _____.
   2. Das Brot ist teuer. Die Butter ist _____. Der Käse ist _____.
   3. Das Zimmer ist groß. Die Wohnung ist _____. Das Haus ist _____.
   4. Ute spricht schnell. Maria spricht _____. Frau Weber spricht _____.
   5. Die Uhr kostet viel. Der Ring kostet _____. Die Brosche kostet _____.
   6. Der Stein ist hart. Der Marmor ist _____. Das Metall ist _____.
   7. Ich sehe Rolf oft. Ich sehe Heinz _____. Ich sehe Paul _____.
   8. Der Käse riecht scharf. Das Gas riecht _____. Die Säure riecht _____.
   9. Er trinkt Wasser gern. Er trinkt Milch _____. Er trinkt Limonade _____.
   10. Das Gebäude ist hoch. Der Turm ist _____. Der Berg ist _____.

Types of Comparison of Adjectives and Adverbs

Comparison of Inequality

Comparisons implying inequality are expressed with the comparative followed by **als** *than*.

Erich ist *größer als* ich.	*Erich is taller than I.*
Der Ring ist *teurer als* die Kette.	*The ring is more expensive than the necklace.*
Er isst *mehr als* sein Vater.	*He eats more than his father.*

61. Complete each of the following sentences, using the comparison of inequality. Follow the model.

   MODEL   Moritz ist intelligent, aber Thomas ist __intelligenter als__ Moritz.

   1. Inge spricht viel, aber ich spreche _____ Inge.
   2. Sie ist dick, aber er ist _____ sie.
   3. Köln ist groß, aber Frankfurt ist _____ Köln.

4. Der BMW ist teuer, aber der Mercedes ist _____ der BMW.
5. Ich trinke Tee gern, aber ich trinke Milch _____ Tee.
6. Der Brocken ist hoch, aber die Zugspitze ist _____ der Brocken.
7. Christian ist nett, aber du bist _____ Christian.
8. Du bist jung, aber ich bin _____ du.
9. Gestern war es dunkel, aber heute ist es _____ gestern.
10. Eisen ist hart, aber Stahl ist _____ Eisen.

62. Write a complete sentence for each of the following groups of elements, showing inequality between the subject of the original sentence and the noun phrase in parentheses. Follow the model.

MODEL   Der Brief ist interessant. (der Artikel)   _Der Brief ist interessanter als der Artikel._

1. Der Februar ist kurz. (der Januar) _____
2. Das Kleid ist teuer. (die Bluse) _____
3. Der Vater isst viel. (das Baby) _____
4. Ute kann gut Spanisch. (Marianne) _____
5. Im Haus ist es warm. (im Garten) _____
6. Das Auto fährt schnell. (das Motorrad) _____
7. Robert ist arm. (Manfred) _____
8. Mein Vater ist stark. (mein Bruder) _____
9. Die Lilie ist schön. (die Geranie) _____
10. Die Limonade ist kalt. (das Wasser) _____
11. Der Kaffee ist heiß. (der Tee) _____
12. Die Schule ist nah. (die Kirche) _____

Immer Plus the Comparative Form

Immer followed by the comparative form expresses an increase in degree.

Es wird *immer kälter.*	*It is getting colder and colder.*
Sie werden *immer reicher.*	*They are getting richer and richer.*
Er spricht *immer schneller.*	*He is talking faster and faster.*

63. Express each of the following sentences in German.

1. *It is getting darker and darker.* _____
2. *She is getting older and older.* _____
3. *He is driving faster and faster.* _____
4. *The days are getting longer and longer.* _____
5. *It is coming closer and closer.* _____

The Superlative

The superlative form **am _____(e)sten** is always used as the superlative of adverbs. It is also used as a predicate adjective.

Ich laufe *am schnellsten.*	*I am running fastest.*
Dieses Messer schneidet *am besten.*	*This knife cuts best.*
Dieses Auto ist *am teuersten.*	*This car is the most expensive.*

64. Write a complete sentence for each of the following groups of elements, using the superlative form of the adjective or adverb. Follow the model.

MODEL   Karl und Hans sind stark. (Gustav)   <u>Gustav ist am stärksten.</u>

  1. Inge und Pia springen hoch. (ich)   _____
  2. Peter und Josef sind groß. (Karl)   _____
  3. Ursel und Bärbel singen gut. (wir)   _____
  4. Laura und Christl sprechen schnell. (meine Mutter)   _____
  5. Renate und Rosa sind krank. (Sabine)   _____
  6. Jochen und Rolf sparen viel. (mein Bruder)   _____
  7. Das Rathaus und das Museum sind nah. (die Kirche)   _____
  8. Gerda und Georg gehen langsam. (Klaus und ich)   _____
  9. Meine Eltern sind reich. (unsere Nachbarn)   _____
10. Der Mantel und das Kleid sind kurz. (der Rock)   _____

65. Write three complete sentences for each of the following groups of elements, using the positive, comparative, and superlative forms of the adjective or adverb. Follow the model.

MODEL   (Das Fahrrad, das Motorrad, das Auto) fährt schnell.

       <u>Das Fahrrad fährt schnell. Das Motorrad fährt schneller. Das Auto fährt am schnellsten.</u>

  1. (Der Brocken, das Matterhorn, die Zugspitze) ist hoch.

     _____

  2. (Wasser, Limonade, Bier) Ich trinke _____ gern.

     _____

  3. (Das Gedicht, die Geschichte, der Roman) ist lang.

     _____

  4. (Der Vogel, der Hubschrauber, das Düsenflugzeug) fliegt schnell.

     _____

  5. (Der Apfel, die Orange, die Zitrone) ist sauer.

     _____

  6. (Das Brot, der Kuchen, die Torte) schmeckt gut.

     _____

  7. (Hans, Josef, Franz) arbeitet viel.

     _____

  8. (Das Wollkleid, die Jacke, der Wintermantel) ist warm.

     _____

Comparison of Equality

Comparisons implying equality are expressed by **so … wie** *as … as.*

Karl ist *so groß wie* **Gerhard.**	*Karl is as tall as Gerhard.*
Der Mantel kostet *so viel wie* **das Kleid.**	*The coat costs as much as the dress.*
Sie fahren *so schnell wie* **wir.**	*They are driving as fast as we are.*

66. Write a complete sentence for each of the following groups of elements, showing equality between the subject of the original sentence and the noun phrase in parentheses. Follow the model.

MODEL   Die Bank ist hoch. (Stuhl)   <u>Die Bank ist so hoch wie der Stuhl.</u>

1. Deine Nägel sind lang. (Katzenkrallen) _____
2. Pia ist groß. (Inge) _____
3. Die Jacke ist nicht warm. (Mantel) _____
4. Deine Augen sind blau. (Himmel) _____
5. Heute ist es kalt. (im Winter) _____
6. Peter ist stark. (Max) _____
7. Die Hose ist teuer. (Pullover) _____
8. Großmutter ist alt. (Großvater) _____
9. Renate schreit laut. (ich) _____
10. Mein Bruder schreibt viel. (sein Freund) _____

Comparative and Superlative Forms as Attributive Adjectives

The comparative and superlative forms of attributive adjectives take the same endings as the positive or base forms of the adjectives.

Dort ist der billigere Mantel.	*There is the cheaper coat.*
Ist das die teuerste Kamera?	*Is that the most expensive camera?*
Das ist ein größerer Wagen.	*That is a larger car.*
Ich kaufe den größeren Koffer.	*I'll buy the larger suitcase.*
Sie hat das größte Zimmer.	*She has the largest room.*
Sie nehmen meine beste Jacke.	*They are taking my best jacket.*
Wir sind in dem modernsten Theater.	*We are in the most modern theater.*
Er hilft einer jüngeren Frau.	*He is helping a younger woman.*
Das ist der Mann meiner jüngsten Schwester.	*That's the husband of my youngest sister.*

mehr and weniger

The comparative forms of **mehr** and **weniger** do not add adjective endings in the singular or plural.

Sie hat *mehr* Bücher *als* du.	*She has more books than you.*
Hast du *weniger* Geld?	*Do you have less money?*

67. Complete each of the following sentences, using the comparative form of the adjective on the right.

1. Das ist der _____ Mantel.   schön
2. Dort liegt die _____ Tasche.   teuer
3. Hier ist das _____ Messer.   scharf
4. Das ist eine _____ Frau.   arm
5. Sein _____ Freund kommt.   jung
6. Ihr _____ Kind spielt.   klein
7. Wo ist euer _____ Teppich?   gut
8. Wann kommt _____ Wetter?   kalt

68. Complete each of the following sentences, using the German comparative form of the English adjective on the right.

1. Ich kaufe den _____ Mantel.   *warmer*
2. Wir brauchen einen _____ Wind.   *stronger*
3. Hast du ein _____ Messer?   *sharper*
4. Ich kaufe eine _____ Tasche.   *larger*
5. Er hat die _____ Kamera.   *better*
6. Ich brauche _____ Geld.   *more*
7. Wir gehen ins _____ Zimmer.   *smaller*
8. Das ist für _____ Leute.   *older*

69. Rewrite each of the following sentences, changing the definite article to the indefinite article.

1. Wir sind in der kleineren Wohnung. _____
2. Er kommt aus dem bekannteren Museum. _____
3. Er fährt mit dem schnelleren Wagen. _____
4. Wir helfen dem kränkeren Patienten. _____
5. Sie erzählt von der besseren Zeit. _____
6. Er spricht mit der kleineren Frau. _____

70. Complete each of the following sentences, using the appropriate comparative form of the adjective on the right.

1. Es liegt jenseits des _____ Berges.   hoch
2. Sie konnte wegen ihres _____ Bruders nicht gehen.   jung
3. Er kam um der _____ Frau willen.   alt
4. Trotz des _____ Windes segeln wir nicht.   stark
5. Es ist innerhalb des _____ Parks.   klein
6. Wir tragen wegen des _____ Wetters Mäntel.   kalt

71. Complete each of the following sentences, using the appropriate superlative form of the adjective on the right.

1. Das ist der _____ Weg.   nah
2. Wie heißt der _____ Berg?   hoch
3. Das ist meine _____ Jacke.   warm
4. Wo ist dein _____ Bild?   teuer
5. Hier ist das _____ Papier.   dünn
6. Wie heißt das _____ Metall?   hart
7. Das ist ihr _____ Freund.   gut
8. Wo ist unsere _____ Tochter?   alt

72. Complete each of the following sentences, using the appropriate German form for the adjective in parentheses.

1. Ich kenne seinen _____ (*youngest*) Sohn.
2. Wir gehen in das _____ (*most modern*) Theater.
3. Er kämpft gegen den _____ (*strongest*) Mann.
4. Ich habe die _____ (*most expensive*) Kette.
5. Er nimmt seine _____ (*best*) Maschine.
6. Sie haben die _____ (*most*) Kinder.

7. Das ist für den _____ (*most intelligent*) Studenten.
8. Ich setze mich neben das _____ (*smallest*) Kind.

73. Complete each of the following sentences, using the appropriate superlative form of the adjective on the right.

1. Er wohnt in der _____ Wohnung.   teuer
2. Sie schreibt mit ihrem _____ Bleistift. kurz
3. Wir helfen dem _____ Mädchen.   arm
4. Ich sitze im _____ Zimmer.   warm
5. Sie glaubt der _____ Frau.   jung
6. Er arbeitet mit seiner _____ Maschine. neu
7. Wir sind im _____ Hotel.   teuer
8. Sie segeln bei _____ Wind.   stark

74. Complete each of the following sentences, using the appropriate German form for the adjective in parentheses.

1. Die Frau meines _____ (*best*) Freundes ist hier.
2. Was ist der Preis des _____ (*most expensive*) Instruments?
3. Wir sind innerhalb der _____ (*oldest*) Stadt.
4. Er macht es um des _____ (*youngest*) Kindes willen.
5. Was war das Thema des _____ (*longest*) Romans?
6. Der Freund ihrer _____ (*prettiest*) Tochter kommt.

Review

75. Complete each of the following sentences, using the appropriate ending. If an ending is not required, place an **X** in the blank.

1. Kennst du seine älter___ Schwester?
2. Dort steht das größt___ Kaufhaus.
3. Wir sind im billigst___ Zimmer.
4. Ich habe mehr___ Zeit.
5. Zieh deinen wärmer___ Mantel an!
6. Ist das der best___ Wein?
7. Habt ihr weniger___ Bücher?
8. Ich brauche das schärfer___ Messer.
9. Ich trinke keinen heiß___ Kaffee.
10. Es ist jenseits des höher___ Berges.
11. Das war der schönst___ Tag meines Lebens.
12. Wie heißt der Mann seiner älter___ Schwester?
13. Sie spricht mit der ärmer___ Frau.
14. Ich fahre mit dem teurer___ Auto.
15. Das war die dunkelst___ Nacht.
16. Die größer___ Jungen bleiben hier.
17. Wir sehen den kürzest___ Film.
18. Trag das länger___ Kleid!
19. Nimm den nächst___ Weg!
20. Das war der kältest___ Winter.

Adverbs

The adverb **sehr** *very* is an intensifier and precedes an adjective or adverb to indicate a high degree of the expressed quality.

Dieses Auto fährt *sehr* schnell. *This car goes very fast.*
Im Sommer ist es *sehr* heiß.   *It is very hot in summer.*
Sie ist eine *sehr* hübsche Frau. *She is a very pretty woman.*
Hier gibt es *sehr* hohe Berge.   *There are very high mountains here.*

76. Express each of the following sentences in German.

1. *He is very old.* _____
2. *They have very good teachers.* _____
3. *He is a very intelligent man.* _____
4. *It is very cold.* _____
5. *She sings very beautifully.* _____

Many German adverbs either do not have a corresponding adjective form at all or do not have an adjective form that can serve as the base for a comparative or superlative. Such adverbs can refer to time, manner, or place. A few of these adverbs follow.

Adverbs Referring to Time

abends	*in the evening*	**morgens**	*in the morning*
bald	*soon*	**nachts**	*at night*
damals	*at that time*	**nie**	*never*
gestern	*yesterday*	**nun**	*now*
heute	*today*	**oft**	*often*
immer	*always*	**selten**	*seldom, rarely*
jetzt	*now*	**spät**	*late*
manchmal	*at times, sometimes*	**täglich**	*daily, every day*

77. Complete each of the following sentences, using the German word for the adverb on the right.

1. Wo ist er _____? *now*
2. Er ist _____ in der Schule. *today*
3. Wir sind _____ zu Hause. *rarely*
4. Was war _____? *yesterday*
5. Sie sind _____ krank. *never*
6. Ich bin _____ müde. *in the evening*
7. Wo waren Sie _____? *at that time*
8. Wir besuchen ihn _____. *every day*
9. Kommen Sie _____? *soon*
10. Sie ist _____ beschäftigt. *always*
11. Er hilft uns _____. *sometimes*
12. Er fährt _____ ins Büro. *in the morning*

Adverbs Referring to Manner

gern	*gladly, like to*	**sicherlich**	*certainly*
hoffentlich	*hopefully*	**so**	*so*
leider	*unfortunately*	**vielleicht**	*perhaps, maybe*
natürlich	*naturally*	**wirklich**	*really*
nicht	*not*	**ziemlich**	*rather*
schon	*already*	**zu**	*too*

78. Complete each of the following sentences, using the German word for the adverb on the right.

1. Er ist _____ reich.   *naturally*
2. Ich lese _____.   *like to*
3. Wir können _____ nicht kommen.   *unfortunately*
4. Sie ist _____ hier.   *not*
5. Warum trinkst du _____ viel.   *so*
6. Es ist _____ heiß.   *really*
7. Du bist _____ klein.   *too*
8. Er ist _____ alt.   *rather*
9. War er _____ hier?   *already*
10. _____ hat sie Kopfweh.   *perhaps*

Adverbs Referring to Place

da	*there*	**links**	*(on to the) left*
dort	*there*	**oben**	*above, upstairs*
draußen	*outside*	**rechts**	*(on to the) right*
drinnen	*inside*	**überall**	*everywhere*
hier	*here*	**weg**	*away*
hinten	*in the back*		

79. Complete each of the following sentences, using the German word for the adverb on the right.

1. Was macht er _____?   *there*
2. Sie arbeitet _____.   *upstairs*
3. Wir sind _____.   *inside*
4. Ich war _____.   *outside*
5. War er _____?   *here*
6. Sie sind _____.   *away*
7. Müssen wir uns _____ halten?   *to the left*
8. Wir bleiben _____.   *in the back*
9. Geht immer _____!   *to the right*
10. Es gab _____ Blumen.   *everywhere*

Position of Adverbs

In German, adverbs usually follow the verb and pronoun (if one is present). If more than one adverb occurs in a series, the following word order is observed: time, manner, place. **Nicht** precedes an adverb of place.

Wir sind *immer* krank.	*We are always ill.*
Er sagt mir *nie* die Wahrheit.	*He never tells me the truth.*
Sie ist *jetzt leider* draußen.	*She is unfortunately outside now.*
Er ist *heute wirklich nicht hier*.	*He is really not here today.*

80. Form a sentence from each of the following groups of words.

1. hier / er / natürlich / bleibt _____
2. Maria / wohnt / unten / nicht _____
3. uns / Karl / sieht / täglich _____
4. drinnen / gestern / waren / wir / wirklich _____
5. nicht / arbeite / ich / abends / draußen _____
6. Vater / suchte / überall / dich / damals _____
7. sitzen / gern / wir / dort / manchmal _____
8. Hunger / ich / wirklich / morgens / habe / großen _____
9. dick / ziemlich / sie / ist / jetzt _____
10. heute / weg / sie / leider / sind _____

81. Express each of the following sentences in German.

1. *We never drink wine.* _____
2. *She was already here today.* _____
3. *I am not there in the evening.* _____
4. *They are unfortunately upstairs now.* _____
5. *She is always inside in the morning.* _____
6. *He was here at that time.* _____
7. *I always sit outside.* _____
8. *He is perhaps in the back.* _____
9. *I am rarely away.* _____
10. *She is certainly everywhere.* _____

Idiomatic Use of Adverbs

German makes frequent use of a number of adverbs such as **denn**, **doch**, **ja**, **noch** to convey the attitude or feelings of the speaker toward a situation or event. Sometimes called *flavoring particles* or *intensifiers*, these adverbs are used in German to indicate the surprise, irritation, emphasis, certainty, uncertainty, doubt, etc., that we in English would express through voice clues such as emphasis and intonation. Consequently, there are often no directly equivalent translations for these adverbs.

denn

Denn usually expresses impatience, curiosity, or interest. It is used in questions.

    Wo ist er *denn*?   *Well, where is he?*

doch

This adverb may be stressed or unstressed. When **doch** is stressed, it expresses that something happened despite expectations to the contrary. It is also used instead of **ja** *yes* as an answer to a negative question.

    Ich habe es *doch* verkauft.   *I sold it after all.*
    „Trinkst du nichts?"   *"Aren't you drinking anything?"*
    „*Doch*, ich trinke Tee."   *"Yes (Sure), I am drinking tea."*

When **doch** is unstressed, it expresses that the opposite of what one is saying is not expected to be true. In an imperative construction, **doch** corresponds to the English *"why don't you...?"* The word **doch** can also be used for emphasis.

Sie ist *doch* nicht in Köln!	*She isn't in Cologne, is she!*
Kauf ihm *doch* etwas!	*Why don't you buy him something?*
Das hast du *doch* schon gesehen.	*After all, you've seen that before.*

ja

This adverb reinforces an idea, observation, or fact.

Sie ist *ja* verrückt.	*Why, she is crazy.*
Wir sind *ja* schon zu Hause.	*We are already home, you know.*
Ich war *ja* krank.	*After all, I was ill.*

noch

Noch corresponds to the English *still, yet*. It indicates that an action is still continuing.

Sie ist *noch* im Krankenhaus.	*She is still in the hospital.*
Das Kind kann *noch* nicht sprechen.	*The child can't talk yet.*

Noch ein frequently means *another*.

Sie wollen *noch ein* Kind.	*They want another child.*
Möchtest du *noch eine* Tasse Tee?	*Would you like another cup of tea?*

82. Complete each of the following sentences, using the appropriate German adverb.

1. Wir haben _____ (*still*) Zeit.
2. Was habt ihr _____ bekommen?
3. Schreib uns _____ bald!
4. Wir sind _____ (*after all*) nicht dumm.
5. Hat sie keine Eltern? _____, sie sind aber verreist.
6. Habt ihr _____ (*another*) Bleistift?
7. Wir wissen es _____ schon (*you know*).
8. Sie hat uns _____ (*after all*) besucht.

CHAPTER 6

Numbers, Dates, Time

Numbers

Cardinal Numbers

The cardinal numbers in German are as follows.

0	null	16	sechzehn	100	hundert
1	eins	17	siebzehn	101	hunderteins
2	zwei	18	achtzehn	102	hundertzwei
3	drei	19	neunzehn	120	hundertzwanzig
4	vier	20	zwanzig	123	hundertdreiundzwanzig
5	fünf	21	einundzwanzig	143	hundertdreiundvierzig
6	sechs	22	zweiundzwanzig	200	zweihundert
7	sieben	30	dreißig	300	dreihundert
8	acht	31	einunddreißig	400	vierhundert
9	neun	35	fünfunddreißig	999	neunhundertneunundneunzig
10	zehn	40	vierzig	1000	tausend
11	elf	50	fünfzig	1001	tausendeins
12	zwölf	60	sechzig	1110	tausendeinhundertzehn
13	dreizehn	70	siebzig	1996	tausendneunhundertsechsundneunzig
14	vierzehn	80	achtzig		(IN DATES) neunzehnhundertsechsundneunzig
15	fünfzehn	90	neunzig	2010	zweitausendzehn

The final **-s** is dropped from **sechs** and the final **-en** from **sieben** in 16 (**sechzehn**), 60 (**sechzig**), 17 (**siebzehn**), and 70 (**siebzig**). **Eins** drops the final **-s** when followed by **und**, e.g., **einundvierzig**. However, when the word **eins** occurs at the end of a number, the final **-s** is always retained: **hunderteins, tausendeins**.

The word **ein** is not usually expressed before **hundert** and **tausend**. When it occurs within a numeral, it is expressed, as in **tausendeinhundert**. Numbers from 1 to 999 999 are written as one word.

345 890 **dreihundertfünfundvierzigtausendachthundertneunzig**

Numbers over 1,000,000

1 000 000	**eine Million**
2 000 000	**zwei Millionen**
1 000 000 000	**eine Milliarde**
1 000 000 000 000	**eine Billion**

Eine Million, eine Milliarde, and **eine Billion** are capitalized and have plural forms because they are nouns. There is a difference between the German **Billion** and the American *billion*: The German **Billion** is equivalent to 1,000,000 millions (10^{12}), while the American *billion* is equivalent to 1,000 millions (10^9).

For convenience in reading large numbers, German uses a period or a space where English would use a comma. For example, *one hundred thousand,* which would normally be written *100,000* in English, is written **100.000** or **100 000** in German. Note that in Swiss usage, this number is written **100′000**.

Measurements, Prices, and Other Decimal Fractions

Decimal fractions used in prices and measurements of various kinds, which would be expressed with a decimal point in English, are represented in German by a comma.

	German	English
2,3	**zwei komma drei**	2.3
4,45	**vier komma fünfundvierzig**	4.45
1,00 DM	**eine Mark**	DM 1.00
6,01 DM	**sechs Mark eins**	DM 6.01
€ 1,00	**ein Euro**	€ 1.00
€ 8,10	**acht Euro zehn**	€ 8.10

The numeral **eins** is treated as an adjective when it is followed by a noun. It takes the ending of the indefinite article: **eine Mark**. When the German noun **Mark** refers to the German currency, it does not have a plural form, e.g., **Es kostet nur 10,00 DM (zehn Mark)**. The abbreviation **DM (Deutsche Mark)** usually follows the amount in nonofficial use.

Germany stopped using the **DM** as its currency on January 1, 2002, when it replaced its national currency with the euro (**der Euro, die Euros**). The euro is broken down into 100 euro cents or, simply, cents (**der Cent, die Cents; der Eurocent, die Eurocents**), abbreviated **c** or **ct**. Like the **Mark** before it, the **Euro** does not use the plural form when referring to the currency.

Das Buch kostet 30 Euro.	*The book costs 30 euros.*

The symbol for the euro is €, which may be placed either before or after the number it refers to. The three-letter code for the euro is **EUR**.

1. Express each of the following numbers in German.

1.	8	_____	11.	101	_____
2.	16	_____	12.	936	_____
3.	21	_____	13.	1274	_____
4.	34	_____	14.	1980 (date)	_____
5.	51	_____	15.	2031	_____
6.	56	_____	16.	10 million	_____
7.	70	_____	17.	8.9	_____
8.	89	_____	18.	17.61	_____
9.	91	_____	19.	€ 20.30	_____
10.	100	_____	20.	€ 191.67	_____

Ordinal Numbers

Ordinal numbers *up to nineteenth* are formed by adding **-t** plus adjective endings to the cardinal numbers. Ordinals *from twentieth upward* add **-st** plus adjective endings to the cardinals. Note that the German words for *first, third,* and *eighth* are irregular. In German, a period following a number indicates that it is an ordinal number.

1. **der, die, das erste**
2. **der, die, das zweite**
3. **der, die, das dritte**

4. **der, die, das vierte**
7. **der, die, das siebente** (OR **siebte**)
8. **der, die, das achte**

11. **der, die, das elfte**	100. **der, die, das hundertste**
19. **der, die, das neunzehnte**	1000. **der, die, das tausendste**
20. **der, die, das zwanzigste**	
21. **der, die, das einundzwanzigste**	
40. **der, die, das vierzigste**	

Ordinal numbers are adjectives in German and therefore require adjective endings. Ordinal numbers are used in titles of rulers.

Nominative   **Wilhelm I., Wilhelm der Erste**

Wilhelm I (der Erste) **wohnte hier.**   *Wilhelm I lived here.*

Accusative   **Wilhelm I., Wilhelm den Ersten**

Er kämpfte gegen *Wilhelm I. (den Ersten)*   *He fought against Wilhelm I.*

Dative   **Wilhelm I., Wilhelm dem Ersten**

Das Schloss gehörte *Wilhelm I. (dem Ersten)*   *The castle belonged to Wilhelm I.*

Genitive   **Wilhelm I., Wilhelms des Ersten**

Wo ist die Krone *Wilhelms I.? (des Ersten)*   *Where is the crown of Wilhelm I?*

2. Complete each of the following sentences, using the appropriate form of the ordinal number in parentheses.

1. Wir wohnen im _____ (8.) Stock.
2. Ich habe ein _____ (2.) Haus gekauft.
3. Das ist seine _____ (4.) Frau.
4. Ich bin der _____ (1.).
5. Er wohnt in der _____ (3.) Straße links.
6. Heinrich _____ _____ (VIII.) hatte viele Frauen.
7. Sie kommen jede _____ (5.) Woche.
8. Wann regierte Friedrich _____ _____ (I.)?
9. Er lebte in der Zeit Ludwigs _____ _____ (XV.).
10. Wir besuchen ein Schloss von Ludwig _____ _____ (II.).

Fractions

Fractions are formed by adding **-el** to the ordinal numbers. Fractions can be used as neuter nouns or as adjectives. No adjective endings are required for fractions. When ¾ is used as an adjective, the numerator and denominator are written as two words. Fractions following whole numbers are written as one word.

FRACTION	NOUN	ADJECTIVE
⅓	**ein (das) Drittel**	**ein drittel**
¼	**ein (das) Viertel**	**ein viertel**
⅕	**ein (das) Fünftel**	**ein fünftel**
¾	**drei Viertel**	**drei viertel**
⅚	**fünf Sechstel**	**fünf sechstel**
10⅓		**zehneindrittel**

Ein Viertel **der Klasse ist abwesend.**   *One quarter of the class is absent.*
Er hat *ein Drittel* **des Kuchens gegessen.**   *He ate one third of the cake.*
Ich habe *drei Viertel* **des Schatzes.**   *I have three quarters of the treasure.*

Wir brauchen *ein viertel* Pfund Butter.	We need one-quarter pound of butter.
Es wiegt *drei viertel* Pfund.	It weighs three-quarter pounds.
Wir müssen noch *fünf einzehntel* Kilometer gehen.	We still have to walk five and one-tenth kilometers.

Forms of "half"

The fraction ½ has the following forms in German, depending on how it is used.

FRACTION	NOUN	ADJECTIVE
½	die (eine) Hälfte	halb

The adjectival form **halb** requires adjective endings.

Er hat *eine halbe* **Stunde gewartet.**	*He waited for a half hour.*
Ich trinke nur *ein halbes* **Glas.**	*I only drink half a glass.*
Sie gibt dir *eine Hälfte.*	*She is giving you one half.*

Special forms of 1½

The fraction 1½ can be written in the following ways.

eineinhalb **Pfund**
anderthalb **Kilo**
ein und ein halbes **Gramm**

3. Express each of the following sentences and phrases in German.

1. *Who has my half?* _____
2. *¾ pound* _____
3. *½ glass* _____
4. *⅓ of the work* _____
5. *2¼ hours* _____
6. *⅝ of the population* _____
7. *1½ pounds* _____
8. *1/20* _____
9. *¼ of the bread* _____
10. *½ pound* _____

Dates

Days of the Week

All days of the week are masculine.

der Montag	*Monday*
der Dienstag	*Tuesday*
der Mittwoch	*Wednesday*
der Donnerstag	*Thursday*
der Freitag	*Friday*
der Samstag OR **Sonnabend**	*Saturday*
der Sonntag	*Sunday*

The Contraction am

In German time expressions, the contraction **am** (**an dem**) is used with the names of the days of the week. **Am**, which corresponds to the English *on,* precedes the name of the day, unless a particular day is to be emphasized. In that case, **an dem** *on that* is used.

Am Sonntag haben wir keine Schule.	*We don't have school on Sunday.*
Er kommt *am* Dienstag.	*He arrives on Tuesday.*
Sie war *an dem* Montag hier.	*She was here on that Monday.*

Months

All months are masculine in gender.

der Januar	*January*	der Juli	*July*
der Februar	*February*	der August	*August*
der März	*March*	der September	*September*
der April	*April*	der Oktober	*October*
der Mai	*May*	der November	*November*
der Juni	*June*	der Dezember	*December*

Seasons

All seasons are masculine.

der Frühling	*spring*
der Sommer	*summer*
der Herbst	*fall*
der Winter	*winter*

The Contraction im

In German time expressions, the contraction **im** (**in dem**) precedes the name of the month or the season, corresponding to the English *in*. When emphasizing a particular month or season, **in dem** *in that* is used.

Ich habe *im* Juli Geburtstag.	*My birthday is in July.*
Im August haben wir Sommerferien.	*We have our summer vacation in August.*
Im Winter ist es sehr kalt.	*It is very cold in winter.*
Er kam *in dem* Herbst.	*He came (in) that fall.*

4. Express each of the following phrases in German.

1. *on Wednesday* _____
2. *in fall* _____
3. *in August* _____
4. *on Tuesday* _____
5. *in winter* _____
6. *in May* _____
7. *on that Thursday* _____
8. *on Friday* _____
9. *in spring* _____
10. *on Monday* _____
11. *on Saturday* _____
12. *in summer* _____
13. *in July* _____
14. *in that September* _____
15. *on that Monday* _____
16. *on Sunday* _____

Days of the Month and Year

The definite article is used with dates in German. A period following the date indicates that the number is an ordinal number. Note that ordinal numbers take adjective endings.

Welches Datum haben wir heute?	*What is today's date?*
Der wievielte ist heute?	*What is today's date?*
Heute ist *der 1.* (*erste*) **Mai 2014.**	*Today is May 1, 2014.*
Den wievielten haben wir heute?	*What is today's date?*
Heute haben wir *den 5.* (*fünften*) **Juni 2010.**	*Today is June 5, 2010.*
Wann hast du Geburtstag?	*When is your birthday?*
Ich habe *am 4.* (*vierten*) **Juli Geburtstag.**	*My birthday is July 4.*
Wann kommst du an?	*When are you arriving?*
Ich komme *am 6.* (*sechsten*) **März an.**	*I'll arrive March 6.*
Ich komme *am Montag, den 10.* (*zehnten*) **August an.**	*I'll arrive on Monday, August 10.*

The Omission of in

The preposition **in** is not expressed in German when referring to a certain year, unless the numeral is preceded by the word **Jahr(e)** *year*. In that case, the dative contraction **im** precedes **Jahr(e)**.

Der Krieg war *1918* **vorbei.**	*The war was over in 1918.*
Er schrieb es *im Jahre* **1935.**	*He wrote it in the year 1935.*

Dating a Letter

Dates in the headings of letters, notes, etc., are preceded by the accusative form of the masculine definite article **den**. In German, the name of the place of origin of the writing may precede the date.

München, *den 14.* (*vierzehnten*) *Juni 2010*	*Munich, June 14, 2010*
Bonn, *den 20. November 2011*	*Bonn, November 20, 2011*

Reversal of Numbers in Dates

Unlike in English, the first number in a German date refers to the day, the second to the month. This is easy to remember since the German pattern progresses from the smallest unit of time to the largest.

Köln, *den 9.3.2013*	*Cologne, 3/9/2013*
Sie starb am 22.12.2009.	*She died 12/22/2009.*
Wir kommen am 13.8.2011 an.	*We'll arrive 8/13/2011.*

5. Express each of the following sentences and phrases in German.

1. *His birthday is January 20.* _____
2. *Today is October 13, 2008.* _____
3. *I'll arrive Friday, March 9.* _____
4. *He died in 1970.* _____
5. *My birthday is December 10.* _____
6. *In the year 1980* _____
7. *5/30/1998* _____
8. *Her birthday is August 10.* _____
9. *I'll arrive February 2.* _____
10. *Today is March 3, 2015.* _____
11. *He died in 1975.* _____

Time

The following expressions answer the questions **Wie viel Uhr ist es?** and **Wie spät ist es?** *What time is it?*

Conversational German

1:00	**Es ist eins (ein Uhr).**	**1.00**
3:00	**Es ist drei Uhr (nachmittags, nachts).**	**3.00**
3:05	**Es ist fünf (Minuten) nach drei.**	**3.05**
3:15	**Es ist (ein) Viertel nach drei.**	**3.15**
3:20	**Es ist zwanzig (Minuten) nach drei.**	**3.20**
	Es ist zehn vor halb vier.	
3:25	**Es ist fünfundzwanzig (Minuten) nach drei.**	**3.25**
	Es ist fünf vor halb vier.	
3:30	**Es ist halb vier.**	**3.30**
3:35	**Es ist fünf nach halb vier.**	**3.35**
3:45	**Es ist (ein) Viertel vor vier.**	**3.45**
	Es ist drei Viertel vier.	
3:50	**Es ist zehn (Minuten) vor vier.**	**3.50**
12:00 (noon)	**Es ist zwölf Uhr (mittags).**	**12.00**
12:00 (midnight)	**Es ist zwölf Uhr (mitternachts).**	**12.00**
9:00	**Es ist neun Uhr (vormittags, abends).**	**9.00**

NOTE: German uses a period instead of a colon between hours and minutes.

In colloquial speech, the words **Uhr** and **Minuten** do not have to be expressed: **Es ist eins (zwei, sechs, neun).** Note that the **-s** of **eins** is dropped when **Uhr** is expressed: **Es ist ein Uhr.** In colloquial speech, adverbs of time are used to clarify A.M. and P.M. when necessary.

Der Zug kommt *um zwei Uhr (nachts, nachmittags)* an.	*The train will arrive at 2 o'clock (in the morning, in the afternoon).*
Er kommt *um 6 Uhr (morgens, abends).*	*He will arrive at 6 o'clock (in the morning, in the evening).*

The half hour is expressed by **halb** plus the next hour.

Es ist *halb zehn.*	*It is 9:30.*

Fifteen minutes before the hour is expressed by **drei Viertel** or **ein Viertel vor** plus the next hour.

Es ist *drei Viertel zehn.*	*It is 9:45.*
Es ist *ein Viertel vor zehn.*	*It is 9:45.*

Twenty and twenty-five minutes after or before the hour can be expressed by referring to 10 and 5 minutes before or after the half hour, respectively.

Es ist *fünf vor halb acht.*	*It is 7:25.*
Es ist *zehn nach halb sechs.*	*It is 5:40.*

6. Express each of the following sentences in German.

1. *It is 8:00 P.M.* _____
2. *It is 10:30 A.M.* _____
3. *It is 5:15.* _____
4. *It is 7:35.* _____
5. *It is 6:25.* _____
6. *It is 4:45.* _____
7. *It is 11:20.* _____
8. *It is 3:10.* _____
9. *It is 1:00 P.M.* _____
10. *It is 12:00 noon.* _____

Official Time

Official time in Germany is based on the 24-hour system. The word **Uhr** is always expressed, but **Minuten** is omitted. Official time is used at railroad stations, at airports, and in public media.

Midnight	**vierundzwanzig Uhr**	**24.00**
12:20 A.M.	**null Uhr zwanzig**	**0.20**
1:00 A.M.	**ein Uhr**	**1.00**
3:30 A.M.	**drei Uhr dreißig**	**3.30**
11:15 A.M.	**elf Uhr fünfzehn**	**11.15**
12:20 P.M.	**zwölf Uhr zwanzig**	**12.20**
1:00 P.M.	**dreizehn Uhr**	**13.00**
2:40 P.M.	**vierzehn Uhr vierzig**	**14.40**
8:00 P.M.	**zwanzig Uhr**	**20.00**

7. Express each of the following sentences and phrases in official German time.

1. *It is 8:30 P.M.* _____
2. *It is 1:00 P.M.* _____
3. *It is 1:00 A.M.* _____
4. *It is midnight.* _____
5. *It is 12:35 A.M.* _____
6. *It is 9:25 P.M.* _____
7. *It is 12:40 P.M.* _____
8. *It is 10:45 A.M.* _____
9. *It is 2:00 P.M.* _____
10. *It is 11:00 P.M.* _____

The Use of um ... Uhr

The idiom **um ... Uhr** corresponds to the English *at ... o'clock.*

Um wie viel Uhr bist du dort?   *At what time will you be there?*
Ich bin *um 10 Uhr* dort.   *I will be there at 10 o'clock.*

8. Express each of the following phrases in colloquial German.

1. *At 5 o'clock.* _____   4. *At 7 o'clock.* _____
2. *At 2 o'clock.* _____   5. *At 11:00.* _____
3. *At 3:30.* _____

Periods of the Day

The periods of the day are preceded by the contraction **am**, corresponding to the English *in* or *at*.

am Morgen	*in the morning*
am Vormittag	*in the morning*
am Mittag	*at noon*
am Nachmittag	*in the afternoon*
am Abend	*in the evening*
BUT **in der Nacht**	*at night*

Ich gehe *am Nachmittag* gern spazieren.	*I like to take a walk in the afternoon.*
Wir besuchen dich *am Abend*.	*We'll visit you in the evening.*
Wo bist du *in der Nacht*?	*Where are you at night?*

9. Complete each of the following sentences, using the German phrase for the English time expression on the right.

1. Er kommt _____.	*in the morning*
2. _____ trinken wir Tee.	*in the afternoon*
3. _____ schlafen wir.	*at night*
4. Wir treffen ihn _____.	*at noon*
5. Ich mache es _____.	*in the evening*

Customary Action

When an adverb of time denotes customary or habitual action, the days of the week and the periods of the day add **-s** and are not capitalized.

Wir gehen *dienstags* zum Kegeln.	*We go bowling on Tuesdays.*
Ich bin *vormittags* zu Hause.	*I am home in the mornings.*

10. Answer each of the following questions, beginning with **Ja** and expressing habitual action. Follow the model.

MODEL   Kommst du am Montag an?   <u>Ja, ich komme immer montags an.</u>

1. Bist du am Abend hier? _____
2. Hast du am Sonntag Zeit? _____
3. Gehst du am Mittwoch mit? _____
4. Schreibst du am Nachmittag? _____
5. Fährst du am Morgen zur Schule? _____

Other Adverbs of Time

The following adverbs of time are not capitalized when used by themselves.

heute	*today*
morgen	*tomorrow*
übermorgen	*the day after tomorrow*
gestern	*yesterday*
vorgestern	*the day before yesterday*

However, when used in combination, the noun is capitalized.

heute Morgen	*this morning*
gestern Abend	*last night*
morgen Nachmittag	*tomorrow afternoon*

Wir haben *gestern Nachmittag* **Tennis gespielt.**	*We played tennis yesterday afternoon.*

11. Express each of the following sentences in German.

1. *He is coming tomorrow evening.* _____
2. *He was home yesterday afternoon.* _____
3. *Otto, did you sleep last night?* _____
4. *They are coming the day after tomorrow.* _____
5. *She departed this morning.* _____
6. *He is coming tomorrow afternoon.* _____

Time Expressions in the Accusative Case

Expressions referring to a definite time or a duration of time require the accusative case.

Ich gehe *jeden Tag* **zur Arbeit.**	*I go to work every day.*
Letzten Sommer **war ich in Spanien.**	*I was in Spain last summer.*
Diesen Monat **ist er zu Hause.**	*He is home this month.*
Wir bleiben *ein ganzes Jahr.*	*We'll stay one entire year.*

12. Complete each of the following sentences, using the appropriate ending(s).

1. Ich bleibe ein___ Tag dort.
2. Letzt___ Herbst war ich in Deutschland.
3. Dies___ Woche bleibe ich dort.
4. Er arbeitet d___ ganz___ Abend.
5. Er trinkt jed___ Stunde Kaffee.
6. Wir singen ein___ ganz___ Stunde lang.

Time Expressions in the Dative Case

Time expressions using the prepositions **an**, **in**, **vor** require the dative case. The prepositions **an** and **in** are usually contracted to **am** and **im** when they precede the names of days, months, seasons, and periods of the day, unless a specific day, month, etc., is being emphasized. *Ago* is expressed by the preposition **vor**. Unlike in English, the preposition **vor** *ago* precedes the time expression.

Wir gehen *am Morgen.*	*We are going in the morning.*
Warst du *an jenem Abend* **dort?**	*Were you there on that evening?*
Sie fahren *am Montag* **ab.**	*They'll leave on Monday.*
Im Sommer **gehen wir schwimmen.**	*We go swimming in the summer.*
Er hat *im Dezember* **Geburtstag.**	*His birthday is in December.*
Sie kommt heute *in vierzehn Tagen.*	*She'll come two weeks from today.*
In acht Tagen **bist du wieder gesund.**	*You'll be well again in one week.*
Er war *vor einer Woche* **in Afrika.**	*A week ago he was in Africa.*
Sie war *vor acht Tagen* **hier.**	*She was here eight days ago.*

13. Complete each of the following sentences, using the appropriate ending.

1. Er war vor ein___ Woche in Kanada.
2. Er war an jen___ Tag krank.
3. Ich war vor ein___ Jahr dort.
4. Ich erwarte sie in acht Tag___.
5. Wir haben euch an jen___ Abend gesehen.
6. Wo war er in jen___ Nacht?
7. Sie besuchte uns vor vierzehn Tag___.
8. Wir spielten an jen___ Samstag Golf.
9. Sie schrieb es vor ein___ Jahr.
10. Sie heirateten in jen___ Mai.

Time Expressions in the Genitive Case

Expressions of indefinite time require the genitive case in German. In English, *someday* (*night, morning,* etc.) is used to refer to future time, and *one day* (*night,* etc.) is used for past time.

Eines Tages erzählte sie die Geschichte.	*One day she told the story.*
Ich zeige es dir *eines Tages.*	*I'll show it to you someday.*
Eines Abends brachte er das Auto.	*He brought the car one evening.*

By way of analogy, the feminine noun **Nacht** also adds **-s** in such indefinite time expressions.

Ich traf ihn *eines Nachts* **im Park.**	*I met him in the park one night.*

14. Complete each of the following sentences, using the German phrase for the English time expression on the right.

1. Ich werde dich _____ besuchen.　　　*someday*
2. Sie wird _____ mitgehen.　　　*some night*
3. Er brachte es _____.　　　*one evening*
4. Ich besuchte sie _____.　　　*one afternoon*
5. Sie wird es _____ lesen.　　　*one morning*

Review

15. Complete each of the following sentences, using the appropriate ending(s), preposition, or time expression.

1. Wir fahren jed___ Winter nach Italien.
2. Ein___ Abend___ wurde er krank.
3. Der Lehrer kommt _____ acht Uhr.
4. Ich bleibe _____ (*this evening*) zu Hause.
5. Ich gehe _____ Sommer gerne baden.
6. Warum arbeitest du d___ ganz___ Nacht?
7. Ich kaufe es _____ Dienstag.
8. Er besucht uns nächst___ Jahr.
9. _____ (*At night*) scheint der Mond.
10. _____ (*Tomorrow afternoon*) fliege ich ab.
11. Kommen Sie doch heute _____ (*in one month*)!
12. _____ wie viel Uhr essen wir?
13. _____ (*In the morning*) war ich in der Schule.
14. Er war _____ (*a week ago*) in der Schweiz.

15. Ich gehe _____ (*Sundays*) nicht zur Arbeit.
16. Du bist ja _____ (*at noon*) im Büro!
17. _____ (*In two weeks*) haben wir Ferien.
18. Wir kaufen _____ (*someday*) ein Auto.
19. Ich warte schon ein___ ganz___ Stunde auf dich.
20. Sie war _____ (*this morning*) in der Stadt.

CHAPTER 7

Verbs

Verb Overview

In German as in English, verbs are words that express an action, a process, or a state of being, e.g., *to read, to redden, to become.*

Transitive and Intransitive Verbs

Also as in English, German verbs are divided into two basic grammatical categories: *transitive verbs* and *intransitive verbs.* A transitive verb is a verb that requires a direct object. Take, for example, the verb *to describe. He describes* is an incomplete statement; it is necessary to specify *what* he describes. An intransitive verb is one that does not require a direct object. An example of an intransitive verb is *to live.* The utterance *he lives* can by itself be a complete sentence and thus can stand alone. Some verbs may be used either as transitive verbs or as intransitive verbs, e.g., *he whistled as he worked* and *he whistled a tune.*

Personal Endings

Unlike most English verbs, German verbs normally take *personal endings,* which indicate both the person and the number of the subject of that verb. Like English, German distinguishes between the *first person,* the *second person,* and the *third person.* Moreover, each of these grammatical persons can be either singular or plural. The present tense personal endings are introduced on page 145, and the past tense personal endings are found on pages 155 and 157.

Certain forms of the verb, such as the infinitive, the present participle, and the past participle, do not take personal endings. However, if the participles are used as adjectives, they take adjective endings (see Chapter 5).

Forms of Address: Formal Versus Informal

There are three ways to express the pronoun *you* in German—the familiar singular **du**, the familiar plural **ihr**, and the formal **Sie**. The **du** form is used when addressing a close friend, relative, child, or animal, or in prayer. The familiar plural **ihr** is used to address two or more friends, relatives, children, animals, or deities. When addressing an acquaintance, a stranger, or a person whom one would address as **Herr** or **Frau**, the formal pronoun **Sie** is used. **Sie** is used for both the formal singular and the formal plural and is always capitalized. The verb has a distinctive personal ending for each form of address (see Chapter 4).

Verb Tenses

In German as in other languages, verbs have *tense*; that is, different forms of the verb indicate the time when the action of the verb takes place, e.g., present, past, or future tense. Tense can be indicated by the personal ending of the verb, as well as by the choice of the auxiliary, or helping, verb used to form the compound tenses.

Strong Verbs and Weak Verbs

There are two basic types of verbs in German: *strong verbs* and *weak verbs*. Weak verbs keep the same stem vowel throughout all their forms, and strong verbs have stem vowel changes in their past tenses. As a *general* rule, the weak verbs have regular and predictable forms, whereas the strong verbs are irregular. Since, however, there are irregular weak verbs and certain predictable patterns for strong verbs, we will not use the terms regular and irregular verbs, but will instead refer to verbs as *weak, strong,* or *mixed.*

Since the patterns for the strong verbs and the irregular weak verbs are not fully predictable, it is essential to learn all the principal parts of such verbs when they are first introduced.

The three principal parts of a verb that must be learned are the *infinitive,* the *past tense,* and the *past participle.* In some cases a fourth form of the German verb must also be memorized—the second- or third-person singular of the present tense, since a small group of strong verbs also have vowel changes in these forms. (The most common strong and mixed German verbs are summarized in the verb chart on pages 297–298.)

Speakers of English are already familiar with the phenomenon that some verbs have no vowel changes in their various forms while others do. Compare, for example, regular verbs such as *play, played, played* and *paint, painted, painted* with irregular verbs such as *sing, sang, sung* and *think, thought, thought.*

Study the principal parts of strong and weak verbs illustrated below by the verbs **spielen** *to play* and **singen** *to sing.*

	WEAK VERB	STRONG VERB
Infinitive	spielen	singen
Past Tense	spielte	sang
Past Participle	gespielt	gesungen

Simple Present Tense

Weak and Strong Verbs

The simple present tense of both the weak and the strong verbs is formed by adding the personal endings for the present tense to the infinitive stem.

Simple present = Infinitive stem + Present tense personal ending

---

In German, the infinitive is the dictionary form of the verb. Typically, an infinitive ends in **-en**, although a few end in **-eln, -ern,** or **-n.** The *infinitive stem* is derived by dropping the **-en** or **-n** from the infinitive.

INFINITIVE	INFINITIVE STEM
denken	denk-
singen	sing-
handeln	handel-
wandern	wander-
tun	tu-

The present tense personal endings that must be added to the infinitive stem are as follows.

	SINGULAR	PLURAL
First Person	-e	-en
Second Person	-st	-t
Third Person	-t	-en

Thus, the fully conjugated present tense of **denken** is as follows.

	SINGULAR	PLURAL
First Person	ich denke	wir denken
Second Person	du denkst	ihr denkt
Third Person	er sie } denkt es	sie denken
		Sie denken

NOTE: Since the same personal ending is used for **er**, **sie**, and **es**, all conjugations presented in this book will list only **er** (third-person singular masculine). Similarly, **Sie** (the form for *you* formal) will not be listed separately, since it takes the same personal ending as **sie** *they*.

Note on Personal Endings

In informal conversational German, the **-e** ending of the first person is often dropped.

Ich tu' das nie.	*I never do that.*
Ich glaub' nicht.	*I don't think so.*
Ich geh' nach Hause.	*I'm going home.*

NOTE: There is only one present tense form in German. Thus, the three forms of the present tense in English, *I think, I do think,* and *I am thinking,* are all translated with **ich denke**.

Below are some examples of present tense verbs used in sentences.

Wir *kaufen* einen Wagen.	*We are buying a car.*
Er *singt* zu laut.	*He is singing too loudly.*
Ich *kenne* den Mann.	*I know the man.*
***Sagst* du die Wahrheit?**	*Are you telling the truth?*
Sie *studieren* Englisch.	*They study English.*
***Trinkt* ihr nichts?**	*Aren't you drinking anything?*
***Suchen* Sie den Hund?**	*Are you looking for the dog?*

Following is a list of weak and strong verbs whose infinitives end in **-en**. They form their present tense according to the pattern just described. Note that weak verbs ending in **-ieren** also belong to this group.

bauen	*to build*	**empfangen**	*to receive*	**kennen**	*to know, be*
beginnen	*to begin*	**empfehlen**	*to recommend*		*acquainted with*
bellen	*to bark*	**entdecken**	*to discover*	**klettern**	*to climb*
besichtigen	*to view*	**erklären**	*to explain*	**kommen**	*to come*
bestellen	*to order*	**erzählen**	*to tell*	**leben**	*to live*
besuchen	*to visit*	**fliegen**	*to fly*	**legen**	*to place, lay*
bezahlen	*to pay*	**fragen**	*to ask*	**lernen**	*to learn*
bleiben	*to stay*	**gehen**	*to go, walk*	**lieben**	*to love*
brauchen	*to need*	**gehören**	*to belong to*	**liegen**	*to lie*
brennen	*to burn*	**glauben**	*to believe*	**machen**	*to do*
bringen	*to bring*	**holen**	*to get*	**malen**	*to paint*
buchstabieren	*to spell*	**hören**	*to hear*	**nennen**	*to call, name*
danken	*to thank*	**kämmen**	*to comb*	**operieren**	*to operate*
denken	*to think*	**kauen**	*to chew*	**parken**	*to park*
drehen	*to turn*	**kaufen**	*to buy*	**probieren**	*to try*

rauchen	*to smoke*	**senden**	*to send*	**vergessen**	*to forget*
reisen	*to travel*	**singen**	*to sing*	**verkaufen**	*to sell*
rennen	*to run*	**springen**	*to jump*	**wandern**	*to wander, hike*
reparieren	*to repair*	**stehen**	*to stand*	**weinen**	*to cry*
riechen	*to smell*	**steigen**	*to climb*	**wissen**	*to know (a fact)*
rufen	*to call*	**stellen**	*to place, put*	**wohnen**	*to live*
sagen	*to say, tell*	**stören**	*to disturb*	**zahlen**	*to pay*
schauen	*to look*	**studieren**	*to study*	**zählen**	*to count*
schenken	*to give*	**suchen**	*to look for*	**zeigen**	*to show*
schicken	*to send*	**tanzen**	*to dance*	**zerstören**	*to destroy*
schreiben	*to write*	**telefonieren**	*to telephone*	**ziehen**	*to pull*
schreien	*to scream*	**träumen**	*to dream*		
schwimmen	*to swim*	**trinken**	*to drink*		

1. Complete each of the following sentences, using the appropriate present tense form of the verb on the right.

1. _____ du Musik?   hören
2. Wir _____ nichts.   trinken
3. Wann _____ er?   kommen
4. Ich _____ etwas.   schicken
5. Die Sängerin _____.   singen
6. Die Fabrik _____.   brennen
7. Ich _____ nach Amerika.   fliegen
8. Dieser Hund _____.   bellen
9. Das Baby _____ hier.   bleiben
10. _____ du an sie?   denken
11. Warum _____ ihr?   weinen
12. Die Touristen _____ vor der Kirche.   stehen
13. Wann _____ die Vorstellung?   beginnen
14. Man _____ Bier.   bringen
15. Ich _____ schnell.   rennen
16. Peter _____ das Auto.   parken
17. Warum _____ ihr so?   schreien
18. _____ Sie schon wieder?   rauchen
19. _____ ihr seine Schwester?   kennen
20. _____ du Richard?   lieben
21. Pia _____ immer.   studieren
22. Seine Eltern _____ ihn.   besuchen
23. Wann _____ ihr das Buch?   holen
24. Der Sportler _____ hoch.   springen
25. Man _____ uns.   rufen
26. Es _____ scharf.   riechen
27. Wir _____ den Brief.   schreiben
28. _____ ihr aufs Dach?   steigen
29. Man _____ ihm.   glauben
30. Ich _____ die Suppe.   probieren
31. Das Kind _____ nicht.   telefonieren
32. Ich _____ etwas.   hören
33. Die Kinder _____ nichts.   brauchen
34. Wo _____ er?   wohnen
35. Wir _____ es.   holen

Variations in Personal Endings

Additional e

When an infinitive stem ends in **-d**, **-t**, **-m**, **-n** preceded by a consonant other than **-l** or **-r**, the endings in the second- and third-person singular and the second-person plural are expanded by adding an **-e-** before the personal endings. The pattern for the personal endings of such verbs is as follows.

	SINGULAR	PLURAL
First Person	-e	-en
Second Person	-*est*	-*et*
Third Person	-*et*	-en

Thus, the fully conjugated present tense for **arbeiten** *work* is as follows.

ich arbeite	wir arbeiten
du arbeitest	ihr arbeitet
er arbeitet	sie arbeiten

Sie *badet* **das Kind.**	*She is bathing the child.*
Er *blutet* **sehr stark.**	*He is bleeding severely.*
***Ordnest* du die Karten?**	*Are you putting the cards in order?*
Er *atmet* **langsam.**	*He is breathing slowly.*
***Zeichnet* ihr oft?**	*Do you draw often?*
Warum *öffnest* **du die Tür?**	*Why are you opening the door?*
Sie *begegnet* **Peter.**	*She meets Peter.*

The following verbs add this additional **e**.

antworten	*to answer*	**bluten**	*to bleed*		**retten**	*to save*
arbeiten	*to work*	**finden**	*to find*		**schneiden**	*to cut*
atmen	*to breathe*	**öffnen**	*to open*		**senden**	*to send*
baden	*to bathe*	**ordnen**	*to put in order*		**warten**	*to wait*
begegnen	*to meet*	**rechnen**	*to figure* (arithmetic)		**wenden**	*to turn*
beobachten	*to observe*	**reden**	*to talk*		**zeichnen**	*to draw*
bitten	*to ask for*	**reiten**	*to ride*			

2. Complete each of the following sentences, using the appropriate present tense form of the verb on the right.

1. Cornelia _____ auf den Bus.   warten
2. _____ du in das Brot?   schneiden
3. Man _____ auch sonntags hier.   arbeiten
4. Worum _____ du?   bitten
5. _____ du Inge oft?   begegnen
6. Ute _____ gut.   reiten
7. _____ ihr alles?   finden
8. _____ ihr gerne?   rechnen
9. Du _____ zu viel.   reden
10. Warum _____ ihr die Katze nicht?   retten
11. Er _____ das Fenster.   öffnen
12. _____ der Spion das Haus?   beobachten
13. Warum _____ du so schnell?   atmen
14. Er _____ die Briefmarken.   ordnen

15. Es _____ stark.   bluten
16. _____ du alles?   senden
17. Warum _____ du nicht?   antworten
18. Paula _____ das Blatt.   wenden

No Additional s Sound

When the stem of the infinitive ends in **-s, -ß, -x, -z**, the personal ending for the second-person singular is **-t** (rather than **-st**). No additional **s** sound is required. Thus, the forms of the second- and third-person singular are identical. All other endings are regular.

Warum *hasst* du ihn?	*Why do you hate him?*
***Tanzt* du gern?**	*Do you like to dance?*

The following verbs belong to this group.

beißen	*to bite*	**heißen**	*to be called*	**setzen**	*to set, place*
grüßen	*to greet*	**mixen**	*to mix*	**sitzen**	*to sit*
hassen	*to hate*	**reisen**	*to travel*	**tanzen**	*to dance*

3. Form a sentence from each of the following groups of words, using the appropriate present tense form of the verb.

1. Wie / heißen / du / ?   _____
2. Was / mixen / du / ?   _____
3. Du / tanzen / gut   _____
4. Warum / grüßen / du / mich / nicht / ? _____
5. Wohin / reisen / du / ?   _____
6. Was / hassen / du / ?   _____
7. Wo / sitzen / du / ?   _____
8. Beißen / du / in den Apfel / ? _____

Infinitives ending in -eln, -ern

If an infinitive ends in **-eln**, the **e** preceding the **-ln** is dropped in the first-person singular. All other forms retain the **e**.

Ich *klingle*.	*I am ringing. / I ring.*

If the infinitive ends in **-eln** or **-ern**, the ending in the first- and third-person plural is **-n**, not **-en**. Thus, these forms are identical to the infinitive.

ich klingle	**wir klingeln**	**ich füttere**	**wir füttern**
du klingelst	**ihr klingelt**	**du fütterst**	**ihr füttert**
er klingelt	**sie klingeln**	**er füttert**	**sie füttern**

Wir *füttern* den Hund.	*We are feeding the dog.*
Sie *klettern* auf den Baum.	*They are climbing the tree.*

The infinitives of the following verbs end in **-eln** or **-ern**.

behandeln	*to treat*	**ändern**	*to change*
klingeln	*to ring*	**bewundern**	*to admire*
lächeln	*to smile*	**füttern**	*to feed*
sammeln	*to collect*	**klettern**	*to climb*
		wandern	*to hike*

4. Complete each of the following sentences, using the appropriate present tense form of the verb on the right.

1. Das Kind _____ auf den Tisch.   klettern
2. Wohin _____ wir?   wandern
3. Ich _____ seine Courage.   bewundern
4. Man _____ Sie sofort.   behandeln
5. Wann _____ du die Katze?   füttern
6. Wir _____ nichts.   ändern
7. Ich _____ doch nicht.   lächeln
8. Die Ärzte _____ sie schon.   behandeln
9. Das Telefon _____.   klingeln
10. Wir _____ alles.   sammeln
11. Ich _____ den Patienten.   behandeln
12. Die Kinder _____ den Hund.   füttern
13. Ich _____ nichts.   sammeln
14. Wir _____ auf den Berg.   klettern

Stem Vowel Changes in Strong Verbs in the Present Tense

Many strong verbs in German have a vowel change in the stem of the present tense in the second- and third-person singular forms. Most strong verbs containing **a**, **au**, **e** undergo this vowel change. They can be grouped according to the changes that take place.

Changes from a, au to ä, äu

Verbs with the stem vowels **a** and **au** change to **ä** and **äu**, respectively, in the second- and third-person singular.

ich fahre	wir fahren	ich laufe	wir laufen
du fährst	ihr fahrt	du läufst	ihr lauft
er fährt	sie fahren	er läuft	sie laufen

The following verbs use the same pattern as **fahren**.

backen	*to bake*	graben	*to dig*	tragen	*to wear, carry*
blasen	*to blow*	halten	*to hold, stop*	wachsen	*to grow*
empfangen	*to receive*	lassen	*to allow, let*	waschen	*to wash*
fallen	*to fall*	schlafen	*to sleep*		
fangen	*to catch*	schlagen	*to hit, beat*		

The following verbs change **au** to **äu**.

laufen	*to run*
saufen	*to drink* (of animals, people in excess)

5. Rewrite each of the following sentences, changing the subject and verb from plural to singular.

1. Schlaft ihr die ganze Nacht? _____
2. Sie wachsen schnell. _____
3. Wascht ihr die Wäsche? _____
4. Wir halten die Ballons. _____
5. Was tragen sie zum Ball? _____
6. Lasst ihr mich gehen? _____
7. Wir backen Brot. _____

8. Warum graben sie ein Loch? _____
9. Sie schlagen das Kind. _____
10. Die Tiere saufen Wasser. _____
11. Sie blasen ins Feuer. _____
12. Wohin lauft ihr? _____
13. Sie fallen. _____
14. Fangt ihr den Ball? _____

Changes from e to i, ie

Most strong verbs with an **e** in the infinitive stem change the **e** to **i** or **ie** in the second-and third-person singular. Study the following forms.

ich breche	**wir brechen**	**ich lese**	**wir lesen**
du brichst	**ihr brecht**	**du liest**	**ihr lest**
er bricht	**sie brechen**	**er liest**	**sie lesen**

The following verbs use the same pattern as **brechen**.

erschrecken	*to frighten*	**geben**	*to give*	**sterben**	*to die*
essen	*to eat*	**helfen**	*to help*	**treffen**	*to meet*
fressen	*to eat* (of animals,	**sprechen**	*to speak, talk*	**vergessen**	*to forget*
	people in excess)	**stechen**	*to sting*	**werfen**	*to throw*

The following verbs use the same pattern as **lesen**.

empfehlen	*to recommend*	**sehen**	*to see*
geschehen	*to happen*	**stehlen**	*to steal*

Important Exceptions

gehen and stehen

Although **gehen** and **stehen** are strong verbs containing **e** in their stems, they do not have the changes in the present tense described above (**du gehst, er geht; du stehst, er steht**).

nehmen

Note that the verb **nehmen** *to take* has an irregular spelling pattern. Study the following forms.

ich nehme	**wir nehmen**
du nimmst	**ihr nehmt**
er nimmt	**sie nehmen**

6. Rewrite each of the following sentences, changing the subject and verb from plural to singular.

1. Helft ihr mir? _____
2. Sie sterben bald. _____
3. Seht ihr uns? _____
4. Wir essen Suppe. _____
5. Die Hunde fressen. _____
6. Was gebt ihr ihm? _____
7. Wir sprechen gern. _____
8. Sie sehen uns. _____
9. Sie stehen beim Haus. _____

10. Geht ihr auch? _____

11. Was nehmt ihr? _____

12. Wann trefft ihr uns? _____

13. Was lesen sie? _____

14. Warum erschreckt ihr? _____

15. Was brechen sie? _____

16. Was stehlt ihr? _____

17. Was werfen sie? _____

18. Warum helfen sie nicht? _____

19. Was vergessen sie? _____

20. Empfehlt ihr dieses Hotel? _____

Irregular Verbs

The present tense of **sein** *to be,* **haben** *to have,* **werden** *to get, become,* **wissen** *to know,* and **tun** *to do* is irregular. Study the following conjugations.

sein	haben	werden	wissen	tun
ich bin	ich habe	ich werde	ich weiß	ich tue
du bist	du hast	du wirst	du weißt	du tust
er ist	er hat	er wird	er weiß	er tut
wir sind	wir haben	wir werden	wir wissen	wir tun
ihr seid	ihr habt	ihr werdet	ihr wisst	ihr tut
sie sind	sie haben	sie werden	sie wissen	sie tun

7. Complete each of the following sentences, using the appropriate present tense form of **sein**.

1. Ich _____ zwanzig Jahre alt.
2. Er _____ in Afrika.
3. Wir _____ jetzt in der Schule.
4. Die Kinder _____ hungrig.
5. Ihr _____ freundlich.
6. _____ Sie auch Schauspielerin?
7. Meine Tante _____ leider krank.
8. _____ du denn glücklich?

8. Complete each of the following sentences, using the appropriate present tense form of **haben**.

1. Meine Eltern _____ kein Auto.
2. Ich _____ keine Angst.
3. _____ du Kopfweh?
4. Die Studenten _____ jetzt Ferien.
5. _____ ihr Durst?
6. Er _____ ja Geld.
7. Wir _____ Besuch.
8. Wann _____ du denn Zeit?

9. Complete each of the following sentences, using the appropriate present tense form of **werden**. Follow the model.

MODEL   Wir werden schon wieder gesund.

1. Ich _____.
2. Ihr _____.
3. Du _____.
4. Frau Sommer, Sie _____.
5. Die Kinder _____.
6. Barbara _____.

10. Complete each of the following sentences, using the appropriate present tense form of **wissen**.

1. Wir _____ ja die Antwort.
2. Die Mädchen _____ es nicht.
3. _____ ihr es?
4. Ich _____, dass er hier ist.
5. Man _____ es schon.
6. _____ du es vielleicht?
7. Er _____ alles.
8. Die Leute _____ es.

11. Complete each of the following sentences, using the appropriate present tense form of **tun**.

1. Was _____ du?
2. Ich _____ immer alles.
3. Wir _____ nichts.
4. Er _____ viel.
5. _____ ihr etwas?
6. _____ Sie nichts?
7. Peter und Sonja _____ wenig.
8. Brigitte _____ etwas.

Special Use of the Present Tense

Future Meaning

As in English, the present tense in German can be used to indicate that an event will take place in the future. The future meaning is conveyed by the context or by an adverbial expression indicating future time.

Ich *gehe* morgen in die Stadt.   *I am going downtown tomorrow.*
Fährst du nächste Woche nach Boston?   *Are you driving to Boston next week?*

12. Answer each of the following questions in the affirmative, using the present tense.

1. Kommst du morgen?   Ja, _____
2. Hat er übermorgen Geburtstag?   Ja, _____
3. Geht ihr morgen Abend ins Theater?   Ja, _____
4. Fliegen Sie im Juli nach Frankfurt? Ja, _____
5. Fährst du nächstes Jahr nach Regensburg? Ja, _____
6. Besuchst du mich heute in acht Tagen? Ja, _____
7. Sind Sie nächsten Monat in Deutschland? Ja, _____
8. Bist du morgen Abend zu Hause?   Ja, _____
9. Habt ihr nächste Woche Zeit?   Ja, _____
10. Spielt sie nächsten Samstag Golf?   Ja, _____

Continued Action

The present tense is used in German to express the fact that an action has been started in the past and continues into the present. In English, one of the past tenses is used to express continued action. In German, the time element is usually introduced by **schon** or **seit**, corresponding to the English *for*.

Ich *wohne schon* zwei Monate hier.   *I have been living here for two months.*
Er *ist seit* einer Woche in Paris.   *He has been in Paris for one week.*

13. Complete each of the following sentences, using the appropriate present tense form of the verb on the right.

1. Ich _____ schon seit einem Monat.   warten
2. Ute _____ seit zehn Jahren hier.   wohnen
3. Er _____ schon eine Stunde dort.   sein
4. Wir _____ schon den ganzen Tag.   arbeiten
5. _____ du schon seit einer Stunde?   singen
6. Ich _____ Robert seit einem Jahr.   kennen
7. Wir _____ seit zehn Minuten hier.   sein
8. Der Pilot _____ schon drei Stunden.   fliegen
9. Es _____ schon zwei Tage.   regnen
10. _____ ihr schon eine Stunde?   schreiben

14. Answer each of the following questions in a complete sentence, using the phrase on the right.

    1. Seit wann liest du schon?   eine Stunde

    _____

    2. Wie lange studiert er schon?   zehn Tage

    _____

    3. Seit wann bist du hier?   fünf Minuten

    _____

    4. Wie lange kennst du ihn schon?   sechs Jahre

    _____

    5. Wie lange telefonierst du schon?   zwanzig Minuten

    _____

Review

15. Complete each of the following sentences, using the appropriate present tense form of the verb on the right.

    1. Warum _____ du ein Loch?   graben
    2. Ich _____ sofort.   kommen
    3. Man _____ hier nicht.   laufen
    4. Was _____ du daran?   ändern
    5. Wir _____ die Vögel.   füttern
    6. _____ ihr auch krank?   sein
    7. Georg _____ Beamter.   werden
    8. Wohin _____ du?   reisen
    9. Hilde _____ schon den ganzen Tag.   arbeiten
  10. _____ du die Zeitung?   lesen
  11. Wir _____ sehr leise.   atmen
  12. Das Tier _____.   fressen
  13. Wohin _____ ihr?   fahren
  14. Das Kind _____ den Ball.   fangen
  15. Ich _____ das Auto.   waschen
  16. Wir _____ ihn nicht.   grüßen
  17. _____ Sie hungrig?   sein
  18. Meine Geschwister _____ die Antwort.   wissen
  19. Warum _____ du so lange?   schlafen
  20. Es _____ schon wieder kalt.   werden
  21. Helga _____ dort.   stehen
  22. Was _____ die Studenten?   studieren
  23. Wo _____ du?   bluten
  24. Ich _____.   klingeln
  25. Wie _____ du?   heißen
  26. Was _____ er?   essen
  27. Wann _____ du Franz das Auto?   geben
  28. Manfred _____ seine Freundin.   sehen
  29. Wir _____ den Kranken.   behandeln
  30. Wo _____ du?   sitzen

Simple Past Tense

In German, the simple past tense (sometimes also referred to as the *imperfect* or *preterit*) is used to describe a completed action or a chain of events that took place in the past. This tense is generally not used in conversation, but is the customary tense used in written narratives. For this reason, it is sometimes referred to as the *narrative* past. (See the usage note on pages 162–163.)

Weak Verbs

The simple past tense of weak verbs is formed by adding the past tense marker **-te** plus the personal endings for weak verbs to the infinitive stem. Note that there are no changes in the stem vowels in the simple past tense of weak verbs.

Simple past of weak verbs =
   Infinitive stem + Past tense marker **-te** + Weak past tense personal ending

The full conjugation pattern for all persons is as follows.

	SINGULAR	PLURAL
First Person	-te-∅	-te-*n*
Second Person	-te-*st*	-te-*t*
Third Person	-te-∅	-te-*n*

Note that the first- and third-person singular forms take no personal ending in the past tense. This no-ending pattern is represented in the chart above by the symbol "∅." The full conjugation of the simple past tense of **bestellen** is as follows.

ich bestellte	wir bestellten
du bestelltest	ihr bestelltet
sie bestellte	sie bestellten

Study the past tense forms in the following sentences.

Wir *tanzten* **den ganzen Abend.**	*We danced the whole night.*
Ich *machte* **damals eine Reise.**	*I made a trip at that time.*
Sie *fragten* **den Lehrer.**	*They asked the teacher.*
Er *bestellte* **Schweinebraten.**	*He ordered pork roast.*

16. Rewrite each of the following sentences in the simple past tense.

1. Sie spielen. _____
2. Er wohnt in Köln. _____
3. Wir glauben daran. _____
4. Ich studiere gern. _____
5. Der Hund bellt. _____
6. Ich bezahle die Rechnung. _____
7. Man gratuliert ihm. _____
8. Wir brauchen Milch. _____
9. Meine Eltern bauen es. _____
10. Das Telefon klingelt. _____

17. Complete each of the following sentences, using the appropriate simple past tense form of the verb on the right.

1. Du _____ damals ein Bild.   malen
2. Wir _____ das Rathaus.   besichtigen
3. Die Mädchen _____ ihn.   fragen
4. Ich _____ ihm etwas.   schenken
5. Wir _____ damals Französisch.   lernen
6. Konrad _____ den Wagen.   reparieren
7. Die Herren _____ mir den Weg.   zeigen
8. Ihr _____ uns damals.   besuchen
9. Unsere Eltern _____ eine Kamera.   kaufen
10. Man _____ sie.   stören

Variations in Personal Endings

Additional e

When an infinitive stem ends in **-d**, **-t**, or in **-m**, **-n** preceded by a consonant other than **-l** or **-r**, an additional **-e-** is inserted before the past tense personal endings. The addition of this **-e-** ensures that the tense marker will be heard clearly. The pattern for such verbs is as follows.

	SINGULAR	PLURAL
First Person	*e*-**te**-∅	*e*-**te**-*n*
Second Person	*e*-**te**-*st*	*e*-**te**-*t*
Third Person	*e*-**te**-∅	*e*-**te**-*n*

Study the full conjugation and sentences that follow.

ich arbeitete	**wir arbeiteten**
du arbeitetest	**ihr arbeitetet**
er arbeitete	**sie arbeiteten**

Er *öffnete* **die Tür.**	*He opened the door.*
Wir *badeten* **das Kind.**	*We bathed the child.*
Sie *ordneten* **Briefmarken.**	*They put stamps in order.*
Ich *begegnete* **dem Mädchen.**	*I met the girl.*

18. Rewrite each of the following sentences in the simple past tense.

1. Ich atme ganz regelmäßig. _____
2. Man tötet ihn. _____
3. Wir retten den Verunglückten. _____
4. Du öffnest die Tür. _____
5. Sie begegnen ihren Eltern. _____
6. Paul beobachtet den Vogel. _____
7. Ich arbeite gern. _____
8. Er ordnet die Bücher. _____
9. Sie antwortet nicht. _____
10. Sie bluten stark. _____

Irregular Weak Verbs

The following weak verbs are irregular in that they have stem vowel changes in the simple past.

INFINITIVE	SIMPLE PAST	INFINITIVE	SIMPLE PAST
brennen	brannte	senden	sandte
kennen	kannte	bringen	brachte
nennen	nannte	denken	dachte
rennen	rannte	wissen	wusste

Er *brachte* **mir Blumen.**	*He brought me flowers.*
Wir *rannten* **ins Haus.**	*We ran into the house.*
Ich *kannte* **den Künstler.**	*I knew the artist.*

19. Rewrite each of the following sentences in the simple past tense.

1. Er weiß das nicht. _____
2. Ich sende ihm einen Brief. _____
3. Es brennt dort. _____
4. Wir bringen Geschenke. _____
5. Sie denken daran. _____
6. Die Kinder rennen. _____
7. Man nennt es. _____
8. Ich kenne ihn auch. _____
9. Sie wissen die Antwort. _____
10. Du kennst uns. _____

Strong Verbs

The past tense of strong verbs is marked by a stem vowel change rather than the tense marker **-te** used to show the past tense in weak verbs. The simple past tense of strong verbs is formed by adding the past tense personal endings for strong verbs to the past tense stem.

Simple past of strong verbs = Past tense stem + Strong past tense personal ending

---

The full pattern for the past tense personal endings of strong verbs is as follows.

	SINGULAR	PLURAL
First Person	-∅	-en
Second Person	-st	-t
Third Person	-∅	-en

Note that the first- and third-person singular forms of both weak and strong verbs take no personal endings in the simple past tense. Note also that the only difference between the personal endings in the past tense of weak and strong verbs is that the first- and third-person plural ending is **-n** for weak verbs and **-en** for strong verbs.

The full conjugation of the simple past tense of the strong verb **bleiben** is as follows.

---

ich blieb	wir blieben
du bliebst	ihr bliebt
er blieb	sie blieben

Vowel Changes in the Stem

As an aid in remembering the different patterns of vowel changes found in the past tense stems of strong verbs, the following groupings can be made.

Changes from a, au, e, ei to ie, i

The following verbs change the stem vowel to **ie** or **i** in the simple past tense.

	INFINITIVE		SIMPLE PAST	PAST PARTICIPLE
a > ie	fallen	*to fall*	fiel	gefallen
	halten	*to stop, hold*	hielt	gehalten
	lassen	*to let*	ließ	gelassen
	schlafen	*to sleep*	schlief	geschlafen
au > ie	laufen	*to run*	lief	gelaufen
ei > ie	bleiben	*to stay*	blieb	geblieben
	leihen	*to loan*	lieh	geliehen
	scheinen	*to shine*	schien	geschienen
	schreiben	*to write*	schrieb	geschrieben
	schreien	*to scream*	schrie	geschrie(e)n
	schweigen	*to be silent*	schwieg	geschwiegen
	steigen	*to climb*	stieg	gestiegen
a > i	fangen	*to catch*	fing	gefangen
e > i	gehen	*to go, walk*	ging	gegangen
ei > i	beißen	*to bite*	biss	gebissen
	leiden	*to suffer*	litt	gelitten
	reiten	*to ride*	ritt	geritten
	schneiden	*to cut*	schnitt	geschnitten

Variations in Personal Endings

If the past tense stem ends in **-d**, **-t**, **-ss (ß)**, **-chs**, an **-e-** is added between the stem and the personal endings of the second-person singular and plural, e.g., **du schnittest, ihr schnittet**. However, these forms, as well as the second-person singular and plural of other verbs in the simple past, are rarely used.

If the past tense stem ends in **-ie**, the first- and third-person plural endings are **-n** instead of **-en**.

Wir *schrien* sehr laut.	*We screamed very loudly.*
Warum *schrien* sie nicht?	*Why didn't they scream?*

20. Rewrite each of the following sentences in the simple past tense.

1. Sie leidet. _____
2. Er schläft schon. _____
3. Sie schreiben Briefe. _____
4. Wir reiten gerne. _____
5. Ich schreie laut. _____
6. Das Buch fällt auf den Boden. _____
7. Der Zug hält dort. _____
8. Ludwig bleibt dort. _____
9. Sie schweigen immer. _____
10. Er schreibt die Aufgabe. _____
11. Sie schweigt nicht. _____
12. Ihr schneidet ins Papier. _____

13. Die Sonne scheint. _____
14. Man leiht dem Kind das Buch. _____
15. Der Hund beißt das Mädchen. _____

21. Form a sentence from each of the following groups of words, using the appropriate simple past tense form of the verb.

1. Ich / lassen / Gudrun / gehen _____
2. Das Pferd / laufen / am schnellsten _____
3. Hubert / reiten / den ganzen Tag _____
4. Wir / leihen / Gisela / das Buch _____
5. Der Rattenfänger / fangen / Ratten _____
6. Ich / schneiden / ins Fleisch _____
7. Meine Eltern / schreiben / den Brief _____
8. Wir / schreien / nicht _____

Changes from au, e, ie to o

The following verbs change the stem vowel to **o** in the simple past tense.

	INFINITIVE		SIMPLE PAST	PAST PARTICIPLE
au > o	**saufen**	*to drink* (of animals)	**soff**	**gesoffen**
e > o	**heben**	*to lift*	**hob**	**gehoben**
ie > o	**biegen**	*to bend*	**bog**	**gebogen**
	fliegen	*to fly*	**flog**	**geflogen**
	fliehen	*to flee*	**floh**	**geflohen**
	fließen	*to flow*	**floss**	**geflossen**
	frieren	*to freeze*	**fror**	**gefroren**
	riechen	*to smell*	**roch**	**gerochen**
	schießen	*to shoot*	**schoss**	**geschossen**
	schließen	*to shut*	**schloss**	**geschlossen**
	verlieren	*to lose*	**verlor**	**verloren**
	wiegen	*to weigh*	**wog**	**gewogen**
	ziehen	*to pull*	**zog**	**gezogen**

22. Complete each of the following sentences, using the appropriate simple past tense form of the verb on the right.

1. Er _____ nach Spanien.   fliegen
2. Ich _____ mein Gepäck.   verlieren
3. Es _____ stark.   riechen
4. Wir _____ die Fensterläden.   schließen
5. Der Jäger _____ auf das Reh.   schießen
6. Du _____ an den Händen.   frieren
7. Man _____ das Gold.   wiegen
8. Die Kinder _____ das Spielzeug.   ziehen
9. Wohin _____ das Wasser?   fließen
10. Ihr _____ damals nach Frankreich.   fliehen
11. Die Tiere _____ Wasser.   saufen
12. Ich _____ in die Schweiz.   fliegen
13. Er _____ den Sack vom Wagen.   heben
14. Die Männer _____ das Metall.   biegen

Changes from e, i, ie, o, u to a

The following verbs change the stem vowel to **a** in the simple past tense.

	INFINITIVE		SIMPLE PAST	PAST PARTICIPLE
e > a	brechen	*to break*	brach	gebrochen
	empfehlen	*to recommend*	empfahl	empfohlen
	essen	*to eat*	aß	gegessen
	fressen	*to eat* (of animals)	fraß	gefressen
	geben	*to give*	gab	gegeben
	helfen	*to help*	half	geholfen
	lesen	*to read*	las	gelesen
	messen	*to measure*	maß	gemessen
	nehmen	*to take*	nahm	genommen
	sehen	*to see*	sah	gesehen
	sprechen	*to speak*	sprach	gesprochen
	stehen	*to stand*	stand	gestanden
	stehlen	*to steal*	stahl	gestohlen
	sterben	*to die*	starb	gestorben
	treffen	*to meet*	traf	getroffen
	treten	*to step*	trat	getreten
	vergessen	*to forget*	vergaß	vergessen
	werfen	*to throw*	warf	geworfen
i > a	beginnen	*to begin*	begann	begonnen
	binden	*to bind*	band	gebunden
	bitten	*to ask*	bat	gebeten
	finden	*to find*	fand	gefunden
	gewinnen	*to win*	gewann	gewonnen
	schwimmen	*to swim*	schwamm	geschwommen
	singen	*to sing*	sang	gesungen
	sinken	*to sink*	sank	gesunken
	sitzen	*to sit*	saß	gesessen
	springen	*to jump*	sprang	gesprungen
	stinken	*to stink*	stank	gestunken
	trinken	*to drink*	trank	getrunken
ie > a	liegen	*to lie*	lag	gelegen
o > a	kommen	*to come*	kam	gekommen
u > a	tun	*to do*	tat	getan

23. Complete each of the following sentences, using the appropriate simple past tense form of the verb on the right.

1. Wir _____ Schokolade.   essen
2. Ich _____ viel Geld.   gewinnen
3. Er _____ über die Hürde.   springen
4. Wir _____ das Haus.   sehen
5. Er _____ am Abend.   kommen
6. Ich _____ das Gedicht.   lesen
7. Er _____ die Zeitung.   nehmen
8. Die Hunde _____ ins Wasser.   springen
9. Ich _____ nichts.   tun

10. Das Schiff _____ schnell.   sinken

11. Der Bandit _____ uns die Hände.   binden

12. Die Frau _____ an Krebs.   sterben

13. Meine Tanten _____ mir nichts.   geben

14. Wir _____ auf dem Sofa.   sitzen

15. Ich _____ die Bilder.   sehen

16. Er _____ die Lektüre.   beginnen

17. Die Leute _____ im Bodensee.   schwimmen

18. Es _____ nach faulen Eiern.   stinken

19. Ihr _____ uns im Zentrum.   treffen

20. Ich _____ Ursel.   bitten

21. Das Kind _____ den Ball.   werfen

22. Du _____ darüber.   sprechen

23. Wir _____ den Film.   sehen

24. Otto _____ das Geld.   stehlen

25. Ich _____ deine Schwester.   treffen

26. Wir _____ dem Kranken.   helfen

27. Die Leute _____ dort.   stehen

28. Herr Kraus _____ seine Aktentasche.   vergessen

29. Der Ingenieur _____ den Wasserstand.   messen

30. Wir _____ nicht auf den Teppich.   treten

24. Form a sentence from each of the following groups of words, using the appropriate simple past tense form of the verb.

1. Der Hund / fressen / das Futter   _____

2. Die Bücher / liegen / auf dem Tisch   _____

3. Wir / springen / aus dem Fenster   _____

4. Ich / sitzen / auf einem Stuhl   _____

5. Die Sängerin / singen / die Arie   _____

6. Die Kinder / trinken / keinen Wein   _____

7. Er / finden / die Diamantbrosche   _____

8. Wir / kommen / um acht Uhr   _____

9. Ich / sehen / Monika / im Kino   _____

10. Er / tun / alles   _____

Changes from a to u

The following verbs change the stem vowel to **u** in the simple past tense.

	INFINITIVE		SIMPLE PAST	PAST PARTICIPLE
a > u	**fahren**	*to drive, go*	**fuhr**	**gefahren**
	graben	*to dig*	**grub**	**gegraben**
	schlagen	*to hit*	**schlug**	**geschlagen**
	tragen	*to carry, wear*	**trug**	**getragen**
	wachsen	*to grow*	**wuchs**	**gewachsen**
	waschen	*to wash*	**wusch**	**gewaschen**

25. Rewrite each of the following sentences in the simple past tense.

1. Die Lehrerinnen fahren in die Stadt. _____

2. Ich schlage ihn nicht. _____

3. Die Arbeiterin gräbt ein Loch. _____
4. Wir tragen Lederhosen. _____
5. Das Baby wächst schnell. _____
6. Tante Ida wäscht die Bettwäsche. _____
7. Er trägt etwas. _____
8. Ich fahre mit dem Zug. _____

Auxiliary Verbs sein, haben, werden

The use of the simple past tense of the auxiliary verbs **sein**, **haben**, **werden** is not restricted to narration, as it is with other verbs. All simple past forms of **sein**, **haben**, and **werden** are freely used in conversation. The simple past forms of these verbs are irregular.

ich war	wir waren	ich hatte	wir hatten	ich wurde	wir wurden
du warst	ihr wart	du hattest	ihr hattet	du wurdest	ihr wurdet
er war	sie waren	er hatte	sie hatten	er wurde	sie wurden

26. Complete each of the following sentences, using the appropriate simple past tense form of **sein**.

1. Wie _____ die Oper?   6. _____ ihr zu Hause?
2. Wo _____ du?   7. Herr Breu, _____ Sie nervös?
3. Ich _____ in Regensburg.   8. Meine Geschwister _____ schon fertig.
4. _____ du krank?   9. _____ ihr auch dort?
5. Wir _____ sehr müde.   10. Mutter _____ sehr böse.

27. Complete each of the following sentences, using the appropriate simple past tense form of **haben**.

1. _____ du Angst?   6. _____ ihr Durst?
2. Die Jungen _____   7. _____ du Glück?
   Hunger.   8. Gisela _____ keinen Freund.
3. Wir _____ Geld.   9. _____ ihr auch Kameras?
4. Ich _____ nichts.   10. _____ Sie ein Auto?
5. _____ du keine Zeit?

28. Complete each of the following sentences, using the appropriate simple past tense form of **werden**.

1. Unsere Eltern _____   5. Ich _____ böse.
   immer älter.   6. Frau Eber _____ nervös.
2. Wir _____ schnell   7. Wann _____ du krank?
   wieder gesund.   8. _____ ihr auch hungrig?
3. Es _____ sehr heiß.   9. _____ er böse?
4. Klaus _____ Doktor.   10. Wann _____ ihr müde?

Usage Notes on the Simple Past Tense

Narrative Past

In German, the simple past tense (narrative past) is used mainly in written materials to narrate or report a chain of events that took place in the past. The simple past is not interchangeable with the present perfect tense (conversational past), which is used when the speaker talks or asks about single past events. The following passages exemplify the different uses of these two past tenses. Note that the simple past of **sein**, **haben**, **werden** is used in narration as well as in conversation.

Narration

„Ich **war** letzten Sonntag mit Bärbel in Garmisch. Wir **trafen** dort ihren Bruder und **machten** zusammen eine Radtour. Ich **wurde** schon nach einer Stunde müde. Endlich **kamen** wir zu einem Rasthaus, wo wir uns ein gutes Essen **bestellten**."

Conversation

„Was **hast** du letzten Sonntag **gemacht**?"

„Ich **war** mit Bärbel in Garmisch."

„**Habt** ihr jemand **getroffen**?"

„Ja, wir **haben** ihren Bruder **getroffen** und **haben** zusammen eine Radtour **gemacht**."

„**Seid** ihr weit **gefahren**?"

„Ja, aber ich **wurde** schon nach einer Stunde müde."

„**Habt** ihr nicht **gerastet**?"

„Doch, endlich **sind** wir zu einem Rasthaus **gekommen**, wo wir uns ein gutes Essen **bestellt haben**."

29. Rewrite the following sentences in paragraph form, using the narrative past (simple past).

    1. Peter hat mich gestern besucht.
    2. Wir haben Limonade getrunken.
    3. Er hat auch ein Stück Schokoladenkuchen gegessen.
    4. Wir sind ins Zentrum gefahren.
    5. Wir haben dort seine Freunde getroffen und wir sind ins Kino gegangen.
    6. Der Film war prima. Er hat mir sehr gefallen.
    7. Wir sind um acht Uhr nach Hause gekommen.
    8. Wir haben eine Stunde CDs gespielt und haben über Musik gesprochen.
    9. Meine Mutter hat noch Wurstbrote gemacht.
    10. Peter ist danach nach Hause gegangen.

Expression of Simultaneous Past Events

The simple past tense is used to express that two actions took place at the same time. The dependent clause is often introduced by **während** *while, during the time which* or **als** *when*. Note that the verb is in final position in clauses introduced by **während** and **als** (i.e., the normal word order for dependent clauses).

Sie *trank* Kaffee, *als* er ins Zimmer *kam*.	She was drinking coffee when he came into the room.
Ich *arbeitete* nicht, *als* ich krank *war*.	I did not work when I was ill.
Er *las* einen Roman, *während* ich *studierte*.	He was reading a novel while I was studying.
Sie *spielte* Klavier, *während* er *schlief*.	She played the piano while he slept.

30. Complete each of the following sentences, using the appropriate simple past tense forms of the verbs on the right.

    1. Ich _____, während er _____.　　schlafen, lesen
    2. Er _____, während Karin _____.　　lächeln, singen
    3. Wir _____, während die Leute _____.　　essen, tanzen
    4. Ich _____, als das Telefon _____.　　schreiben, klingeln
    5. Er _____ Wein, als er mich _____.　　kaufen, treffen
    6. Wir _____ nach Hause, als es kalt _____.　　gehen, werden
    7. Er _____, als ich die Geschichte _____.　　lachen, erzählen

8. Wir _____ draußen, als du _____.   sein, kommen
9. Ich _____ Klaus, als er im Garten _____.   helfen, arbeiten
10. Wir _____, während er das Gras _____.   schwimmen, schneiden

Customary Past Occurrence

The German simple past tense is used to express habitual past action. Words like **gewöhnlich** *usually* and **immer** *always* occur in such sentences. In English, the habitual action is expressed by *used to*.

Er *schlief gewöhnlich* **die ganze Nacht.**   *He usually slept the whole night.*
Wir *besuchten sie* *immer.*   *We always used to visit her.*

31. Form a sentence from each of the following groups of words, using the appropriate simple past tense form of the verb to show customary occurrence.

1. Wir / fahren / gewöhnlich / in die Schweiz   _____
2. Ich / sein / immer / krank   _____
3. Die Damen / trinken / gewöhnlich / Tee   _____
4. Die Schauspielerin / werden / immer /   _____
   nervös
5. Wir / gehen / sonntags / gewöhnlich /   _____
   zur Kirche
6. Er / arbeiten / immer   _____
7. Karin / trinken / gewöhnlich / Limonade   _____
8. Wir / geben / den Kindern / immer / Geld   _____
9. Ich / helfen / Renate / immer   _____
10. Wir / spielen / gewöhnlich / moderne   _____
    Musik

Review

32. Complete each of the following sentences, using the appropriate simple past tense form(s) of the verb(s) on the right.

1. Wann _____ du krank?   werden
2. Inge _____ an einer schlimmen Krankheit.   leiden
3. Ich _____ dort ein ganzes Jahr.   arbeiten
4. Er _____ das Autofenster.   öffnen
5. Der Mechaniker _____ es.   reparieren
6. Die Touristen _____ das Schloss.   besichtigen
7. _____ ihr böse?   sein
8. Ich _____ den Film.   sehen
9. Er _____, als ich _____.   schlafen, kommen
10. _____ du keine Zeit?   haben
11. Herr Wimmer, _____ Sie auch dort?   sein
12. Thomas _____ das Geld.   nehmen
13. Ich _____ viel Wasser, während ich krank _____. trinken, sein
14. Wir _____ ihm das Bild.   zeigen
15. Man _____ immer.   klingeln
16. Das Kind _____ durch den Garten.   laufen
17. Die Haushälterin _____ die Wäsche.   waschen
18. Ich _____ seine Adresse.   vergessen
19. Wir _____ gewöhnlich um zehn Uhr dort.   sein
20. Ich _____ ein Buch, während Ulrich _____.   lesen, studieren

Present Perfect Tense

The present perfect tense of German verbs consists of the present tense inflected forms of the auxiliary **haben** or **sein** plus the past participle of the main verb.

The verbs that take **haben** as their auxiliary include the transitive verbs (those that take a direct object), the reflexive verbs, and the modal auxiliaries. The verbs that take **sein** as their auxiliary include the intransitive verbs (those without a direct object) indicating a change of condition or a change in location.

NOTE: When used as part of the verb (rather than as an adjective), the past participle never takes an ending, and in independent clauses the past participle is in final position (see Chapter 10).

The German present perfect tense can refer to completed actions in the past, as well as to actions that have begun in the past and continue into the present (as is the case for the present perfect tense in English). In German, the present perfect tense, also called the *conversational past,* is the past tense that is most frequently used to describe past events in normal conversation. In this situation, it is best translated by the simple past tense in English.

Present perfect tense = Present tense of **sein** or **haben** + Past participle

---

Formation of the Past Participle

Past Participle of Weak Verbs

The past participle of most weak verbs is formed by placing the prefix **ge-** in front of the infinitive stem and adding **-t** or **-et** at the end of the stem.

Past participle (weak verbs) = **ge-** + Infinitive stem + **-t** or **-et**

---

spielen	*ge* + **spiel** + *t* = **gespielt**
lachen	*ge* + **lach** + *t* = **gelacht**
arbeiten	*ge* + **arbeit** + *et* = **gearbeitet**

Past Participle of Strong Verbs

The past participle of most strong verbs is formed by placing the prefix **ge-** in front of the past participle stem and adding **-en** at the end of the stem.

Past participle (strong verbs) = **ge-** + Past participle stem + **-en**

---

singen	*ge* + **sung** + *en* = **gesungen**

As we learned in the section on the simple past tense, strong verbs are characterized by a stem vowel change in the past tense. This characteristic is also reflected in the past participle. However, the stem vowel of the past participle is not always the same as the vowel in the simple past tense form of a strong verb. *The stem vowel of the past participle can be the same as the stem vowel in the simple past, the same as the stem vowel in the infinitive, or a different vowel altogether.* Thus, although there are some basic sound patterns that help predict the stem vowel of a past participle, it is necessary to learn the principal parts for each strong verb.

Regular Weak Verbs

The present perfect tense of most regular weak verbs is formed with the present tense of **haben** or **sein** and the past participle of the main verb.

INFINITIVE	THIRD-PERSON SINGULAR	PAST PARTICIPLE
arbeiten	er arbeitet	gearbeitet
lieben	er liebt	geliebt
machen	er macht	gemacht
öffnen	er öffnet	geöffnet

Study the following conjugation.

ich habe gemacht	wir haben gemacht
du hast gemacht	ihr habt gemacht
er hat gemacht	sie haben gemacht

Wir *haben* einen Wagen *gekauft.*	*We bought a car.*
Er *hat* die Wahrheit *gesagt.*	*He told the truth.*
Ich *habe* den Lehrer *gefragt.*	*I asked the teacher.*
Habt ihr auch *gearbeitet?*	*Did you also work?*
Er weiß, dass ich den Brief *geschickt habe.*	*He knows that I sent the letter.*

Weak Verbs Without the **ge-** Prefix

Verbs ending in **-ieren**

The past participle of weak verbs ending in **-ieren** does not take the **ge-** prefix.

INFINITIVE	PAST PARTICIPLE
probieren	probiert
studieren	studiert
telefonieren	telefoniert

Additional Verbs Without the **ge-** Prefix

Verbs with the following inseparable prefixes do not take the **ge-** prefix in the past participle: **be-**, **emp-**, **ent-**, **er-**, **ge-**, **ver-**, **zer-** (see the section on inseparable prefix verbs, pages 179–180).

    NOTE: Inseparable prefix verbs can be either weak or strong.

WEAK VERBS		STRONG VERBS	
INFINITIVE	PAST PARTICIPLE	INFINITIVE	PAST PARTICIPLE
bestellen	bestellt	bestehen	bestanden
entdecken	entdeckt	entnehmen	entnommen
erklären	erklärt	erfahren	erfahren
gehören	gehört	gefallen	gefallen
verkaufen	verkauft	verbergen	verborgen

Study the following conjugations.

ich habe zerstört	wir haben zerstört	ich habe zerbrochen	wir haben zerbrochen
du hast zerstört	ihr habt zerstört	du hast zerbrochen	ihr habt zerbrochen
er hat zerstört	sie haben zerstört	er hat zerbrochen	sie haben zerbrochen

33. Complete each of the following sentences, using the appropriate present perfect tense form of the verb on the right.

1. Wir _____ den Kellner _____. fragen
2. Wo _____ Sie _____? wohnen
3. Wir _____ alles _____. glauben
4. _____ du den Mantel _____? kaufen
5. Gisela _____ ihren Freund _____. lieben
6. Die Leute _____ die Geschichte _____. hören
7. Ich _____ den Hund _____. suchen

34. Complete each of the following sentences, using the appropriate present perfect tense form of the verb on the right.

1. Warum _____ ihr _____? bezahlen
2. _____ du die Maschine _____? verkaufen
3. Die Jungen _____ das Auto _____. reparieren
4. Unsere Lehrerin _____ alles _____. erzählen
5. Ich _____ die ganze Nacht _____. studieren
6. Wir _____ die Suppe _____. probieren
7. Wer _____ die Stadt _____? zerstören
8. _____ dir der Fußball _____? gehören
9. _____ du _____? telefonieren
10. Meine Eltern _____ schon _____. bestellen

35. Rewrite each of the following sentences in the present perfect tense.

1. Wir studieren viel. _____
2. Brauchst du Geld? _____
3. Warum bellt der Hund? _____
4. Er arbeitet viel. _____
5. Man zerstört das Haus. _____
6. Suchen Sie den Jungen? _____
7. Träumt ihr oft? _____
8. Sie atmet sehr laut. _____
9. Ich blute stark. _____
10. Die Kinder baden gerne. _____
11. Wo wohnt ihr? _____

Irregular Weak Verbs

Some weak verbs have a vowel change in the past stem. The past participles of these irregular weak verbs also have a stem vowel change.

INFINITIVE		SIMPLE PAST	PAST PARTICIPLE
brennen	*to burn*	**brannte**	**gebrannt**
bringen	*to bring*	**brachte**	**gebracht**
denken	*to think*	**dachte**	**gedacht**
kennen	*to know* (a person)	**kannte**	**gekannt**
nennen	*to name*	**nannte**	**genannt**
senden	*to send*	**sandte**	**gesandt**
wenden	*to turn*	**wandte**	**gewandt**
wissen	*to know* (a fact)	**wusste**	**gewusst**

36. Form a sentence from each of the following groups of words, using the appropriate present perfect tense form of the verb.

1. Er / kennen / meine Schwester   _____
2. Die Kinder / wissen / die Antwort   _____
3. Ich / bringen / Blumen   _____
4. Denken / du / daran / ?   _____
5. Die Häuser / brennen   _____
6. Wir / senden / das Paket   _____
7. Nennen / ihr / den höchsten Berg / ?   _____
8. Ich / wenden / das Blatt   _____

Intransitive Verbs

The present perfect tense of some German verbs is formed with the present tense of the auxiliary verb **sein** instead of **haben**. Such verbs are referred to as intransitive verbs (verbs that do not take a direct object). They usually denote a change of location or condition. The following weak verbs are conjugated with **sein**.

INFINITIVE		PAST PARTICIPLE
begegnen	*to meet*	**ist begegnet**
klettern	*to climb*	**ist geklettert**
reisen	*to travel*	**ist gereist**
rennen	*to run*	**ist gerannt**
wandern	*to wander*	**ist gewandert**

Note that the irregular weak verb **rennen** has a vowel change in the past participle.

Intransitive verbs are conjugated as follows.

ich bin gereist	**wir sind gereist**
du bist gereist	**ihr seid gereist**
er ist gereist	**sie sind gereist**

Wir *sind* auf den Baum *geklettert*.	*We climbed the tree.*
Ich *bin* nach Deutschland *gereist*.	*I traveled to Germany.*
***Bist* du deinem Freund *begegnet*?**	*Did you meet your friend?*

37. Complete each of the following sentences, using the appropriate present perfect tense form of the verb on the right.

1. Wir _____ sehr schnell _____.   rennen
2. Wohin _____ ihr _____?   reisen
3. Ich _____ auf den Berg _____.   klettern
4. _____ er durch die Schweiz _____?   reisen
5. _____ ihr ins Dorf _____?   wandern
6. Ich _____ nicht _____.   rennen
7. Die Kinder _____ ihrem Lehrer _____.   begegnen
8. Meine Mutter _____ nach München _____.   reisen
9. _____ du auch auf den Baum _____?   klettern
10. Ich _____ ihrem Freund _____.   begegnen

Strong Verbs

The present perfect tense of most strong verbs is formed with the present tense of **haben** and the past participle of the main verb. Note that some are conjugated with **sein**. Remember also that the past participle of a strong verb may have the same stem vowel as the infinitive, the same stem vowel as the simple past tense, or a completely different stem vowel.

sehen, sah, gesehen	beißen, biss, gebissen	finden, fand, gefunden
ich habe gesehen	ich habe gebissen	ich habe gefunden
du hast gesehen	du hast gebissen	du hast gefunden
er hat gesehen	er hat gebissen	er hat gefunden
wir haben gesehen	wir haben gebissen	wir haben gefunden
ihr habt gesehen	ihr habt gebissen	ihr habt gefunden
sie haben gesehen	sie haben gebissen	sie haben gefunden

Remember also that the past participles of verbs beginning with one of the inseparable prefixes (**be-, emp-, ent-, er-, ge-, ver-, zer-**) do not take the **ge-** prefix.

Past Participles with No Vowel Change

The past participles of the following strong verbs consist of the prefix **ge-** and the infinitive stem plus **-en**. Note the extra **g** in **gegessen**.

INFINITIVE		SIMPLE PAST	PAST PARTICIPLE
backen	*to bake*	**backte** (OLD FORM: **buk**)	gebacken
essen	*to eat*	**aß**	gegessen
fahren	*to drive, go*	**fuhr**	(ist) gefahren
fallen	*to fall*	**fiel**	(ist) gefallen
fangen	*to catch*	**fing**	gefangen
fressen	*to eat* (of animals)	**fraß**	gefressen
geben	*to give*	**gab**	gegeben
graben	*to dig*	**grub**	gegraben
halten	*to hold*	**hielt**	gehalten
kommen	*to come*	**kam**	(ist) gekommen
lassen	*to let*	**ließ**	gelassen
laufen	*to run*	**lief**	(ist) gelaufen
lesen	*to read*	**las**	gelesen
messen	*to measure*	**maß**	gemessen
schlafen	*to sleep*	**schlief**	geschlafen
schlagen	*to hit*	**schlug**	geschlagen
sehen	*to see*	**sah**	gesehen
tragen	*to carry, wear*	**trug**	getragen
treten	*to step*	**trat**	(ist) getreten
vergessen	*to forget*	**vergaß**	vergessen
wachsen	*to grow*	**wuchs**	(ist) gewachsen
waschen	*to wash*	**wusch**	gewaschen

Note that the past participles preceded by **(ist)** take **sein** as their auxiliary verb in the present perfect tense.

ich bin gewachsen	wir sind gewachsen
du bist gewachsen	ihr seid gewachsen
er ist gewachsen	sie sind gewachsen

Er *ist* nach Hamburg *gefahren*.   *He went (by car or train) to Hamburg.*
Ich *bin* ins Zimmer *getreten*.   *I stepped into the room.*
Sie *sind* schnell *gewachsen*.   *They grew fast.*

38. Complete each of the following sentences, using the appropriate present perfect tense form of the verb on the right.

1. _____ du den Roman _____?   lesen
2. Er _____ den Jungen _____.   schlagen
3. Ich _____ es meinem Lehrer _____. geben
4. Wann _____ ihr den Film _____?   sehen
5. Wir _____ einen Kuchen _____.   backen
6. Ich _____ die Strecke _____.   messen
7. Was _____ das Tier _____?   fressen
8. Die Männer _____ nach Gold _____.   graben
9. Die Frau _____ keinen Hut _____.   tragen
10. Ich _____ mir die Hände _____.   waschen
11. _____ ihr den Tiger _____?   fangen
12. Wer _____ die Bananen _____?   essen
13. _____ du den Mantel zu Hause _____? lassen
14. Warum _____ ihr nicht _____?   schlafen

39. Form a sentence from each of the following groups of words, using the appropriate present perfect tense form of the verb.

1. Mein Bruder / fahren / schnell   _____
2. Treten / du / ins Haus / ?   _____
3. Wir / wachsen / schon wieder   _____
4. Fahren / ihr / nach Bremen / ?   _____
5. Die Kinder / wachsen / immer   _____
6. Ich / fahren / gestern   _____
7. Laufen / ihr / in Haus / ?   _____
8. Wann / du / kommen / ?   _____
9. Die Leute / laufen / schnell   _____
10. Ich / ins Wasser / fallen   _____

Past Participles with a Vowel Change

Many strong verbs change the stem vowel in the past participle. The participles of such verbs can be grouped according to these vowel changes. The following groups may facilitate learning these past participles.

Changes from ei to ie or i

The **ei** of the infinitive stem is changed to **ie** or **i** in the past participles of the following verbs.

	INFINITIVE		SIMPLE PAST	PAST PARTICIPLE
ei > ie	bleiben	*to stay*	blieb	(ist) geblieben
	leihen	*to loan*	lieh	geliehen
	scheinen	*to shine, seem*	schien	geschienen
	schreiben	*to write*	schrieb	geschrieben
	schreien	*to scream*	schrie	geschrien
	schweigen	*to be silent*	schwieg	geschwiegen
	steigen	*to climb*	stieg	(ist) gestiegen

	INFINITIVE		SIMPLE PAST	PAST PARTICIPLE
ei > i	beißen	*to bite*	biss	gebissen
	leiden	*to suffer*	litt	gelitten
	reiten	*to ride*	ritt	(ist) geritten
	schneiden	*to cut*	schnitt	geschnitten

NOTE: The stem vowels in the past participles in the groups of verbs above are the same as the stem vowels in the simple past tense.

40. Rewrite each of the following sentences in the present perfect tense.

1. Reitest du oft? _____
2. Wir schreien laut. _____
3. Warum schreibt ihr nicht? _____
4. Die Sonne scheint. _____
5. Warum beißt er? _____
6. Bleibt ihr lange? _____
7. Die Kranken leiden. _____
8. Warum schweigt ihr? _____
9. Steigst du auf die Leiter? _____
10. Ich leihe dir Geld. _____
11. Er schneidet dem Kind die Haare. _____
12. Leidet ihr nicht? _____
13. Ich schreie nicht. _____
14. Schreibst du den Brief? _____

Changes from ie, au to o or e

The **ie, au** of the infinitive stem is changed to **o** or **e** in the past participles of the following verbs.

	INFINITIVE		SIMPLE PAST	PAST PARTICIPLE
ie > o	biegen	*to bend*	bog	gebogen
	fliegen	*to fly*	flog	(ist) geflogen
	fliehen	*to flee*	floh	(ist) geflohen
	fließen	*to flow*	floss	(ist) geflossen
	frieren	*to freeze*	fror	gefroren
	riechen	*to smell*	roch	gerochen
	schießen	*to shoot*	schoss	geschossen
	schließen	*to shut*	schloss	geschlossen
	verlieren	*to lose*	verlor	verloren
	wiegen	*to weigh*	wog	gewogen
	ziehen	*to pull*	zog	gezogen
au > o	saufen	*to drink* (of animals)	soff	gesoffen

NOTE: The stem vowels in the past participles in the groups of verbs above are the same as the stem vowels in the simple past tense.

ie > a/e	liegen	*to lie* (of animals)	lag	gelegen

NOTE: The stem vowel in the past participle of **liegen** is different from those in the infinitive and the simple past tense.

41. Complete each of the following sentences, using the appropriate present perfect tense form of the verb on the right.

1. _____ du den Schlüssel _____?   verlieren
2. Er _____ den Braten _____.   riechen
3. _____ ihr nach Nürnberg _____?   fliegen
4. Ein Beamter _____ den Koffer _____.   wiegen
5. Warum _____ du auf den Hasen _____?   schießen
6. Er _____ sie an den Haaren _____.   ziehen
7. Ein Gefangener _____ gestern _____.   fliehen
8. Wohin _____ das Wasser _____?   fließen
9. Warum _____ du die Augen _____?   schließen
10. Wir _____ an den Beinen _____.   frieren
11. Der Wind _____ die Bäume _____.   biegen
12. Er _____ im Schatten _____.   liegen
13. Der Hund _____ das Wasser _____.   saufen
14. Ich _____ das Geld _____.   verlieren

Changes from i to u, o, or e

The **i** of the infinitive stem is changed to **u, o,** or **e** in the past participles of the following verbs.

	INFINITIVE		SIMPLE PAST	PAST PARTICIPLE
i > a/u	binden	*to bind*	band	gebunden
	finden	*to find*	fand	gefunden
	singen	*to sing*	sang	gesungen
	sinken	*to sink*	sank	(ist) gesunken
	springen	*to jump*	sprang	(ist) gesprungen
	stinken	*to stink*	stank	gestunken
	trinken	*to drink*	trank	getrunken
i > a/o	beginnen	*to begin*	begann	begonnen
	gewinnen	*to win*	gewann	gewonnen
	schwimmen	*to swim*	schwamm	(ist) geschwommen
i > a/e	bitten	*to ask*	bat	gebeten
	sitzen	*to sit*	saß	gesessen

NOTE: The stem vowels in the past participles in the groups of verbs above are different from the stem vowels in both the infinitive and the simple past tense.

42. Form a sentence from each of the following groups of words, using the appropriate present perfect tense form of the verb.

1. Die Sonne / sinken / ins Meer _____
2. Die Vorlesung / beginnen _____
3. Springen / ihr / von der Brücke / ? _____
4. Ich / singen / das Lied _____
5. Schwimmen / du / über die Nordsee / ? _____
6. Er / gewinnen / den Preis _____
7. Das Gas / stinken _____
8. Binden / du / den Hund / an den Baum / ? _____
9. Die Männer / springen / über die Hürde _____

10. Singen / ihr / oft? _____
11. Ich / trinken / Wasser _____
12. Wir / beginnen / gestern _____
13. Er / sitzen / auf dem Sofa _____
14. Bitten / ihr / die Frau / ? _____
15. Wer / finden / den Schmuck / ? _____
16. Er / trinken / kaltes Bier _____

Changes from e, u to o or a

The **e** or **u** of the infinitive stem is changed to **o** or **a** in the past participles of the following verbs.

	INFINITIVE		SIMPLE PAST	PAST PARTICIPLE
e > a/o	brechen	to break	brach	gebrochen
	empfehlen	to recommend	empfahl	empfohlen
	helfen	to help	half	geholfen
	nehmen	to take	nahm	genommen
	sprechen	to talk, speak	sprach	gesprochen
	stehlen	to steal	stahl	gestohlen
	sterben	to die	starb	(ist) gestorben
	treffen	to meet	traf	getroffen
	werfen	to throw	warf	geworfen
e > i/a	gehen	to go	ging	(ist) gegangen

NOTE: The stem vowels in the past participles in the groups of verbs above are different from the stem vowels in both the infinitive and the simple past tense.

e > a	stehen	to stand	stand	(ist OR hat) gestanden
u > a	tun	to do	tat	getan

43. Rewrite each of the following sentences in the present perfect tense.

1. Trefft ihr sie? _____
2. Sie werfen den Ball. _____
3. Warum brichst du es in Stücke? _____
4. Ich helfe ihr. _____
5. Das Kind nimmt nichts. _____
6. Der Verletzte stirbt. _____
7. Warum stiehlst du? _____
8. Frau Knauer, Sie sprechen zu schnell. _____
9. Wir helfen dem Kranken. _____
10. Sprichst du viel? _____
11. Gehst du ins Kino? _____
12. Ich stehe hier. _____
13. Wir empfehlen die Suppe. _____
14. Der Kran hebt das Auto. _____
15. Was tust du? _____

Auxiliary Verbs sein, haben, werden

The present perfect tense of the auxiliary verbs **sein**, **haben**, **werden** is as follows.

sein	haben	werden
ich bin gewesen	ich habe gehabt	ich bin geworden
du bist gewesen	du hast gehabt	du bist geworden
er ist gewesen	er hat gehabt	er ist geworden
wir sind gewesen	wir haben gehabt	wir sind geworden
ihr seid gewesen	ihr habt gehabt	ihr seid geworden
sie sind gewesen	sie haben gehabt	sie sind geworden

Wir *sind* in Japan *gewesen*.	*We were in Japan.*
Ich *bin* müde *geworden*.	*I became tired.*
Hast du Geld *gehabt*?	*Did you have money?*
Seid ihr krank *geworden*?	*Did you become ill?*
Er *ist* in der Schule *gewesen*.	*He was in school.*

44. Rewrite each of the following sentences, changing the verb to the present perfect tense.

1. Hast du Hunger? _____
2. Ich bin krank. _____
3. Wir haben Hunger. _____
4. Sie werden immer dicker. _____
5. Er wird wieder gesund. _____
6. Wann sind Sie dort? _____
7. Ich habe Kopfweh. _____
8. Wir werden nass. _____
9. Bist du auch müde? _____
10. Ich werde böse. _____
11. Habt ihr Geld? _____
12. Ich habe Sorgen. _____
13. Sie ist unglücklich. _____
14. Die Pferde sind unruhig. _____
15. Wirst du nervös? _____
16. Seid ihr krank? _____

Review

45. Complete each of the following sentences, using the appropriate present perfect tense form of the verb on the right.

1. _____ Sie den Turm _____?   besichtigen
2. Er _____ mir nichts _____.   geben
3. Wie lange _____ du dort _____?   wohnen
4. Otto _____ etwas _____.   kaufen
5. Die Leute _____ mich _____.   kennen
6. Was _____ du _____?   backen
7. _____ ihr ihn _____?   sehen
8. Die Kinder _____ laut _____.   schreien
9. Er _____ vor einer Stunde _____.   telefonieren
10. Ich _____ den ganzen Tag _____.   arbeiten
11. _____ ihr schon _____?   bestellen

12. Wem _____ du _____? begegnen
13. Warum _____ er _____? schweigen
14. Wir _____ nichts _____. verloren
15. Die Katze _____ es _____. fressen
16. Du _____ aber _____! wachsen
17. _____ ihr auch ins Wasser _____? springen
18. Ich _____ von dir _____. träumen
19. Man _____ es ganz _____. zerstören
20. _____ du schon _____? studieren
21. Wann _____ du _____? kommen
22. Ich _____ alles _____. erzählen
23. _____ ihr den Kuchen _____? essen
24. _____ Sie lange _____? warten
25. Die Kinder _____ Limonade _____. trinken
26. Wir _____ das Haus _____. verkaufen
27. _____ du stark _____? bluten
28. Ich _____ auf die Leiter _____. steigen
29. Er _____ alles _____. sagen
30. Der Mechaniker _____ den Wagen _____. reparieren
31. _____ du die Suppe _____? empfehlen
32. Warum _____ das Boot _____? sinken
33. Wen _____ ihr nach der Arbeit _____? treffen
34. Wie lange _____ du _____? schlafen
35. Die Kinder _____ die Tür _____. schließen

Past Perfect Tense

Weak and Strong Verbs

The past perfect tense of both weak and strong verbs is formed with the simple past tense form of the auxiliary **haben** or **sein** plus the past participle. The past perfect tense is sometimes referred to as the *pluperfect* tense.

Past perfect tense = Simple past tense of **sein** or **haben** + Past participle

---

Study the following conjugations.

---

ich hatte gesucht	wir hatten gesucht	ich war gegangen	wir waren gegangen
du hattest gesucht	ihr hattet gesucht	du warst gegangen	ihr wart gegangen
er hatte gesucht	sie hatten gesucht	er war gegangen	sie waren gegangen

---

Ich *hatte* die Geschichte *gehört.*   *I had heard the story.*
Wir *waren* zu Hause *geblieben.*   *We had stayed at home.*
Er *war* schon dort *gewesen.*   *He had already been there.*
Sie *hatten* den Hund *gefüttert.*   *They had fed the dog.*

46. Rewrite each of the following sentences in the past perfect tense.

1. Wir haben getanzt. _____
2. Hast du gesungen? _____
3. Sie sind gefahren. _____
4. Habt ihr gefragt? _____

5. Man hat es genommen. _____
6. Sie haben viel getrunken. _____
7. Hast du studiert? _____
8. Ich habe es repariert. _____
9. Wann ist er gekommen? _____
10. Er hat mich besucht. _____
11. Hast du den Wagen gewaschen? _____
12. Konrad ist dort geblieben. _____
13. Ich habe die Jacke getragen. _____
14. Sie ist in Rom gewesen. _____
15. Hat er dem Kranken geholfen? _____
16. Wir haben gearbeitet. _____

Use of the Past Perfect Tense

In German as in English, the past perfect tense is used to report events that took place prior to another event in the past. Note that the conjunction **denn** *for* does not affect the word order of the clause that contains the past perfect form of the verb. The simple past tense is used in the main clause. Study the following examples.

Ich war müde, denn ich *hatte* den ganzen Tag *gearbeitet*.	*I was tired, for I had worked the entire day.*
Er hatte Hunger, denn er *hatte* nichts *gegessen*.	*He was hungry, for he had not eaten anything.*

47. Combine each of the following pairs of sentences, using the simple past tense in the first clause and **denn** and the past perfect tense in the second. Follow the model.

MODEL　Ich bin glücklich. Ich habe Geld gewonnen.

　　　　Ich war glücklich, denn ich hatte Geld gewonnen.

1. Wir sind arm. Wir haben alles verloren.

_____

2. Sie hat Angst. Sie ist schon oft im Krankenhaus gewesen.

_____

3. Ich weiß alles. Ich habe viel studiert.

_____

4. Sie bestellen viel. Sie haben den ganzen Tag nichts gegessen.

_____

5. Laura ist traurig. Ihr Freund hat sie nicht besucht.

_____

6. Sie sind schwach. Sie waren krank.

_____

7. Ich bin müde. Ich habe schlecht geschlafen.

_____

8. Wir haben Durst. Wir haben nichts getrunken.

_____

9. Es riecht nach Wein. Er hat die Flasche zerbrochen.

_____

10. Ich habe kein Geld. Ich habe viel gekauft.

_____

Future Tense

Weak and Strong Verbs

The future tense of both weak and strong verbs is formed with the auxiliary verb **werden** plus the infinitive. The infinitive is in final position, unless it occurs in a dependent clause.

Future tense = Present tense of **werden** + Infinitive

Study the following conjugation.

ich werde suchen	**wir werden suchen**
du wirst suchen	**ihr werdet suchen**
er wird suchen	**sie werden suchen**

Ich *werde* dich nicht *vergessen*.	*I shall not forget you.*
Werdet *ihr auch* kommen?	*Will you also come?*
Wir *werden* einen Hund *kaufen*.	*We are going to buy a dog.*
Ich weiß, dass du *kommen wirst*.	*I know that you will come.*

48. Complete each of the following sentences, using the appropriate future tense form of the verb on the right.

1. _____ ihr hier _____?   bleiben
2. _____ du _____?   telefonieren
3. Die Leute _____ es nicht _____.   glauben
4. Ich _____ die Rechnung _____.   bezahlen
5. Er _____ es _____.   lesen
6. Wir _____ es _____.   machen
7. _____ ihr uns _____?   helfen
8. Die Kinder _____ den Brief _____.   schreiben
9. Ich _____ die Tür _____.   öffnen
10. _____ du den Mantel _____?   kaufen
11. Was _____ ihr _____?   bestellen
12. Warum _____ er nicht _____?   kommen
13. Ich _____ es nicht _____.   vergessen
14. Wir _____ das Metall _____.   biegen
15. Die Leute _____ laut _____.   schreien
16. Du _____ in der Kälte _____.   frieren

Use of the Future Tense

The future tense is used to indicate actions that will take place entirely in the future. If an adverb or adverbial phrase indicating future time is not expressed, the future using **werden** is commonly used. If an adverbial indicator is present or if it is obvious from the context that the future is clearly intended, the present tense (with a future meaning) is frequently encountered, particularly in spoken German.

Wir *werden* unsere Freunde *besuchen*.	*We will visit our friends.*
Ich *fahre morgen* nach Stuttgart.	*I am going to Stuttgart tomorrow.*

49. Rewrite each of the following sentences in the future tense, omitting the adverbs of time.

1. Wir bringen morgen das Auto.   _____
2. Ich fahre nächste Woche nach Berlin.   _____
3. Kommst du übermorgen?   _____

4. Er schreibt das Gedicht morgen Abend. _____

5. Zeigt ihr euren Eltern das Haus
nächsten Monat? _____

6. Sie arbeiten heute Abend. _____

7. Ich esse morgen bei Inge. _____

8. Kaufst du es morgen Nachmittag? _____

Probability

The German future tense may also indicate present or future probability or likelihood, particularly when used in conjunction with adverbs such as **sicher**, **schon**, **vielleicht**, **wohl**.

Ingo ist nicht zur Schule gekommen. Er *wird* **sicher** krank *sein*.	*Ingo didn't come to school. He's probably sick.*
Du hast schwer gearbeitet. Du *wirst wohl* müde *sein*.	*You've worked hard. You're probably tired.*
Die Wolken sind sehr dunkel. Es *wird wohl* bald *regnen*.	*The clouds are very dark. It will probably rain soon.*

The future tense in German can also be used to show determination. When used in this way, the verb **werden** is usually stressed.

Sag was du willst. Ich *werde* **das Buch zu Ende** *schreiben*.	*Say what you want. I will finish writing my book.*

50. Express each of the following sentences in German.

1. *Perhaps she is ill.* _____
2. *We are probably coming.* _____
3. *Perhaps they are crying.* _____
4. *Children, you are probably hungry.* _____
   (Hunger haben)
5. *Peter, you probably know it.* _____
6. *I am probably going.* _____
7. *He is probably working.* _____
8. *Perhaps they are helping.* _____

Future Perfect Tense

Weak and Strong Verbs

The future perfect tense is formed with the present tense of **werden** plus the past participle plus the auxiliary verb **haben** or **sein**.

Future perfect tense = Present tense of werden + Past participle + Infinitive of haben or sein

---

Study the following conjugations.

ich werde gemacht haben	**ich werde gefahren sein**
du wirst gemacht haben	**du wirst gefahren sein**
er wird gemacht haben	**er wird gefahren sein**
wir werden gemacht haben	**wir werden gefahren sein**
ihr werdet gemacht haben	**ihr werdet gefahren sein**
sie werden gemacht haben	**sie werden gefahren sein**

Use of the Future Perfect Tense

The future perfect tense is used to indicate an action that will end at or prior to a specified time in the future. It is most frequently used to express past probability or likelihood. When used in this way, an adverb such as **sicher**, **vielleicht**, **wahrscheinlich**, **wohl** often occurs in the same sentence. Otherwise, this tense is rarely used.

Sie *werden vielleicht* dort *geblieben sein.*	*They probably stayed there.*
Er *wird wohl* lange *geschlafen haben.*	*He probably slept late.*

51. Rewrite each of the following sentences, using the future perfect tense with the word **wohl**.

1. Ihr habt getanzt.   _____
2. Sie sind gekommen.   _____
3. Maria hat geschlafen.   _____
4. Wir haben es nicht gesehen. _____
5. Du hast nicht gefragt.   _____
6. Er hat das Gedicht geschrieben. _____
7. Sie hat sich gefreut.   _____
8. Du hast lange gewartet.   _____

Verbs with Inseparable Prefixes

Verbs beginning with the prefixes **be-**, **emp-**, **ent-**, **er-**, **ge-**, **ver-**, **zer-** are called *inseparable prefix verbs*, because these prefixes are never separated from the verb stem. The inseparable prefixes do not have an independent meaning by themselves, and they cannot stand alone. They do, however, change the meaning of the stem verb to which they are prefixed.

Inseparable prefix verbs can be either strong or weak, following the same conjugational patterns of the verb stem, except that they do not take the characteristic **ge-** prefix in the past participle. Therefore, those verbs beginning with the inseparable prefix **ge-** have the same past participle form as the infinitive from which they are derived.

INFINITIVE		SIMPLE PAST	PAST PARTICIPLE
fallen	*to fall*	**fiel**	**(ist) gefallen**
gefallen	*to please*	**gefiel**	**(hat) gefallen**
langen	*to be sufficient, suffice*	**langte**	**gelangt**
gelangen	*to reach, attain*	**gelangte**	**gelangt**

In spoken German, the inseparable prefix does not receive any stress. The primary stress is given to the first syllable of the verb stem.

Only the prefix **zer-** has a predictable meaning. It denotes destruction or reduction to small parts or components: **drücken** *to squeeze*, **zerdrücken** *to squash*. The prefix **be-** makes a verb transitive. (The verb can be followed by a direct object and is conjugated with **haben**.)

Er *ist* gekommen.	*He has arrived.*
BUT **Er *hat* Geld *bekommen.***	*He has received money.*

Note how the different prefixes alter the meanings of the following verbs.

stehen *to stand*

bestehen	*to pass, persist*	**Ich *habe* das Examen *bestanden.***
entstehen	*to originate*	**Wie *entsteht* das Gas?**
gestehen	*to confess*	**Er *gestand* alles.**
verstehen	*to understand*	**Sie *werden* das Problem *verstehen.***

fallen *to fall*

entfallen	*to fall out of, slip*	**Sein Name ist mir *entfallen*.**
gefallen	*like, to be pleasing*	**Das Kleid *hat* ihr *gefallen*.**
verfallen	*to decline, fall into disrepair*	***Verfällt* das Schloss?**
zerfallen	*to fall apart*	**Der Kuchen *ist zerfallen*.**

52. Complete each of the following sentences, using the appropriate present tense form of the verb on the right.

 1. Ute _____ ein Klavier.   bekommen
 2. Ich _____ alles.   zerbrechen
 3. Er _____ das Bild.   verkaufen
 4. Wir _____ die Antwort.   verstehen
 5. Ich _____ die Gäste.   empfangen
 6. Er _____ Kuchen.   bestellen
 7. _____ dir das Motorrad?   gefallen
 8. _____ ihr eure Eltern?   besuchen
 9. Ich _____ das Problem.   erklären
10. _____ du alles?   erzählen
11. Wir _____ das Hotel.   empfehlen
12. Du _____ alles.   vergessen

53. Rewrite each of the following sentences, using the present perfect tense.

 1. Wir verstehen das Wort.   _____
 2. Es gefällt mir nicht.   _____
 3. Sie gestehen die Wahrheit.   _____
 4. Warum zerfällt es?   _____
 5. Ich bestehe das Examen.   _____
 6. Wer besucht dich?   _____
 7. Verkauft ihr das Haus?   _____
 8. Er empfängt den Brief.   _____
 9. Warum erzählst du alles?   _____
10. Was entdeckt er?   _____

Verbs with Separable Prefixes

Another group of verbs is known as *separable prefix verbs,* because the prefix is separated from the verb stem under certain conditions, which will be explained below. Many separable prefixes are prepositions (**an**, **auf**, **nach**) or adverbs (**zurück**, **heim**, **vorbei**); others are verbs (**kennen**, **spazieren**, **stehen**). Occasionally, adjectives (**frei**, **kalt**, **wach**) and nouns (**Rad**, **Schlittschuh**) also function as separable prefixes. The separable prefixes have definite meanings, very often denoting direction.

Like inseparable prefix verbs, separable prefix verbs can be either strong or weak, following the same conjugational patterns of the verb stems. However, unlike inseparable prefix verbs, they take the past participle prefix **ge-** in addition to the separable prefix.

Unlike inseparable prefix verbs, separable prefix verbs always have their main stress on the prefix.

Study the following list of common separable prefixes and their basic meanings. Note that it is also possible for the added prefix to change the meaning of the stem verb in very subtle ways.

ab	*off, down*	**abfliegen** *to take off,* **abschreiben** *to copy down*
an	*at, on*	**anschauen** *to look at,* **anziehen** *to put on*

auf	up, open	**aufstehen** *to get up*, **aufmachen** *to open up*
aus	out	**ausbrechen** *to break out*, **ausbrennen** *to burn out*
ein	into, in	**eintreten** *to step into*, **einsteigen** *to get into*
fort	away	**fortgehen** *to go away*, **fortbleiben** *to stay away*
heim	home	**heimkommen** *to come home*, **heimgehen** *to go home*
her	toward the speaker, hither	**hersehen** *to look toward*, **herkommen** *to come toward*
hin	away from the speaker, there	**hingehen** *to go there*, **hinwerfen** *to throw there*
mit	with, along	**mitfahren** *to ride along*, **mitlachen** *to laugh along*
nach	after	**nachschauen** *to look after*, **nachkommen** *to come after*
nieder	down	**niederlegen** *to lie down*, **niedersetzen** *to sit down, set down*
vor	before	**vorsetzen** *to set before*, **vorlegen** *to put before*
weg	away	**weglaufen** *to run away*, **wegnehmen** *to take away*
zu	to, close	**zuhören** *to listen to*, **zumachen** *to close*
zurück	back	**zurücknehmen** *to take back*, **zurückgeben** *to give back*
zusammen	together	**zusammenkommen** *to come together*, **zusammennähen** *to stitch together*

Not all German prefixes can be translated into idiomatic English by using these equivalents.

ausbessern	*to repair, mend*	**nachmachen**	*to imitate*
aussehen	*to look like*	**zusammenlegen**	*to fold*

Following the Orthographic Reform, **spazieren gehen** and **spazieren fahren** are written as two words. On the other hand, **kennenlernen** can now be written either as one word (**kennenlernen**) or as two (**kennen lernen**). Most importantly, however, in terms of grammatical usage, all three still behave like standard separable prefix verbs.

Position of the Separable Prefix

A separable prefix is always the final element of a sentence or main clause when the verb is in the present tense, the simple past tense, or the imperative. Study the following examples.

Present Tense

Ich *gehe* oft *aus.*	*I often go out.*
Kommst du auch *heim*?	*Are you coming home too?*
Geht ihr morgen *mit*?	*Are you going along tomorrow?*

54. Complete each of the following sentences, using the appropriate present tense form of the verb on the right.

1. Er _____ in den Zug _____.	einsteigen
2. Wir _____ oft _____.	zusammenkommen
3. Ich _____ auch _____.	mitfahren
4. Warum _____ du den warmen Mantel _____?	anziehen
5. _____ ihr euch schon _____?	niederlegen
6. Wann _____ ihn deine Eltern _____?	kennenlernen
7. Wann _____ du _____?	zurückkommen
8. Ich _____ nicht gern _____.	hingehen
9. Wann _____ ihr _____?	aufstehen
10. Deine Freunde _____ mit uns _____.	spazieren fahren

Simple Past Tense

> **Sie** *ging* abends *spazieren.* She used to go for a walk in the evening.
> **Warum** *schaute* sie es *an?* Why did she look at it?

55. Form a sentence from each of the following groups of words, using the appropriate simple past tense form of the verb.

1. Er / aufessen / alles _____
2. Ich / abschreiben / das Lied _____
3. Wir / kennenlernen / ihn _____
4. Arnim / einsammeln / für die Armen _____
5. Die Kinder / nachmachen / alles _____
6. Wer / zumachen / das Fenster / ? _____
7. Wie / zusammennähen / er / das Leder / ? _____
8. Wann / heimgehen / die Studenten / ? _____

Imperative

See the section on the imperative, pages 204–207.

> *Geh* mit uns *spazieren!* Go walking with us.
> *Kommt* bald *zurück!* Come back soon.
> *Lernen* Sie Arnold *kennen!* Meet Arnold!

56. Form an imperative sentence from each of the following groups of words. Follow the model.

MODEL Irmgard / herkommen / schnell __Irmgard, komm schnell her!__

1. Gisela / weglaufen / nicht _____
2. Frau Bayer / zumachen / schnell _____
3. Konrad / mitfahren / bitte _____
4. Ursula und Theo / eintreten / leise _____
5. Frau Breuer / aufstehen / langsam _____
6. Helga / herkommen / doch _____
7. Mutter / zumachen / die Schachtel _____
8. Arno / anschauen / es / nicht _____

Infinitive

A separable prefix does not separate from the verb stem in the infinitive. However, in infinitive clauses with **zu**, the **zu** comes between the separable prefix and the verb stem.

> **Ich will** *anfangen.* I want to start.
> **Ich bin nicht bereit** *anzufangen.* I'm not ready to start.

Compound Tenses

Future Tense

> **Er** *wird* wohl *mitessen.* He will probably eat with us.
> **Ich** *werde* nicht *ausgehen.* I won't go out.

57. Rewrite each of the following sentences, using the future tense.

1. Wir gehen fort. _____
2. Ich gehe hinaus. _____
3. Er bringt es zurück. _____
4. Sie nehmen nichts weg. _____
5. Gehst du aus? _____
6. Ich schaue das Album an. _____

Present Perfect Tense

Note that separable prefix verbs, unlike inseparable prefix verbs, take the **ge-** prefix in the past participle form. However, it is placed between the separable prefix and the past participle stem. For this reason, the **-ge-** in this position is sometimes referred to as an *infix*.

STRONG VERBS	WEAK VERBS
an*ge*kommen	ein*ge*kauft
aus*ge*laufen	an*ge*macht

Der Zug *ist* endlich *angekommen.*	*The train has finally arrived.*
Mutter *hat* schon *eingekauft.*	*Mother has already gone shopping.*
Sie *sind* schon *angekommen.*	*They have already arrived.*

58. Rewrite each of the following sentences, using the present perfect tense.

1. Sie lachten auch mit. _____
2. Wir schauten bei ihr nach. _____
3. Ich lernte ihn kennen. _____
4. Der Zug kam bald an. _____
5. Wir gingen spazieren. _____
6. Ich fuhr mit ihm heim. _____
7. Gudrun stand dann auf. _____
8. Sie schauten bald nach. _____

Past Perfect Tense

Ich *hatte* es schon *aufgemacht.*	*I had already opened it.*
Der Vorrat *war ausgelaufen.*	*The supply had run out.*
Der Lehrer *hatte* das Licht *angemacht.*	*The teacher had turned the light on.*

59. Complete each of the following sentences, using the appropriate past perfect form of the verb on the right.

1. Er _____ sofort _____.   einsteigen
2. Ich _____ das Licht _____.   ausmachen
3. Wir _____ es _____.   abschreiben
4. Die Kinder _____ die Bücher _____.   niederlegen
5. _____ ihr _____?   zusammenkommen
6. Ich _____ ihn _____.   kennenlernen
7. Unsere Eltern _____ lange _____.   fortbleiben
8. Wer _____ uns _____?   zuhören

Separable Prefix Verbs in Dependent Clauses

A separable prefix is never separated from its verb when it occurs in a dependent clause. Study the following examples.

Present	Ich weiß, dass er bald *ankommt.*	*I know that he is arriving soon.*
Simple Past	Er lachte, als ich *hinfiel.*	*He laughed when I fell.*
Future	Sie weiß, warum ich *mitgehen werde.*	*She knows why I'm going along.*
Present Perfect	Ich freue mich, dass du *heimgekommen bist.*	*I'm happy that you came home.*
Past Perfect	Sie weiß, dass er *abgeschrieben hatte.*	*She knows that he had copied/ cheated.*

60. Rewrite each of the following sentences, introducing the sentence with **Ich weiß, dass**.

1. Er ist fortgegangen. _____
2. Sie wird herkommen. _____
3. Wir fliegen morgen ab. _____
4. Ihr habt Peter kennengelernt. _____
5. Der Zug war angekommen. _____
6. Ich komme nach. _____
7. Er ging aus. _____
8. Wir werden heimkommen. _____
9. Du fährst mit. _____
10. Er hatte nachgeschaut. _____

Case Following Verbs

Accusative and Dative Cases for Direct and Indirect Objects

Many transitive verbs can take an indirect object in addition to a direct object. The direct object can be identified by asking *who* or *what* receives the action of the verb, that is, who/what is given, shown, brought, etc. In German, the answer to this question will normally be the direct object in the accusative case. The indirect object can be identified by asking *to or for whom,* or *to or for what,* was the action of the verb undertaken, that is, to or for whom/what is something being given, shown, brought, etc. In German, the indirect object is in the dative case.

The following verbs are common examples of verbs that can take both a direct object in the accusative and an indirect object in the dative.

bringen	*to bring, take*	**Sie bringt** *dem Kranken Suppe.*
geben	*to give*	**Er gibt** *seiner Tochter das Gold.*
holen	*to get*	**Wir holen** *dem Hasen eine Karotte.*
kaufen	*to buy*	**Ich kaufte** *den Kindern das Spielzeug.*
sagen	*to say, tell*	**Sie sagen** *ihren Eltern die Wahrheit.*
schenken	*to give, present*	**Ich habe** *meinem Vater eine Krawatte* **geschenkt.**
schicken	*to send*	**Wer hat** *dir das Paket* **geschickt?**
schreiben	*to write*	**Er hat** *seiner Freundin einen Brief* **geschrieben.**
zeigen	*to show*	**Sie zeigten** *den Touristen den Hafen.*

Dative Case

A small number of German verbs take their direct objects in the dative rather than the accusative case. These verbs are called dative verbs and must be memorized. Following are common examples.

antworten	*to answer*	**Wir antworten *dem Lehrer*.**
danken	*to thank*	**Er dankte *seiner Tante*.**
folgen	*to follow, obey*	**Folgst du *deiner Mutter*?**
gefallen	*to like, be pleasing to*	**Der Film hat *den Kindern* gefallen.**
gehören	*to belong to*	**Das gehört *seiner Freundin*.**
glauben	*to believe*	**Ich glaube *meinem Freund*.**
gratulieren	*to congratulate*	**Wir gratulieren *ihr* zum Geburtstag.**
helfen	*to help*	**Er hilft *seiner Mutter*.**
schmecken	*to taste, taste good*	**Dieses Fleisch schmeckt *mir*.**

61. Form a sentence from each of the following groups of words, using the appropriate present tense form of the verb.

1. Ich / zeigen / das Kind / das Buch _____
2. Er / schicken / deine Mutter / eine Karte _____
3. Wir / glauben / der Mann _____
4. Ich / bringen / die Studentin / der Roman _____
5. Danken / du / dein Lehrer / ? _____
6. Wir / helfen / unsere Großmutter _____
7. Das Haus / gehören / meine Eltern _____
8. Antworten / ihr / die Lehrerin / ? _____
9. Maria / kaufen / ihre Freundin / eine Kette _____
10. Der Wagen / gehören / mein Bruder _____
11. Wer / holen / der Kranke / eine Pille / ? _____
12. Die Blumen / gefallen / unsere Tante _____
13. Warum / gratulieren / du / deine Schwester / ? _____
14. Er / schenken / das Baby / eine Puppe _____
15. Wir / schicken / der Präsident / ein Protest _____
16. Die Kinder / folgen / der Großvater _____

Prepositional Objects

Like English, German has a number of verb + preposition combinations; however, in German, a decision must be made as to whether the object of such a preposition should be in the dative or the accusative case. Also, German preposition usage often does not correspond to English preposition usage following verbs that have the same meaning.

Accusative Objects after an, auf, über

When a verb is followed by the preposition **an**, **auf**, **über**, the preposition takes the accusative case. Study the following examples.

antworten auf	*to reply to* (*something*)	**Wir *antworten auf* seine Frage.**
denken an	*to think of*	**Ich *denke* oft *an* meine Freundin.**
glauben an	*to believe in*	**Wir *glaubten an* seine Unschuld.**
hoffen auf	*to hope for*	**Er hat *auf* gutes Wetter *gehofft*.**
lachen über	*to laugh about*	**Sie hat nicht *über* das Thema *gelacht*.**
sprechen über	*to talk about in detail*	***Sprecht* ihr *über* das Instrument?**
warten auf	*to wait for*	**Warum *hast* du nicht *auf* deine Eltern *gewartet*?**

Dative Objects after von, zu, nach, vor

The dative case is used after the following verb + preposition combinations.

fragen nach	*to ask about*	**Er** *fragte nach* **meiner Mutter.**
gehören zu	*to be a part/member of, belong to*	**Otto** *gehört* **auch** *zum* **Klub.**
halten von	*to think of (something, somebody)*	**Was** *hältst* **du** *von* **dem Programm?**
hören von	*to hear from*	**Ich** *habe* **heute** *von* **meiner Schwester** *gehört.*
sprechen von	*to talk about*	**Er** *hat von* **seiner Reise** *gesprochen.*
suchen nach	*look for*	**Ich** *suche nach* **meinen Eltern.**
träumen von	*dream about*	**Sie** *träumte von* **ihrem Hund.**
wissen von	*to know about*	**Er** *weiß* **nichts** *von* **diesem Thema.**

62. Complete each of the following sentences, using the appropriate ending(s).

1. Er fragte nach mein___ Adresse.
2. Er weiß nichts von d___ Thema.
3. Sie lachte über d___ Frage.
4. Sie brachte ihr___ Mann ein___ Krawatte.
5. Wir glauben d___ Kind.
6. Was hältst du von sein___ Frau?
7. Das Buch gehört zu dies___ Sammlung.
8. Hast du dein___ Freund geholfen?
9. Warum dankst du nicht sein___ Mutter?
10. Ich habe mein___ Bruder nicht geantwortet.
11. Dieses Bild gefällt mein___ Freundin.
12. Wer wartet auf d___ Zug?
13. Sucht ihr nach d___ Schule?
14. Ich träume von mein___ Reise.
15. Wir antworten auf sein___ Brief.
16. Ich schenke mein___ Großmutter ein___ Orchidee.
17. Hast du d___ Geburtstagskind gratuliert?
18. Die Torte schmeckte mein___ Mutter.

Reflexive Verbs

A reflexive verb expresses that the action of the verb is both performed by and received by the subject, that is, the object of the verb is identical to the subject of the verb: *He amuses himself easily.* The object pronoun used to show this relationship is called a *reflexive pronoun,* because it refers or reflects back to the subject of the sentence or clause.

In English, this relationship is often implied rather than expressly stated: *He is shaving (himself).* Many verbs and verb idioms in German require a reflexive pronoun (**Er erholt sich.** *He is getting better. / He is recovering.*). There are other verbs, however, that may be used both reflexively (**Er amüsiert sich leicht.** *He amuses himself easily.*) and nonreflexively (**Er amüsiert sein Enkelkind.** *He amuses his grandchild.*).

In German, reflexive pronouns may be in either the accusative or the dative case, depending on the particular verb and how the reflexive pronoun functions within the sentence. When the reflexive pronoun functions as a direct object, the accusative is generally used.

Reflexive Verbs Governing the Accusative Case

Following are common reflexive verbs followed by an accusative reflexive pronoun.

sich amüsieren	*to enjoy/amuse oneself*	sich gewöhnen an	*to get used to*
sich anziehen	*to dress*	sich interessieren für	*to be interested in*
sich aufregen	*to get excited*	sich legen	*to lie down*
sich ausziehen	*to undress*	sich rasieren	*to shave*
sich benehmen	*to behave*	sich setzen	*to sit down*
sich bewegen	*to move*	sich stellen	*to place oneself*
sich entscheiden	*to decide*	sich umziehen	*to change (clothes)*
sich entschuldigen	*to apologize, excuse oneself*	sich unterhalten	*to converse, enjoy oneself*
sich erinnern an	*to remember*	sich verletzen	*to hurt oneself*
sich erkälten	*to catch a cold*	sich verspäten	*to be late*
sich freuen	*to be glad*	sich vorstellen	*to introduce oneself*
sich freuen auf	*to look forward to*	sich waschen	*to wash oneself*
sich freuen über	*to be glad about*	sich wundern über	*to be surprised at*
sich fürchten vor	*to be afraid of*	sich zuwenden	*to turn to*

Accusative Reflexive Pronouns

The accusative reflexive pronouns are identical to the accusative personal pronouns, except in the third-person singular and plural forms and for the formal form of address **Sie**.

	ACCUSATIVE CASE		
	PERSONAL PRONOUNS	REFLEXIVE PRONOUNS	
ich	mich	mich	*myself*
du	dich	dich	*yourself*
er	ihn	*sich*	*himself*
sie	sie	*sich*	*herself*
es	es	*sich*	*itself*
wir	uns	uns	*ourselves*
ihr	euch	euch	*yourselves*
sie	sie	*sich*	*themselves*
Sie	Sie	*sich*	*yourselves*

Note that **sich**, the reflexive pronoun used with the formal form of address **Sie**, is not capitalized.
Study the following conjugation.

ich wasche mich	wir waschen uns
du wäschst dich	ihr wascht euch
er wäscht sich	sie waschen sich

Er *interessiert sich* **für klassische Musik.**	*He is interested in classical music.*
Ich *fürchte mich* **vor großen Hunden.**	*I'm afraid of large dogs.*
Sie *werden sich* **wohl an ihn** *erinnern.*	*They probably remember him.*
Ich *habe mich* **schon** *rasiert.*	*I have already shaved.*
Sie *legte sich* **aufs Sofa.**	*She lay down on the sofa.*
Warum *hast du dich* **nicht** *entschuldigt?*	*Why didn't you excuse yourself?*

The reflexive pronoun is placed as close as possible to the subject. However, it never comes between a pronoun subject and the verb.

Rasierst du *dich* **jeden Tag?**	*Do you shave every day?*
Ich habe *mich* **darüber gewundert.**	*I was surprised at that.*

Reflexive Verbs with Separable Prefixes

The separable prefix of reflexive verbs acts like the separable prefix of verbs used nonreflexively. (See Separable Prefix Verbs, pages 180–184.)

Ich *ziehe mich* **nicht** *aus.*	*I'm not getting undressed.*
Er *zog sich an.*	*He got dressed.*
Sie *werden sich* **wohl** *umziehen.*	*They are probably changing clothes.*
Warum *hast* **du** *dich aufgeregt?*	*Why did you get upset?*

63. Complete each of the following sentences, using the present tense of the reflexive verb on the right.

1. Ich _____ für Chemie.   sich interessieren
2. Wir _____ über Politik.   sich unterhalten
3. Du _____ so _____.   sich aufregen
4. Wohin _____ ihr _____?   sich setzen
5. Ich _____ sehr oft.   sich erkälten
6. Wann _____ du _____?   sich vorstellen
7. Die Eltern _____.   sich umziehen
8. Er _____.   sich freuen
9. Ursula _____ aufs Sofa.   sich legen
10. Wir _____ über das Geschenk.   sich freuen
11. Unser Vater _____.   sich rasieren
12. Ich _____ immer.   sich amüsieren
13. Das Tier _____ schnell.   sich bewegen
14. _____ du _____ auf die Ferien?   sich freuen
15. _____ ihr _____?   sich waschen
16. Er _____ nicht.   sich entscheiden
17. Ich _____ oft.   sich verspäten
18. _____ Sie _____ an meinen Onkel?   sich erinnern
19. Der Junge _____ schon _____.   sich anziehen
20. _____ du _____ immer?   sich entschuldigen

64. Rewrite each of the following sentences in the present perfect tense.

1. Er fürchtet sich vor Pferden.   _____
2. Wir interessieren uns für die Sammlung.   _____
3. Sie benehmen sich ganz nett.   _____
4. Freut ihr euch über das Geschenk?   _____
5. Ich ziehe mich schon um.   _____
6. Wir stellen uns heute vor.   _____
7. Erkältest du dich oft?   _____
8. Sie wäscht sich schon.   _____
9. Die Männer rasieren sich.   _____
10. Verspätet ihr euch?   _____

65. Answer each of the following questions, using the prepositional phrase on the right.

1. Worauf hast du dich gefreut?   auf seine Ankunft

   _____

2. Wohin legt ihr euch denn?   aufs Bett

   _____

3. Wann hast du dich verletzt?   am Freitag

   _____

4. Wofür interessierst du dich?   für Briefmarken

   _____

5. Woran hast du dich schon gewöhnt?   an die Arbeit

   _____

6. Wann hat er sich erkältet?   im Winter

   _____

7. Worüber wundern Sie sich?   über die Explosion

   _____

8. Wovor fürchten sich die Kinder?   vor dem Gewitter

   _____

Reflexive Imperative Forms

In German, the reflexive pronoun is always expressed in commands and is placed following the imperative form of the verb. (See Imperatives, page 204.)

Setz *dich*!	*Sit down.*
Zieht *euch* **um!**	*Change your clothes.*
Fürchten Sie *sich* **nicht!**	*Don't be afraid!*
Waschen wir *uns*!	*Let's wash (ourselves).*

66. Express each of the following sentences in German.

1. *Don't get excited.*   _____
2. *Children, don't be late.*   _____
3. *Peter, don't catch a cold.*   _____
4. *Mr. Ziegler, introduce yourself.* _____
5. *Let's sit down.*   _____
6. *Gisela, wash yourself.*   _____
7. *Girls, excuse yourselves.*   _____
8. *Mrs. Klein, hurry up.*   _____
9. *Ute, don't be afraid of the dog.* _____
10. *Father, shave.*   _____

Reflexive Versus Nonreflexive Use of Verbs

As mentioned above, some German reflexive verbs can be used nonreflexively as well. The reflexive pronoun is used only when the action is received by the subject.

Reflexive Use	**Ich amüsiere mich.**	*I am amusing myself.*
Nonreflexive Use	**Ich amüsiere das Baby.**	*I am amusing the baby.*

67. Complete each of the following sentences, using the appropriate reflexive pronoun. If no reflexive pronoun is required, place an **X** in the blank.

1. Leg _____ den Mantel auf den Stuhl!
2. Er stellt _____ meiner Mutter vor.
3. Ich unterhalte _____ mit ihm.
4. Sie haben _____ verletzt.
5. Er zieht _____ aus.
6. Die Mutter wäscht _____ das Kind.
7. Wir waschen _____.
8. Sie haben _____ das Tier verletzt.
9. Ich ziehe _____ das Baby an.
10. Sie setzt _____ hin.

Reflexive Verbs Governing the Dative Case

When a verb has a direct object in the accusative case, the reflexive pronoun is in the dative case. Note that in such cases, the reflexive functions as an indirect object. Study the difference between the following two constructions.

Accusative Reflexive Pronoun	Ich wasche *mich.*	*I wash (myself).*
Dative Reflexive Pronoun	Ich wasche *mir die Hände.*	*I wash my hands.*

A dative reflexive pronoun is also used when a verb can only take a dative object.

Dative Reflexive Pronoun	Ich konnte *mir* nicht helfen.	*I couldn't help myself.*
Dative Object after Dative Verb	Ich helfe *meiner Mutter.*	*I help my mother.*

The dative case is required after the following reflexive verbs.

sich einbilden	*to imagine*
sich etwas vorstellen	*to imagine something*
sich weh tun	*to hurt oneself*

Dative Reflexive Pronouns

The dative reflexive pronouns are identical to the dative personal pronouns, except in the third-person singular and plural and for the formal form of address **Sie**. Here, as in the accusative, the reflexive pronoun is **sich**.

	DATIVE CASE		
	PERSONAL PRONOUNS	**REFLEXIVE PRONOUNS**	
ich	mir	mir	*myself*
du	dir	dir	*yourself*
er	ihm	sich	*himself*
sie	ihr	sich	*herself*
es	ihm	sich	*itself*
wir	uns	uns	*ourselves*
ihr	euch	euch	*yourselves*
sie	sie	sich	*themselves*
Sie	Sie	sich	*yourselves*

Note that **sich**, the reflexive pronoun used with the formal form of address **Sie**, is not capitalized.

Study the following conjugation.

ich tue mir weh	wir tun uns weh
du tust dir weh	ihr tut euch weh
er tut sich weh	sie tun sich weh

The dative reflexive pronoun is also frequently used with verbs like **kaufen**, **holen**, **bestellen**, **machen**, **nehmen**. The pronoun is rendered in English by *for myself* (*yourself*, etc.).

Ich *kaufe mir* ein Auto.	*I am buying a car for myself.*
Er *holte sich* etwas.	*He got something for himself.*

Dative Reflexive Pronouns with Parts of the Body

To show possession when referring to parts of the body or articles of clothing, German often uses the definite article coupled with a dative reflexive pronoun in place of the possessive adjective. In English, the possessive adjective is used in such situations.

Ich *habe mir* die Zähne *geputzt*.	*I brushed my teeth.*
Ich *ziehe mir* die Schuhe *an*.	*I am putting on my shoes.*
Wäschst du *dir* den Kopf?	*Are you washing your hair?*

68. Complete each of the following sentences, using the present tense of the reflexive verb on the right.

1. Du _____ bestimmt _____.   sich weh tun
2. Wir _____ die Schuhe.   putzen
3. Ich _____ die Uhr.   kaufen
4. Warum _____ ihr _____ nicht die Hände?   waschen
5. Das Mädchen _____ so viel _____.   sich einbilden
6. Die Dame _____ den Hut _____.   aufsetzen
7. Er _____ Bier.   bestellen
8. Ich _____ die Reise _____.   sich vorstellen
9. Wir _____ das Motorrad.   kaufen
10. Er _____ Kaffee.   holen
11. _____ ihr _____ etwas?   nehmen

69. Answer each of the following questions, using the word or phrase on the right.

1. Was stellst du dir vor? _____ das Haus
2. Was haben Sie sich geholt? _____ das Papier
3. Wann bestellt ihr euch das Essen? _____ bald
4. Wo hast du dir weh getan? _____ am Fuß
5. Wo ziehen sich die Gäste an? _____ im Schlafzimmer
6. Wer bildet sich etwas ein? _____ Gisela

70. Form an imperative sentence from each of the following groups of words, using the dative reflexive pronoun. Follow the model.

MODEL   Inge / waschen / Gesicht   Inge, wasch dir das Gesicht!

1. Herr Müller / bestellen / Buch _____
2. Kinder / putzen / Zähne _____
3. Peter und Heinz / kaufen / etwas _____
4. Marlene / weh tun / nicht _____
5. Kinder / waschen / Hände _____
6. Frau Wimmer / nehmen / etwas _____

Modal Auxiliary Verbs

Unlike most other verbs in German, the modal auxiliaries do not by themselves express an action, process, or change in condition; instead, they affect the meaning of the main verb. It is often said that they indicate an attitude toward the main verb.

The modal auxiliaries are usually used with a dependent infinitive. The six modal auxiliaries and their basic meanings are as follows.

dürfen	permission	*may, to be allowed to*
	(in the negative) prohibition	*must NOT*
müssen	necessity, obligation	*must, to have to, be obliged to*
können	ability	*can, to be able to, know how to*
mögen	inclination, desire, liking	*to like to, care for, want to*
	(in the negative) not liking	*NOT to like to, care for, want to*
wollen	desire, intention	*to want to*
sollen	obligation	*should, ought, to be supposed to*

Present Tense

The present tense of the modal auxiliary verbs is irregular. Study the following conjugations.

dürfen		müssen		können	
ich darf	**wir dürfen**	**ich muss**	**wir müssen**	**ich kann**	**wir können**
du darfst	**ihr dürft**	**du musst**	**ihr müsst**	**du kannst**	**ihr könnt**
er darf	**sie dürfen**	**er muss**	**sie müssen**	**er kann**	**sie können**

mögen		wollen		sollen	
ich mag	**wir mögen**	**ich will**	**wir wollen**	**ich soll**	**wir sollen**
du magst	**ihr mögt**	**du willst**	**ihr wollt**	**du sollst**	**ihr sollt**
er mag	**sie mögen**	**er will**	**sie wollen**	**er soll**	**sie sollen**

Note that all modals except **sollen** use different stem vowels for the singular and the plural in the present tense. The plural stem agrees with the infinitive. The first- and third-person singular forms have no personal endings in the present tense.

The modal auxiliary verbs are used with the infinitive. The infinitive occurs in final position in the sentence, unless the modal plus infinitive is used in a dependent clause. In a negative sentence, **nicht** usually precedes the infinitive.

Wir *dürfen* dem Techniker *helfen*.	*We may help the technician.*
***Darfst* du *rauchen*?**	*Are you allowed to smoke?*
Ich *darf* mir eine Zeitung *nehmen*.	*I am allowed to take a newspaper.*
Ihr *dürft* nicht *bleiben*.	*You must not stay.*
***Musst* du noch *studieren*?**	*Do you still have to study?*
Ich *muss* nach Hause *gehen*.	*I have to go home.*
Werner *kann* gut *singen*.	*Werner can sing well.*
Du *kannst* nicht *mitkommen*.	*You cannot come along.*
Wir *mögen* es nicht *sehen*.	*We don't want to see it.*
Ich *mag* es auch *hören*.	*I like to hear it also.*
***Wollt* ihr bei uns *bleiben*?**	*Do you want to stay with us?*
Ich *will* es nicht *machen*.	*I don't want to do it.*
Wir *sollen* etwas *mitbringen*.	*We are supposed to bring something.*
Du *sollst* die Wahrheit *sagen*.	*You ought to tell the truth.*

71. Complete each of the following sentences, using the appropriate present tense form of **dürfen**.

1. Wir _____ nicht bleiben.
2. Die Kinder _____ gehen.
3. Dieter, du _____ nicht rauchen.
4. _____ ich das Geschenk aufmachen?
5. Er _____ die Geschichte erzählen.
6. Anna, du _____ heute helfen.
7. _____ ihr das Radio kaufen?
8. Du _____ nicht gehen.

72. Rewrite each of the following sentences, using the appropriate form of the present tense of **müssen**.

1. Er arbeitet schwer. _____
2. Sie holen Brot. _____
3. Studierst du? _____
4. Singen Sie heute? _____
5. Wir stehen auf. _____
6. Wann seid ihr im Büro? _____
7. Die Kinder bleiben zu Hause. _____
8. Ich bestelle das Essen. _____

73. Form a sentence from each of the following groups of words, using the appropriate present tense form of the verb.

1. Ich / können / glauben / die Geschichte / nicht _____
2. Können / ihr / mitkommen / morgen / ? _____
3. Wir / helfen / können / unserem Freund / nicht _____
4. Max / können / gut / tanzen _____
5. Können / du / langsamer / sprechen / ? _____
6. Ich / können / alles / hören _____

74. Complete each of the following sentences, using the appropriate present tense form of **mögen**.

1. Ich _____ nicht studieren.
2. Er _____ nicht helfen.
3. Wir _____ nicht arbeiten.
4. _____ du nicht helfen?
5. _____ ihr das Auto sehen?
6. Inge _____ alles essen.
7. _____ Sie nichts anschauen?
8. Die Kinder _____ nicht schlafen.

75. Express each of the following sentences in German, using the modal verb **wollen**.

1. *We want to help.* _____
2. *I don't want to see it.* _____
3. *He wants to come.* _____
4. *Do they want to sleep?* _____
5. *Ursel, do you want to go?* _____
6. *She wants to study.* _____
7. *Erika and Franz, do you want to work?* _____
8. *I want to visit the museum.* _____

76. Rewrite each of the following sentences, using the appropriate form of the present tense of **sollen**.

1. Ich kaufe dem Kind etwas. _____
2. Er kommt schnell. _____
3. Sagst du die Wahrheit? _____
4. Die Studenten lernen. _____
5. Man stiehlt nicht. _____
6. Wir kommen nicht. _____
7. Bleibt ihr? _____
8. Ich repariere das Auto. _____

Omission of the Dependent Infinitive with Modal Auxiliaries

In colloquial German, the dependent infinitive is often omitted when the meaning of the sentence is clear from the context. This occurs most frequently with verbs such as **machen**, **tun** and with verbs indicating motion, such as **fahren**, **gehen**.

Er *muss* nach Hause.	*He has to go home.*
Wir *müssen* in die Stadt.	*We have to go downtown.*
Musst du zur Arbeit/Schule?	*Do you have to go to work/school?*
Gerda *kann* Deutsch.	*Gerda knows German.*
Kannst du Französisch?	*Do you know French?*
Wir *wollen* ins Kino / nach Hause.	*We want to go to the movies / home.*
Das *darfst* du (machen).	*You may (do it).*

77. Express each of the following sentences in German without using the infinitive.

1. *We know English.* _____
2. *I don't want any soup.* _____
3. *They have to go home.* _____
4. *Does he know German?* _____
5. *She has to go downtown.* _____
6. *He doesn't want any milk.* _____

Simple Past Tense

The simple past tense of the modal verbs is formed by taking the infinitive stem, dropping the umlaut if there is one, and then adding the past tense marker **-te** plus the past tense personal verb endings for weak verbs (see page 155). Study the following simple past tense conjugations.

dürfen		müssen		können	
ich durfte	wir durften	ich musste	wir mussten	ich konnte	wir konnten
du durftest	ihr durftet	du musstest	ihr musstet	du konntest	ihr konntet
er durfte	sie durften	er musste	sie mussten	er konnte	sie konnten

mögen		wollen		sollen	
ich mochte	wir mochten	ich wollte	wir wollten	ich sollte	wir sollten
du mochtest	ihr mochtet	du wolltest	ihr wolltet	du solltest	ihr solltet
er mochte	sie mochten	er wollte	sie wollten	er sollte	sie sollten

Note that **dürfen**, **müssen**, **können**, **mögen** drop their umlauts in the past tense. In addition, **mögen** has a consonant change: In the past tense, **mögen** becomes **mochten**.

Wir *konnten* die Geschichte nicht verstehen. — *We couldn't understand the story.*
Er *durfte* nicht kommen. — *He wasn't allowed to come.*
Sie *wollte* nicht aufmachen. — *She didn't want to open up.*
Ich *musste* ihn tragen. — *I had to carry him.*

78. Rewrite each of the following sentences in the simple past tense.

1. Wir wollen mitmachen. _____
2. Ich mag keinen Reis. _____
3. Kannst du bleiben? _____
4. Dürft ihr denn rauchen? _____
5. Du kannst nicht heimgehen. _____
6. Luise will bezahlen. _____
7. Warum wollen Sie helfen? _____
8. Musst du studieren? _____
9. Ich will es sehen. _____
10. Könnt ihr das machen? _____

79. Form a sentence from each of the following groups of words, using the appropriate simple past tense form of the verb.

1. können / ihr / ihm / helfen / ? _____
2. ich / wollen / etwas / kaufen _____
3. sollen / er / auch / mitmachen / ? _____
4. wir / müssen / ihn / anrufen _____
5. die Kinder / mögen / kein / Gemüse _____
6. dürfen / du / nicht / gehen / ? _____

Use of the Simple Past Tense

The simple past tense of the modal verbs is not restricted to narration, but is used freely in conversation and posing questions.

80. Rewrite each of the following questions, using the simple past tense of the modal verb on the right. Follow the model.

MODEL   du abfahren?   __Musstest du abfahren?__   müssen

1. Herr Maier, Sie schlafen? _____ wollen
2. ihr rauchen? _____ dürfen
3. du ausgehen? _____ können
4. ihr Bananen? _____ mögen
5. Frau Lang, Sie daran glauben? _____ sollen
6. ihr helfen? _____ müssen
7. du es kaufen? _____ sollen
8. ihr fragen? _____ wollen
9. du mitmachen? _____ dürfen
10. ihr es sehen? _____ können
11. Sie alles nehmen? _____ müssen
12. ihr Bier bestellen? _____ sollen
13. du keine Milch? _____ mögen
14. Sie Konrad kennenlernen? _____ wollen

Compound Tenses

Present Perfect Tense

Past Participles of Modals

The modal auxiliary verbs are unique, because they have two different past participles. One is formed the conventional way with a **ge-** prefix, the other is identical to the infinitive. In both cases, the perfect tenses are formed with **haben**.

Past Participles Formed with a ge- Prefix

When no dependent infinitive is needed to convey the meaning in context, the following past participles of the modals are used.

dürfen	**gedurft**	**müssen**	**gemusst**
können	**gekonnt**	**sollen**	**gesollt**
mögen	**gemocht**	**wollen**	**gewollt**

Ich *habe* Französisch *gekonnt.*	*I knew French.*
Er *hat* nach Hause *gemusst.*	*He had to go home.*
Wir *haben* keinen Spinat *gemocht.*	*We didn't like any spinach.*

81. Rewrite each of the following sentences, using the present perfect tense of the verb.

1. Ich mag ihn nicht. _____
2. Sie will nach Köln. _____
3. Darfst du das? _____
4. Wir müssen zur Schule. _____
5. Kann er das? _____
6. Die Leute mögen nicht. _____
7. Ihr könnt doch Deutsch. _____
8. Sie können Englisch. _____
9. Ich muss zur Arbeit. _____
10. Wir dürfen es. _____
11. Magst du keine Limonade? _____
12. Ich soll in die Stadt. _____

Double Infinitive Construction

When a modal verb is followed by the infinitive of another verb, the present perfect tense is formed with **haben** plus the infinitive of the verb plus the infinitive of the modal. This construction is called *double infinitive construction,* because the two infinitives occur together in final position in the sentence.

Sie *haben* es nicht *sehen dürfen.*	*They weren't allowed to see it.*
Ich *habe* nicht *arbeiten können.*	*I was not able to work.*
Hast du den Roman *lesen müssen?*	*Did you have to read the novel?*
Er *hat* Gisela *kennenlernen wollen.*	*He wanted to get acquainted with Gisela.*

82. Rewrite each of the following sentences, using the present perfect tense of the verb.

1. Wir sollten nicht mitfahren. _____
2. Ich konnte nicht schreiben. _____
3. Musstet ihr hier bleiben? _____
4. Warum wollte er anrufen? _____
5. Ich durfte es bringen. _____
6. Man konnte Musik hören. _____

7. Sie mochten nicht aufstehen. _____
8. Warum wolltest du es zerstören? _____
9. Er durfte es sehen. _____
10. Wolltet ihr dort parken? _____
11. Ich wollte heimgehen. _____
12. Musstest du zu Hause bleiben? _____
13. Sie konnten gut lesen. _____
14. Hubert musste studieren. _____

Past Perfect Tense

As in the present perfect tense, the past perfect tense of modal verbs can be formed with two different past participles. Compare the following sentences.

Er *hatte* Deutsch *gekonnt*.   *He had known German.*
Wir *hatten* es *machen dürfen*.   *We had been allowed to do it.*

83. Rewrite each of the following sentences, changing the verb to the past perfect tense.

1. Wir konnten es. _____
2. Ich musste abfahren. _____
3. Er wollte es. _____
4. Sie mochten keinen Kuchen. _____
5. Sie sollte mich anrufen. _____
6. Durftest du sie besuchen? _____
7. Ich wollte nicht davon sprechen. _____
8. Ihr durftet es ja wissen. _____
9. Sie konnte das Fenster aufmachen. _____
10. Ich musste zur Schule. _____
11. Wir mochten Peter nicht. _____
12. Wolltest du hinausgehen? _____
13. Ich konnte Russisch. _____
14. Er musste den Wagen reparieren. _____

Future Tense

The future tense of modal verbs is formed with **werden** plus the infinitive plus the infinitive of the modal.

Er *wird* wohl nicht *fahren können*.   *He will probably not be able to go.*
Ich *werde* nicht *kommen dürfen*.   *I will not be allowed to come.*

84. Rewrite each of the following sentences, changing the verb to the future tense.

1. Sie können nicht schlafen. _____
2. Wir müssen den ganzen Tag studieren. _____
3. Er will es sehen. _____
4. Ich muss klingeln. _____
5. Ihr dürft nichts kaufen. _____
6. Kannst du es schicken? _____
7. Gudrun will nicht mitmachen. _____
8. Wollt ihr die Suppe probieren? _____
9. Sie dürfen nicht schreien. _____
10. Wir können nicht arbeiten. _____

Dependent Infinitives

Simple Tenses—Present and Past

Like modals, the verbs **hören** *to hear,* **sehen** *to see,* **helfen** *to help,* **lassen** *to let, allow, leave* can be used either alone or with the infinitive of another verb. This infinitive is referred to as a *dependent infinitive.* Note that the verb **lassen** means *to leave* when used alone. When used with a dependent infinitive, it means *to let, allow.* Compare the following pairs of sentences.

Ich *lasse* den Mantel hier.	*I leave the coat here.*
Ich *lasse* Robert *kommen.*	*I let Robert come.*
Wir *hörten* Musik.	*We heard music.*
Wir *hörten* Anita *singen.*	*We heard Anita sing.*
Er *sah* die Parade.	*He saw the parade.*
Er *sah* Inge *tanzen.*	*He saw Inge dance.*
Hilfst du Peter?	*Are you helping Peter?*
Hilfst du Peter *schreiben?*	*Are you helping Peter write?*

85. Form a sentence from each of the following groups of words, using the appropriate present tense form of the verb.

1. Wir / lassen / das Bild / in der Schule _____
2. Ich / helfen / Rita / den Hund / suchen _____
3. Sehen / du / deine Schwester / arbeiten / ? _____
4. Hören / Sie / die Sonate / ? _____
5. Er / hören / seine Frau / schreien _____
6. Lassen / ihr / Hans / gehen / ? _____
7. Die Leute / hören / uns / sprechen _____
8. Ich / sehen / die Kirche _____
9. Frau Berger / helfen / heute _____
10. Er / lassen / Gerda / mitkommen _____

Compound Tenses—Present Perfect and Past Perfect

When the verbs **hören, sehen, helfen, lassen** are used in a perfect tense with a dependent infinitive, the double infinitive construction is used. If used without a dependent infinitive, the regular past participle is used. (See Double Infinitive Construction, page 196.) Compare the following pairs of sentences.

Ich *habe* das Lied *gehört.*	*I heard the song.*
Ich *habe* sie *schreien hören.*	*I heard her scream.*
Wir *haben* das Museum *gesehen.*	*We saw the museum.*
Wir *haben* Agnes *malen sehen.*	*We saw Agnes paint.*
Hast du das Buch dort *gelassen?*	*Did you leave the book there?*
Hast du Ute *probieren lassen?*	*Did you let Ute try?*

86. Rewrite each of the following sentences, changing the verb to the present perfect tense.

1. Ich ließ es liegen. _____
2. Wir hörten sie lachen. _____
3. Er sah seinen Freund. _____
4. Sie halfen Heinz das Auto reparieren. _____
5. Er hörte nichts.

6. Ich sah Pia reiten. _____

7. Sie hörten Sonja weinen. _____

8. Wir ließen die Zeitungen zu Hause. _____

9. Wir halfen den Kindern. _____

10. Vater ließ uns gehen. _____

Future Tense

When the future tense is formed with one of the preceding verbs and a dependent infinitive, the double infinitive construction occurs at the end of the sentence.

Ich *werde* die Sängerin *hören*.	*I will hear the singer.*
Ich *werde* das Kind *weinen hören*.	*I will hear the child cry.*
Wir *werden* das Bild hier *lassen*.	*We will leave the painting here.*
Wir *werden* das Bild *reparieren lassen*.	*We will have the picture repaired.*

87. Rewrite each of the following sentences, adding the verb on the right.

1. Er wird Peter sehen. _____ schreiben

2. Ich werde Otto hören. _____ kommen

3. Wir werden den Kindern helfen. _____ zeichnen

4. Wirst du Dieter sehen? _____ lachen

5. Sie werden Rainer hören. _____ sprechen

6. Werden Sie Anneliese helfen? _____ lesen

7. Ich werde den Mantel hier lassen. _____ liegen

8. Werdet ihr Großmutter hören? _____ rufen

Dependent Clauses

When the double infinitive construction occurs in dependent clauses, the conjugated form of the auxiliary **haben** or **werden** is not moved into final position, as might be expected. Instead, the conjugated form of the auxiliary precedes the double infinitive.

Er sagt, dass er *hat kommen dürfen*.	*He says that he was allowed to come.*
Ich bin glücklich, weil ich Ursel *werde singen hören*.	*I'm happy, because I will hear Ursel sing.*

88. Change each of the following sentences to a dependent clause, introducing it with **Er sagt, dass**. Follow the model.

MODEL   Ich habe Anna lachen sehen.   _Er sagt, dass ich Anna habe lachen sehen._

1. Du hast die Jacke liegen lassen. _____

2. Wir haben Josef studieren helfen. _____

3. Sie haben Franz singen hören. _____

4. Ich habe es machen lassen. _____

5. Sie hat das Geschenk öffnen dürfen. _____

6. Du hast den Bleistift zurückgeben wollen. _____

7. Wir haben Peter kommen lassen. _____

8. Ihr habt das Auto bringen müssen. _____

Infinitives Preceded by zu *to*

Dependent infinitives are never preceded by **zu** *to* when used in the future tense, or when used with the modals or the verbs **sehen, hören, helfen, lassen**. However, dependent infinitives are preceded by **zu** in the following instances.

After Certain Prepositions

The following prepositions introduce infinitive phrases in which the dependent infinitive is preceded by **zu** in German. Note that the gerund ending in *-ing* is used in English for the first two.

(an)statt ... zu *instead of _____ing*

> **Wir haben gemalt, anstatt *zu studieren*.**　　　*We were painting instead of studying.*

ohne ... zu *without _____ing*

> **Er kam ins Zimmer, ohne *zu klopfen*.**　　　*He came into the room without knocking.*

um ... zu *in order to*

> **Sie ging hinaus, um den Brief *zu lesen*.**　　　*She went outside in order to read the letter.*

Note that the dependent infinitive is in final position in German. The infinitive phrase is set off by a comma when it consists of more elements than **zu** plus infinitive.

When a separable prefix verb occurs in an infinitive phrase, **zu** comes between the prefix and infinitive.

> **Er telefonierte, um uns einzuladen.**　　　*He called in order to invite us.*

89. Complete each of the following sentences, using the German equivalent of the English phrase on the right.

1. Er geht vorbei, _____.　　　*without seeing Norma*
2. Sie bleibt zu Hause, _____.　　　*instead of going to school*
3. Ich bin gelaufen, _____.　　　*in order to help Gertrud*
4. Sie sind gekommen, _____.　　　*without calling* (anrufen)
5. Ich gehe auf mein Zimmer, _____.　　　*in order to change*
6. Er hat telefoniert, _____.　　　*in order to invite the children*
7. Sie gibt es ihrem Bruder, _____.　　　*instead of bringing it to Helga*
8. Sie geht aus, _____.　　　*without putting on a coat*
9. Wir haben sie besucht _____.　　　*in order to ask*
10. Ich konnte das Gedicht, _____.　　　*without learning it*

With Anticipatory da(r)-compounds Followed by zu + Dependent Infinitive

Introductory phrases containing an anticipatory **da(r)**-compound are completed by an infinitive preceded by **zu**. In English, **da(r)-** is not translated. Note that the infinitive is in final position in the German sentence.

> **Ich warte darauf, das Auto *zu* sehen.**　　　*I am waiting to see the car.*
> **Er hofft darauf, sein Geld wieder*zu*finden.**　　　*He is hoping to find his money.*
> **Sie wartet darauf, sich *zu* setzen.**　　　*She is waiting to sit down.*

90. Complete each of the following sentences, using the German equivalent of the English phrase on the right.

1. Er denkt nicht daran, _____.	*to apologize*
2. Er denkt nicht daran, _____.	*to ask us*
3. Er denkt nicht daran, _____.	*to help the children*
4. Er denkt nicht daran, _____.	*to tell the story*
5. Er denkt nicht daran, _____.	*to shave*
6. Er denkt nicht daran, _____.	*to come along*
7. Er denkt nicht daran, _____.	*to get it*
8. Er denkt nicht daran, _____.	*to take money*
9. Er denkt nicht daran, _____.	*to feed the dog*
10. Er denkt nicht daran, _____.	*to eat the cake*

With Certain Verbs Introducing zu + Infinitive

Following are some of the verbs that introduce **zu** plus infinitive.

anfangen	*to start, begin*	**helfen**	*to help*
aufhören	*to stop*	**hoffen**	*to hope*
bitten	*to ask*	**vergessen**	*to forget*
erlauben	*to allow*	**versprechen**	*to promise*
etwas schön (nett,	*to find/consider something*	**vorschlagen**	*to propose*
etc.) **finden**	pretty (*nice*, etc.)	**wünschen**	*to wish*

Er *hörte auf*, Golf *zu spielen*.	*He stopped playing golf.*
Ich *hoffe*, euch bald *zu sehen*.	*I hope to see you soon.*
Sie *findet es dumm*, ihn *zu fragen*.	*She considers it stupid to ask him.*

91. Complete each of the following sentences, using the appropriate form of the infinitive on the right.

1. Ich verspreche dir, dich oft _____.	anrufen
2. Er fängt an, seine Aufgaben _____.	schreiben
3. Sie vergaß, mir die Zeitung _____.	mitgeben
4. Sie hat mich gebeten, ihn auch _____.	einladen
5. Wir helfen dir gern, das Gras _____.	schneiden
6. Ich finde es toll, bei euch _____.	sein
7. Ich schlage vor, es _____.	lesen
8. Wir hoffen, Oma _____.	besuchen
9. Versprecht ihr, meinen Freund _____?	begleiten
10. Er bittet, seine Mutter _____.	mitnehmen
11. Sie finden es schön, ihren Onkel _____.	sehen
12. Ich höre auf, die Geschichte _____.	glauben

With the Verb brauchen + nicht zu + Dependent Infinitive

The verb **brauchen** plus **nicht zu** plus infinitive corresponds to the English *not to have to*. This construction is usually used instead of the negative form of **müssen**. Note that **nicht zu** plus infinitive occurs at the end of the sentence.

Muss ich kommen?	*Do I have to come?*
Nein, du *brauchst nicht zu kommen*.	*No, you don't have to come.*

Muss ich deinem Vater helfen?	*Do I have to help your father?*
Nein, du *brauchst* ihm *nicht zu helfen*.	*No, you don't have to help him.*
Müssen wir heute Abend singen?	*Do we have to sing tonight?*
Nein, ihr *braucht* heute Abend *nicht zu singen*.	*No, you don't have to sing tonight.*

92. Rewrite each of the following sentences in the negative, using **brauchen**.

1. Er muss studieren. _____
2. Ich muss lesen. _____
3. Wir müssen das Buch zurückgeben. _____
4. Sie muss arbeiten. _____
5. Ihr müsst es machen. _____
6. Du musst Herbert helfen. _____
7. Ich muss Bert besuchen. _____
8. Renate muss lesen. _____
9. Sie müssen die Geschichte erzählen. _____
10. Ich muss es bestellen. _____

Verbs as Other Parts of Speech

Infinitives Used as Nouns

German infinitives used as nouns are neuter in gender and are always capitalized. They often correspond to the English gerund, which ends in *-ing*.

Ihr *Lachen* machte mich nervös.	*Her laughing/laughter made me nervous.*
Das viele *Rauchen* ist ungesund.	*Smoking a lot is unhealthy.*

The contraction **beim** plus infinitive noun means *while _____ing* or *in the act of*.

Er hat sich *beim Schwimmen* verletzt.	*He got hurt while swimming.*

93. Complete each of the following sentences, using the German equivalent of the English phrase on the right.

1. Ich habe mich _____ amüsiert.   *while walking*
2. Ich habe mich _____ amüsiert.   *while dancing*
3. Ich habe mich _____ amüsiert.   *while singing*
4. Ich habe mich _____ amüsiert.   *while working*
5. Ich habe mich _____ amüsiert.   *while painting*
6. Ich habe mich _____ amüsiert.   *while repairing*
7. Ich habe mich _____ amüsiert.   *while studying*
8. Ich habe mich _____ amüsiert.   *while playing*
9. Ich habe mich _____ amüsiert.   *while telephoning*
10. Ich habe mich _____ amüsiert.   *while swimming*

Present Participles Used as Adjectives and Adverbs

The present participle is formed by adding **-d** to the infinitive. It can be used as an adjective or as an adverb. Remember to add adjective endings when appropriate.

Ist das *weinende* Kind krank?	*Is the crying child ill?*
Er kam *lachend* ins Zimmer.	*He came into the room laughing.*

94. Complete each of the following sentences, using the appropriate present participle form of the verb on the right.

1. Sie sieht _____ aus.   leiden
2. Der _____ Student wartet auf den Professor.   lesen
3. Wir brauchen ein Zimmer mit _____ Wasser.   fließen
4. Hörst du den _____ Hund?   bellen
5. _____ lief er ins Haus.   bluten
6. Wie heißt die _____ Frau?   singen
7. Kennst du den _____ Jungen?   weinen
8. Dort liegt das _____ Kind.   schlafen
9. Wer ist das _____ Mädchen?   lächeln
10. _____ geht er vorbei.   grüßen

Past Participles Used as Adjectives and Adverbs

The past participles of many weak and strong verbs can be used as adjectives and adverbs.

Ich möchte ein *weichgekochtes* Ei.   *I would like a soft-boiled egg.*
Das Mädchen ist *verletzt*.   *The girl is hurt.*

95. Complete each of the following sentences, using the appropriate past participle form of the verb on the right.

1. Die _____ Stadt wird aufgebaut.   zerstören
2. Die Suppe ist _____.   anbrennen
3. Was macht ihr mit dem _____ Geld?   stehlen
4. Hier ist deine _____ Arbeit.   schreiben
5. Frisch _____ Brötchen schmecken herrlich.   backen
6. Wo ist die _____ Arbeit?   beginnen
7. Das Tier ist _____.   fangen
8. Der _____ Hund schläft.   füttern
9. Wo steht das _____ Auto?   reparieren
10. Mach das _____ Fenster zu!   öffnen

Participles Used as Nouns

Many present and past participles can be used as nouns. They are capitalized and take adjective endings.

Der *Reisende* hatte große Koffer.   *The (male) traveler had large suitcases.*
Seine *Verwandte* ist angekommen.   *His (female) relative arrived.*

96. Complete each of the following sentences, using the appropriate adjective ending.

1. Wo sind die Verletzt___?   6. Die Reisend___ sind müde.
2. Ein Gefangen___ ist ausgebrochen.   7. Die Verliebt___ tanzen.
3. Der Sterbend___ ließ seine Kinder   8. Das Gefroren___ ist gut.
   kommen.   9. Wie heißt der Gefallen___?
4. Eine Verwundet___ lag auf der Straße.   10. Das Neugeboren___ schreit.
5. Wo wohnt der Gesandt___?

Imperatives

Weak and Strong Verbs

The imperative expresses commands, requests, or orders. Just as there are three different forms of address (**Sie**, **ihr**, **du**), there are three corresponding imperative forms. The imperative verb is the first element in a command. However, it may be preceded by **bitte** *please*, which can also occur within the sentence or in final position. The word **doch** softens the command, corresponding to the English *why don't you?* In written German commands, an exclamation point is used.

Imperative = (Bitte) Verb + Personal pronoun (if required)

Study the examples of the imperative forms below.

Sie	Spielen Sie!	Helfen Sie mir!
ihr	Spielt!	Helft mir!
du	Spiel(e)!	Hilf mir!

Formal Commands (Singular and Plural) (Sie)

Formal commands are formed by using the infinitive plus **Sie**. The pronoun **Sie** is always expressed. The same form is used for addressing one or more individuals.

Kommen Sie!	*Come.*
Bitte *parken Sie* hier!	*Please park here.*
Rauchen Sie bitte nicht!	*Please don't smoke.*
Antworten Sie doch!	*Why don't you answer?*
Herr Müller, *erzählen Sie* die Geschichte bitte!	*Mr. Müller, please tell the story.*
Meine Herren, *nehmen Sie* bitte nichts!	*Gentlemen, please don't take anything.*

Familiar Commands

Plural (ihr)

The familiar plural command corresponds to the **ihr** form of the present tense. Note that the pronoun **ihr** is not expressed.

Macht die Aufgaben!	*Do your homework.*
Lest doch den Roman!	*Why don't you read the novel?*
Bitte *holt* die Bücher!	*Please get the books.*
Öffnet bitte das Fenster!	*Please open the window.*
Sprecht langsamer bitte!	*Talk slower, please.*
Kommt doch am Abend!	*Why don't you come in the evening?*

Singular (du)

The familiar singular command is formed by using the infinitive stem plus **-e**. In colloquial speech, this **-e** is usually dropped (except in the cases noted below on pages 205–206). Note that the pronoun **du** is normally not expressed except for special emphasis.

Frag deinen Vater!	*Ask your father.*
Komm mit deinem Bruder bitte!	*Please come with your brother.*
Gudrun, bitte *kauf* die Kamera!	*Gudrun, please buy the camera.*
Trink doch Wasser!	*Why don't you drink water?*
Such das Bild bitte!	*Look for the picture, please.*
Geh ins Zimmer!	*Go into the room.*
BUT *Geh du* nach Hause!	*Go home! (you, and not one of the others)*

97. Answer each of the following questions, using the appropriate formal command beginning with **Ja**. Follow the model.

MODEL Essen? ___Ja, essen Sie bitte.___

1. Schreiben? _____
2. Schlafen? _____
3. Gehen? _____
4. Tanzen? _____
5. Lächeln? _____

6. Reden? _____
7. Arbeiten? _____
8. Erzählen? _____
9. Singen? _____
10. Fahren? _____

98. Complete each of the following sentences, using the appropriate familiar plural command form of the verb on the right.

1. _____ es!   finden
2. _____ lauter!   sprechen
3. _____ weniger!   trinken
4. _____ den Mantel! holen
5. _____ gut!   schlafen
6. _____ das Auto!   parken
7. _____ mehr!   studieren
8. _____ zur Schule! gehen

9. _____ dort!   bleiben
10. _____ den Arzt!   rufen
11. _____ den Braten! essen
12. _____ das Geld!   nehmen
13. _____ langsamer! reiten
14. _____ Milch!   bestellen
15. _____ bald!   schreiben

99. Rewrite each of the following commands, changing the verb from plural to singular.

1. Singt lauter! _____
2. Kommt jetzt! _____
3. Sucht das Geld! _____
4. Bleibt hier! _____
5. Macht es! _____
6. Grüßt Tante Ida! _____
7. Geht ins Haus! _____
8. Probiert die Wurst! _____
9. Weint nicht! _____
10. Springt ins Wasser! _____
11. Schwimmt schneller! _____
12. Sagt die Wahrheit! _____
13. Ruft die Polizei! _____
14. Fragt den Lehrer! _____
15. Raucht nicht! _____

Variations of the Familiar Singular Command

-e Ending

When the infinitive stem ends in **-d**, **-t**, **-ig**, or **-m**, **-n** preceded by a consonant other than **-l** or **-r**, the **-e** ending is not dropped in the familiar singular command form.

Öffne **die Tür!**   *Open the door.*
Entschuldige **bitte!**   *Excuse me, please.*
Antworte **bitte!**   *Answer, please.*
Wende **es!**   *Turn it.*
Atme **regelmäßig!**   *Breathe normally.*

Infinitives Ending in -eln and -ern

When the infinitive ends in **-eln**, the **e** preceding **-ln** is dropped and the **-e** ending is kept.

Klingle **nicht!**	*Don't ring.*
Lächle **doch!**	*Why don't you smile?*
Behandle **das Kind!**	*Treat the child.*

When the infinitive ends in **-ern**, the **-e** ending is kept.

Ändere **nichts!**	*Don't change anything.*
Füttere **die Katze!**	*Feed the cat.*
Wandere **nicht!**	*Don't hike.*

100. Answer each of the following questions, using the familiar singular command beginning with **Ja**. Follow the model.

MODEL   Arbeiten?   __Ja, arbeite!__

1. Warten? _____	8. Es ändern? _____
2. Reden? _____	9. Es beobachten? _____
3. Lächeln? _____	10. Rechnen? _____
4. Es füttern? _____	11. Es schneiden? _____
5. Ihn behandeln? _____	12. Es sammeln? _____
6. Es öffnen? _____	13. Wandern? _____
7. Antworten? _____	14. Arbeiten? _____

Stem Vowel e Changes to i or ie

Strong verbs that have a stem vowel change from **e** to **i** or **ie** in the second- and third-person singular forms of the present tense, have the same change in the familiar singular command.

Gib **Gisela den Brief!**	*Give the letter to Gisela.*
Hilf **uns!**	*Help us.*
Iss **die Suppe!**	*Eat your soup.*
Sprich **langsamer!**	*Speak more slowly.*
Lies **doch das Buch!**	*Why don't you read the book?*
Nimm **nichts!**	*Don't take anything.*

101. Rewrite each of the following commands, changing the formal command to the familiar singular.

1. Helfen Sie dem Kind! _____
2. Sprechen Sie lauter! _____
3. Geben Sie es dem Lehrer! _____
4. Stehlen Sie nicht! _____
5. Lesen Sie die Zeitung! _____
6. Brechen Sie es nicht! _____
7. Treffen Sie die Frau! _____
8. Sterben Sie nicht! _____
9. Erschrecken Sie nicht! _____
10. Essen Sie das Fleisch! _____
11. Nehmen Sie den Schmuck! _____
12. Vergessen Sie nichts! _____

Irregular Imperative Forms

The imperative forms of **haben**, **sein**, **werden**, **wissen** are slightly irregular. Study the following forms.

		haben	sein	werden	wissen
Formal	Sie	Haben Sie!	Seien Sie!	Werden Sie!	Wissen Sie!
Familiar Plural	ihr	Habt!	Seid!	Werdet!	Wisst!
Familiar Singular	du	Hab(e)!	Sei!	Werde!	Wisse!

102. Complete each of the following commands, using the appropriate form of the verb on the right.

1. Peter und Hans, _____ keine Angst!   haben
2. Ilse, _____ nicht frech!   sein
3. Herr Koch, _____ ja nicht krank!   werden
4. Kinder, _____ morgen die Antwort!   wissen
5. Frau Bucher, _____ bitte ruhig!   sein
6. Du liebes Kind, _____ bald wieder gesund!   werden
7. Christa, _____ nur vorsichtig!   sein
8. Fritz, _____ doch Geduld!   haben
9. Herr Knauer, _____ keine Angst!   haben
10. Frau Bremer, _____ es nächste Woche!   wissen

First-Person Command (*Let's*)

The idea of *let's* is expressed by the first-person plural. The pronoun **wir** follows the conjugated verb.

Singen wir!	*Let's sing.*
Gehen wir!	*Let's go.*
Fahren wir mit dem Auto!	*Let's go by car.*

103. Answer each of the following questions, using the appropriate first-person command. Follow the model.

MODEL   Pferd füttern?   Füttern wir das Pferd!

1. Das Abendessen kochen? _____
2. Den Lehrer fragen? _____
3. Warme Milch trinken? _____
4. Wein kaufen? _____
5. Jetzt gehen? _____
6. Die Aufgaben schreiben? _____
7. Den Hund rufen? _____
8. Das Buch holen? _____
9. Viel arbeiten? _____
10. Nichts ändern? _____

Impersonal Imperative

Instructions to the public are expressed by an infinitive command form. In this construction, the infinitive occurs in final position and the exclamation point is not used.

Bitte *anschnallen.*	*Please fasten your seat belts.*
Rechts *fahren.*	*Drive on the right side.*
Nicht *aufstehen.*	*Do not get up.*
Einfahrt *freihalten.*	*Keep the driveway clear.*

The Conditional

Weak and Strong Verbs

The German conditional is formed with the auxiliary **würden** plus infinitive, and corresponds to the English verb pattern *would* plus infinitive. The conditional expresses what would happen if it were not for another circumstance. As is customary for dependent infinitives, the infinitive of the conditional is in final position, unless it occurs in a dependent clause. Study the following conjugation and examples.

ich würde sagen	wir würden sagen
du würdest sagen	ihr würdet sagen
er würde sagen	sie würden sagen

Sie *würden* das Haus nicht *kaufen.*	*They would not buy the house.*
Ich *würde* dem Kind *helfen.*	*I would help the child.*
Würdest du das Geld *nehmen*?	*Would you take the money?*
Er weiß, dass ich es *sagen würde.*	*He knows that I would say it.*

104. Rewrite each of the following sentences, using the conditional.

1. Wir nehmen nichts. _____
2. Bezahlst du? _____
3. Ich schwimme den ganzen Tag. _____
4. Sie arbeiten viel. _____
5. Er studiert nicht. _____
6. Fahrt ihr nach Deutschland? _____
7. Singen Sie laut? _____
8. Ich springe nicht ins Wasser. _____
9. Liest du das Buch? _____
10. Er repariert den Wagen. _____
11. Kommt ihr? _____
12. Sie bringen das Geschenk. _____
13. Helft ihr mir? _____
14. Ich gehe auch. _____
15. Tragen Sie die Jacke? _____
16. Laufen die Kinder? _____

Use of the Conditional

In both English and German, the conditional is used in the conclusion of contrary-to-fact *if* clauses. It is used increasingly in place of the subjunctive in the conclusion of the condition in spoken and informal German. (See pages 210, 211, and 216–217.)

The conditional is also used as a polite form of request.

Würden Sie bitte einen Moment *warten*?	*Would you please wait a moment?*
Würdest du mir bitte *helfen*?	*Would you please help me?*
Würdet ihr *singen* bitte?	*Would you please sing?*

105. Rewrite each of the following commands, changing the command to the conditional.

1. Kommen Sie bitte! _____
2. Nimm das bitte! _____
3. Bleibt hier bitte! _____

4. Fahren Sie bitte schneller! _____
5. Gib mir bitte das Messer! _____
6. Sprechen Sie bitte langsamer! _____
7. Gehen Sie bitte! _____
8. Park bitte das Auto! _____
9. Bestellt das Essen bitte! _____
10. Zeigen Sie es den Kindern bitte! _____
11. Besuchen Sie Ihren Vater bitte! _____
12. Warte hier bitte! _____

The Subjunctive

Whereas the *indicative mood* is used to make statements of fact, ask questions, and generally describe reality, the *subjunctive mood* is used to express conditions and situations that are contrary to fact, unlikely, uncertain, or hypothetical.

The indicative is used for actions that have taken place, are taking place, or will very likely take place.

Er hat großen Hunger.	*He is very hungry.*
Ich weiß, dass sie krank ist.	*I know that she is ill.*
Wir werden ihn besuchen.	*We will visit him.*
Er hat es genommen.	*He took it.*

The subjunctive is used to express that a certain action has not taken place or may not take place, because it is a supposition, conjecture, or desire, rather than a fact. When a statement is contrary to fact or when it implies a possibility rather than a probability, the subjunctive mood is used.

Ich wollte, er *wäre* hier!	*I wish he were here.*
Er sagte, er *würde* keine Zeit haben.	*He said he would have no time.*
Sie tut, als ob sie Geld *hätte*.	*She acts as if she had money.*

Subjunctive Forms in German

In German, there are two forms of the subjunctive, for convenience often referred to as *Subjunctive I* and *Subjunctive II*.

Subjunctive I was given its name because it is based on the infinitive stem (the first principal part of the verb). *Subjunctive II* derives its name from the fact that it is based on the simple past tense stem of the verb (the second principal part of the verb).

Principal Parts of the Verb

FIRST PART (INFINITIVE)	SECOND PART (SIMPLE PAST)	THIRD PART (PAST PARTICIPLE)
machen	**machte**	**gemacht**
gehen	**ging**	**gegangen**

Subjunctive I (sometimes called the *special subjunctive*) is used primarily to render indirect speech in formal situations. It calls attention to the fact that these are not the exact words of the original speaker, but are only someone else's report of those words. This form of the subjunctive is commonly encountered in newspapers, magazines, and other media, as well as in very formal speech; in colloquial speech, however, native speakers often use the indicative instead.

Subjunctive II (sometimes called the *general subjunctive* or the *imperfect subjunctive*) is used in a wider variety of situations, mainly to express the following.

(1) contrary-to-fact conditions
(2) wishes and desires
(3) hypothetical questions
(4) polite requests and questions
(5) as a substitute for *Subjunctive I* when those forms are identical to the past indicative and for that reason might be confusing

Each of these uses is explained below.

It is possible to indicate different timeframes in the subjunctive through the addition and choice of an auxiliary verb. Because both *Subjunctive I* and *Subjunctive II* can be expressed in a variety of timeframes, it is perhaps misleading to refer to them as the "present subjunctive" and "past subjunctive" simply because of the verb stem that each form is based on.

For convenience of presentation, we will start with *Subjunctive II*.

Subjunctive II—Present-Time

Subjunctive II is used to express wishes, unreal conditions, and hypothetical events in the present or future. It is formed by adding the subjunctive personal endings to the stem of the simple past tense. To obtain the past stem, drop the **-en** from the first-person plural form of the simple past tense. Note that this rule applies to both strong and weak verbs.

Present-time Subjunctive II = Past stem + Subjunctive personal ending

---

The subjunctive personal endings that must be added to the past stem are as follows.

	SINGULAR	PLURAL
First Person	-e	-en
Second Person	-est	-et
Third Person	-e	-en

Thus, the fully conjugated present-time subjunctive for **sagen** is as follows.

ich sagte	**wir sagten**
du sagtest	**ihr sagtet**
er sagte	**sie sagten**

> **Ich wollte, er *sagte* mir die Wahrheit.**   *I wished he would tell me the truth.*

Weak Verbs

The German present-time Subjunctive II of weak verbs is identical to the simple past indicative. This is also true in English. The subjunctive of all English verbs, except *to be,* is identical to the past indicative: *If* I had *the money* …; *If* he lost *everything* …; BUT *If* she were *rich*….

In German as well as in English, these present-time Subjunctive II forms are ambiguous. Only the context makes clear whether the forms are past indicative or subjunctive. For this reason, the present conditional **würden** plus infinitive is often substituted for the subjunctive in German. (See The Conditional, page 208.) The German present-time Subjunctive II corresponds to the English present conditional *would* plus infinitive (*would run*) or to the present-time subjunctive (*ran*), depending on its use in the sentence. Although the present-time subjunctive looks like the simple past indicative, it always refers to present or future time.

106. Rewrite each of the following sentences, substituting the Subjunctive II for the present conditional.

1. Sie würden uns besuchen. _____
2. Wir würden viel machen. _____
3. Würdet ihr es kaufen? _____
4. Ich würde es erzählen. _____
5. Würdest du es zerstören? _____
6. Würden Sie dort arbeiten? _____
7. Ich würde ihn fragen. _____
8. Wir würden zahlen. _____
9. Er würde es glauben. _____
10. Ich würde es sagen. _____
11. Würdest du dort wohnen? _____
12. Würdet ihr es hören? _____
13. Sie würden es lernen. _____
14. Wir würden nicht weinen. _____
15. Ich würde bezahlen. _____
16. Er würde studieren. _____
17. Würdet ihr das Haus bauen? _____
18. Würden Sie dort spielen? _____
19. Sie würden alles hören. _____
20. Würdest du malen? _____

107. Express each of the following sentences in German, using the Subjunctive II.

1. *I would cry.* _____
2. *We would play.* _____
3. *They would get it.* _____
4. *He would not believe it.* _____
5. *Children, would you play?* _____
6. *Gerda, would you buy flowers?* _____
7. *Mrs. Treibl, would you live there?* _____
8. *She would work.* _____
9. *We would learn.* _____
10. *They would try the soup.* _____

Irregular Weak Verbs

The irregular weak verbs **brennen**, **kennen**, **nennen**, **rennen**, **senden**, **wenden** do not form the Subjunctive II from their simple past tense stems; instead, they retain the vowel of the infinitive stem. These forms, however, are increasingly rare and are being replaced by the conditional (**würden** plus infinitive).

ich rennte	**wir rennten**
du renntest	**ihr renntet**
er rennte	**sie rennten**

    Ich *wollte*, die Kerze *brennte* den ganzen Tag.   *I wished the candle would burn all day.*
    Ich *wünschte*, ich *kennte* die Frau besser.   *I wished I knew the woman better.*

The irregular weak verbs **bringen**, **denken**, **wissen** use the simple past tense stems but add an umlaut to the stem vowel in addition to the subjunctive endings to form the Subjunctive II.

ich brächte	wir brächten	ich dächte	wir dächten	ich wüsste	wir wüssten
du brächtest	ihr brächtet	du dächtest	ihr dächtet	du wüsstest	ihr wüsstet
er brächte	sie brächten	er dächte	sie dächten	er wüsste	sie wüssten

Ich *wünschte*, sie *brächte* ihm nichts.   *I wished she wouldn't bring him anything.*
Ich *wünschte*, er *dächte* nicht daran.   *I wished he would not think of it.*
Ich *wünschte*, wir *wüssten* alles.   *I wished we would know everything.*

108. Rewrite each of the following sentences, substituting the Subjunctive II for the present conditional.

1. Das Haus würde brennen.   _____
2. Würdet ihr daran denken?   _____
3. Ich würde etwas bringen.   _____
4. Würdest du es nennen?   _____
5. Sie würden schnell rennen.   _____
6. Wir würden es wissen.   _____
7. Ich würde den Brief senden.   _____
8. Wir würden das Blatt wenden.   _____
9. Ich würde das wissen.   _____
10. Würdest du das Buch bringen?   _____

Strong Verbs

The Subjunctive II of strong verbs is also formed by adding the subjunctive endings **-e**, **-est**, **-e**, **-en**, **-et**, **-en** to the simple past tense stem. However, strong verbs containing the vowels **a**, **o**, **u** in the past stems add an umlaut to the vowel.

NO UMLAUT	UMLAUT	UMLAUT	UMLAUT
ich bliebe	ich nähme	ich flöge	ich führe
du bliebest	du nähmest	du flögest	du führest
er bliebe	er nähme	er flöge	er führe
wir blieben	wir nähmen	wir flögen	wir führen
ihr bliebet	ihr nähmet	ihr flöget	ihr führet
sie blieben	sie nähmen	sie flögen	sie führen

Ich *wünschte*, er *käme* am Samstag.   *I wished he would come on Saturday.*
Ich *wünschte*, wir *flögen* nach Paris.   *I wished we would fly to Paris.*
Ich *wünschte*, du *gingest* nach Hause.   *I wished you would go home.*
Ich *wünschte*, ich *führe* in die Schweiz.   *I wished I would go to Switzerland.*
Ich *wünschte*, sie *schrieben* die Karte.   *I wished they would write the card.*

109. Form a sentence from each of the following groups of words, using the Subjunctive II.

1. ich / schreiben / das Gedicht   _____
2. wir / trinken / nichts   _____
3. lassen / du / ihn / gehen / ?   _____
4. die Alten / gehen / zur Kirche   _____
5. die Sonne / scheinen / nicht   _____
6. die Studenten / lesen / das Buch   _____

    7. er / fliegen / auch   _____

    8. schlafen / du / lange / ?   _____

    9. ich / geben / Anna / alles   _____

  10. er / laufen / schnell   _____

  11. die Leute / fahren / mit dem Auto   _____

  12. wir / schreien / laut   _____

  13. er / schneiden / das Haar   _____

  14. ich / bleiben / hier   _____

  15. wir / kommen / auch   _____

  16. nehmen / du / das Papier / ?   _____

  17. ich / essen / Brot   _____

  18. das Pferd / ziehen / den Schlitten   _____

  19. er / verlieren / das Geld   _____

  20. wir / springen / hoch   _____

Irregular Strong Verbs

The following strong verbs require a change in their past tense stem vowels to form the Subjunctive II.

helfen	**ich hülfe**	**sterben**	**ich stürbe**
stehen	**ich stünde**	**werfen**	**ich würfe**

These forms, however, are rarely used; the **würden**-plus-infinitive construction is generally used in informal German instead.

Ich *stünde* **dort.**	*I would stand there.*
Wer *hülfe* **dem Kind?**	*Who would help the child?*
Wir *würfen* **den Ball.**	*We would throw the ball.*
Er *stürbe* **vor Angst.**	*He would die of fright.*

110. Express each of the following sentences in German, using the Subjunctive II.

    1. *He would die.*   _____

    2. *They would help.*   _____

    3. *We would throw the ball.*   _____

    4. *She would stand here.*   _____

    5. *I would help.*   _____

    6. *They would die.*   _____

    7. *We would stand here.*   _____

    8. *Helga, would you help?*   _____

Subjunctive II Auxiliaries **haben** and **sein**

Study the following conjugations.

ich hätte	**wir hätten**	**ich wäre**	**wir wären**
du hättest	**ihr hättet**	**du wärest**	**ihr wäret**
er hätte	**sie hätten**	**er wäre**	**sie wären**

Ich *hätte* **kein Geld.**	*I would not have any money.*
Wir *hätten* **Ferien.**	*We would have a vacation.*
Er *wäre* **zu klein.**	*He would be too small.*
***Wärest* du dort?**	*Would you be there?*

111. Rewrite each of the following sentences, substituting the Subjunctive II for the indicative.

1. Wir haben kein Auto. _____
2. Ich bin reich. _____
3. Sie haben keine Ferien. _____
4. Du bist nicht glücklich. _____
5. Ich habe keinen Hund. _____
6. Sie ist böse. _____
7. Sie sind nicht intelligent. _____
8. Ihr habt kein Geld. _____
9. Er hat nichts. _____
10. Habt ihr Geld? _____
11. Wir sind krank. _____
12. Hast du Angst? _____
13. Wir haben alles. _____
14. Seid ihr müde? _____
15. Bist du froh? _____
16. Ich bin arm. _____

Modal Verbs

Modal auxiliary verbs retain the vowels of the infinitive in the Subjunctive II stems. Note the consonant change in **mögen**.

dürfen	**ich dürfte**	*might, would be permitted, may I?, could I? (in polite questions)*
können	**ich könnte**	*were able, would be able*
mögen	**ich möchte**	*would like*
müssen	**ich müsste**	*ought to, would have to*
sollen	**ich sollte**	*should, would have to*
wollen	**ich wollte**	*wanted, would want to*

The subjunctive form of the modals is frequently used to express possibility or an opinion, and to phrase questions and requests politely. In English, the modals are usually expressed with *would* plus the meaning of the modal.

Du *solltest* zu Hause bleiben.	*You should stay at home.*
***Müsstest* du nicht arbeiten?**	*Wouldn't you have to work?*
***Möchtest* du ein Stück Kuchen?**	*Would you like a piece of cake?*
***Dürfte* ich es sehen?**	*Could I see it?*

112. Rewrite each of the following questions, using the Subjunctive II to form polite requests or questions.

1. Können Sie mir helfen? _____
2. Willst du auch zeichnen? _____
3. Musst ihr nicht studieren? _____
4. Darf er mitgehen? _____
5. Sollst du Marianne besuchen? _____
6. Kann ich ein Stück nehmen? _____
7. Musst du nicht lernen? _____
8. Wollt ihr den Film sehen? _____
9. Kann sie es holen? _____
10. Darf ich bleiben? _____

113. Complete each of the following sentences, using the appropriate Subjunctive II form of **mögen**.

1. _____ du noch etwas?   6. _____ du dort leben?
2. Ich _____ Schokolade.   7. _____ Sie etwas haben?
3. Wir _____ gehen.   8. Ich _____ fliegen.
4. Die Kinder _____ reiten.   9. _____ ihr essen?
5. _____ Sie mitmachen?   10. _____ du etwas bestellen?

Wishes

Contrary-to-fact Wishes

Contrary-to-fact wishes may be introduced by the Subjunctive II of verbs of wishing, e.g., **ich wollte**, **ich wünschte**. When using a contrary-to-fact wish, the speaker expresses his or her dissatisfaction with an actual situation and expresses how he or she would like it to be.

Fact	**Er ist nicht zu Hause.**	*He is not at home.*
Wish	***Ich wollte,* er wäre zu Hause.**	*I wish he were at home.*

114. Rewrite each of the following sentences, beginning with **Ich wollte** and using the Subjunctive II to change the fact to a contrary-to-fact wish. Follow the model.

MODEL   Sie ist krank.   <u>Ich wollte, sie wäre nicht krank.</u>

1. Er bleibt dort. _____
2. Sie können abfahren. _____
3. Wir leben in einem Dorf. _____
4. Ich habe Zahnweh. _____
5. Ihr arbeitet so viel. _____
6. Ich muss studieren. _____
7. Wir sind nicht zu Hause. _____
8. Du kaufst dir nichts. _____
9. Sie weint. _____
10. Ich bin arm. _____
11. Wir haben es. _____
12. Er nimmt es. _____
13. Er sieht Paula. _____
14. Sie besuchen Oma. _____

Contrary-to-fact Wishes Introduced by wenn *if*

When a contrary-to-fact wish is expressed in a **wenn** *if* clause, the conjugated verb is in final position, as is required in dependent clauses. Such wishes often contain the words **nur** or **doch**, corresponding to the English *only*.

Wenn sie nur daran *glaubten*!   *If only they believed in it.*
Wenn er doch nicht *rauchte*!   *If only he wouldn't smoke.*
Wenn ich es nur nicht tun *müsste*!   *If only I didn't have to do it.*

115. Form a wish from each of the following groups of words, beginning with **Wenn** and using the Subjunctive II. Follow the model.

MODEL   ich / nur mehr Geld / haben   <u>Wenn ich nur mehr Geld hätte!</u>

1. wir / nur in München / sein _____
2. er / nur das Fenster / öffnen _____

3. ihr / doch ein Auto / kaufen   _____

4. die Leute / nur nicht so laut / schreien   _____

5. ich / nur alles / wissen   _____

6. er / nur nicht krank / sein   _____

7. die Kinder / nur zu Hause / bleiben   _____

8. ich / nur Deutsch / können   _____

9. ihr / nur mehr / haben   _____

10. Georg / nur nicht / abfahren   _____

Contrary-to-fact Wishes Not Introduced by wenn *if*

The introductory **wenn** of the wishes above can also be omitted. In that case, the conjugated verb is in first position.

Hätte **ich nur mehr Zeit!**	*If only I had more time.*
Gäbe **es nur besseres Essen!**	*If only there were better food.*
Dürfte **ich nur heimgehen!**	*If only I could go home.*

116.   Rewrite each of the following wishes, omitting **wenn**.

1. Wenn sie nur die Wahrheit sagte!   _____

2. Wenn ich doch schlafen könnte!   _____

3. Wenn er nur das Auto reparierte!   _____

4. Wenn sie nur nicht so viel tränken!   _____

5. Wenn er doch schwiege!   _____

6. Wenn wir nur keine Angst hätten!   _____

7. Wenn du nur hier wärest!   _____

8. Wenn er nur hier bliebe!   _____

9. Wenn sie es nur glaubte!   _____

10. Wenn ihr nur mehr lerntet!   _____

Conditional Sentences

Contrary-to-fact Conditions

Conditional sentences consist of a conditional clause, introduced by **wenn** *if,* and a conclusion. The verbs in a conditional sentence may be in the indicative or the subjunctive mood.

    If the speaker wants to express that the condition is factual, real, or fulfillable, the indicative is used.

Wenn ich Geld *habe, kaufe* **ich es.**	*If I have money, I'll buy it.*
	When I have money, I'll buy it.

In this sentence, the speaker does not yet have money, but there is a good probability that he or she will have it in the future.

    If a condition is contrary to fact, unreal, unlikely, or unfulfillable, the subjunctive is used.

Wenn ich Geld *hätte, kaufte* **ich es.**	*If I had money, I would buy it.*

By using the subjunctive, the speaker expresses that he or she does not have the money now, nor is he or she likely to have it in the future. The subjunctive is used in both the condition and the conclusion.

    Variations from the patterns above are possible in German. The present conditional is frequently used in place of the ambiguous subjunctive form of weak verbs, when the subjunctive and the past indicative forms are identical.

Wenn ich reich *wäre,* *machte* **ich eine Weltreise.**	
OR *würde* **ich eine Weltreise** *machen.*	

In colloquial speech, the present conditional is increasingly used to replace the subjunctive of strong verbs in the conclusion of the conditional sentence.

Wenn es kälter *wäre*,   *zöge* ich den Pelzmantel an.
OR ***würde* ich den Pelzmantel *anziehen*.**

The Subjunctive II of **haben**, **sein**, and the modal verbs is not replaced by the present conditional.

117. Rewrite each of the following clauses, replacing the Subjunctive II with the conditional.

Wenn ich kein Geld hätte, …
1. arbeitete ich. _____
2. wohnte ich nicht hier. _____
3. gäbe ich dir nichts. _____
4. flöge ich nicht nach Hamburg. _____
5. bestellte ich mir nichts. _____

Wenn er käme, …
6. tränken wir Kaffee. _____
7. unterhielten wir uns. _____
8. freute ich mich. _____
9. zöge ich mich um. _____
10. fürchtete ich mich nicht. _____

118. Complete each of the following sentences, using the appropriate Subjunctive II forms of the verbs on the right.

1. Wenn ich Zeit _____, _____ ich dir.   haben, helfen
2. Wenn er hier _____, _____ ich glücklich.   sein, sein
3. Wenn Ute etwas _____, _____ sie es.   sehen, beschreiben
4. Wenn du zu Hause _____, _____ wir dich.   bleiben, besuchen
5. Wenn ihr _____, _____ ihr es.   studieren, wissen
6. Wenn wir Essen _____, _____ wir es.   bestellen, essen
7. Wenn du Deutsch _____, _____ du es.   lernen, können

Omission of **wenn** in Contrary-to-fact Conditional Sentences
The conjugated verb is in first position in the sentence when **wenn** is omitted.

***Wäre* das Radio kaputt, (dann) *würde* er es reparieren.**   *If the radio were broken, (then) he would fix it.*
***Machtest* du das Fenster *auf*, (dann) *würde* es kalt *werden*.** *If you opened the window, (then) it would get cold.*

119. Rewrite each of the following sentences, omitting **wenn** and adding **dann** at the beginning of the main clause.

1. Wenn du mir hülfest, wäre ich froh. _____
2. Wenn er käme, bliebe ich dort. _____
3. Wenn wir ihn fragten, würde er uns antworten. _____
4. Wenn sie es wollte, gäbe ich es ihr. _____
5. Wenn ich Angst hätte, würde ich schreien. _____

120. Express each of the following sentences in German, using the Subjunctive II in both clauses and omitting **wenn**.

1. *If I were ill, I would stay at home.*   _____
2. *If we knew it, we would tell Alexander.*   _____
3. *If she had money, she would buy the coat.*   _____
4. *If they worked, they would be happier.*   _____
5. *If he arrived, I would pick him up.*   _____

Clauses Introduced by als ob

The subjunctive is used in clauses introduced by **als ob** or **als wenn** *as if*, because the speaker makes an unreal comparison. Note that if the word **ob** is omitted, the verb follows **als**.

Er sieht aus, *als ob* **er krank wäre.**	*He looks as if he were ill.*
Sie tun, *als ob* **sie Angst hätten.**	*They act as if they were afraid.*
Sie sehen aus, *als* **wären Sie krank.**	*You look as if you were ill.*

121. Complete each of the following sentences, using the appropriate Subjunctive II form of the verb on the right.

1. Wir tun, als ob wir Zeit _____.   haben
2. Du tust, als ob du sie _____.   lieben
3. Er tut, als ob er ins Haus _____.   gehen
4. Sie tun, als ob sie krank _____.   sein
5. Ich tue, als ob ich bleiben _____.   wollen
6. Ich tue, als ob ich es _____.   können
7. Sie tut, als ob sie hier _____.   bleiben
8. Sie tun, als ob sie _____.   arbeiten
9. Er tut, als ob er alles _____.   sehen
10. Wir tun, als ob wir es _____.   nehmen

Hypothetical Statements and Questions

Study the use of the Subjunctive II in the following examples.

So etwas *täte* **sie nicht.**	*She wouldn't do something like that.*
Tätest **du so etwas?**	*Would you do something like that?*
Das *wäre* **schrecklich!**	*That would be terrible!*

Polite Requests and Questions

Könntest **du mir bitte etwas Geld leihen?**	*Could you please lend me some money?*
Möchten **Sie noch ein Stück Kuchen?**	*Would you like another piece of cake?*
Würden **Sie mir das Messer geben?**	*Would you give me the knife?*

Subjunctive II—Compound Forms to Indicate Past Time

The past-time subjunctive is used to express wishes, unreal conditions, and hypothetical events relating to any time in the past. It is formed with the subjunctive forms of **hätte** or **wäre** plus the past participle.

Past-time subjunctive = Subjunctive II of **haben** or **sein** (**hätte** or **wäre**) + Past participle

Study the following conjugations.

ich hätte gesungen	wir hätten gesungen	ich wäre gegangen	wir wären gegangen
du hättest gesungen	ihr hättet gesungen	du wärest gegangen	ihr wäret gegangen
er hätte gesungen	sie hätten gesungen	er wäre gegangen	sie wären gegangen

The German past-time subjunctive corresponds to the English *had* plus participle (*had run, had gone*) or to the English past conditional *would* plus *have* plus past participle (*would have run, would have gone*), depending on its use in the sentence. Since the past-time subjunctive in German is not ambiguous, there is no need to use the past conditional.

The past-time subjunctive is used with contrary-to-fact wishes, contrary-to-fact conditional clauses, and **als ob** clauses referring to past time.

Wenn sie nur *mitgeholfen hätte*!	*If only she had helped.*
Hätte **ich nur den Roman** *gelesen*!	*If only I had read the novel.*
Wenn wir *studiert hätten*, *hätten* **wir die Antworten** *gewusst*.	*If we had studied, we would have known the answers.*
Wäre **er krank** *gewesen*, *hätte* **er nicht** *gearbeitet*.	*If he had been ill, he wouldn't have worked.*
Sie tut, als ob sie dort *gewesen wäre*.	*She acts as if she had been there.*

122. Rewrite each of the following sentences, changing the fact to a contrary-to-fact wish using the appropriate form of the past-time subjunctive. Follow the model.

MODEL   Ich hatte keinen Schlüssel.   <u>Wenn ich nur einen Schlüssel gehabt hätte!</u>

1. Wir waren nicht in der Schule. _____
2. Du hast nicht angerufen. _____
3. Ich habe nicht gebadet. _____
4. Er hatte keine Angst. _____
5. Ihr seid nicht gekommen. _____

123. Rewrite each of the following wishes, omitting **wenn**.

1. Wenn du nur geschrien hättest! _____
2. Wenn wir ihr nur begegnet wären! _____
3. Wenn ich nur hingegangen wäre! _____
4. Wenn er nur nicht gestorben wäre! _____
5. Wenn sie nur geschrieben hätte! _____

124. Complete each of the following sentences with the appropriate form of the past-time subjunctive of the verb on the right.

1. Wenn er alles _____ _____, _____ er keinen Hunger _____.   essen, haben
2. Wenn du es _____ _____, _____ ich es nicht _____.   zurückbringen, holen
3. Wenn ihr das Fenster _____ _____, _____ ihr euch nicht _____.   zumachen, erkälten
4. Wenn du mich _____ _____, _____ ich es dir _____.   anrufen, sagen
5. Wenn das Kind nicht so _____ _____, _____ es nicht so laut _____.   bluten, schreien

125. Rewrite each of the following contrary-to-fact conditional clauses, omitting **wenn**.

1. Wenn es geklingelt hätte, hätten wir aufgemacht.

   _____

2. Wenn du angerufen hättest, wäre ich gekommen.

   _____

3. Wenn wir es gefunden hätten, hätten wir es wieder zurückgegeben.

   _____

4. Wenn ihr geschrieben hättet, hätten wir euch dort getroffen.

   _____

126. Express each of the following sentences in German.

1. *He acts as if he had bought it.*   _____
2. *They act as if they had not slept.* _____
3. *She acts as if she had been ill.*   _____
4. *He acts as if he had come along.*   _____

Modal Auxiliaries

When a modal auxiliary is used with a dependent infinitive in the past-time subjunctive, the double infinitive construction is used.

> **Hätte** ich es nur *machen können*!   *If only I could have done it!*

If the double infinitive occurs in a **wenn** clause or an **als ob** clause, the conjugated form of the auxiliary (**hätte**, **wäre**) precedes the double infinitive.

> **Wenn ich nur** *hätte kommen dürfen*!   *If only I had been allowed to come!*
> **Wenn du es** *hättest machen wollen*, **wäre ich**   *If you had wanted to do it, I would have been*
>   **glücklich gewesen.**   *happy.*
> **Sie tun, als ob sie alles** *hätten tun dürfen*.   *They act as if they should have done everything.*

127. Rewrite each of the following sentences, using the appropriate form of the modal verb on the right in the wish or dependent clause.

1. Wäre er nur geblieben! _____ dürfen
2. Wenn ich doch nicht gegangen wäre!   müssen

   _____

3. Er tut, als ob er es gesehen hätte!   können

   _____

4. Du tust, als ob ich es geschrieben hätte.   sollen

   _____

5. Wenn ich geritten wäre, hätte ich es dir gesagt.   wollen

   _____

6. Hätte er nur gesungen! _____ können
7. Wenn du nur nichts gegessen hättest!   wollen

   _____

8. Wenn wir gefragt hätten, hätten wir die Antwort gewusst. dürfen

   _____

9. Hätte sie nur geholfen! _____ können
10. Sie tun, als ob sie auf mich gewartet hätten.   müssen

   _____

Indirect Speech

There are two ways to report what another person has said. One method is to quote the exact words of the original speaker. In written materials, quotation marks set off the speaker's exact words. (Note the position of the opening quotation marks in German.)

> **Sie sagte: „Er hat die Schlüssel gefunden."**   *She said, "He found the keys."*

It is, however, also possible to report the substance of the original speaker's utterance as an indirect quotation. Note the difference in word order in the two examples below.

> **Sie sagte, *dass* er die Schlüssel *gefunden hätte.***   *She said that he had found the keys.*
> **Sie sagte, er *hätte* die Schlüssel *gefunden.***   *She said he had found the keys.*

In the examples of indirect speech, the use of the subjunctive makes it clear that the information reported here is secondhand and that the speaker is merely passing it on. The use of *Subjunctive I* can imply a certain skepticism, or it can merely be a device to distance the speaker from events for which he or she was not present.

Note also that the use of the subjunctive to indicate indirect speech can be continued throughout long passages without any other signal that the entire passage is an indirect quotation.

Direct Quotation

Robert sagt: „Heidi *ist* zu spät gekommen, und *meine* Freunde *sind* ohne sie ins Kino gegangen. Dies *ist* nichts Ungewöhnliches, sie *kommt* immer zu spät. *Ich habe* kein Verständnis dafür. So etwas *ärgert mich* maßlos. Sie *muss* sich bessern."

Indirect Speech

Robert sagte, Heidi *sei* zu spät gekommen, und *seine* Freunde *seien* ohne sie ins Kino gegangen. Dies *sei* nichts Ungewöhnliches, sie *käme* immer zu spät. *Er habe* kein Verständnis dafür. So etwas *ärgere ihn* maßlos. Sie *müsse* sich bessern.

As illustrated by the passages above, not only have the verb forms been changed from the indicative to the *Subjunctive I* forms in indirect speech, but restating the material as indirect speech also requires logical changes in the pronouns and possessive adjectives used, e.g., changing *I* to *he*, *my* to *his*, etc.

In English, we do not use the subjunctive to mark indirect speech. The indicative mood is used for both direct quotations and indirect speech, though frequently a change in verb tense helps to indicate indirect speech in English. It should be noted, however, that the indicative is also heard in indirect speech in German, particularly if there is absolutely no doubt regarding the accuracy of the information reported.

> **Ingo sagte: „*Ich bin* glücklich."**   *Ingo said, "I am happy."*
> **Ingo sagte, *dass* er glücklich *ist.***   *Ingo said that he is happy.*

In colloquial German, there is an increasing tendency in indirect speech either to use the *Subjunctive II* or to avoid subjunctive forms altogether and use the indicative instead.

In formal writing, however, *Subjunctive I* remains the preferred form in indirect speech unless the *Subjunctive I* form is identical to the present indicative form, in which case the *Subjunctive I* form is replaced by the *Subjunctive II* form. In current practice, however, the trend is to use *Subjunctive II* in indirect speech.

Subjunctive I
Weak and Strong Verbs

The subjunctive endings **-e, -est, -e, -en, -et, -en** are added to the infinitive stems of both weak and strong verbs.

WEAK VERB		STRONG VERB	
ich sage	wir sagen	ich gehe	wir gehen
du sagest	ihr saget	du gehest	ihr gehet
er sage	sie sagen	er gehe	sie gehen

All verbs except **sein** follow the above pattern.

Subjunctive I of sein
Study the following conjugation.

ich sei	wir seien
du seiest	ihr seiet
er sei	sie seien

128. Complete each of the following sentences, replacing the Subjunctive II form in parentheses with the appropriate Subjunctive I present-time tense form.

1. Sie sagt, er _____ (wäre) in Kanada.
2. Sie sagt, er _____ (bliebe) in Kanada.
3. Sie sagt, er _____ (wohnte) in Kanada.
4. Sie sagt, er _____ (studierte) in Kanada.
5. Sie sagt, er _____ (arbeitete) in Kanada.
6. Sie sagt, sie _____ (gäbe) uns etwas.
7. Sie sagt, sie _____ (kaufte) uns etwas.
8. Sie sagt, sie _____ (brächte) uns etwas.
9. Sie sagt, sie _____ (schickte) uns etwas.
10. Sie sagt, sie _____ (schenke) uns etwas.
11. Er sagte, ich _____ (hätte) nichts.
12. Er sagte, ich _____ (wüsste) nichts.
13. Er sagte, ich _____ (könnte) nichts.
14. Er sagte, ich _____ (wollte) nichts.
15. Er sagte, ich _____ (fände) nichts.
16. Er sagte, ich _____ (tränke) nichts.

Subjunctive I—Compound Forms to Indicate Past Time

The past-time of Subjunctive I is formed with the subjunctive forms of **sein** or **haben** plus the past participle.

Past-time subjunctive = Subjunctive I of **haben** or **sein** (**habe** or **sei**) + Past participle

---

Study the following conjugations.

ich habe gesehen	wir haben gesehen	ich sei gegangen	wir seien gegangen
du habest gesehen	ihr habet gesehen	du seiest gegangen	ihr seiet gegangen
er habe gesehen	sie haben gesehen	er sei gegangen	sie seien gegangen

129. Rewrite each of the following sentences, changing the Subjunctive II form to the Subjunctive I form.

1. Er sagt, er hätte schon geschrieben. _____
2. Er sagt, ich wäre ins Kino gegangen. _____
3. Er sagt, sie wäre im Krankenhaus gewesen. _____
4. Er sagt, er hätte etwas geholt. _____
5. Er sagt, er hätte nicht kommen dürfen. _____

Use of Subjunctive I

The use of Subjunctive I is rather limited. Some German speakers use it in indirect statements; others never use it. Moreover, Subjunctive I is mainly used in the first- and third-person singular.

Whether the present-time or the past-time subjunctive is used in the indirect quotation depends on the tense of the verb in the direct quotation. When the original statement is in the present tense, the present-time Subjunctive I or II is used. In German, unlike in English, the tense of the introductory verb does not influence the choice of the subjunctive form in the indirect statement. The verb of the framing clause, e.g., **er sagt**, may be any tense in German. Study the following examples.

DIRECT STATEMENT	INDIRECT STATEMENT
„Ich *bin* krank."	Er sagt, Er sagte, Er hat gesagt, Er hatte gesagt, } er *sei* (*wäre*) krank.

When the verb of the original statement is in the future tense, the present-time subjunctive or the present conditional may be used in the indirect statement.

„Ich *werde* ihn *fragen*."	Sie sagt, Sie sagte, Sie hat gesagt, Sie hatte gesagt, } sie *würde* ihn *fragen*. sie *frage* (*fragte*) ihn.

When the verb of the original statement is in the simple past, the present perfect, or the past perfect, the past-time subjunctive is used.

„Ich *kam* gestern *an*." „Ich *bin* gestern *angekommen*." „Ich *war* gestern *angekommen*."	Er sagt, Er sagte, Er hat gesagt, Er hatte gesagt, } er *sei* (*wäre*) gestern *angekommen*.

130. Rewrite each of the following direct statements as an indirect statement, starting with **Sie sagte** and using the appropriate Subjunctive II form.

1. „Mutter ist krank gewesen." _____
2. „Großvater hatte Geld." _____
3. „Peter hat Angst." _____
4. „Sie war allein." _____
5. „Er hatte ihn gesehen." _____
6. „Christa war nach Köln gefahren." _____
7. „Onkel Werner ist in Hamburg." _____
8. „Ich hatte dich besucht." _____

131. Rewrite each of the following direct statements as an indirect statement, starting with **Er hat gesagt** and using the appropriate Subjunctive I form.

1. „Mutter ist krank gewesen." _____
2. „Großvater hatte Geld." _____
3. „Peter hat Angst." _____
4. „Sie war allein." _____
5. „Er hatte ihn gesehen." _____
6. „Christa war nach Köln gefahren." _____
7. „Onkel Werner ist in Hamburg." _____
8. „Ich hatte dich besucht." _____

Passive Voice

The passive voice in German consists of a form of **werden** plus the past participle of the main verb. Note that all tenses in German can be expressed in the passive.

In German as in English, passive constructions shift the emphasis from the subject of the active sentence to the direct object. What had been the direct object of the active sentence becomes the subject of the passive sentence. In an active sentence, the subject performs an action, whereas in a passive sentence the subject is acted upon by an agent that had been the subject of the active sentence. This agent might or might not be expressed in the passive sentence. If the agent is expressed in a passive construction in German, it is preceded by either **von** or **durch**. If the agent is a person, it is preceded by **von** and is in the dative case. If the agent is an impersonal means by which something is done, it is preceded by **durch** and is in the accusative case. In English, the word *by* is used to introduce the agent, whether it is a person or an impersonal means.

Active	**Die Eltern fragen den Jungen.**	*The parents ask the boy.*
Passive	**Der Junge** *wird von den Eltern gefragt.*	*The boy is asked by his parents.*
Active	**Der Sturm zerstört die Ernte.**	*The storm is destroying the harvest.*
Passive	**Die Ernte** *wird durch den Sturm zerstört.*	*The harvest is destroyed by the storm.*

Many passive sentences in German do not express an agent, however. They simply consist of a subject and the passive verb pattern.

Die Tür *wird geschlossen.*	*The door is (being) closed.*
Die Vorlesung *wird gehalten.*	*The lecture is (being) held.*

In German, the indirect object of the active sentence cannot become the subject of the passive sentence; it must remain the indirect object. The German passive construction does not need a subject. **Es** may be placed in first position in the sentence. It functions merely as a filler and not as a subject. Otherwise, the indirect object or other elements may be in first position when no subject is present.

Active	**Der Arzt hilft dem Verwundeten.**	*The doctor is helping the wounded (man).*
Passive	**Dem Verwundeten** *wird vom Arzt geholfen.*	*The wounded man is being helped by the doctor.*
	Es wird **dem Verwundeten vom Arzt geholfen.**	*The wounded man is helped by the doctor.*

Present Tense Passive

The present tense of the passive is constructed from the present tense of **werden** plus the past participle of the main verb.

Present passive tense = Present tense of **werden** + Past participle

---

Study the following conjugation.

ich werde gefragt	wir werden gefragt
du wirst gefragt	ihr werdet gefragt
er wird gefragt	sie werden gefragt

132. Complete each of the following passive sentences, using the appropriate present passive form of the verb on the right, preposition, and article or contraction (when necessary).

1. Das Brot _____ Bäcker _____.   backen
2. Die Kranke _____ Arznei _____.   retten

3. Das Abendessen _____ schon _____.   servieren
4. Die Bücher _____ ihm _____.   anschauen
5. Es _____ uns _____.   nehmen
6. Dem Kranken _____ Arzt _____.   helfen
7. Die Aufgabe _____ dem Mädchen _____.   schreiben
8. Die Wäsche _____ Mutter _____.   waschen
9. Das Loch _____ den Männern _____.   graben
10. Das Hotel _____ die Bombe _____.   zerstören
11. Wir _____ Vater _____.   sehen
12. Ich _____ dem Jungen _____.   schlagen
13. Er _____ seiner Freundin _____.   hören
14. Das Haus _____ den Sturm _____.   zerstören
15. Das Auto _____ dem Mechaniker _____.   reparieren

133. Rewrite each of the following sentences, changing the verb from the active to the passive voice.

1. Der Hund beißt das Kind.   _____
2. Das Feuer zerstört das Haus.   _____
3. Meine Freunde trinken den Kaffee. _____
4. Er füttert das Pferd.   _____
5. Der Vater hilft dem Kranken.   _____

Past Tense Passive

The simple past tense of the passive is constructed from the past tense of **werden** plus the past participle of the main verb.

Past passive tense = Past tense of werden + Past participle

Study the following conjugation.

---

ich wurde gefragt	**wir wurden gefragt**
du wurdest gefragt	**ihr wurdet gefragt**
er wurde gefragt	**sie wurden gefragt**

Wir *wurden* **von ihm** *gesehen.*   *We were seen by him.*
Die Geschichte *wurde* **von dem Lehrer** *erzählt.*   *The story was told by the teacher.*
Wann *wurdest* **du** *gefragt?*   *When were you asked?*

134. Rewrite each of the following sentences, changing the present passive tense to the past passive.

1. Wir werden abgeholt.   _____
2. Die Rechnung wird von Renate bezahlt.   _____
3. Wirst du beobachtet?   _____
4. Das Auto wird geparkt.   _____
5. Es wird schon von den Leuten gemacht.   _____
6. Das Museum wird von der Klasse besucht.

_____

7. Das Wort wird von dem Studenten buchstabiert.

_____

8. Ich werde gesehen.   _____
9. Die Maschine wird von dem Mechaniker repariert.

_____

135. Express each of the following sentences in German.

  1. *He was seen.* _____

  2. *The window was opened by Marlene.* _____

  3. *They were asked by their father.* _____

  4. *She was heard.* _____

  5. *It was washed by my aunt.* _____

  6. *We were helped by the boy.* _____

  7. *I was observed.* _____

  8. *The city was destroyed by a bomb.* _____

Compound Tenses

Present Perfect and Past Perfect Passive

The simple present tense and the simple past tense of the auxiliary verb **sein** are used in the formation of the present perfect and the past perfect passive. The past participle of **werden** is **geworden**, but the **ge-** prefix is dropped in these tenses. Thus, the perfect tenses in the passive consist of a form of **sein** plus the past participle of the main verb plus **worden**.

Present perfect passive = Present tense of sein + Past participle of main verb + worden

---

Study the following conjugation.

ich bin gefragt worden	**wir sind gefragt worden**
du bist gefragt worden	**ihr seid gefragt worden**
er ist gefragt worden	**sie sind gefragt worden**

Past perfect passive = Past tense of sein + Past participle of main verb + worden

---

Study the following conjugation.

ich war gefragt worden	**wir waren gefragt worden**
du warst gefragt worden	**ihr wart gefragt worden**
er war gefragt worden	**sie waren gefragt worden**

Das Auto *ist* vom Mechaniker *repariert worden*.	*The car was repaired by the mechanic.*
Ich *bin* von meiner Mutter *gefragt worden*.	*I was asked by my mother.*
Das Haus *war* von meinem Bruder *verkauft worden*.	*The house had been sold by my brother.*

136. Rewrite each of the following sentences, changing the verb to the present perfect tense.

  1. Das Museum wurde 1911 erbaut. _____

  2. Es wurde ihr darüber erzählt. _____

  3. Das Kleid wurde rot gefärbt. _____

  4. Es wurde ihm gegeben. _____

  5. Du wurdest überall gesucht. _____

  6. Ich wurde von ihm gesehen. _____

  7. Er wurde vom Arzt behandelt. _____

Future Tense Passive

The future passive is constructed from the present tense of **werden** plus the past participle of the main verb plus **werden**.

Future passive = Present tense of werden + Past participle of main verb + werden

Study the following conjugation.

ich werde gefragt werden	wir werden gefragt werden
du wirst gefragt werden	ihr werdet gefragt werden
er wird gefragt werden	sie werden gefragt werden

Er *wird* wohl *abgeholt werden.*	*He will probably be picked up.*
Die Möbel *werden* wohl *gebracht werden.*	*The furniture will probably be delivered.*
Ich *werde* **von meinem Freund** *besucht werden.*	*I'll be visited by my friend.*

The future passive is used chiefly to express probability.

If an adverb of time referring to the future occurs in the sentence, the present passive is preferred.

Die Äpfel *werden* **morgen von den Männern** *gepflückt.*	*The apples will be picked by the men tomorrow.*

137. Rewrite each of the following sentences, changing the verb to the future tense and omitting the adverb of time.

1. Das Haus wird nächstes Jahr von meinen Freunden gebaut.

   _____

2. Die Geschichte wird morgen erzählt.

   _____

3. Der Patient wird bald durch Medikamente geheilt.

   _____

4. Das Geschenk wird morgen Abend von den Kindern bewundert.

   _____

5. Die Rechnung wird später von meinem Vater bezahlt.

   _____

6. Der Brief wird morgen geholt.

   _____

7. Das Haus wird am Sonntag beobachtet.

   _____

8. Der Brief wird morgen vom Lehrer geschrieben.

   _____

9. Rudi wird nächsten Monat gefragt.

   _____

10. Franz wird in einer Stunde abgeholt.

    _____

Substitute for the Passive

Passive constructions are not used as frequently in German as they are in English. Especially in spoken German, the active construction is preferred. One common substitute for the passive is an active sentence containing the indefinite pronoun **man** as subject. **Man** can only be used in an active sentence. However, such sentences are often rendered as passive sentences in English. Note that in the following pairs of sentences, the subject of the passive sentence is the direct object in the active sentence.

Passive	**Ich** *bin gesehen worden.*	*I was seen.*
Active	*Man hat* **mich** *gesehen.*	
Passive	**Peter** *wird gefragt.*	*Peter is asked.*
Active	*Man fragt* **Peter.**	

Passive	**Der Wagen *wurde repariert*.**	*The car was repaired.*
Active	**Man *reparierte* den Wagen.**	
Passive	**Das Haus *wird* wohl *verkauft werden*.**	*The house will probably be sold.*
Active	**Man *wird* wohl das Haus *verkaufen*.**	

138. Rewrite each of the following sentences, changing the passive construction to an active construction using **man**.

    1. Die Ruine wird zerstört.   _____
    2. Wir werden angerufen.   _____
    3. Das Essen wird bestellt.   _____
    4. Die Geschichte wurde erzählt.   _____
    5. Der Arzt wurde geholt.   _____
    6. Der Katalog wurde geschickt.   _____
    7. Das Bild ist verkauft worden.   _____
    8. Der Mann ist angerufen worden. _____
    9. Der Brief war geschrieben worden. _____
  10. Die Limonade war getrunken worden. _____
  11. Die Stadt wird wohl aufgebaut werden. _____

Passive Versus False (or Apparent) Passive

In German, unlike in English, a distinction is made between the action itself and the state resulting from the action. The English sentence *it was taken* may express the action or the result of the action. In German, such ambiguity is not possible. The action or process is expressed by the genuine passive, formed by **werden** plus the past participle.

Es *wird* gekocht.	*It is (being) cooked.*
Es *wurde* gezählt.	*It was (being) counted.*

If the German speaker wants to express the result of that action, the verb **sein** plus the past participle is used. Such a construction is referred to as the *false* or *apparent passive*. Note that it describes a state of being rather than a process.

Es *ist* gekocht.	*It is cooked.*
Es *war* gezählt.	*It was counted.*

Compare the following forms of the true passive and the apparent passive.

	PROCESS	RESULT
Present	Es *wird* gebaut.	Es *ist* gebaut.
Simple Past	Es *wurde* gebaut.	Es *war* gebaut.
Present Perfect	Es *ist* gebaut *worden*.	Es *ist* gebaut *gewesen*.
Past Perfect	Es *war* gebaut *worden*.	Es *war* gebaut *gewesen*.
Future	Es *wird* gebaut *werden*.	Es *wird* gebaut.

139. Express each of the following sentences in German, using the genuine passive.

1. *It is found.* _____	6. *It is begun.* _____
2. *It was destroyed.* _____	7. *It will be cut.* _____
3. *It was shown.* _____	8. *It had been built.* _____
4. *It was saved.* _____	9. *It was paid.* _____
5. *It is repaired.* _____	10. *It is said.* _____

140. Express each of the following sentences in German, using the apparent passive.

1. *It is found.* _____
2. *It was destroyed.* _____
3. *It was shown.* _____
4. *It was saved.* _____
5. *It is repaired.* _____

6. *It is begun.* _____
7. *It will be cut.* _____
8. *It had been built.* _____
9. *It was paid.* _____
10. *It is said.* _____

Verbs with Special Meanings

Kennen, wissen, können

The verb *to know* can be expressed in German by three different verbs.

kennen *to know people or things* (**to be acquainted with**)

Hast du ihn gut *gekannt*?	*Did you know him well?*
Ich *kenne* diese Stadt.	*I know this city.*

wissen *to know a fact*

This verb frequently introduces dependent clauses.

Er *wusste* es schon.	*He already knew it.*
Weißt du, wo er wohnt?	*Do you know where he lives?*

können *to know how* (**to have mastered something**)

Er *kann* gut Deutsch.	*He knows German well.*
Ich *habe* die Aufgabe *gekonnt*.	*I knew the lesson.*

141. Complete each of the following sentences, using the appropriate present tense form of **kennen**, **wissen**, or **können**.

1. Seit wann _____ du deinen Freund?
2. Ich _____ die Schauspielerin.
3. Wir _____ auch Englisch.
4. _____ ihr, wo er wohnt?
5. Er _____, dass sie krank ist.
6. Das Mädchen _____ uns nicht.
7. Ich _____, wo er ist.
8. _____ du Deutsch?
9. _____ ihr den Präsidenten?
10. Die Kinder _____, dass ich hier bin.

142. Express each of the following sentences in German.

1. *We know the president.* _____
2. *They know French.* _____
3. *Inge, did you know my aunt?* _____
4. *I know the answer.* _____
5. *He knows everything.* _____

Liegen, sitzen, stehen

These three verbs are used intransitively (that is, they cannot be followed by a direct object). They denote location and, if used with the either/or (accusative/dative) prepositions, are followed by the dative case. All three are strong verbs.

liegen *to lie*

Sie *liegt* stundenlang im Bett.	*She lies in bed for hours.*
Er *hat* unter dem Auto *gelegen.*	*He was lying under the car.*

sitzen *to sit*

Warum *sitzt* du hinter ihr?	*Why are you sitting behind her?*
Er *hat* dort *gesessen.*	*He was sitting there.*

stehen *to stand*

Sie *standen* unter dem Apfelbaum.	*They were standing under the apple tree.*
Sie *steht* vor dem Bild.	*She is standing in front of the picture.*

Legen, setzen, stellen

In contrast to the preceding verbs, these three verbs are followed by the accusative case when used with accusative/dative prepositions. All three are weak verbs and can be used reflexively.

legen, sich legen *to lay, put, lie down*

Ich *habe* es auf den Tisch *gelegt.*	*I put it on the table.*
Er *legte sich* aufs Sofa.	*He lay down on the sofa.*

setzen, sich setzen *to set, sit down*

Sie *setzt* das Baby in den Hochstuhl.	*She sets the baby in the highchair.*
Setz dich auf den Boden!	*Sit down on the floor.*

stellen, sich stellen *to place, put (oneself), stand*

Wer *hat* die Vase auf den Tisch *gestellt?*	*Who put the vase on the table?*
Stell dich neben mich!	*Stand (place yourself) beside me.*

143. Complete each of the following sentences, using the appropriate present tense form of **liegen** or **legen**.

1. Wo _____ das Buch?
2. Ich _____ auf dem Boden.
3. _____ er noch im Bett?
4. Warum _____ du dich nicht aufs Sofa?
5. Anna, _____ die Zeitung auf den Tisch!
6. Wir _____ unter dem Baum.
7. Er _____ das Messer neben den Teller.
8. Ich _____ das Papier auf den Tisch.

144. Complete each of the following sentences, using the appropriate present tense form of **sitzen** or **setzen**.

1. Er _____ sich vor Günther.
2. Wo _____ ihr?

3. Ich _____ mich ins Auto.
4. Peter _____ sich neben seine Tante.
5. Wohin _____ du dich?
6. Ich _____ auf dem Sofa.
7. Er _____ neben dem Mädchen.
8. _____ du in der Küche?

145. Complete each of the following sentences, using the appropriate present tense form of **stehen** or **stellen**.

1. Die Leute _____ an der Haltestelle.
2. Wohin _____ Mutter die Vase?
3. Ich _____ mich hinter Martin.
4. _____ du dich neben den Jungen?
5. Ich _____ den Teller auf den Tisch.
6. Wo _____ dein Freund?
7. Wir _____ den Stuhl ins Zimmer.
8. _____ du vor dem Auto?

Lassen

The verb **lassen** can be used with or without a dependent infinitive. When it is used without a dependent infinitive, it has the meaning *to leave (something in some place)*. The past participle is prefixed with **ge-** in this case.

Ich *lasse* den Hund zu Hause.	*I leave the dog at home.*
Er *hat* sein Auto in der Garage *gelassen*.	*He left his car in the garage.*

When **lassen** is used with a dependent infinitive, it means *to let, allow (someone to do something)*. In this case, the double infinitive construction is used in the compound tenses.

Bitte *lasst* ihn doch *gehen*!	*Please let him go.*
Er *hat* mich *mitkommen lassen*.	*He allowed me to come along.*

146. Complete each of the following sentences, using the appropriate present tense form of **lassen** to express the verb phrase on the right.

1. Wir _____ die Kinder dort. *leave*
2. Er _____ Irene hier _____. *allow to live*
3. Herr Weiß, bitte _____ Sie Marianne _____! *let go*
4. Ich _____ Herbert _____. *let sing*
5. _____ du das Auto in der Garage? *leave*
6. Frau Hauptmann _____ ihre Tochter _____. *allow to call*
7. Thomas, _____ den Mantel hier! *leave*
8. Ich _____ die Tasche zu Hause. *leave*

147. Rewrite each of the following sentences, changing the verb to the present perfect tense.

1. Wir lassen die Kinder spielen. _____
2. Er lässt das Fahrrad dort. _____
3. Lässt du die Jacke zu Hause? _____
4. Sie lassen uns mitmachen. _____
5. Rudi lässt Inge mitmachen. _____
6. Ich lasse die Katze im Garten. _____

CHAPTER 8

Negative Words and Constructions

Negation

In German, negation is most commonly expressed by the negative adverb **nicht**. The word **nicht** can be used to negate an entire sentence or an individual element within a sentence.

Nicht in Final Position

Nicht always *follows* these four elements.

    (1) The inflected form of the verb (the form with the personal ending)
    (2) Noun objects (direct or indirect objects)
    (3) Pronoun objects (direct or indirect objects)
    (4) Adverbs of definite time

    Study the examples below. Note that in each example in this chapter, the sentence is first presented in the affirmative and then negated.

Subject + Verb

Sie liest.	Sie liest *nicht*.
Anton fragte.	Anton fragte *nicht*.

Subject + Verb + Direct object (noun or pronoun)

Wir besuchten die Dame.	Wir besuchten die Dame *nicht*.
Gisela holte es.	Gisela holte es *nicht*.
Wir freuten uns.	Wir freuten uns *nicht*.

Subject + Verb + Direct object (pronoun) + Indirect object (noun or pronoun)

Sie gab es dem Kind.	Sie gab es dem Kind *nicht*.
Ich erklärte es ihr.	Ich erklärte es ihr *nicht*.

Subject + Verb + Indirect object (noun or pronoun) + Direct object (noun)

Ich gab dem Jungen die Birne.	Ich gab dem Jungen die Birne *nicht*.
Werner kaufte ihr die Vase.	Werner kaufte ihr die Vase *nicht*.

Subject + Verb + Objects + Adverb of time

Er besuchte uns heute.	**Er besuchte uns heute** *nicht*.

1. Rewrite each of the following sentences in the negative.

    1. Er kennt den Herrn.   _____

    2. Wir geben es den Leuten.   _____

    3. Ich wasche mich.   _____

    4. Heinz weiß es.   _____

    5. Sie kamen vorgestern.   _____

    6. Ich kaufe den Mantel.   _____

    7. Sie nimmt es.   _____

Nicht Preceding Certain Other Elements in the Sentence

Nicht *precedes* most other elements.

    (1) Predicate adjectives
    (2) Predicate nouns
    (3) Separable prefixes
    (4) Noninflected verb forms (past participles in compound tenses, dependent infinitives, double infinitives)
    (5) Adverbs (except those of definite time)
    (6) Prepositional phrases

Predicate adjectives and nouns

Er ist krank.	**Er ist** *nicht* **krank.**
Das sind meine Kinder.	**Das sind** *nicht* **meine Kinder.**

Separable prefixes

Das Flugzeug flog ab.	**Das Flugzeug flog** *nicht* **ab.**

Past participles

Sie sind gefahren.	**Sie sind** *nicht* **gefahren.**

Dependent infinitives

Wir hören sie lachen.	**Wir hören sie** *nicht* **lachen.**
Ich darf kommen.	**Ich darf** *nicht* **kommen.**
Ich hoffe, es zu sehen.	**Ich hoffe, es** *nicht* **zu sehen.**

Double infinitives

Er hat es machen wollen.	**Er hat es** *nicht* **machen wollen.**

Adverbs of place or prepositional phrases

Er wohnte hier.	**Er wohnte** *nicht* **hier.**
Wir sind im Wohnzimmer.	**Wir sind** *nicht* **im Wohnzimmer.**
Ich freue mich darauf.	**Ich freue mich** *nicht* **darauf.**

When a past participle and a prepositional phrase or adverb of place occur in the same sentence, **nicht** precedes the prepositional phrase or adverb of place.

Ich habe im Sand gelegen.	**Ich habe** *nicht* **im Sand gelegen.**
Er war zu Hause gewesen.	**Er war** *nicht* **zu Hause gewesen.**
Sie hat dort gespielt.	**Sie hat** *nicht* **dort gespielt.**

Nicht in Dependent Clauses

Since German word order requires the inflected form of the verb to be in final position in a dependent clause (see exceptions on pages 199 and 257), **nicht** must precede the verb or verb combination at the end of a dependent clause.

Ich weiß, dass er arbeitet.	**Ich weiß, dass er *nicht* arbeitet.**
Sie sagt, dass er kommen kann.	**Sie sagt, dass er *nicht* kommen kann.**
Ich hoffe, dass er es gesehen hat.	**Ich hoffe, dass er es *nicht* gesehen hat.**

2. Rewrite each of the following sentences in the negative.

1. Sie haben gespielt. _____
2. Ich wollte die Rechnung bezahlen. _____
3. Wir haben sie schreien hören. _____
4. Maria hat neben dem Hotel gewartet. _____
5. Ich weiß, dass er fliegen will. _____
6. Das ist meine Tante. _____
7. Er sagt, dass er sie gesucht hätte. _____
8. Das Mädchen fährt heim. _____
9. Wir sind zur Schule gegangen. _____
10. Ich bin dort geblieben. _____
11. Wir sind im Kino. _____
12. Ich sehe sie kommen. _____
13. Er kommt mit. _____
14. Ihr könnt es sehen. _____
15. Sie sind reich. _____
16. Er hat hier gewartet. _____
17. Wir haben es geholt. _____
18. Das sind meine Bücher. _____
19. Ich hoffe, Inge zu sehen. _____
20. Du hast sie genommen. _____

Nicht with sondern

As noted above, when **nicht** is used to negate a specific sentence element, it precedes the element it negates. In this case, **nicht** is often followed by a clause introduced by the coordinating conjunction **sondern** *but rather, but on the contrary.* (See Chapter 10.) Note that **sondern** is used only if the first clause is negated *and* a contrast is stated. Note also that whenever the two clauses share any of the same elements, it is not necessary to repeat these elements.

Sie raucht *nicht* Zigaretten, *sondern* Zigarren.	*She doesn't smoke cigarettes, but cigars.*
Er hat *nicht* sie besucht, *sondern* ihre Schwester.	*He didn't visit her, but her sister.*
Sie singt *nicht*, *sondern* spielt die Gitarre.	*She doesn't sing, but plays the guitar.*
Sie geht *nicht* ins Kino, *sondern* ins Theater.	*She's not going to the movies, but to the theater.*

3. Rewrite each of the following sentences in the negative, placing **nicht** in the appropriate position. Take your cue from the clause introduced by **sondern**. Follow the model.

MODEL   Er hat das Flugzeug gesehen.   <u>Er hat das Flugzeug nicht gesehen</u>, sondern gehört.

1. Sie ist bei ihrer Tante geblieben.

   _____, sondern bei ihrer Schwester.

2. Er hat das Auto repariert.

   _____, sondern das Fahrrad.

3. Wir haben das rote Buch gekauft.

_____, sondern das blaue.

4. Ich brauche den Löffel.

_____, sondern das Messer.

5. Ihr habt das Radio gewonnen.

_____, sondern gestohlen.

6. Ich lese die Zeitung.

_____, sondern den Roman.

Nicht with Interrogative

The rules for negation with **nicht** also apply to the position of **nicht** in a negative interrogative construction.

Arbeitest du?	**Arbeitest du *nicht*?**
Gehst du mit?	**Gehst du *nicht* mit?**
Hast du ihn dort kennengelernt?	**Hast du ihn *nicht* dort kennengelernt?**

4. Rewrite each of the following questions in the negative.

1. Habt ihr ihnen geholfen? _____
2. Sind sie abgefahren? _____
3. Holt sie es? _____
4. Macht sie mit? _____
5. Darfst du bleiben? _____
6. Hast du ihn gefragt? _____
7. Ist das dein Freund? _____
8. Hast du mitgesungen? _____
9. Rasiert er sich? _____
10. Hat sie es vergessen? _____
11. Willst du ihm helfen? _____
12. War das seine Frau? _____
13. Ist sie schön? _____
14. Kaufst du die Blumen? _____
15. Kann er sich daran erinnern? _____

Answering Affirmative and Negative Questions (ja, doch)

When the answer to an affirmative question is affirmative, **ja** is used.

Fährst du nach Hause?	***Ja,* ich fahre nach Hause.**
Kann sie lesen?	***Ja,* sie kann lesen.**

When the answer to an affirmative question is negative, **nein** is used.

Fährst du nach Hause?	***Nein,* ich fahre nicht nach Hause.**
Kann sie lesen?	***Nein,* sie kann nicht lesen.**

When the answer to a negative question is affirmative, **doch** is used instead of **ja**.

Fährst du *nicht* nach Hause?	***Doch,* ich fahre nach Hause.**
Kann sie *nicht* lesen?	***Doch,* sie kann lesen.**

5. Answer each of the following questions, using **ja** or **doch**.

1. War er krank? _____
2. Ist er nicht gestorben? _____
3. Hast du es gekonnt? _____
4. Braucht ihr es nicht? _____
5. Hat er es nicht gefressen? _____
6. Ist sie nicht intelligent? _____

The Negative Form of brauchen

To express *not to have to,* the negative form of **brauchen** (**brauchen** plus **nicht zu** plus infinitive) is usually preferred to the negative form of **müssen**. (See Chapter 7, pages 201–202).

Muss er hier bleiben?	**Nein, er *braucht nicht* hier *zu* bleiben.**
Muss er Cornelia helfen?	**Nein, er *braucht* Cornelia *nicht zu* helfen.**

6. Rewrite each of the following sentences in the negative.

1. Sie muss kommen. _____
2. Hans muss schreiben. _____
3. Ihr müsst abfahren. _____
4. Wir müssen gehen. _____
5. Ich muss studieren. _____
6. Sie müssen arbeiten. _____
7. Wir müssen springen. _____
8. Du musst den Roman lesen. _____

Other Negative Words

The following negatives follow the same rules for position that apply to **nicht**.

gar nicht *not at all*

   Das ist *gar nicht* teuer.   *That is not at all expensive.*

nicht mehr *no more, no longer, not anymore*

   Sie wohnen *nicht mehr* hier.   *They don't live here anymore.*

nie *never*

   Er hilft uns *nie*.   *He never helps us.*

noch nicht *not yet*

   Wir haben uns *noch nicht* umgezogen.   *We haven't changed (our clothes) yet.*

noch nie *not ever, never*

   Wir waren *noch nie* dort.   *We were never there.*

7. Rewrite each of the following sentences, adding the German equivalent of the English word or phrase on the right.

1. Er fragt uns. _____ *never*
2. Wir sind müde. _____ *not at all*

3. Sie wohnt in Bonn.   _____   *no longer*
4. Ich kann fahren.   _____   *not yet*
5. Er hat sie gesehen.   _____   *not ever*
6. Er hilft.   _____   *never*
7. Sie geht ins Kino.   _____   *no more*
8. Er war in Deutschland.   _____   *not ever*
9. Wir sind nach Hause geflogen. _____   *not yet*
10. Sie sind freundlich.   _____   *not at all*
11. Ich habe Schnecken gegessen. _____   *not ever*
12. Er kennt mich.   _____   *no longer*
13. Sie lernte den Präsidenten kennen. _____   *never*
14. Wir machen mit.   _____   *not at all*
15. Er hat die Sammlung verkauft. _____   *not yet*

The Negative Article kein-

Kein- *no, not any, not a* precedes a noun object or a predicate noun. It is used when the noun in the affirmative statement has an indefinite article or no article. **Kein** takes the same endings as the indefinite article (**ein** words). (See Chapter 5.)

Er hat einen Bruder.   **Er hat *keinen* Bruder.**
Wir trinken Milch.   **Wir trinken *keine* Milch.**

When the noun in the affirmative is preceded by a definite article, a "**der**" word, or a possessive adjective, the negative **nicht** is used instead.

Dieses Bier schmeckt gut.   **Dieses Bier schmeckt *nicht* gut.**
Meine Tochter ist hier.   **Meine Tochter ist *nicht* hier.**
Der Hund bellt.   **Der Hund bellt *nicht*.**

8. Rewrite each of the following sentences in the negative, using **kein-** or **nicht**.

1. Er erzählte ein Märchen.   _____
2. Wir besuchten eine bekannte Stadt. _____
3. Er hat unser Kind gesehen.   _____
4. Hat sie Blumen gekauft?   _____
5. Trinkt er Wasser?   _____
6. Ich habe einen warmen Mantel.   _____
7. Das sind Haselnüsse.   _____
8. Ich habe mich auf die Ferien gefreut. _____
9. Wir essen Bananen.   _____
10. Ich habe einen Freund.   _____
11. Ich kenne den Herrn.   _____
12. Sie singt das Lied.   _____
13. Er hat Kinder.   _____
14. Dieser Ring ist teuer.   _____
15. Hier liegt ein Buch.   _____
16. Wer isst Brot?   _____
17. Das ist ein Tachometer.   _____
18. Die Lehrerin schreibt.   _____
19. Ist die Milch sauer?   _____
20. Ich habe Zeit.   _____

The Pronouns nichts, niemand

Nichts *nothing* and **niemand** *nobody* are used only in the singular. **Nichts** has no endings, and no endings are required for **niemand**. Note, however, that endings are sometimes used with **niemand**, e.g., **Ich habe niemanden gesehen. Nichts** can be followed by a neuter adjective used as a noun.

Er hat *nichts* **gekauft.**	*He bought nothing.*
Er gab mir *nichts* **Kostbares.**	*He gave me nothing valuable.*
Ich kenne *niemand.*	*I know nobody.*

9. Express each of the following sentences in German.

1. *He can see nothing.* _____
2. *Nobody helps us.* _____
3. *I have nothing old.* _____
4. *They know nothing.* _____
5. *He asks nobody.* _____

CHAPTER 9

Interrogative Words and Constructions

General Questions

Formation of Questions by Inversion

General questions are questions that can be answered by **ja** *yes* or **nein** *no*. This type of question is formed by simply *inverting the subject and the verb* of a declarative sentence so that the verb is in first position. No interrogative word or phrase is used in forming this type of question. In German, any subject-verb combination may be inverted to form a general question.

Compare the following patterns.

Statement = Subject + Verb (+ Remainder of sentence).

S	+ V	(+ remainder of sentence).
Das Kind	**kommt**	**(nach Hause).**

General question = Verb + Subject (+ Remainder of sentence)?

V	+ S	(+ remainder of sentence)?
Kommt	**das Kind**	**(nach Hause)?**

NOTE: In English, a general question usually requires the use of an auxiliary verb (such as *to do, to be,* e.g., *Does she sing?, Is he going too?*), whereas in the German simple tenses (simple present, simple past), the main verb is used by itself to introduce such questions (**Singt sie?, Kommt er auch?**). In the German compound tenses, however, it is the auxiliary verb (i.e., the verb form with a personal ending) that is inverted and put in first position to introduce a general question.

Simple Tenses

STATEMENT	QUESTION
Robert reparierte das Auto.	*Reparierte* **Robert das Auto?**
Horst, du bist krank.	**Horst,** *bist* **du krank?**
Sie fährt auch mit.	*Fährt* **sie auch mit?**
Konrad kann Deutsch.	*Kann* **Konrad Deutsch?**

1. Rewrite each of the following statements as questions.

    1. Er kommt morgen. _____

    2. Herbert bringt es zurück. _____

3. Er setzte sich aufs Bett. _____

4. Du weißt alles. _____

5. Die Männer arbeiteten viel. _____

6. Ihr braucht es. _____

7. Ihr amüsiert euch. _____

8. Petra bestellte auch Bier. _____

9. Die Touristen besichtigen das Schloss. _____

10. Er will nicht. _____

11. Du hörst nichts. _____

12. Sie muss in die Stadt. _____

13. Sie bleiben dort. _____

14. Er rauchte viel. _____

15. Du schwimmst nicht. _____

Compound Tenses and Dependent Infinitives

In compound tenses, the subject and the auxiliary verb bearing a personal ending are inverted to form a question. In sentences containing dependent infinitives, the modal or similarly used verb, such as **hören**, **sehen**, **helfen**, **lassen**, is inverted with the subject. The dependent infinitive is in final position in questions.

STATEMENT	QUESTION
Er würde helfen.	*Würde* **er** *helfen*?
Robert, du hast es gesehen.	**Robert,** *hast* **du es** *gesehen*?
Ihr hättet gelesen.	*Hättet* **ihr** *gelesen*?
Sie hat sich niedergesetzt.	*Hat* **sie sich** *niedergesetzt*?
Du kannst es machen.	*Kannst* **du es** *machen*?
Sie sehen ihren Vater kommen.	*Sehen* **sie ihren Vater** *kommen*?

2. Rewrite each of the following sentences as a question.

1. Er hat schon geschrieben. _____

2. Sie haben sich gestern kennengelernt. _____

3. Ihr habt alles verloren. _____

4. Sie wird es aufmachen. _____

5. Du darfst es nehmen. _____

6. Er hat sich verletzt. _____

7. Ihr werdet euch umziehen. _____

8. Du hättest es gekauft. _____

9. Er ist gestorben. _____

10. Sie können nicht dort bleiben. _____

11. Du lässt Peter helfen. _____

12. Sie sieht die Kinder spielen. _____

Use of doch in Answer to Negative Questions

In the answer to a negative question, **doch** is used instead of **ja**. **Doch** is stressed when used this way. (See page 235.)

Hast du *kein* **Buch?**	*Doch,* **natürlich habe ich ein Buch.**
Könnt ihr *nicht* **lesen?**	*Doch,* **wir können lesen.**
Bist du *nicht* **krank?**	*Doch,* **ich bin krank.**

3. Write the question for each of the following answers. Follow the model.

MODEL ___Kannst du nicht schwimmen?___ Doch, ich kann schwimmen.

1. _____ Doch, er ist hier.
2. _____ Doch, ich fahre mit.
3. _____ Doch, wir dürfen nach Bonn fahren.
4. _____ Doch, ich komme mit.
5. _____ Doch, sie hilft den Kindern.

Specific Questions

Specific questions are questions that ask for specific information. In both English and German, this type of question is introduced by an interrogative word or phrase that seeks information about time, manner, place, or cause (as well as who or what may be the actor or the recipient of some action).

Interrogative Adverbs and Adverbial Expressions

When a question is introduced by an adverb or an adverbial expression, the subject and verb are also inverted. However, in this case the verb is not in first position in the sentence, but is in second position following the interrogative adverb or adverbial expression that introduces the question.

Compare the following patterns.

Statement = Subject + Verb (+ Remainder of sentence).

S	+ V	(+ remainder of sentence).
Das Kind	**kommt**	**(nach Hause).**

Specific question = Interrogative + Verb + Subject (+ Remainder of sentence)?

I	+ V	+ S	(+ remainder of sentence)?
Wann	**kommt**	**das Kind**	**(nach Hause)?**
Warum	**kommt**	**das Kind**	**(nach Hause)?**
Wie	**kommt**	**das Kind**	**(nach Hause)?**
Um wie viel Uhr	**kommt**	**das Kind**	**(nach Hause)?**

The following interrogative adverbs are used to introduce questions.

Wann?	*When?*	**Wie oft?**	*How often?*
Warum?	*Why?*	**Wie viel?**	*How much? How many?*
Wie?	*How?*	**Wie viele?**	*How many?*
Wie lange?	*How long?*	**Um wie viel Uhr?**	*At what time?*

Wann kommt der Zug an?	*When is the train arriving?*
Warum hast du nichts gesagt?	*Why didn't you say anything?*
Wie ist das Wetter?	*How is the weather?*
Wie lange bleibst du dort?	*How long are you staying there?*
Wie oft besuchst du sie?	*How often do you visit her?*
Wie viel kostet es?	*How much does it cost?*
Wie viel (Wie viele) Hunde habt ihr?	*How many dogs do you have?*
Um wie viel Uhr kommst du?	*At what time are you coming?*

Wie viel or wie viele

Wie viel *how much* is used in specific questions and before singular nouns; **wie viele** *how many* is used before plural nouns.

Wie viel **kostet das?**	*How much does that cost?*
Wie viel **Zeit hast du?**	*How much time do you have?*
Wie viel **Geld hast du?**	*How much money do you have?*
Wie viele **Kinder sind hier?**	*How many children are here?*
Wie viele **Äpfel hast du gegessen?**	*How many apples did you eat?*

NOTE: In colloquial speech, one often hears **wie viel** when, strictly speaking, one would expect to hear **wie viele**.

Wie viel (Wie viele) **Planeten gibt es?**	*How many planets are there?*
Wie viel (Wie viele) **Katzen hast du?**	*How many cats do you have?*

4. Complete each of the following questions, using the appropriate interrogative adverb or adverbial expression.

 1. Sie fliegt morgen ab. _____ fliegt sie ab?
 2. Peter ist klug. _____ ist Peter?
 3. Er besucht uns dreimal die Woche. _____ besucht er uns?
 4. Der Film war lang. _____ war der Film?
 5. Ich habe zehn Minuten gewartet. _____ hast du gewartet?
 6. Das Hemd kostet zehn Mark. _____ kostet das Hemd?
 7. Er heißt Hans. _____ heißt er?
 8. Ich habe es dreimal gesehen. _____ hast du es gesehen?
 9. Ich bleibe eine Woche dort. _____ bleibst du dort?
10. Er kommt um drei Uhr. _____ kommt er?
11. Sie ist am Nachmittag gekommen. _____ ist sie gekommen?
12. Wir kommen nächste Woche. _____ kommt ihr?
13. Ich komme nicht, weil ich krank bin. _____ kommst du nicht?
14. Wir treffen Johann um zehn Uhr. _____ trefft ihr Johann?

Wo, wohin, woher

In German, there are three different interrogatives to ask about place: **wo**, **wohin**, **woher**. These words are *not* interchangeable; each has its own distinct meaning.

The interrogative **wo** asks about *location* (*in what place?*). Normally, **wo** is used when there is no movement (or only movement or activity within a place). The answer usually contains a preposition followed by the dative case.

Wo **seid ihr?**	**Wir sind in der Schule.**
Wo **wandert er?**	**Er wandert im Wald.**
Wo **ist das Buch?**	**Es liegt auf dem Tisch.**

The interrogative **wohin** asks about *destination* or *direction* (*to what place?*). **Wohin** expresses movement to or toward a place. The answer usually contains a preposition followed by the accusative case.

Wohin **geht ihr?**	**Wir gehen ins Theater.**
Wohin **fahren wir?**	**Wir fahren in die Stadt.**

The interrogative **woher** asks about *origin* (*from what place?*).

Woher **kommst du?**	**Ich komme aus dem Wald.**
Woher **kommst du?**	**Ich komme aus den USA.**

NOTE: Although modern English uses the word *where* for all of these situations, earlier English made the same distinctions as German (*where, whence = from where, whither = to where*).

5. Complete each of the following questions with **wo**, **wohin**, or **woher**.

1. Bärbel ist in Düsseldorf. _____ ist Bärbel?
2. Ich komme aus Zürich. _____ kommst du?
3. Wir fahren nach England. _____ fahrt ihr?
4. Er kommt von seiner Großmutter. _____ kommt er?
5. Wir gehen ins Kino. _____ geht ihr?
6. Wir sind in der Küche. _____ seid ihr?
7. Therese kommt aus Deutschland. _____ kommt Therese?
8. Anna läuft ins Geschäft. _____ läuft Anna?

Review

6. Form a question that elicits the bold elements in the each of the following responses, using the appropriate interrogative word. Follow the model.

MODEL ____Wann kommt Anna?____ Anna kommt **morgen**.

1. _____ Sie fährt **nach Kanada**.
2. _____ Sie bringen es **übermorgen**.
3. _____ Alexander besuchte uns **dreimal**.
4. _____ Heute ist es **heiß**.
5. _____ Sie ist **in Holland**.
6. _____ Ella kommt **aus München**.
7. _____ Sie bleiben **drei Monate** dort.
8. _____ Es kostet **zehn Mark**.

Interrogative Pronouns

Wer, wen, wem, wessen

The interrogative pronoun **wer** *who* is used in questions that refer to people. **Wer** takes the same case endings as the definite article **der**. Study the following forms.

Nominative	**Wer?**	*Who?*
Accusative	**Wen?**	*Whom?*
Dative	**Wem?**	*Whom?*
Genitive	**Wessen?**	*Whose?*

NOTE: There are no plural forms of these interrogative pronouns. The answer, however, may be in the singular or the plural.

Wer kommt?	*Who is coming?*
Wen hast du gesehen?	*Whom did you see?*
Für wen kaufst du es?	*For whom are you buying it?*
Wem gehört die Kamera?	*To whom does the camera belong?*
Bei wem bleibst du?	*With whom are you staying?*
Wessen Mantel ist das?	*Whose coat is that?*

Was

The interrogative pronoun **was** is used in questions that refer to things, ideas, or actions. The form **was** is the same for the nominative and the accusative. There are no dative or genitive singular forms, and there is no plural. The answer, however, may be in the singular or the plural.

Was ist das?	*What is that?*
Was machst du?	*What are you doing?*

7. Complete each of the following questions, using the appropriate interrogative pronoun.

1. _____ hat er dir gegeben?
2. _____ bringst du Blumen?
3. _____ habt ihr gegessen?
4. Bei _____ hast du gewohnt?
5. _____ arbeitet dort?
6. Mit _____ gehst du?
7. _____ besucht ihr?
8. _____ Wagen ist das?
9. Für _____ machst du das?
10. Von _____ hast du das?

11. _____ hast du geholfen?
12. _____ habt ihr getroffen?
13. _____ kann das machen?
14. _____ hat sie gedankt?
15. _____ Hut liegt dort?
16. Zu _____ geht ihr?
17. Gegen _____ bist du?
18. _____ Buch ist das?
19. _____ sagte er?
20. _____ tust du?

Wo-compounds

The interrogative pronoun **was** is usually avoided after dative and accusative prepositions. Instead, **wo(r)-** is prefixed to the preposition to form the question. (See Chapter 3.)

Worauf wartest du?	*What are you waiting for?*
Wovor fürchten Sie sich?	*What are you afraid of?*
Wofür interessierst du dich?	*What are you interested in?*

Wo-compounds can be used with all accusative and dative prepositions except **entlang, ohne, außer, gegenüber, seit, hinter, neben, zwischen**.

Wo-compounds cannot refer to people. The interrogative pronouns must be used in such cases.

An wen erinnerst du dich?	**An Hedwig.**
Woran erinnerst du dich?	**An letzten Sommer.**

8. Complete each of the following questions, using the appropriate interrogative pronoun, preposition plus interrogative pronoun, or **wo**-compound. Take your cue from the phrase on the right.

1. _____ sprecht ihr?   von dem Sportwagen
2. _____ repariert er?   die Uhr
3. _____ fahrt ihr?   mit dem Zug
4. _____ habt ihr gefragt?   Herrn Böll
5. _____ habt ihr gefragt?   nach dem Weg
6. _____ brauchst du Geld?   für die Karten
7. _____ hofft er?   Auf gutes Wetter
8. _____ hast du das gekauft?   für Susi
9. _____ wundert er sich?   über Ursula
10. _____ brauchst du?   den Schlüssel
11. _____ sprecht ihr?   mit Frau Kröger
12. _____ interessiert er sich?   für moderne Musik
13. _____ liegt es?   in der Schachtel
14. _____ brauchst du das?   zum Reparieren
15. _____ setzt du dich?   hinter die dicke Dame

Welch- *which, which one*

The interrogative **welch-** may be used attributively as an interrogative adjective or as an interrogative pronoun. **Welch-** takes the same endings as the definite article (**der** words). All forms in both the singular and the plural are used.

Interrogative Adjective	Interrogative Pronoun
Welches Haus gehört euch?	*Welches* möchtest du haben?
Welchen Wein hat er getrunken?	*Welchen* hat sie gekauft?
Mit *welchem* Auto wollen wir fahren?	Aus *welchem* ist sie gestiegen?
Welche Blumen soll ich abschneiden?	*Welche* kann er bringen?

9. Complete each of the following questions, using the appropriate form of **welch-**.

1. _____ Kinder haben es genommen?
2. Bei _____ Leuten seid ihr geblieben?
3. Nach _____ Straße hat er gefragt?
4. _____ Teppich habt ihr gekauft?
5. Mit _____ Studentin kommst du zusammen?
6. Für _____ Roman interessierst du dich?
7. Aus _____ Land kommt er?
8. _____ Buch gehört dir?
9. In _____ Haus wohnen Sie?
10. _____ Blume gefällt dir?
11. _____ Wagen ist kaputt?
12. _____ Kette hat er gekauft?

10. Complete each of the following questions, using the appropriate form of the interrogative pronoun **welch-** and taking your cue from the statement that precedes. Follow the model.

MODEL   Hier sind schöne Äpfel. __Welchen__ möchtest du haben?

1. Dort sind viele Hunde. _____ gehört dir?
2. Ich habe zwei Autos. Mit _____ möchtest du fahren?
3. Wir besuchen unsere Tanten. Für _____ kaufst du ein Geschenk?
4. Dort sind viele Taschen. _____ gehört dir?
5. Dort liegen viele Bleistifte. _____ brauchst du?

11. Rewrite each of the following questions, changing the form of **welch-** from singular to plural.

1. Welches nimmst du?   _____
2. Welche hat er gekauft?   _____
3. Von welcher erzählt er?   _____
4. Welchen brauchst du?   _____
5. Für welche kauft er es?   _____

Interrogative Adjective

Was für ein- *what kind of* is usually used as an interrogative adjective. In the singular, the indefinite article **ein-** takes adjective endings, which are determined by how the following noun is used grammatically in the sentence. **Für** does not act as a preposition in these expressions. In the plural, the expression is **was für**.

Was für eine Maschine habt ihr gekauft?	Eine Drehmaschine.
Mit was für einem Herrn hast du gesprochen?	Mit einem alten Herrn.
Was für Leute sind das?	Das sind Touristen.

12. Express each of the following questions in German.

1. *What kind of car is that?*   _____
2. *What kind of girl is that?*   _____
3. *With what kind of people does he go to Germany?*   _____
4. *In what kind of house do they live?*   _____
5. *What kind of books does he write?*   _____

CHAPTER 10

Word Order and Conjunctions

Word Order

There are four basic sentence types in German, each with its own characteristic word order. These basic sentence types are the following.

(1) Declarative sentences (statements)
(2) Interrogative sentences (questions)
(3) Imperative sentences (commands)
(4) Exclamatory sentences (exclamations)

In general, word order in German is more flexible than in English. This is possible because German contains many grammatical clues, such as case, gender, and verb endings, that permit one to analyze the relationships between the words of a sentence without having to depend primarily on word order. English, which in most cases lacks these grammatical markers, depends more on word order to clarify the relationships between the words of a sentence.

Although in some respects there is more flexibility in German word order, there are nonetheless cardinal rules for word order that must be followed in forming sentences.

Statements
Regular Word Order (S + V)

The regular word order used in declarative sentences in German is as follows.

Statement (regular word order) = Subject + Verb (+ Other sentence parts).

Simple Tenses

In statements in the simple present or simple past tense, the verb is in second position, preceded by the subject and followed by the objects and other sentence parts. The subject may be a noun, pronoun, or other noun phrase. Words such as **danke**, **ja**, **nein**, **doch** do not affect word order.

SUBJECT	CONJUGATED VERB	OTHER SENTENCE PARTS
Der Mann	ist	**unser Lehrer.**
Die Erde	dreht	**sich um die Sonne.**
Ja, mein kleiner Bruder	gab	**ihm das Buch.**

Compound Tenses

In statements containing compound tenses, the conjugated verb (the verb form with a personal ending) or the auxiliary is in second position. The dependent infinitive, the double infinitive, or the past participle is in final position, preceded by the other sentence parts.

SUBJECT	CONJUGATED VERB	OTHER SENTENCE PARTS	INFINITIVE(S) OR PAST PARTICIPLE(S)
Inge	wird	ihm	helfen.
Meine Eltern	wollten	sich einen Ofen	kaufen.
Ich	habe	es ihr	zeigen wollen.
Seine Schwester	hat	ihm gestern das Buch	gekauft.
Das rote Auto	wurde	von ihm	gestohlen.

Separable Prefixes

Simple Tenses

In simple tenses, the prefix is separated from the verb and occurs in final position.

SUBJECT	CONJUGATED VERB	OTHER SENTENCE PARTS	PREFIX
Wir	gehen	jeden Sonntag	spazieren.
Die Studenten	kamen	mit dem Zug	an.

Compound Tenses

In compound tenses, the prefix is attached to the verb and occurs in final or next-to-final position.

SUBJECT	CONJUGATED VERB	OTHER SENTENCE PARTS	INFINITIVE(S) OR PAST PARTICIPLE(S)
Er	wird	bald	heimgehen.
Ich	habe	das Geschenk	aufmachen dürfen.
Der Junge	ist	gestern Abend	weggelaufen.

1. Form a sentence from each of the following groups of words, beginning with the subject.

1. vor einer Stunde / der Schnellzug / angekommen / ist _____
2. bei uns / bleibt / Norma _____
3. mitmachen / will / der kleine Junge _____
4. von ihm / wurde / zurückgebracht / die Goldkette _____
5. wir / ihn / können / haben / sehen _____
6. mit Klaus / Gerda / geht / spazieren _____
7. den Jungen / der Hund / beißt _____
8. es / ich / habe / dürfen / kaufen _____
9. die Geschichte / wird / er / erzählen _____
10. er / mich / kommen / sieht _____

2. Rewrite each of the following sentences, using the present perfect tense of the verb.

1. Sie mussten schneller laufen. _____
2. Wir machten die Schachtel auf. _____
3. Er wollte nicht heimgehen. _____
4. Ich wollte es ihm zeigen. _____
5. Seine Großeltern brachten es mit. _____
6. Mein Vater ließ mich gehen. _____
7. Er konnte gut singen. _____
8. Der Alte setzte sich auf die Bank. _____
9. Der Zug fuhr vor einer Stunde ab. _____

Inverted Word Order (X + V + S)

Simple Tenses

As noted above, German word order is in some respects quite flexible, and it is not required that the subject be the first component of a sentence. For special emphasis, the direct object, the indirect object, an adverb, a prepositional phrase, or any other logical element can be placed in first position, which is here denoted by X. However, when the subject is no longer the first element in a declarative sentence, the regular S + V word order changes, as follows.

Statement (inverted word order) = X + Verb + Subject (+ Other sentence parts).

Note that although the conjugated verb remains in second position, the order of the subject and verb is inverted, and the subject is followed by any other sentence parts that may be present.

Compound Tenses

If the verb is in a compound tense, the conjugated form of the auxiliary verb is in second position and the past participle, dependent infinitive, or double infinitive is in final position.

In the case of separable prefix verbs, the separable prefix is attached to the verb stem in the infinitive and past participle (see Chapter 7). The separable prefix form is placed in final position, just like any other past participle or infinitive.

It is important to remember that the X element can be of any length. It can be a single word, a prepositional phrase, a dependent clause, or even a combination of long and involved dependent clauses. However, *no matter how long or short this X element is, the subject and the verb of the main clause that follows must be inverted.*

ANY ELEMENT	CONJUGATED VERB	SUBJECT	OTHER SENTENCE PARTS
Vor zwei Tagen	reiste	**mein Freund**	nach Indien.
Trotz des Regens	sind	**wir**	mit ihm ausgegangen.
Dadurch	wollte	**er**	viel Geld gewinnen.
Nach dem Essen	will	**sie**	abfahren.
Wie immer	hat	**sie**	ihn warten lassen.
Wenn ich Zeit hätte,	besuchte	**ich**	sie.
Weil sie krank war,	kam	**sie**	nicht.

Thus, the X element can be as simple as **gestern** *yesterday,* **heute** *today,* or **am Mittwoch** *on Wednesday,* or as complex as **nach einer gut vorbereiteten und wohl schmeckenden Mahlzeit** *after a well-prepared and good-tasting meal* or **weil er immer geglaubt hatte, dass er nicht genug Geld hatte, um eine lange Reise zu machen** *because he had always believed that he did not have enough money to take a long trip.*

Questions

Specific Questions (X + V + S?)

Specific questions (sometimes referred to as *informational questions*) are questions that ask for particular information. This type of question is introduced by an interrogative word or phrase seeking specific information: **Wann? Warum? Wo? Wie? Wovon? Wieso? Um wie viel Uhr?** Specific questions also follow the word order pattern below.

Specific question = X (interrogative) + Verb + Subject (+ Other sentence parts)?

INTERROGATIVE ADVERB	CONJUGATED VERB	SUBJECT	OTHER SENTENCE PARTS
Wann	hat	**das Konzert**	begonnen?
Wohin	habt	**ihr**	es gelegt?

3. Rewrite each of the following sentences, beginning with the bold element.

    1. Wir wollten **das Auto** in Deutschland kaufen. _____

    2. Sie kommen **heute** zurück. _____

    3. Er hat es **im Kino** vergessen. _____

    4. Er ist am Abend **meistens** müde. _____

    5. Meine Eltern waren **leider** zu Hause. _____

    6. Ich konnte **wegen meiner Erkältung** nicht kommen. _____

    7. Wir haben es **gestern Abend** gemacht. _____

    8. Sie fahren **mit dem Zug** in die Schweiz. _____

    9. Das Museum ist **im Zentrum**. _____

    10. Ich habe es **oft** hören müssen. _____

4. Form a question from each of the following groups of words, beginning with the interrogative adverb and using the present tense.

    1. Wann / du / zumachen / das Fenster / ? _____

    2. Was / das Kind / dürfen / wissen / ? _____

    3. Wie viel / die Kamera / kosten / ? _____

    4. Wo / die Leute / wollen / wohnen / ? _____

    5. Warum / du / nicht / niedersetzen / dich / ? _____

    6. Wohin / du / fahren / mit dem Auto / ? _____

    7. Worauf / die Bücher / sollen / liegen / ? _____

    8. Woher / die Kinder / kommen / ? _____

5. Rewrite each of the following sentences, beginning with the bold dependent clause.

    1. Ich kann nicht mit ins Kino, **weil ich viel zu tun habe**.

    _____

    2. Sie las ein Buch, **als ihre Mutter ins Zimmer kam**.

    _____

    3. Ich werde meine Tante besuchen, **wenn ich Zeit habe**.

    _____

    4. Ich habe viel lernen müssen, **während ich studierte**.

    _____

    5. Du sollst deiner Großmutter helfen, **bevor du abreist**.

    _____

Variations in the Position of the Noun Subject

In sentences using inverted word order, the noun subject may be preceded by a pronoun object. An accusative, dative, or reflexive pronoun may thus come between the verb and the subject. When the subject is a pronoun, this variation is not possible; in this case, the object pronoun must follow the subject.

Wo hat *dich* Peter kennengelernt?	*Where did Peter meet you?*
OR **Wo hat Peter *dich* kennengelernt?**	
Gestern Abend hat *ihm* Anton geholfen.	*Yesterday evening Anton helped him.*
OR **Gestern Abend hat Anton *ihm* geholfen.**	
Am Sonntag hat *sich* Paula schön angezogen.	*On Sunday Paula dressed up beautifully.*
OR **Am Sonntag hat Paula *sich* schön angezogen.**	
BUT **Wo hat er *dich* gesehen?**	*Where did he see you?*
Warum gibst du *ihm* etwas?	*Why are you giving him something?*

6. Rewrite each of the following sentences, placing the accusative, dative, or reflexive pronoun before the subject. If this word order is not possible, place an **X** in the blank.

1. Morgen bringt er mir die Leiter. _____
2. Vor einer Woche hat Axel uns besucht. _____
3. Im Theater hat Konrad sich amüsiert. _____
4. Jeden Tag schickt Mutter ihr etwas. _____
5. Wo hat Ursel dich getroffen? _____
6. Wann kannst du es machen? _____
7. Warum helft ihr mir nicht? _____
8. Gestern hat Vater uns etwas gebracht. _____
9. Um neun Uhr trifft ihr Freund sie. _____
10. In der Stadt kaufte ich ihm die Krawatte. _____

General Questions (V + S?)

General questions (sometimes referred to as *alternative questions*) are questions that ask whether something is true or false. They can be answered by **ja** *yes* or **nein** *no*. This type of question is formed by inverting the subject and the verb of the declarative sentence so that the conjugated form of the verb is in first position.

General question = Verb + Subject (+ Other sentence parts)?

In the case of compound tenses, the past participle, dependent infinitive, double infinitive, or separable prefix is in final position.

NOTE: No interrogative word or phrase is used in forming this type of question.

Kennst **du meine Freundin?**   *Do you know my girlfriend?*
Hat **er es nehmen dürfen?**   *Was he permitted to take it?*
Wirst **du ihn dort treffen?**   *Will you meet him there?*
Kommt **er bald heim?**   *Is he coming home soon?*

When the verb is in first position, the noun subject may be preceded or followed by a pronoun object.

Hat ihn **dein Bruder gesehen?**   *Did your brother see him?*
OR *Hat* **dein Bruder** *ihn* **gesehen?**

7. Rewrite each of the following sentences, changing the statements to questions and placing a pronoun object before the subject when possible.

1. Du hast ihm den Brief geschrieben. _____
2. Peter kennt mich. _____
3. Gerda wollte das Museum besuchen. _____
4. Ihr helft ihm den Baum pflanzen. _____
5. Herr Klein macht die Tür auf. _____
6. Er kann Deutsch. _____
7. Erika hat sich bei ihr entschuldigt. _____
8. Du hast dir das schnelle Auto gekauft. _____
9. Ihr habt es ihm genommen. _____
10. Man hat dich gefragt. _____

Commands (V (+ S))

The imperative verb is the first element in commands in German. The subject is not normally expressed in informal commands in the second-person singular (**du**) and second-person plural (**ihr**) imperative forms. In formal commands, the subject (**Sie**) is expressed directly after the imperative verb. The subject in **wir** commands is expressed, also directly following the imperative verb. Separable prefixes are in final position.

Command = Verb (+ Subject) (+ Other sentence parts)!

Commands are generally indicated by an exclamation mark.

Geh hinters Haus!	*Go behind the house.*
Steht bitte *auf*!	*Please get up.*
Setzen Sie *sich* bitte!	*Please sit down.*
Fahren wir mit dem Motorrad!	*Let's go by motorcycle.*
Bitte *fahren* Sie bald *ab*!	*Please depart soon.*
Macht auf!	*Open up.*

NOTE: The second-person subject of an informal command may be expressed for special emphasis.

Geh du mal vor!	You *go first.*

8. Complete each of the following commands, using the appropriate form of the familiar singular or plural imperative.

1. _____ mir das Bild!   zeigen
2. _____ uns die Tür!   öffnen
3. _____ ihn!   fragen
4. _____ bald _____!   heimkommen
5. _____ es sofort _____!   nachmachen

9. Answer each of the following questions, using a formal command beginning with **Ja**. Follow the model.

MODEL   Darauf warten?   _Ja, warten Sie darauf!_

1. Das Bier trinken?   _____
2. Darüber lachen?   _____
3. Es mir schicken?   _____
4. Den warmen Mantel anziehen?   _____

Exclamations

Exclamations are utterances expressing great feeling, surprise, irritation, and a whole range of other emotional responses. Exclamations, which are generally indicated by an exclamation mark at the end, do not have to be complete sentences, as the following examples demonstrate.

Was für ein braves Mädchen!	*What a good girl!*
So was ärgerliches!	*How irritating!*
Wie lieb von dir!	*How nice of you!*

Coordinating Conjunctions

A coordinating conjunction links words, phrases, or clauses that are parallel and equal. Because coordinating conjunctions are merely links and do not become a part of any of the clauses they connect, they have no effect on the word order of the clauses they introduce. A coordinating conjunction is normally followed by regular word order according to the following pattern.

Word order with coordinating conjunction = Subject + Verb (+ Other sentence parts) + Coordinating conjunction + Subject + Verb (+ Other sentence parts)

If, however, another element X (adverb, prepositional phrase, etc.) directly follows the coordinating conjunction, the word order of the clause following the conjunction is inverted. This is not due to the coordinating conjunction, but rather to the rule X + V + S.

In written texts, coordinating conjunctions are usually preceded by a comma.

Er singt Lieder, *und* ich spiele Gitarre.	*He sings songs, and I play guitar.*

However, a comma is not used before **und** and **oder** when either the subject or the verb of the clauses is identical but is not expressed in the second clause.

Er singt Lieder *und* spielt die Gitarre.	*He sings songs and plays guitar.*
Er spielt Klavier *und* Gitarre.	*He plays piano and guitar.*

NOTE: Coordinating conjunctions never change their form.
The most common coordinating conjunctions are the following.

aber *but*

Er musste hier bleiben, *aber* ich durfte ins Kino gehen.	*He had to stay here, but I could go to the movies.*

denn *because, since, for*

Sie geht nicht mit, *denn* sie ist krank.	*She isn't going along, because she is ill.*

oder *or*

Sag ihm die Wahrheit, *oder* er wird sie von mir hören.	*Tell him the truth, or he'll hear it from me.*

sondern *but (on the contrary)*
Sondern follows a negative.

Sie fuhr *nicht* in die Stadt, *sondern* sie blieb zu Hause.	*She did not go downtown, but stayed home.*

und *and*

Ich habe im Gras gelegen, *und* er hat gearbeitet.	*I was lying in the grass, and he was working.*

10. Combine each of the following pairs of sentences, using the coordinating conjunction on the right.

1. Er ist arm. Seine Eltern sind reich.   aber

   _____

2. Ich freute mich. Er wollte sofort mit der Arbeit anfangen.   denn

   _____

3. Wir sind nicht dort geblieben. Wir sind ausgegangen.   sondern

   _____

4. Sei vorsichtig! Es geht kaputt.   oder

   _____

5. Ich spiele Golf. Er spielt Tennis.   und
   _____

6. Er ist glücklich. Er hat Geld gewonnen.   denn
   _____

7. Wir sind nicht in Deutschland. Wir sind in Spanien.   sondern
   _____

8. Du kannst zu Hause bleiben. Ich muss zur Schule.   aber
   _____

9. Er trinkt Milch. Ich trinke Limonade.   und
   _____

Subordinating Conjunctions

Subordinating conjunctions introduce dependent clauses (sometimes also referred to as *subordinate clauses*) and establish the relationship between the main clause and the dependent clause(s) in the sentence. A dependent clause is not a complete sentence and cannot stand alone.

Unlike coordinating conjunctions, subordinating conjunctions do become a part of the clause they introduce, and they do have an effect on the word order of the clause. Thus, the conjugated verb is normally placed in final position in the dependent clause. The pattern for dependent clause word order is as follows.

Dependent clause word order =
   Subordinating conjunction + Subject (+ Other sentence parts) + Verb

---

All dependent clauses introduced by subordinating conjunctions are separated from the main clause by a comma.

Er weiß, *dass* **ich zu Hause** *bin.*	*He knows that I'm at home.*
Weil **ich mich nicht gut** *fühle,* **bin ich heute zu Hause geblieben.**	*Because I don't feel well, I stayed home today.*

NOTE: Like coordinating conjunctions, subordinating conjunctions never change their form.
   The most common subordinating conjunctions include the following.

als *when*

Als **er ins Zimmer** *kam,* **standen alle auf.**	*When he came into the room, everyone stood up.*

als ob *as if*

Sie sieht aus, *als ob* **sie krank** *gewesen wäre.*	*She looks as if she had been ill.*

bevor *before*

Bevor **du ins Kino** *gehst,* **musst du mir noch helfen.**	*Before you go to the movies, you have to help me.*

bis *until*

Ich arbeitete, *bis* **ich müde** *wurde.*	*I worked until I became tired.*

da *since, as*

Ich musste warten, *da* **sie noch nicht angezogen war.**	*I had to wait, since she wasn't dressed yet.*

damit *in order to, so that*

> Ich rufe ihn an, *damit* er nicht *kommt*.   *I'll call him so that he won't come.*

dass *that*

> Ich weiß, *dass* er einen Hund *hat*.   *I know that he has a dog.*

je ... desto *the (comparative) ... the (comparative)*

> *Je mehr* er Klavier *spielt, desto weniger*   *The more he plays the piano, the fewer*
>   Fehler macht er.   *mistakes he makes.*
> *Je länger* sie in den USA *lebt, desto besser*   *The longer she lives in the USA, the better*
>   spricht sie Englisch.   *she speaks English.*

This two-part subordinating conjunction is always used with the comparative.

Note the word order used with this two-part conjunction. The clause beginning with **je** has its verb in final position, as is expected for dependent clauses introduced by subordinating conjunctions, whereas the clause introduced by **desto** follows the X + V + S rule for word order.

nachdem *after*

> Er grüßte mich, *nachdem* ich ihn *gegrüßt hatte*.   *He greeted me after I had greeted him.*

ob *whether, if*

> Sie wollen wissen, *ob* sie *rauchen dürfen*.   *They want to know whether they may smoke.*

obwohl *although*

> Er ging, *obwohl* es sein Vater *verboten hatte*.   *He went, although his father had forbidden it.*

seit, seitdem *since*

> *Seitdem* wir weniger Geld *haben*, bleiben wir   *Since we have less money, we stay home*
>   öfters zu Hause.   *more often.*

während *while*

> Ich arbeitete, *während* er einen Roman *las*.   *I worked while he read a novel.*

weil because

> Wir konnten nichts kaufen, *weil* wir kein   *We couldn't buy anything, because we had*
>   Geld *hatten*.   *no money.*

wenn when

> *Wenn* er nach Hause *kommt*, gehen wir   *When he comes home, we will go to the theater.*
>   ins Theater.

Als, wenn, wann

English *when* can be expressed three ways in German: **als**, **wenn**, **wann**. Each has a definite use, and they are not interchangeable.

Als refers to a single action in the past. It is used with the simple past, the present perfect, and the past perfect tenses.

> Ich freute mich, *als* er die Goldmedaille   *I was glad when he won the gold medal.*
>   gewann.

Wenn corresponds to English *if* in conditional clauses. In time clauses, it may be rendered with *when*; it is then used with the present tense, referring to the future.

Wenn ich Zeit *hätte,* **würde ich schwimmen gehen.**	*If I had time, I would go swimming.*
Ich gehe schwimmen, *wenn* **es heiß** *wird.*	*I'll go swimming when it gets hot.*

Wenn may also be used with the simple past tense. It then has the meaning of *whenever*.

***Wenn* er hier** *war,* **gingen wir spazieren.**	*Whenever he was here, we went for a walk.*

Wann is an interrogative, meaning *when*. It is used in direct and indirect questions.

***Wann erwartest* du ihn?**	*When do you expect him?*
Weißt du, *wann* **Ilse** *kommt?*	*Do you know when Ilse is coming?*

11. Express each of the following sentences in German, using **als**, **wenn**, or **wann**.

1. *When are you reading the book?*
   _____

2. *When she is ill, she stays home.*
   _____

3. *Whenever he visited me, he brought me something.*
   _____

4. *Do you know when he is arriving?*
   _____

5. *When it got cold, I went into the house.*
   _____

6. *If he had more money, he would go to Germany.*
   _____

12. Combine each of the following pairs of sentences, introducing the second sentence with the subordinating conjunction on the right.

1. Sie hat Kopfweh. Die Kinder haben viel Lärm gemacht.   weil
   _____

2. Er ist in Berlin. Seine Frau ist noch hier.   während
   _____

3. Ich fragte ihn. Sie sind wieder gesund.   ob
   _____

4. Es war sehr kalt. Wir waren in Alaska.   als
   _____

5. Sie konnte gut Deutsch. Sie hatte in Deutschland studiert.   nachdem
   _____

6. Wir kauften alles. Wir hatten viel Geld gewonnen.   da
   _____

7. Wir blieben im Wald. Es wurde dunkel.   bis
   _____

8. Konrad musste mithelfen. Er konnte ausgehen.   bevor
   _____

9. Er trägt einen Pullover. Er erkältet sich nicht.   damit
   _____

10. Sie ist immer müde. Sie kann nicht gut schlafen.   seitdem
    _____

13. Complete each of the following sentences, using the German conjunction equivalent to the English word(s) on the right.

1. Ich weiß, _____ er in Köln ist.	*that*
2. _____ es kalt ist, trägt er keinen Mantel.	*although*
3. Ich wartete, _____ er fertig war.	*until*
4. Sie tut, _____ sie reich wäre.	*as if*
5. Weißt du, _____ sie dort ist?	*whether*
6. _____ wir arbeiten, haben wir keine Zeit.	*since*
7. _____ weniger sie isst, desto schlanker wird sie.	*the*
8. Er studiert, _____ er alles weiß.	*so that*
9. Ich konnte nicht kommen, _____ ich in Rom war.	*since*
10. Wir waren im Theater, _____ du studiert hast.	*while*

Words Functioning as Subordinating Conjunctions

Dependent clauses can also be introduced by words functioning as subordinating conjunctions, such as relative pronouns, interrogative pronouns, and interrogative adverbs. These constructions also require dependent clause word order with the conjugated verb in final position. Remember, separable prefixes are always prefixed to the verb in dependent clauses.

Relative Pronouns and Interrogatives

The conjugated verb is in final position in relative clauses and in indirect questions introduced by interrogative words.

Dort steht der Student, *den* **ich in Paris kennengelernt** *habe.*	*The student whom I met in Paris is standing there.*
Du bekommst alles, *was* **du** *willst.*	*You will get everything you want.*
Weißt du, *wann* **der Zug** *ankommt?*	*Do you know when the train will arrive?*
Ich möchte wissen, *wie viel* **du davon getrunken** *hast.*	*I'd like to know how much of it you drank.*

14. Rewrite each of the following sentences, changing the direct question to an indirect question starting with **Ich weiß nicht**.

1. Wo hat er gewohnt?   _____
2. Wie viel muss sie noch machen?   _____
3. Wovon lebt er?   _____
4. Warum bringt er es mit?   _____
5. Worüber wird er erzählen?   _____

15. Combine each of the following pairs of sentences, using the appropriate form of the relative pronoun **der**. Follow the model.

MODEL   Kennst du die Leute? Du hast ihnen das Bild gezeigt.

        Kennst du die Leute, denen du das Bild gezeigt hast?

1. Wo ist der Mantel? Ich habe ihn gekauft.

   _____

2. Die Kinder spielen mit der Puppe. Er hat sie mitgebracht.

   _____

3. Dort steht das Flugzeug. Ich fliege damit ab.

   _____

4. Hilfst du dem Mädchen? Sein Vater ist gestorben.

   _____

5. Wo sind die Karten? Er hat sie mir geschenkt.

   _____

Haben or werden with the Double Infinitive

If a double infinitive construction occurs in a dependent clause, the conjugated form of the auxiliary **haben** or **werden** does not move to final position. Instead, the conjugated verb precedes the double infinitive.

Ich freute mich, weil er *hat kommen können.*	*I was happy, because he was able to come.*
Ich weiß, dass er sie *wird singen hören.*	*I know that he will hear her sing.*

16. Rewrite each of the following sentences, changing the verb to the present perfect tense. Follow the model.

   MODEL   Weißt du, ob er schreiben wollte?   ___Weißt du, ob er hat schreiben wollen?___

   1. Er ist glücklich, weil er gehen durfte. _____
   2. Ich glaube, dass er fragen wollte. _____
   3. Kennst du den Mann, den ich schreien _____
      hörte?
   4. Weißt du, ob er arbeiten musste? _____
   5. Ich weiß, was er machen sollte. _____

Conditional Sentences

Any real or contrary-to-fact condition may start with **wenn** or with the conjugated verb. When the conjugated verb is in first position, the dependent infinitive, the double infinitive, the past participle, and the separable prefix move to final position.

Wenn er nach Hause *käme,* wäre ich froh.	*If he came home, I would be happy.*
Käme er nach Hause, wäre ich froh.	
Wenn sie abfahren *will,* rufe ich das Taxi.	*If she wants to leave, I'll call a taxi.*
Will sie abfahren, rufe ich das Taxi.	

17. Rewrite each of the following sentences, omitting **wenn**.

   1. Wenn ich daran denke, bestelle ich es.

   _____

   2. Wenn er es gewollt hätte, hätte ich es ihm gekauft.

   _____

   3. Wenn es kalt wird, heizen wir das Haus.

   _____

   4. Wenn du mitmachen willst, musst du dich umziehen.

   _____

   5. Wenn ich es ihr wegnehme, weint sie.

   _____

Main Clauses Following Dependent Clauses

When the main clause follows the dependent clause, the conjugated verb is in first position in the main clause.

Wenn ich Zeit hätte, *besuchte* **ich sie.**	*If I had time, I would visit her.*
Weil sie krank war, *kam* **sie nicht.**	*Because she was sick, she didn't come.*

18. Rewrite each of the following sentences, starting with the dependent clause.

1. Ich konnte es nicht machen, da ich keine Zeit hatte.

   _____

2. Sie spielte Klavier, als er ins Zimmer kam.

   _____

3. Ich werde euch besuchen, wenn ich das Auto habe.

   _____

4. Ich musste viel schlafen, während ich krank war.

   _____

5. Du musst mir helfen, bevor du gehst.

   _____

Position of the Object

Noun and pronoun objects are usually arranged in the following manner, regardless of the position of the verb.

(1) Dative nouns precede accusative nouns.

Der Professor erklärte *den Studenten* *das Problem.*	*The professor explained the problem to the students.*

(2) Pronoun objects precede noun objects, regardless of their case.

Weißt du, ob sie *es ihren Eltern* **zeigt?**	*Do you know whether she is showing it to her parents?*
Hast du *dir die Hände* **gewaschen?**	*Did you wash your hands?*
Sie kauft *ihm das Auto.*	*She is buying the car for him.*

19. Rewrite each of the following sentences, changing the dative noun object to a pronoun.

1. Wir zeigten der Dame die Lampe.

   _____

2. Wann hat er dem Hasen die Karotte gegeben?

   _____

3. Ich habe meiner Tante eine Vase geschenkt.

   _____

4. Hat er seinem Sohn das Motorrad gekauft?

   _____

5. Wer hat den Leuten das Geld genommen?

   _____

6. Weißt du, ob er den Kindern die Schokolade gegeben hat?

   _____

20. Rewrite each of the following sentences, changing the accusative noun object to a pronoun.

1. Wir zeigten der Dame die Lampe.

   _____

2. Wann hat er dem Hasen die Karotte gegeben?

   _____

3. Ich habe meiner Tante eine Vase geschenkt.

   _____

4. Hat er seinem Sohn das Motorrad gekauft?

   _____

5. Wer hat den Leuten das Geld genommen?

   _____

6. Weißt du, ob er den Kindern die Schokolade gegeben hat?

   _____

(3) Accusative pronoun objects precede dative pronoun objects.

Wir bestellten *es uns*.	*We ordered it (for ourselves).*
Ich war krank, als er *sie mir* brachte.	*I was sick when he brought it to me.*

21. Rewrite each of the following sentences, changing both noun objects to pronouns.

1. Willst du deiner Mutter das Gedicht vorlesen?

   _____

2. Wann hat er seinen Eltern den Brief gebracht?

   _____

3. Weißt du, ob er seinem Vater die Geschichte erzählt hat?

   _____

4. Wann hat er den Touristen das Museum gezeigt?

   _____

5. Ich habe Frau Hartmann die Zeitschrift gegeben.

   _____

(4) Pronoun objects may precede or follow noun subjects if the subject is not in first position.

Ich glaube, dass *ihn der Lehrer* gesehen hat.	*I believe that the teacher has seen him.*
Er weiß, warum *Angelika mir* das Geschenk gegeben hat.	*He knows why Angelika gave me the present.*
Kann *dir der Junge* helfen?	*Can the boy help you?*
Hat *das Mädchen sich* verletzt?	*Did the girl hurt herself?*

22. Rewrite each of the following sentences, placing the pronoun object before the subject.

1. Gibt Peter dir den Ring?

   _____

2. Warum kann Ursula uns nicht besuchen?

   _____

3. Kennt der Professor ihn?

   _____

4. Hat Frau Schafft sich schon umgezogen?

   _____

5. Sie weint, weil die Leute sie auslachten.

   _____

Position of the Adverb

Adverbs follow pronoun objects.

Ich habe es *ihr gestern* gebracht.	*I brought it to her yesterday.*
Hast du *sie dort* getroffen?	*Did you meet her there?*

Adverbs may precede or follow noun objects. The item of greater news value follows the item of less news value.

Ich weiß, dass du *deinem Freund gestern* geschrieben hast.	*I know that you wrote your friend yesterday.*
Ich weiß, dass du *gestern deinem Freund* geschrieben hast.	*I know that yesterday you wrote your friend.*

23. Rewrite each of the following sentences, changing the noun object to a pronoun.

1. Er sieht täglich seine Freunde.

   _____

2. Wir geben natürlich den Leuten alles zurück.

   _____

3. Sie besucht abends ihre Freundin.

   _____

4. Ich habe wirklich den Schauspieler getroffen.

   _____

5. Er kann leider seine Eltern nicht abholen.

   _____

If more than one adverb or adverbial phrase is used in a sentence, they occur in the following order: time, manner, place.

Ich bin *um acht Uhr mit dem Zug nach Bonn* gefahren.	*I traveled by train to Bonn at 8 o'clock.*

24. Answer each of the following questions, using a complete sentence that incorporates the phrase on the right.

1. Wann bist du nach Hause gekommen?   am Nachmittag

   _____

2. Wo trefft ihr sie um zehn Uhr?   im Hotel

   _____

3. Wann warst du dort?   jeden Tag

   _____

4. Mit wem gehst du heute Abend spazieren?   mit Ursel

   _____

5. Wie bist du in die Stadt gefahren?   sehr schnell

   _____

6. Womit seid ihr gestern ins Kino gefahren?   mit dem alten Wagen

If there are several time expressions in one sentence, the general time precedes the specific time.

Er ist *gestern Vormittag um elf Uhr*   *He came yesterday morning at 11 o'clock.*
gekommen.

25. Answer each of the following questions, beginning with **Ja**. Follow the model.

    MODEL   War er gestern Abend hier?   um sieben Uhr

              Ja, er war gestern Abend um sieben Uhr hier.

    1. Besucht ihr mich morgen?   um drei Uhr
    _____

    2. Fahrt ihr diesen Sommer in die Berge?   im Juli
    _____

    3. Gehst du nächste Woche ins Theater?   am Mittwoch
    _____

    4. Fliegt ihr heute Abend ab?   um sechs Uhr
    _____

    5. Bist du morgen zu Hause?   zwischen sieben und acht Uhr
    _____

Answers to Exercises

Chapter 1

1. See the German alphabet on page 1.

2. See the German alphabet on page 1.

3. See the list of code words developed by the German Post Office on page 2.

4.
1. wann	6. lang
2. hastig	7. Bank
3. rasch	8. Ball
4. Stadt	9. Gedanke
5. Hand	10. Handtasche

5.
1. beten	6. fehlen
2. Kopfweh	7. Mehlwurm
3. Vorlesung	8. Seemann
4. dem	9. mehr
5. Regenwasser	10. Beet

6.
1. Dienstag	6. ihnen
2. mir	7. Bier
3. Lieder	8. Briefträger
4. ihm	9. hier
5. wir	10. antik

7.
1. Spott	6. Norden
2. morgen	7. Oktett
3. Segelsport	8. Stock
4. offen	9. Topf
5. sorgfältig	10. Wochentag

8.
1. Fuß	6. Natur
2. Stuhl	7. Bluse
3. Kuh	8. Anzug
4. gut	9. Ruhm
5. Juli	10. trug

9.
1. älter	6. Bett
2. Eltern	7. fern
3. Wände	8. kälter
4. Unterwäsche	9. beschäftigen
5. ändern	10. Ärzte

10.
1. blöd	6. Böhmen
2. Möbel	7. Fön
3. Löwe	8. Föhn
4. aushöhlen	9. Öl
5. öd	10. Vermögen

11.
1. Müller	6. schüchtern
2. müssen	7. beglücken
3. Mütter	8. Lücke
4. benützen	9. Müll
5. Früchte	10. Idyll

12.
1. sich	6. Nichte
2. nichts	7. leichter
3. schlecht	8. Becher
4. besichtigen	9. Löcher
5. wöchentlich	10. Bäuche

13.
1. gewesen	6. Besuch
2. Käsekuchen	7. Eisen
3. Nase	8. sechzehn
4. also	9. so
5. ansehen	10. Süden

14.
1. Abend	6. Phantasie
2. Leute	7. Suppe
3. Musik	8. Universität
4. sagen	9. beenden
5. Bäckerei	10. studieren

15.
1. Anrufbe / antworter
2. Post / amt
3. eines / Abends
4. in / Aachen
5. was / esst / ihr?
6. auf / Englisch
7. Ebbe / und Flut
8. Verkehrs / ampel
9. be / enden
10. die / Ei / erkuchen

16.
1. ba-cken	6. Res-tau-rants
2. Würst-chen	7. lang-wei-lig
3. Om-ni-bus	8. Ha-se
4. Pro-gram-me	9. au-ßer
5. Ra-dier-gum-mi	10. Wasch-lap-pen

Chapter 2

1.
1. Der	7. Das
2. Das	8. Die
3. Die	9. Der
4. Der	10. Die
5. Das	11. Der
6. Die	12. Das

13. Die
14. Die
15. Das
16. Der

17. Der
18. Das
19. Die
20. Das

2.
1. Der
2. Der
3. Der, der
4. Der
5. Der

6. Der
7. Der
8. Der
9. Der, der
10. Der

3.
1. Die, die
2. Die, die
3. Die
4. Die
5. Die

6. der
7. Die
8. Die
9. Die
10. Die

4.
1. die
2. der
3. X
4. Die
5. Das

6. Die
7. Die
8. X
9. das
10. Die

5.
1. Das
2. Das
3. der
4. Das
5. Das

6. Das
7. Das
8. Das
9. Das
10. Das

6.
1. Das
2. das
3. Der
4. Der
5. Der
6. Der
7. Der
8. Der
9. Das
10. Der, die

11. Die
12. Das
13. die
14. Der
15. Der
16. Die
17. Die
18. Die
19. Das
20. Der

7.
1. Der
2. das
3. Der
4. Die, der, das
5. Der
6. Der, das
7. Der
8. Der, der
9. Der

10. der
11. Das
12. Der
13. Der
14. die
15. Der
16. Die, die
17. Das
18. das

8.
1. Der
2. Der
3. Der
4. Der
5. Der

6. Der
7. Der
8. Der
9. Der
10. Der

9.
1. Die
2. die
3. Die
4. Die
5. Die
6. Die
7. Die
8. Die
9. die
10. Die

11. Die
12. Die
13. Die
14. Die
15. Die
16. die
17. Die
18. Die
19. Die
20. Die

10.
1. Das
2. das
3. Das
4. das
5. Das

6. Das
7. das
8. Das
9. Das
10. Das

11.
1. Die, das
2. Die, das, der
3. Die
4. Der
5. Die
6. Das
7. Der, der
8. die
9. Die, die
10. Die

11. Das, das
12. Der
13. Die, die
14. der, der
15. Die
16. Das
17. Die
18. Die
19. Der
20. Der

12.
1. Der
2. Die
3. Der
4. Der
5. Das
6. das
7. Die
8. Das

9. Die
10. Der
11. Das
12. Der
13. Die
14. Die
15. Das

13.
1. Der Geburtstagskuchen
2. Der Wintermantel
3. Der Autobus
4. Das Hotelzimmer
5. Der Sportsmann
6. Die Blumenvase
7. Das Kinderzimmer
8. Der Krankenwagen
9. Die Straßenlampe
10. Die Universitätsprofessorin
11. Das Tagebuch
12. Die Mitgliedskarte
13. Die Wasserfarbe
14. Das Staatsexamen
15. Die Zahnbürste
16. Der Rotstift
17. Die Rundfahrt

14.
1. Das Obst ist frisch.
2. Die Musik ist modern.
3. Das Fleisch ist frisch.
4. Die Butter ist teuer.
5. Der Honig ist süß.
6. Die Milch ist sauer.
7. Das Vieh ist hungrig.
8. Das Gold ist kostbar.

15.
1. Die Kissen sind weich.
2. Die Onkel kommen.
3. Die Töchter sind klein.
4. Die Zimmer sind kalt.
5. Die Brüder rauchen.
6. Die Mäntel sind neu.
7. Die Fenster sind geschlossen.
8. Die Äpfel sind rot.
9. Die Lehrer sind alt.
10. Die Koffer sind aus Leder.
11. Die Messer sind rostig.
12. Die Segel sind weiß.
13. Die Teller stehen dort.
14. Die Schlüssel sind alt.
15. Die Mädchen sind hübsch.
16. Die Mütter warten.
17. Die Wagen stehen hier.
18. Die Theater sind modern.
19. Die Löffel sind teuer.
20. Die Schüler lernen.

16.
1. Die Würste schmecken gut.
2. Die Monate sind lang.
3. Die Hände sind nass.
4. Die Gedichte sind kurz.
5. Die Hunde sind braun.
6. Die Züge kommen an.
7. Die Tische sind aus Holz.
8. Die Städte sind modern.
9. Die Berge sind hoch.
10. Die Tiere sind verletzt.
11. Die Kriege sind brutal.
12. Die Söhne sind groß.
13. Die Briefe sind interessant.
14. Die Schuhe sind aus Leder.
15. Die Tage sind kurz.
16. Die Freunde lachen.
17. Die Nächte sind kalt.
18. Die Jahre gehen vorüber.

17.
1. Die Würmer sind lang.
2. Die Bücher sind interessant.
3. Die Eier schmecken gut.
4. Die Länder sind neutral.
5. Die Gläser sind kalt.
6. Die Blätter sind grün.
7. Die Männer rauchen.
8. Die Häuser sind teuer.

9. Die Kleider passen nicht.
10. Die Kinder weinen.
11. Die Völker sind hungrig.
12. Die Bilder sind billig.
13. Die Lieder sind melodisch.
14. Die Götter sind alt.

18.
1. Die Herren sind alt.
2. Die Damen sind freundlich.
3. Die Katzen sind schwarz.
4. Die Nationen sind progressiv.
5. Die Jungen sind hier.
6. Die Studentinnen lernen.
7. Die Türen sind offen.
8. Die Straßen sind breit.
9. Die Studenten sind arm.
10. Die Freundinnen sind krank.
11. Die Hasen sind weiß.
12. Die Blumen blühen.
13. Die Fabriken sind grau.
14. Die Tassen sind gelb.
15. Die Wohnungen sind kalt.
16. Die Präsidenten sind alt.
17. Die Namen sind lang.
18. Die Antworten sind falsch.
19. Die Helden sind stark.
20. Die Zeitungen liegen hier.

19.
1. Die Kameras sind teuer.
2. Die Bars sind geschlossen.
3. Die Radios sind kaputt.
4. Die Hotels sind teuer.
5. Die Sofas sind weich.
6. Die Parks sind groß.
7. Die Jobs sind interessant.
8. Die Fotos sind alt.

20.
1. Die Firmen sind bekannt.
2. Sind die Wörter auf der Liste?
3. Die Bänke sind im Park.
4. Die Dramen sind interessant.
5. Die Museen sind modern.
6. Die Busse kommen.
7. Die Banken sind geschlossen.
8. Die Zentren sind groß.

21.
1. Der Teller ist weiß.
2. Die Lehrerin ist hübsch.
3. Das Glas ist leer.
4. Der Mantel hängt hier.
5. Das Zimmer ist warm.
6. Der Student lernt.
7. Das Geschäft ist geschlossen.
8. Die Nacht ist lang.
9. Der Held ist bekannt.
10. Die Bar ist billig.
11. Das Gymnasium ist progressiv.

12. Das Sofa ist rot.
13. Die Mutter ist freundlich.
14. Das Segel ist weiß.
15. Die Stadt ist übervölkert.
16. Das Radio ist kaputt.
17. Die Zeitung ist alt.
18. Der Mann ist krank.
19. Die Hand ist schmutzig.
20. Das Theater ist modern.
21. X
22. X

22.
1. X
2. Die Schuhe sind schwarz.
3. Die Freundinnen sind nett.
4. X
5. Die Äpfel sind sauer.
6. Die Schlüssel sind rostig.
7. Die Mädchen sind freundlich.
8. Die Busse sind rot.
9. Die Mütter schreiben.
10. Die Würste sind lecker.
11. Die Autos sind neu.
12. Die Briefe sind lang.
13. Die Hände sind nass.
14. Die Zimmer sind groß.
15. Die Tiere sind wild.
16. Die Gläser sind teuer.
17. Die Bücher sind interessant.
18. Die Straßen sind eng.
19. Die Freunde sind reich.
20. Die Lieder sind kurz.

23.
1. Die   6. Das
2. Der   7. das
3. das   8. Die
4. Der   9. Der
5. Die   10. Der

24.
1. Diese   6. Dieses
2. Dieser   7. dieses
3. dieses   8. Diese
4. Dieser   9. Dieser
5. Diese   10. Dieser

25.
1. Diese Länder sind reich.
2. Welche Männer kommen?
3. Jene Häuser sind alt.
4. Wo sind die Zeitungen?
5. Welche Studentinnen sind hübsch?
6. Jene Frauen sind krank.
7. Dort liegen die Äpfel.
8. Diese Mädchen lernen.
9. Diese Städte sind modern.
10. Wo sind die Bücher?

26.
1. ein   6. eine
2. Eine   7. eine
3. ein   8. Eine
4. Ein   9. ein
5. ein   10. ein

27.
1. kein   6. keine
2. Keine   7. keine
3. kein   8. Keine
4. Kein   9. kein
5. kein   10. kein

28.
1. e   6. X
2. X   7. X
3. X   8. X
4. e   9. e
5. X   10. e

29.
1. Ist das seine Firma?
2. Sein Job ist schwer.
3. Sein Glas ist leer.
4. Sein Hund bellt.
5. Wo ist seine Frau?
6. Sein Auto ist neu.
7. Sein Bus kommt.
8. Sein Drama ist lang.
9. Wo ist sein Junge?
10. Seine Freundin ist hübsch.

30.
1. Meine Freundinnen lachen.
2. Ihre Brüder sind krank.
3. Wo sind seine Lehrer?
4. Deine Messer liegen dort.
5. Wo sind unsere Schlüssel?
6. Sind das eure Häuser?
7. Wo sind Ihre Zeitungen?
8. Dort sind meine Onkel.
9. Sind das deine Kinder?
10. Wo sind eure Lehrerinnen?

31.
1. e, e   6. e
2. X   7. er, X
3. e   8. X
4. X   9. e
5. es   10. e

32.
1. den   6. das
2. das   7. die
3. die   8. den
4. die   9. das
5. das   10. den

33.
1. diesen   6. dieses
2. dieses   7. diese
3. diese   8. diesen
4. diese   9. dieses
5. dieses   10. diesen

34.
1. Wir kennen die Dichter.
2. Ich bekomme die Briefe.
3. Er kauft die Würste.
4. Ich sehe die Tiere.
5. Sie treffen die Freunde.
6. Wir besuchen die Städte.
7. Ich kenne die Berge.
8. Er schreibt die Gedichte.
9. Ich kaufe die Blumen.
10. Wir singen die Lieder.

35.
1. einen
2. eine
3. ein
4. ein
5. einen
6. eine
7. einen
8. einen
9. ein
10. eine

36.
1. keinen
2. keine
3. kein
4. kein
5. keinen
6. keine
7. keinen
8. keinen
9. kein
10. keine

37.
1. Kaufst du unser Auto?
2. Ich sehe unsere Katze.
3. Wir besuchen unser Kind.
4. Er ruft unseren Lehrer.
5. Ich nehme unseren Schlüssel.
6. Wir kennen unsere Lehrerin.

38.
1. en
2. e
3. en
4. X
5. e
6. e
7. e
8. X
9. X
10. e

39.
1. Hat er meine Bilder?
2. Brauchst du deine Bücher?
3. Seht ihr unsere Freundinnen?
4. Ich nehme seine Zeitungen.
5. Hast du deine Mäntel?
6. Wir kennen ihre Kinder.
7. Ich habe ihre Schuhe.
8. Verkaufst du unsere Wagen?
9. Sie brauchen ihre Freunde.
10. Treffen Sie Ihre Lehrer?

40.
1. en, en
2. en, en
3. en, en
4. en, n
5. en, n
6. en, n
7. en, en
8. en, en
9. en, n
10. en, n

41.
1. e, en
2. X
3. en, n
4. en, n
5. er, X, en
6. e, en
7. er, X, e
8. as, e
9. e, en
10. er, X

11. X, es
12. e, en, en
13. e, en
14. X, X, e
15. e, e
16. e
17. e
18. en, n
19. e, es
20. en

42.
1. dem
2. der
3. dem
4. dem
5. der
6. dem
7. dem
8. der
9. der
10. der

43.
1. jenem
2. jener
3. jenem
4. jenem
5. jener
6. jenem
7. jenem
8. jener
9. jener
10. jener

44.
1. einer
2. einer
3. einem
4. einer
5. einem
6. einer
7. einem
8. einem
9. einem
10. einem

45.
1. keiner
2. keiner
3. keinem
4. keiner
5. keinem
6. keiner
7. keinem
8. keinem
9. keinem
10. keinem

46.
1. er
2. em
3. er
4. em
5. em
6. er
7. em
8. em
9. er
10. em

47.
1. keinem
2. unserem
3. dieser
4. meinem
5. eurer
6. unserer
7. jenem
8. jedem
9. seiner
10. Ihrer

48.
1. em, en
2. em, en
3. em, en
4. em, n
5. em, n
6. em, n
7. em, en
8. em, n

49.
1. Schreibst du deinen Freundinnen?
2. Er hilft jenen Kindern.
3. Es gefällt seinen Lehrern.
4. Sie zeigt es ihren Brüdern.
5. Er antwortet den Männern.
6. Ich hole den Babys Milch.
7. Es gehört diesen Jungen.
8. Wir glauben den Frauen.
9. Sie dankt ihren Freunden.
10. Es gehört euren Studenten.

50.
1. jenen
2. meinem
3. unseren
4. ihrem
5. deinen
6. dieser
7. Welchem
8. keinem
9. einem
10. jedem

51.
1. X, em
2. er, ie
3. en
4. er
5. es, er
6. e, em, en
7. em, es
8. en
9. er, em, ie
10. X, er
11. en, n, en
12. er, em
13. en, X
14. em, ie
15. en, n, e

52.
1. der, X
2. des, s
3. des, s
4. des, es
5. der, X
6. des, (e)s
7. des, ns
8. des, n
9. des, (e)s
10. des, en

53.
1. dieser, X
2. dieses, s
3. dieses, s
4. dieses, es
5. dieser, X
6. dieses, (e)s
7. dieses, ns
8. dieses, n
9. dieses, (e)s
10. dieses, en

54.
1. eines, en
2. eines, n
3. eines, (e)s
4. eines, en
5. eines, s
6. eines, s
7. einer, X
8. eines, s
9. eines, n
10. einer, X

55.
1. seines, s
2. meiner, X
3. unseres, en
4. eures, n
5. ihres, s
6. deiner, X
7. ihrer, X
8. meines, (e)s
9. seines, (e)s
10. Ihrer, X

56.
1. Die Kinder jener Frauen sind krank.
2. Die Sitze seiner Autos sind bequem.
3. Das sind die Fotos unserer Töchter.
4. Die Bücher jener Studenten liegen hier.
5. Wann beginnt der Bau eurer Häuser?
6. Die Museen dieser Städte sind modern.
7. Die Kleider meiner Freundinnen sind neu.
8. Der Wagen der Herren steht dort.
9. Die Betonung der Namen ist schwer.
10. Die Gemälde jener Museen sind bekannt.

57.
1. Die Schneide von diesem Messer ist scharf.
2. Die Dokumente von unserem Präsidenten sind im Museum.
3. Wir haben die Hälfte von dem Gedicht gelesen.
4. Hier ist ein Bild von meinen Freunden.
5. Der Preis von dem Auto ist zu hoch.

58.
1. Das Wasser jenes Sees ist eiskalt.
2. Peters Hund bellt.
3. Die Ohren solcher Hasen sind sehr lang.
4. Die Mutter des Mädchens steht dort.
5. Die Produkte dieser Fabrik sind teuer.

59.
1. ie, er, X
2. as, er, X
3. ie, es, (e)s
4. es, s
5. ie, es, s
6. ie, es, (e)s
7. s
8. er, es, s
9. ie, er, X
10. ie, es, n
11. ie, er, X
12. as, es, es
13. ie, er, X
14. en, es, en
15. en, es, s

60.
1. Der
2. Die
3. Das
4. Die
5. Die
6. Der
7. Der
8. Die

61.
1. Der
2. die
3. Die
4. die
5. Der
6. Der
7. der
8. Das
9. die
10. Die
11. X
12. Das

62.
1. das
2. das
3. die
4. die
5. das
6. die

63.
1. die
2. die
3. die
4. den
5. das
6. den
7. den
8. die

64.
1. die
2. die
3. Die
4. das
5. Die
6. Der
7. den
8. Der
9. die
10. Die
11. die
12. Die
13. Das
14. Die
15. Das
16. die
17. die
18. Die

65.
1. Ich habe Fieber.
2. Er ist Lehrer.
3. Sie ist eine gute Lehrerin.
4. Hat er Zahnweh?
5. Er ist als Student in Berlin.
6. Er ist Professor.
7. Sie wird Pianistin.
8. Ich habe Halsweh.

66.
1. ie, es, (e)s, en
2. es, es, er, X, en
3. ie, es, s
4. X, e
5. e, er, er, X
6. e, e
7. e, en, X, X
8. er, es, n
9. em, en, en
10. es, er, es, s

67.
1. Wir haben keine Fotos.
2. Wo sind seine Brüder?
3. Wer hat jene Bilder genommen?
4. Welche Lieder soll ich singen?
5. Wer hilft den Babys?
6. Das gefällt den Mädchen.
7. Meine Freundinnen kommen.
8. Unsere Autos sind rot.
9. Wann kommen Ihre Töchter?
10. Die Kinder unserer Lehrer sind hier.
11. Wo sind unsere Hotels?
12. Manche Länder sind arm.
13. Wo sind die Museen?
14. Die Bücher der Studenten liegen hier.
15. Werden diese Geschichten euren Freunden gefallen?

68.
1. X
2. X
3. X
4. das
5. Die
6. Die
7. ein
8. Der
9. die
10. Der
11. den
12. die
13. Der
14. Das
15. die
16. X

Chapter 3

1.
1. durch
2. entlang
3. um
4. gegen
5. ohne
6. bis
7. für
8. für
9. durch
10. ohne

2.
1. en
2. s
3. en
4. e
5. en
6. e
7. s
8. e
9. ie
10. s
11. s
12. e
13. e
14. en
15. e
16. s
17. en
18. ie
19. ie
20. e

3.
1. meine
2. ihren
3. unsere
4. seinen
5. jenen
6. diese
7. ihren
8. euer

4.
1. mit, nach
2. bei
3. zum
4. seit
5. gegenüber
6. Nach, zur
7. von
8. mit
9. von
10. von

5.
1. em
2. er
3. em
4. m
5. em
6. em
7. m
8. X
9. er
10. er
11. em
12. em
13. en, X
14. er
15. em
16. en
17. vom
18. em
19. er
20. en

6.
1. seiner
2. einem
3. jenem
4. einem
5. Dieser
6. unserem
7. eurem
8. dem
9. der
10. dem
11. meiner
12. seinem
13. ihren
14. deiner

7.
1. im
2. die
3. unters
4. unseren
5. im
6. der
7. Am
8. ins
9. diesem
10. die
11. Im
12. einem
13. ans
14. deinen
15. seinen
16. jener
17. Am
18. ins
19. deine
20. dem
21. im
22. meinen
23. ihren
24. Im
25. hinters
26. den
27. einem
28. eurem
29. meinem
30. deine
31. jenem
32. unsere
33. ins
34. den
35. der

8.
1. darin
2. damit
3. daneben
4. dabei
5. darunter
6. dahinter
7. daran
8. darauf
9. darüber
10. dazu
11. danach
12. davon

9.
1. herein
2. hinaus
3. hinein
4. herein
5. heraus
6. herein
7. hinein
8. hinaus
9. hinein
10. hinaus

10.
1. Womit
2. Worauf
3. Worin
4. Woran
5. Woraus
6. Wovon
7. Worum
8. Worüber
9. Wovor
10. Wozu
11. Worauf
12. Wobei
13. Wogegen
14. Womit
15. Wofür

11.
1. er
2. er
3. es
4. er
5. es
6. er
7. er
8. er
9. es
10. er
11. er
12. es
13. es
14. er
15. er
16. er
17. es
18. er
19. es
20. er

12.
1. Seiner
2. des
3. des
4. die
5. der
6. den
7. der
8. Der
9. Des
10. dem

13.
1. ie
2. im, nach
3. en
4. er
5. em
6. es
7. X
8. ie
9. ie
10. er
11. ie
12. em
13. es
14. em
15. em
16. es
17. m
18. er
19. ie
20. em
21. e
22. e
23. es
24. as (OR ums)
25. en, nach

14.
1. Worin
2. Wozu
3. Womit
4. Wogegen
5. Worüber
6. Worauf
7. Wovon
8. Wovor

15.
1. darin
2. daneben
3. davor
4. darauf
5. darunter

Chapter 4

1.
1. er
2. du
3. Sie
4. sie
5. du
6. Ihr OR ihr (eure)
7. Es
8. Sie
9. ihr
10. Sie
11. Sie
12. Sie
13. Sie
14. Sie
15. es
16. ihr
17. Sie
18. du

2.
1. er, ihn
2. sie, sie
3. wir, sie
4. sie, es
5. sie, sie
6. er, sie
7. ich, ihn
8. sie, sie
9. ich, es
10. wir, ihn
11. ich, dich
12. er, sie
13. wir, ihn
14. ich, es

3.
1. Renate braucht es.
2. Wir kaufen ihn.
3. Ich setzte mich neben sie.
4. Wir essen sie.
5. Ich darf ihn lesen.
6. Wer hat ihn gefüttert?

4.
1. Ja, er hat dich erkannt.
2. Ja, er schreibt uns.
3. Ja, ich habe es für dich gekauft.
4. Ja, er geht ohne uns.
5. Ja, wir können euch dort besuchen.

5.
1. Er gab es ihr.
2. Wir helfen ihm.
3. Gibst du ihm das Futter?
4. Wir unterhielten uns mit ihr.
5. Er erzählte von ihm.
6. Wohnst du bei ihnen?
7. Ich schrieb ihnen Ansichtskarten.
8. Sie holte ihm Medizin.
9. Es gehört ihnen.
10. Sie bringen ihr Essen.
11. Es gefällt ihm.
12. Ich kaufe ihr etwas.
13. Er kommt von ihm.
14. Wir stehen hinter ihm.

6.
1. Ja, er hat mir etwas gebracht.
2. Ja, ich zeige euch die Stadt.
3. Ja, wir sagen euch die Wahrheit.
4. Ja, er hat mir geholfen.
5. Ja, ich bringe dir etwas mit.
6. Ja, er hat mir dafür gedankt.
7. Ja, sie hat uns geholfen.
8. Ja, ich kaufe (OR wir kaufen) ihm etwas.
9. Ja, das Bild gefällt mir.
10. Ja, wir kaufen dir den Wagen.

7.
1. Er gab es seiner Mutter.
2. Ich habe ihr ein Paket geschickt.
3. Sie zeigte sie ihrem Kind.
4. Sie erzählen ihnen die Neuigkeit.
5. Sie bringen sie den Kranken.
6. Er kauft sie seiner Tante.
7. Ich schreibe ihm eine Karte.
8. Sie glaubt ihm die Geschichte.
9. Ich gebe sie der Dame.
10. Wir kaufen ihnen Geschenke.

8.
1. Wir bringen es ihm.
2. Ich hole ihn ihm.
3. Wir erzählten sie ihnen.
4. Er gibt ihn ihm.
5. Er hat sie ihr geglaubt.
6. Johann zeigte es ihnen.
7. Der Professor erklärte sie ihnen.
8. Ich kaufe sie ihnen.
9. Er schreibt sie ihm.
10. Dieter holt es ihm.

9.
1. Ja, er hat sie mir geschenkt.
2. Ja, ich habe sie ihnen gezeigt.
3. Ja, er hat sie uns gekauft.
4. Ja, ich bringe ihn dir.
5. Ja, sie hat ihn uns gegeben.

10.
1. Hilft ihnen Ellen?
2. Ich glaube, dass es Maria gekauft hat.
3. Wir wissen nicht, ob er sie besichtigt hat.
4. Ich habe Zeit, weil ihn Norma abholt.
5. Morgen kauft ihr Susi den Pullover.

11.
1. Jeden Tag holt Pia ihm die Zeitung.
2. Ich weiß, wann Peter ihr geholfen hat.
3. Bringt Gabriele es?
4. Hat er es genommen?
5. Weißt du, wo Dieter sie getroffen hat?

12.
1. Er lachte über sie.
2. Wir sprechen von ihnen.
3. Er fragt nach ihr.
4. Was weißt du von ihm?
5. Er denkt an sie.
6. Warten Sie auf ihn?
7. Warum hast du Angst vor ihm?
8. Wir sprechen über ihn.
9. Ich habe von ihm gehört.
10. Er lädt sie zu ihnen ein.

13.
1. dir
2. ihm
3. uns
4. sie
5. uns
6. ihm
7. dir
8. dich
9. euch
10. mich
11. uns
12. dir
13. sie
14. Sie

14.
1. Ja, ich denke daran.
2. Ja, ich liege darunter.
3. Ja, ich warte auf sie.
4. Ja, wir sprechen darüber.
5. Ja, ich spreche von ihr.
6. Ja, ich fahre damit.
7. Ja, ich stehe davor.
8. Ja, ich warte darauf.
9. Ja, wir stehen neben ihnen.
10. Ja, er denkt an sie.
11. Ja, sie fragt nach ihr.

12. Ja, ich sitze hinter ihm.
13. Ja, ich arbeite damit.
14. Ja, wir fahren mit ihnen.
15. Ja, ich weiß etwas davon.
16. Ja, ich habe Angst vor ihm.

15.
1. mich
2. sich
3. uns
4. euch
5. sich
6. sich
7. dich
8. dich
9. mich
10. sich

16.
1. euch
2. mir
3. sich
4. dir
5. mir
6. dir
7. sich
8. mir
9. dir
10. uns

17.
1. Heute morgen haben sich die Kinder weh getan.
2. Auf die Ferien freut sich Max.
3. Wegen des Unfalls hat sich der Beamte verspätet.
4. Vor einer Stunde hat Vater sich das Auto gekauft.
5. An seine Ferien erinnert sich mein Freund.
6. Am Abend putzt Barbara sich die Zähne.
7. Ein Motorrad kauft sich Herr Obermeyer.
8. Am Morgen rasiert sich Vater.

18.
1. deine
2. eurer
3. unsere
4. mein(e)s
5. deinen
6. seine
7. ihren
8. unserem
9. meinen
10. ihrem

19.
1. der dort/da
2. dem hier
3. die dort/da
4. dem hier
5. die hier
6. denen dort/da

20.
1. diese dort/da
2. diesem hier
3. diese dort/da
4. dieser hier
5. dieses hier

21.
1. niemand(en)
2. etwas
3. Wenige
4. einigen
5. Jeder
6. nichts
7. Man
8. Viele
9. alle
10. einem nichts
11. viel
12. wenig
13. Jemand
14. andere
15. einige OR mehrere
16. Viele OR Manche
17. alles
18. Man

22.
1. das
2. der
3. die
4. die
5. der
6. das
7. die
8. der

23.
1. den
2. die
3. den
4. das
5. die
6. die
7. das
8. den

7. dem
8. den
9. wo
10. der
11. das
12. was
13. dessen
14. Wer
15. das
16. die
17. wo
18. denen
19. deren
20. was
21. die
22. die
23. dem
24. was
25. dem

24.
1. Liest du das Buch, das er gebracht hat?
2. Brauchst du die Zeitung, die auf dem Tisch liegt?
3. Kennst du den Herrn, den wir getroffen haben?
4. Heute kam der Junge, der uns damals geholfen hatte.
5. Kennst du die Leute, die dort spazieren gehen?
6. Wo sind die Blumen, die ich gekauft habe?

25.
1. dem
2. dem
3. denen
4. dem
5. der
6. der
7. denen
8. dem

26.
1. Dort sitzt der Tourist, welchem du das Essen bringen sollst.
2. Kennst du meine Geschwister, bei welchen ich wohne?
3. Die Leiter, auf welcher er steht, ist kaputt.
4. Hier ist das Auto, mit welchem wir spazieren fahren.
5. Der Stuhl, auf welchem du sitzt, ist alt.

27.
1. deren
2. dessen
3. dessen
4. deren
5. deren
6. deren
7. dessen
8. dessen

28.
1. Wer
2. Was
3. Wer
4. Was
5. Wer

29.
1. was
2. wo
3. wo
4. was
5. was
6. was
7. wo
8. was

30.
1. Der Stuhl, worauf du sitzt, ist eine Rarität.
2. Wir besuchen das Haus, worin Goethe geboren wurde.
3. Ist das das Spielzeug, womit sie sich so amüsiert?
4. Dort ist die Kirche, wonach er fragte.
5. Sind das die Bücher, wofür du dich interessierst?
6. Wo ist der Brief, worauf er wartet?
7. Das Problem, worüber ihr sprecht, ist schwer.
8. Wo ist die Ruine, wovon er erzählt?

31.
1. was
2. den
3. Wer
4. dem
5. deren
6. das

Chapter 5

1.
1. das
2. der
3. der
4. den
5. dem
6. Die
7. den
8. den
9. den
10. die

2.
1. Dieser Mantel dort gehört mir.
2. Wir holen etwas für dieses Mädchen hier.
3. Ich helfe diesem Mann da.
4. Es liegt unter diesen Büchern da.
5. Mit diesem Wagen hier fahren wir nicht.
6. Ursula hat diese Kamera da.
7. Ich schlafe nicht in diesem Bett da.
8. Kennst du diesen Mann dort?
9. Diese Frauen hier kaufen nichts.
10. Er kauft diese Blumen hier.

3.
1. heiß
2. süß
3. faul
4. lang
5. krank
6. reich
7. schmutzig
8. leicht
9. hässlich
10. billig
11. dick
12. langsam
13. schlecht
14. alt
15. klein

4.
1. er, e
2. as, e, e
3. es, e
4. ie, e
5. er, e
6. er, e, e
7. er, e
8. er, e

5.
1. Welche deutsche
2. Jenes kleine
3. Jedes neue
4. die junge
5. dieser amerikanische
6. jener blonde
7. das dünne, rote
8. jeder gesunde
9. das leere
10. jene große
11. der interessante
12. Diese kalte

6.
1. Jener französische Dichter ist weltbekannt.
2. Der rote Bus wartet.
3. Manches deutsche Drama ist lang.
4. Wie viel kostet jenes schnelle Auto?
5. Jedes moderne Museum braucht Geld.
6. Welche alte Maschine ist kaputt?
7. Wo ist die weiße Katze?
8. Wo steht die frische Milch?

7.
1. es, e
2. ie, e
3. en, en
4. es, e
5. en, en
6. e, e, e
7. en, en
8. en, en

8.
1. die lange
2. jenes moderne
3. diesen großen
4. Welchen interessanten
5. das scharfe
6. die kleine
7. jenes fremde, junge
8. jedes kranke
9. den schmutzigen
10. jenen heißen
11. den großen, blonden
12. jenen klugen

9.
1. Er restaurierte manches historische Haus.
2. Wer hat den alten Lederkoffer?
3. Bring dieses schmutzige Glas in die Küche!
4. Wir kaufen jenes schnelle Motorboot.
5. Welchen roten Apfel möchtest du?
6. Wir wandern durch die kleine Stadt.
7. Sie bringt Blumen für das kranke Kind.
8. Ich brauche jede neue, deutsche Briefmarke.

10.
1. em, en
2. er, en
3. em, en
4. em, en, en
5. er, en
6. em, en
7. er, en
8. em, en

11.
1. jenem internationalen
2. jeder interessanten
3. dieser netten
4. dem schmutzigen
5. jenem kurzen
6. dem großen, amerikanischen
7. welchem fremden
8. der hübschen
9. jenem reichen
10. dem kleinen
11. jeder kranken
12. dem hässlichen

12.
1. Wir schlafen in dem modernen Schlafwagen.
2. Mit welchem neuen Handy soll ich telefonieren?
3. Er wohnt bei jener netten Dame.
4. Der Ball liegt unter dem blauen Sessel.
5. Trink nicht aus jenem roten Glas!
6. Wir gehen bei diesem kalten Wetter nicht aus.
7. Wer sitzt auf der alten, rostigen Bank?
8. Wir bekamen von manchem amerikanischen Studenten Post.

13.
1. es, en
2. er, en
3. es, en
4. es, en
5. er, en
6. es, en
7. es, en
8. er, en

14.
1. des blauen
2. jenes exotischen
3. des deutschen
4. dieses billigen
5. der kranken
6. dieses bequemen
7. jener bekannten
8. dieser kleinen
9. der dicken
10. des gesunden
11. jenes großen
12. jener interessanten

15.
1. Wo ist der Besitzer dieses schmutzigen Mantels?
2. Die Gedichte manches deutschen Dichters sind kompliziert.
3. Die Mutter jenes kranken Kindes ist hier.
4. Der Park ist jenseits des großen Monuments.
5. Trotz dieser starken Explosion gab es keine Verwundete.
6. Die Straßen jener alten Stadt sind eng.
7. Die Zimmer der neuen Wohnung sind modern.

16.
1. Welche deutschen Städte hat er besucht?
2. Ohne diese warmen Kleider fahre ich nicht.
3. Wir steigen auf jene bekannten Berge.
4. Es gehört jenen interessanten, jungen Frauen.
5. Er schenkt etwas in alle leeren Gläser.
6. Ich liege unter den schattigen Bäumen.
7. Er erzählt den kleinen Mädchen Geschichten.
8. Ich komme um der kranken Lehrer willen.
9. Alle gesunden Patienten dürfen nach Hause.
10. Sie hat die grünen Äpfel.

17.
1. dem dunklen
2. die bittere
3. jenen teuren (teueren)
4. dieses hohen
5. die saubere
6. die saure (sauere)
7. das saubere
8. dieses teure (teuere)
9. die sauren (saueren)
10. dieser hohe
11. Nürnberger
12. Frankfurter
13. Dortmunder
14. Berliner
15. Kölner

18. 1. ie, en, en, en
2. en, en, em, en
3. en, en, er, en
4. ie, e, em, en
5. es, en
6. ie, e, em, en, en
7. e, en, m, en
8. en, en, as, e
9. ie, e, es, e
10. er, e, es, e

19. 1. Dieses deutsche, jener netten
2. Alle eleganten, diese kurzen
3. Jener blonde, dieses teure (teuere)
4. Die hübsche, dem dicken
5. Der neue, des teuren (teueren)
6. die schmutzigen, des kleinen
7. Jener amerikanische, diese billige
8. Der schwarze, dem runden
9. Die jungen, der dunklen
10. Die hungrige, den großen

20. 1. X, er
2. e, e, e
3. e, e
4. X, er
5. e, e
6. X, es
7. X, er
8. e, e
9. e, e, e
10. X, es
11. X, er
12. X, es
13. X, er
14. X, es
15. e, e
16. X, er

21. 1. Wo ist ein weiches Kissen?
2. Ein alter Freund ist hier.
3. Wann schläft ein wildes Tier?
4. Eine neue Maschine steht dort.
5. Hier ist ein schmutziger Teller.
6. Wo ist ein kleines Buch?
7. Hier liegt eine deutsche Zeitung.
8. Wie viel kostet ein schnelles Auto?

22. 1. Mein altes Radio ist kaputt.
2. Wo wohnt deine nette Freundin?
3. Wie viel kostet Ihr neuer Wagen?
4. Wann kommt sein reicher Onkel?
5. Das ist keine enge Straße.
6. Ist unser deutsches Foto interessant?
7. Wo ist eure schmutzige Wäsche?
8. Hier ist ihr alter Wein.

23. 1. en, en
2. X, es
3. e, e, e, e
4. e, e
5. en, en, en
6. e, e
7. en, en, en
8. X, es
9. e, e
10. e, e
11. X, es
12. X, es

24. 1. Er kauft einen hässlichen Teppich.
2. Wann bekommst du einen neuen Mantel?
3. Wir besuchen eine historische Stadt.
4. Siehst du ein rotes Auto?
5. Ich kaufe es für ein krankes Kind.

6. Er geht durch einen langen Tunnel.
7. Der Bus fuhr gegen eine alte Mauer.
8. Ich möchte ein weißes Bonbon.

25. 1. Sie geht in ihre dunkle Wohnung.
2. Wir verkaufen unser blaues Sofa.
3. Haben Sie ein billiges Zimmer?
4. Ich habe einen bequemen Stuhl.
5. Braucht er seine neue Kamera?
6. Wir gehen durch einen langen Tunnel.
7. Ich schreibe einen kurzen Brief.
8. Kennst du keine hübsche Studentin?

26. 1. em, en
2. em, en, en
3. er, en
4. em, en
5. er, en, en
6. er, en
7. em, en
8. er, en
9. er, en
10. em, en
11. er, en
12. em, en

27. 1. Er sitzt auf einem harten Stuhl.
2. Sie wohnt in einem modernen Haus.
3. Ich bin bei einer netten Frau.
4. Sie spielt mit einem süßen Baby.
5. Wir stehen neben einem großen Mann.
6. Ich liege auf einem weichen Bett.
7. Hilfst du einem fremden Mann?
8. Sie kommt von einer langen Reise zurück.

28. 1. Er kam mit einem interessanten Freund.
2. Wir kennen uns seit unserer glücklichen Kindheit.
3. Er schnitt das Brot mit seinem scharfen Messer.
4. Warum sitzt du auf einem unbequemen Stuhl?
5. Die Katze liegt auf meinem schwarzen Mantel.
6. Sie kommt aus ihrem dunklen Zimmer.
7. Was steht in seinem langen Brief?
8. Sie sitzt in meinem neuen Auto.

29. 1. einer dunklen
2. meines alten
3. seiner schlimmen
4. eines amerikanischen
5. ihrer wichtigen
6. eures kranken
7. deiner neuen
8. eines teuren (teueren)

30. 1. Das ist die Frau eines bekannten Dichters.
2. Es ist die Geschichte eines fremden Volkes.
3. Der Preis eines antiken Perserteppichs ist hoch.
4. Ich singe die Melodie eines deutschen Liedes.
5. Der Direktor einer großen Fabrik kommt.

31. 1. Trotz meiner langen Reise war ich nicht müde.
2. Die Farbe deines neuen Pullovers ist hübsch.
3. Sie ist die Frau eines amerikanischen Präsidenten.
4. Hier ist das Foto seines bekannten Bruders.
5. Wo ist das Haus Ihres reichen Onkels?
6. Wir konnten wegen seiner langen Verspätung nicht essen.
7. Der Bus ist jenseits eines hohen Turm(e)s.

32. 1. Er hat keine teuren Ringe gekauft.
2. Er glaubt seinen kleinen Söhnen.
3. Ich telefonierte mit meinen deutschen Freundinnen.
4. Unsere neuen Nähmaschinen waren teuer.
5. Wer hat meine roten Bleistifte?
6. Wegen seiner faulen Brüder darf er nicht kommen.
7. Wir trinken keine kalten Getränke.
8. Wo sind ihre warmen Jacken?
9. Willst du deine alten Lehrer besuchen?
10. Wo sind eure progressiven Gymnasien?

33. 1. X, er, e, e
2. er, en, X, er
3. ie, e, em, en
4. er, en, es, en
5. en, en, er, en, e, en
6. e, e, em, en
7. e, e, er, en
8. as, e, e, e
9. X, es, en, en
10. en, en, ie, e
11. e, en, e, e
12. em, en, ie, en

34. 1. der jungen, einen interessanten
2. Mein kranker, unserem guten
3. ihrem kleinen, die leere
4. deine reiche, dieses teure (teuere)
5. jener langen, ihre neuen
6. das neue, des bekannten
7. Meine amerikanischen, keinen bitteren
8. sein kaputtes, die dunkle
9. ihren netten, eine kurze
10. Die armen, ihrer kalten

35. 1. Welch
2. viel
3. wenig
4. viel
5. Solch
6. viel
7. solch
8. Wenig

36. 1. armes
2. bittere
3. Liebe
4. viel schmutzige
5. Lieber
6. wenig japanisches
7. Guter alter
8. gutes
9. neues
10. kaltes
11. Lieber
12. armer
13. teures (teueres)
14. typische

37. 1. Welch interessantes Gedicht!
2. Das ist teures Leder.
3. Frische Butter schmeckt gut.
4. Moderne Musik ist schnell.
5. Ist das billiger Schmuck?
6. Kalte Limonade ist erfrischend.
7. Du süßes Baby!

38. 1. viel saure (sauere)
2. wenig schwarzes
3. Guten, Gute, Guten
4. große
5. weißen
6. wenig süßen
7. schönes
8. schwarzen
9. dünnes
10. Frische holländische
11. pikanten französischen
12. große
13. viel amerikanisches
14. viel heißes

39. 1. Was hast du gegen klassische Musik?
2. Leg es in kaltes Wasser!
3. Ich esse frisches Brot.
4. Wir brauchen japanisches Geld.
5. Er hat großen Hunger.
6. Warum trinkst du kalten Kaffee?
7. Sie nimmt braunen Zucker.
8. Sie hat viel teuren Schmuck.

40. 1. großer
2. langer
3. guter
4. viel warmer
5. großem
6. schönem, sonnigem
7. rostfreiem
8. großer
9. wenig weißem
10. viel heißem
11. bitterem, kaltem
12. hartem

41. 1. Bei schlechtem Wetter fliege ich nicht.
2. Wer schreibt mit grüner Kreide?
3. Nach kurzer Zeit wurde es still.
4. Das Messer ist aus rostfreiem Stahl.
5. Warum schwimmst du in eiskaltem Wasser?
6. Der Dieb kam bei helllichtem Tag.
7. Ich kenne ihn seit langer Zeit.
8. Er trank nichts außer viel starkem Kaffee.

42. 1. klassischer
2. dichten
3. freundlicher
4. Traurigen
5. alten
6. wahrer
7. langer
8. neuen
9. großer
10. kurzer

43. 1. Trotz bitterer Kälte spielten die Kinder im Schnee.
2. Er ist Liebhaber moderner Musik.
3. Der Preis guten alten Weins ist hoch.
4. Wegen schlechten Wetters hat er Verspätung.
5. Trotz guter Ausbildung fand er keine Stelle.
6. Trotz netter Hilfe kam sie nicht vorwärts.

44.
1. es, es	8. es
2. em	9. es
3. er	10. er
4. er	11. e
5. e	12. en
6. e, er	13. e, en, en
7. em	14. em

45.
1. einige	4. viele
2. Andere	5. Wenige
3. Mehrere	6. Viele

46. 1. gelbe
2. viele gute
3. einige bekannte
4. braune
5. einige graue
6. Mehrere große, frische
7. andere neue
8. Alte
9. wenige teure (teuere)

47. 1. alten
2. einigen deutschen
3. netten
4. einigen amerikanischen
5. mehreren kleinen
6. dicken
7. vielen intelligenten
8. anderen alten

48. 1. einiger hoher
2. mehrerer wilder
3. alter
4. vieler alter
5. einiger reicher
6. mancher primitiver
7. hoher
8. armer
9. herbstlicher
10. einiger moderner

49.
1. er	5. e, e
2. e, e	6. en, en, e
3. em	7. er
4. er, e, e	8. e

9. er, e	15. e, e
10. es	16. e, e
11. en	17. em
12. en, en	18. er, er
13. em	19. en
14. en	20. e

50.
1. kochende	6. fließendem
2. bellenden	7. sterbenden
3. kommenden	8. brennenden
4. weinende	9. leidende
5. Fliegende	10. schreiende

51.
1. gekochte	6. geschnittenen
2. geöffneten	7. Vereinigten
3. geschriebene	8. angebrannte
4. gefrorenen	9. bezahlte
5. reparierte	10. zerbrochene

52.
1. Kleinen	6. Reichen
2. Blonde	7. Arme (Armen)
3. Schnelle	8. Kranken
4. Alten	9. Hübsche
5. Fremden	10. Glücklichen

53.
1. e	9. e
2. en	10. en
3. e	11. en
4. e	12. e
5. er	13. e
6. e	14. e
7. en	15. en
8. e	16. en

54.
1. Billiges	6. Persönliches
2. Neues	7. Altes
3. Süßes	8. Modernes
4. Interessantes	9. Kaltes
5. Gutes	10. Wichtiges

55.
1. Seine	6. Ihr
2. Unsere	7. Ihre
3. Ihr	8. eure
4. mein	9. Unser
5. dein	10. Ihre

56.
1. unseren	6. ihren
2. meine	7. sein
3. dein	8. meine
4. eure	9. unser
5. Ihre	10. eure

57.
1. er	6. em
2. er	7. er
3. em	8. en
4. en	9. em
5. em	10. em

58.
1. seines
2. ihrer
3. unseres
4. meiner
5. ihres
6. deines
7. eures
8. Ihrer
9. unseres
10. ihrer

59.
1. seine
2. mein
3. deine
4. Ihre
5. unsere
6. ihrer
7. seinem
8. eure
9. Ihrem
10. eure
11. Meine
12. seiner

60.
1. länger, am längsten
2. teurer, am teuersten
3. größer, am größten
4. schneller, am schnellsten
5. mehr, am meisten
6. härter, am härtesten
7. öfter, am öftesten
8. schärfer, am schärfsten
9. lieber, am liebsten
10. höher, am höchsten

61.
1. mehr als
2. dicker als
3. größer als
4. teurer als
5. lieber als
6. höher als
7. netter als
8. jünger als
9. dunkler als
10. härter als

62.
1. Der Februar ist kürzer als der Januar.
2. Das Kleid ist teurer als die Bluse.
3. Der Vater isst mehr als das Baby.
4. Ute kann besser Spanisch als Marianne.
5. Im Haus ist es wärmer als im Garten.
6. Das Auto fährt schneller als das Motorrad.
7. Robert ist ärmer als Manfred.
8. Mein Vater ist stärker als mein Bruder.
9. Die Lilie ist schöner als die Geranie.
10. Die Limonade ist kälter als das Wasser.
11. Der Kaffee ist heißer als der Tee.
12. Die Schule ist näher als die Kirche.

63.
1. Es wird immer dunkler.
2. Sie wird immer älter.
3. Er fährt immer schneller.
4. Die Tage werden immer länger.
5. Es kommt immer näher.

64.
1. Ich springe am höchsten.
2. Karl ist am größten.
3. Wir singen am besten.
4. Meine Mutter spricht am schnellsten.
5. Sabine ist am kränksten.
6. Mein Bruder spart am meisten.
7. Die Kirche ist am nächsten.
8. Klaus und ich gehen am langsamsten.
9. Unsere Nachbarn sind am reichsten.
10. Der Rock ist am kürzesten.

65.
1. Der Brocken ist hoch. Das Matterhorn ist höher. Die Zugspitze ist am höchsten.
2. Ich trinke Wasser gern. Ich trinke lieber Limonade. Ich trinke Bier am liebsten.
3. Das Gedicht ist lang. Die Geschichte ist länger. Der Roman ist am längsten.
4. Der Vogel fliegt schnell. Der Hubschrauber fliegt schneller. Das Düsenflugzeug fliegt am schnellsten.
5. Der Apfel ist sauer. Die Orange ist saurer. Die Zitrone ist am sauersten.
6. Das Brot schmeckt gut. Der Kuchen schmeckt besser. Die Torte schmeckt am besten.
7. Hans arbeitet viel. Josef arbeitet mehr. Franz arbeitet am meisten.
8. Das Wollkleid ist warm. Die Jacke ist wärmer. Der Wintermantel ist am wärmsten.

66.
1. Deine Nägel sind so lang wie Katzenkrallen.
2. Pia ist so groß wie Inge.
3. Die Jacke ist nicht so warm wie der Mantel.
4. Deine Augen sind so blau wie der Himmel.
5. Heute ist es so kalt wie im Winter.
6. Peter ist so stark wie Max.
7. Die Hose ist so teuer wie der Pullover.
8. Großmutter ist so alt wie Großvater.
9. Renate schreit so laut wie ich.
10. Mein Bruder schreibt so viel wie sein Freund.

67.
1. schönere
2. teurere
3. schärfere
4. ärmere
5. jüngerer
6. kleineres
7. besserer
8. kälteres

68.
1. wärmeren
2. stärkeren
3. schärferes
4. größere
5. bessere
6. mehr
7. kleinere
8. ältere

69.
1. Wir sind in einer kleineren Wohnung.
2. Er kommt aus einem bekannteren Museum.
3. Er fährt mit einem schnelleren Wagen.
4. Wir helfen einem kränkeren Patienten.
5. Sie erzählt von einer besseren Zeit.
6. Er spricht mit einer kleineren Frau.

70.
1. höheren
2. jüngeren
3. älteren
4. stärkeren
5. kleineren
6. kälteren

71.
1. nächste
2. höchste
3. wärmste
4. teuerstes
5. dünnste
6. härteste
7. bester
8. älteste

72.
1. jüngsten
2. modernste
3. stärksten
4. teuerste
5. beste
6. meisten
7. intelligentesten
8. kleinste

73.
1. teuersten
2. kürzesten
3. ärmsten
4. wärmsten
5. jüngsten
6. neuesten
7. teuersten
8. stärkstem

74.
1. besten
2. teuersten
3. ältesten
4. jüngsten
5. längsten
6. hübschesten

75.
1. e
2. e
3. en
4. X
5. en
6. e
7. X
8. e
9. en
10. en
11. e
12. en
13. en
14. en
15. e
16. en
17. en
18. e
19. en
20. e

76.
1. Er ist sehr alt.
2. Sie haben sehr gute Lehrer.
3. Er ist ein sehr intelligenter Mann.
4. Es ist sehr kalt.
5. Sie singt sehr schön.

77.
1. nun OR jetzt
2. heute
3. selten
4. gestern
5. nie
6. abends
7. damals
8. täglich
9. bald
10. immer
11. manchmal
12. morgens

78.
1. natürlich
2. gern
3. leider
4. nicht
5. so
6. wirklich
7. zu
8. ziemlich
9. schon
10. Vielleicht

79.
1. da OR dort
2. oben
3. drinnen
4. draußen
5. hier
6. weg
7. links
8. hinten
9. rechts
10. überall

80.
1. Er bleibt natürlich hier.
2. Maria wohnt nicht unten.
3. Karl sieht uns täglich.
4. Wir waren gestern wirklich drinnen.
5. Ich arbeite abends nicht draußen.
6. Vater suchte dich damals überall.
7. Wir sitzen manchmal gern dort.
8. Ich habe morgens wirklich großen Hunger.
9. Sie ist jetzt ziemlich dick.
10. Sie sind heute leider weg.

81.
1. Wir trinken nie Wein.
2. Sie war heute schon hier.
3. Ich bin abends nicht dort (da).
4. Sie sind jetzt leider oben.
5. Sie ist morgens immer drinnen.
6. Er war damals hier.
7. Ich sitze immer draußen.
8. Er ist vielleicht hinten.
9. Ich bin selten weg.
10. Sie ist sicherlich überall.

82.
1. noch
2. denn
3. doch
4. doch
5. Doch
6. noch einen
7. ja
8. doch

Chapter 6

1.
1. acht
2. sechzehn
3. einundzwanzig
4. vierunddreißig
5. einundfünfzig
6. sechsundfünfzig
7. siebzig
8. neunundachtzig
9. einundneunzig
10. hundert
11. hunderteins
12. neunhundertsechsunddreißig
13. tausendzweihundertvierundsiebzig
14. neunzehnhundertachtzig
15. zweitausendeinunddreißig
16. zehn Millionen
17. acht komma neun
18. siebzehn komma einundsechzig
19. zwanzig Euro dreißig
20. hunderteinundneunzig Euro siebenundsechzig

2.
1. achten
2. zweites
3. vierte
4. erste
5. dritten
6. der Achte
7. fünfte
8. der Erste
9. des Fünfzehnten
10. dem Zweiten

3.
1. Wer hat meine Hälfte?
2. dreiviertel Pfund
3. ein halbes Glas
4. ein Drittel der Arbeit
5. zweieinviertel Stunden
6. fünf Achtel der Bevölkerung
7. eineinhalb Pfund OR anderthalb Pfund OR ein und ein halbes Pfund
8. ein Zwanzigstel
9. ein Viertel des Brotes
10. ein halbes Pfund

4. 1. am Mittwoch
2. im Herbst
3. im August
4. am Dienstag
5. im Winter
6. im Mai
7. an dem Donnerstag
8. am Freitag
9. im Frühling
10. am Montag
11. am Samstag OR am Sonnabend
12. im Sommer
13. im Juli
14. in dem September
15. an dem Montag
16. am Sonntag

5. 1. Er hat am 20. (zwanzigsten) Januar Geburtstag.
2. Heute ist der 13. (dreizehnte) Oktober 2008.
3. Ich komme am Freitag, den 9. (neunten) März an.
4. Er ist 1970 gestorben.
5. Ich habe am 10. (zehnten) Dezember Geburtstag.
6. Im Jahre 1980
7. 30. 5. 1998
8. Sie hat am 10. (zehnten) August Geburtstag.
9. Ich komme am 2. (zweiten) Februar an.
10. Heute ist der 3. (dritte) März 2015.
11. Er ist 1975 gestorben.

6. 1. Es ist acht Uhr abends.
2. Es ist halb elf Uhr vormittags.
3. Es ist (ein) Viertel nach fünf.
4. Es ist fünf nach halb acht.
5. Es ist fünfundzwanzig nach sechs. OR Es ist fünf vor halb sieben.
6. Es ist (ein) Viertel vor fünf. OR Es ist drei Viertel fünf.
7. Es ist zwanzig nach elf. OR Es ist zehn vor halb zwölf.
8. Es ist zehn nach drei.
9. Es ist ein Uhr nachmittags.
10. Es ist zwölf Uhr mittags.

7. 1. Es ist zwanzig Uhr dreißig.
2. Es ist dreizehn Uhr.
3. Es ist ein Uhr.
4. Es ist vierundzwanzig Uhr.
5. Es ist null Uhr fünfunddreißig.
6. Es ist einundzwanzig Uhr fünfundzwanzig.
7. Es ist zwölf Uhr vierzig.
8. Es ist zehn Uhr fünfundvierzig.
9. Es ist vierzehn Uhr.
10. Es ist dreiundzwanzig Uhr.

8. 1. Um fünf Uhr.
2. Um zwei Uhr.
3. Um halb vier Uhr.
4. Um sieben Uhr.
5. Um elf Uhr.

9. 1. am morgen
2. Am Nachmittag
3. In der Nacht
4. am Mittag
5. am Abend

10. 1. Ja, ich bin immer abends hier.
2. Ja, ich habe immer sonntags Zeit.
3. Ja, ich gehe immer mittwochs mit.
4. Ja, ich schreibe immer nachmittags.
5. Ja, ich fahre immer morgens zur Schule.

11. 1. Er kommt morgen Abend.
2. Er war gestern Nachmittag zu Hause.
3. Otto, hast du gestern Abend geschlafen?
4. Sie kommen übermorgen.
5. Sie ist heute Morgen abgefahren.
6. Er kommt morgen Nachmittag.

12. 1. en
2. en
3. e
4. en, en
5. e
6. e, e

13. 1. er
2. em
3. em
4. en
5. em
6. er
7. en
8. em
9. em
10. em

14. 1. eines Tages
2. eines Nachts
3. eines Abends
4. eines Nachmittags
5. eines Morgens

15. 1. en
2. es, s
3. um
4. heute Abend
5. im
6. ie, e
7. am
8. es
9. In der Nacht
10. Morgen Nachmittag
11. in einem Monat
12. Um
13. Am Morgen
14. vor einer Woche OR vor acht Tagen
15. sonntags
16. am Mittag
17. In vierzehn Tagen OR In zwei Wochen
18. eines Tages
19. e, e
20. heute Morgen

Chapter 7

1.
1. Hörst
2. trinken
3. kommt
4. schicke
5. singt
6. brennt
7. fliege
8. bellt
9. bleibt
10. Denkst
11. weint
12. stehen
13. beginnt
14. bringt
15. renne
16. parkt
17. schreit
18. Rauchen
19. Kennt
20. Liebst
21. studiert
22. besuchen
23. holt
24. springt
25. ruft
26. riecht
27. schreiben
28. Steigt
29. glaubt
30. probiere
31. telefoniert
32. höre
33. brauchen
34. wohnt
35. holen

2.
1. wartet
2. Schneidest
3. arbeitet
4. bittest
5. Begegnest
6. reitet
7. Findet
8. Rechnet
9. redest
10. rettet
11. öffnet
12. Beobachtet
13. atmest
14. ordnet
15. blutet
16. Sendest
17. antwortest
18. wendet

3.
1. Wie heißt du?
2. Was mixt du?
3. Du tanzt gut.
4. Warum grüßt du mich nicht?
5. Wohin reist du?
6. Was hasst du?
7. Wo sitzt du?
8. Beißt du in den Apfel?

4.
1. klettert
2. wandern
3. bewundere
4. behandelt
5. fütterst
6. ändern
7. lächle
8. behandeln
9. klingelt
10. sammeln
11. behandle
12. füttern
13. sammle
14. klettern

5.
1. Schläfst du die ganze Nacht?
2. Er/Sie wächst schnell.
3. Wäschst du die Wäsche?
4. Ich halte die Ballons.
5. Was trägt er/sie zum Ball?
6. Lässt du mich gehen?
7. Ich backe Brot.
8. Warum gräbt er/sie ein Loch?
9. Er/Sie schlägt das Kind.
10. Das Tier säuft Wasser.
11. Er/Sie bläst ins Feuer.
12. Wohin läufst du?
13. Er/Sie fällt.
14. Fängst du den Ball?

6.
1. Hilfst du mir?
2. Er/Sie stirbt bald.
3. Siehst du uns?
4. Ich esse Suppe.
5. Der Hund frisst.
6. Was gibst du ihm?
7. Ich spreche gern.
8. Er/Sie sieht uns.
9. Er/Sie steht beim Haus.
10. Gehst du auch?
11. Was nimmst du?
12. Wann triffst du uns?
13. Was liest er/sie?
14. Warum erschrickst du?
15. Was bricht er/sie?
16. Was stiehlst du?
17. Was wirft er/sie?
18. Warum hilft er/sie nicht?
19. Was vergisst er/sie?
20. Empfiehlst du dieses Hotel?

7.
1. bin
2. ist
3. sind
4. sind
5. seid
6. Sind
7. ist
8. Bist

8.
1. haben
2. habe
3. Hast
4. haben
5. Habt
6. hat
7. haben
8. hast

9.
1. werde schon wieder gesund.
2. werdet schon wieder gesund.
3. wirst schon wieder gesund.
4. werden schon wieder gesund.
5. werden schon wieder gesund.
6. wird schon wieder gesund.

10.
1. wissen
2. wissen
3. Wisst
4. weiß
5. weiß
6. Weißt
7. weiß
8. wissen

11.
1. tust
2. tue
3. tun
4. tut
5. Tut
6. Tun
7. tun
8. tut

12. 1. ich komme morgen.
2. er hat übermorgen Geburtstag.
3. wir gehen morgen Abend ins Theater.
4. ich fliege im Juli nach Frankfurt.
5. ich fahre nächstes Jahr nach Regensburg.
6. ich besuche dich heute in acht Tagen.
7. ich bin nächsten Monat in Deutschland.
8. ich bin morgen Abend zu Hause.
9. wir haben nächste Woche Zeit.
10. sie spielt nächsten Samstag Golf.

13. 1. warte   6. kenne
2. wohnt   7. sind
3. ist   8. fliegt
4. arbeiten   9. regnet
5. Singst   10. Schreibt

14. 1. Ich lese schon seit einer Stunde.
2. Er studiert schon zehn Tage.
3. Ich bin seit fünf Minuten hier.
4. Ich kenne ihn schon sechs Jahre.
5. Ich telefoniere schon zwanzig Minuten.

15. 1. gräbst   16. grüßen
2. komme   17. Sind
3. läuft   18. wissen
4. änderst   19. schläfst
5. füttern   20. wird
6. Seid   21. steht
7. wird   22. studieren
8. reist   23. blutest
9. arbeitet   24. klingle
10. Liest   25. heißt
11. atmen   26. isst
12. frisst   27. gibst
13. fahrt   28. sieht
14. fängt   29. behandeln
15. wasche   30. sitzt

16. 1. Sie spielten.
2. Er wohnte in Köln.
3. Wir glaubten daran.
4. Ich studierte gern.
5. Der Hund bellte.
6. Ich bezahlte die Rechnung.
7. Man gratulierte ihm.
8. Wir brauchten Milch.
9. Meine Eltern bauten es.
10. Das Telefon klingelte.

17. 1. maltest   6. reparierte
2. besichtigten   7. zeigten
3. fragten   8. besuchtet
4. schenkte   9. kauften
5. lernten   10. störte

18. 1. Ich atmete ganz regelmäßig.
2. Man tötete ihn.
3. Wir retteten den Verunglückten.
4. Du öffnetest die Tür.
5. Sie begegneten ihren Eltern.
6. Paul beobachtete den Vogel.
7. Ich arbeitete gern.
8. Er ordnete die Bücher.
9. Sie antwortete nicht.
10. Sie bluteten stark.

19. 1. Er wusste das nicht.
2. Ich sandte ihm einen Brief.
3. Es brannte dort.
4. Wir brachten Geschenke.
5. Sie dachten daran.
6. Die Kinder rannten.
7. Man nannte es.
8. Ich kannte ihn auch.
9. Sie wussten die Antwort.
10. Du kanntest uns.

20. 1. Sie litt.
2. Er schlief schon.
3. Sie schrieben Briefe.
4. Wir ritten gerne.
5. Ich schrie laut.
6. Das Buch fiel auf den Boden.
7. Der Zug hielt dort.
8. Ludwig blieb dort.
9. Sie schwiegen immer.
10. Er schrieb die Aufgabe.
11. Sie schwieg nicht.
12. Ihr schnittet ins Papier.
13. Die Sonne schien.
14. Man lieh dem Kind das Buch.
15. Der Hund biss das Mädchen.

21. 1. Ich ließ Gudrun gehen.
2. Das Pferd lief am schnellsten.
3. Hubert ritt den ganzen Tag.
4. Wir liehen Gisela das Buch.
5. Der Rattenfänger fing Ratten.
6. Ich schnitt ins Fleisch.
7. Meine Eltern schrieben den Brief.
8. Wir schrien nicht.

22. 1. flog   8. zogen
2. verlor   9. floss
3. roch   10. floht
4. schlossen   11. soffen
5. schoss   12. flog
6. frorst   13. hob
7. wog   14. bogen

23.
1. aßen
2. gewann
3. sprang
4. sahen
5. kam
6. las
7. nahm
8. sprangen
9. tat
10. sank
11. band
12. starb
13. gaben
14. saßen
15. sah
16. begann
17. schwammen
18. stank
19. traft
20. bat
21. warf
22. sprachst
23. sahen
24. stahl
25. traf
26. halfen
27. standen
28. vergaß
29. maß
30. traten

24.
1. Der Hund fraß das Futter.
2. Die Bücher lagen auf dem Tisch.
3. Wir sprangen aus dem Fenster.
4. Ich saß auf einem Stuhl.
5. Die Sängerin sang die Arie.
6. Die Kinder tranken keinen Wein.
7. Er fand die Diamantbrosche.
8. Wir kamen um acht Uhr.
9. Ich sah Monika im Kino.
10. Er tat alles.

25.
1. Die Lehrerinnen fuhren in die Stadt.
2. Ich schlug ihn nicht.
3. Die Arbeiterin grub ein Loch.
4. Wir trugen Lederhosen.
5. Das Baby wuchs schnell.
6. Tante Ida wusch die Bettwäsche.
7. Er trug etwas.
8. Ich fuhr mit dem Zug.

26.
1. war
2. warst
3. war
4. Warst
5. waren
6. Wart
7. waren
8. waren
9. Wart
10. war

27.
1. Hattest
2. hatten
3. hatten
4. hatte
5. Hattest
6. Hattet
7. Hattest
8. hatte
9. Hattest
10. Hatten

28.
1. wurden
2. wurden
3. wurde
4. wurde
5. wurde
6. wurde
7. wurdest
8. Wurdet
9. Wurde
10. wurdet

29. Peter besuchte mich gestern. Wir tranken Limonade. Er aß auch ein Stück Schokoladenkuchen. Wir fuhren ins Zentrum. Wir trafen dort seine Freunde und (wir) gingen ins Kino. Der Film war prima. Er gefiel mir sehr. Wir kamen um acht Uhr nach Hause. Wir spielten eine Stunde CDs und sprachen über Musik. Meine Mutter machte noch Wurstbrote. Peter ging danach nach Hause.

30.
1. schlief, las
2. lächelte, sang
3. aßen, tanzten
4. schrieb, klingelte
5. kaufte, traf
6. gingen, wurde
7. lachte, erzählte
8. waren, kamst
9. half, arbeitete
10. schwammen, schnitt

31.
1. Wir fuhren gewöhnlich in die Schweiz.
2. Ich war immer krank.
3. Die Damen tranken gewöhnlich Tee.
4. Die Schauspielerin wurde immer nervös.
5. Wir gingen sonntags gewöhnlich zur Kirche.
6. Er arbeitete immer.
7. Karin trank gewöhnlich Limonade.
8. Wir gaben den Kindern immer Geld.
9. Ich half Renate immer.
10. Wir spielten gewöhnlich moderne Musik.

32.
1. wurdest
2. litt
3. arbeitete
4. öffnete
5. reparierte
6. besichtigten
7. Wart
8. sah
9. schlief, kam
10. Hattest
11. waren
12. nahm
13. trank, war
14. zeigten
15. klingelte
16. lief
17. wusch
18. vergaß
19. waren
20. las, studierte

33.
1. haben, gefragt
2. haben, gewohnt
3. haben, geglaubt
4. Hast, gekauft
5. hat, geliebt
6. haben, gehört
7. habe, gesucht

34.
1. habt, bezahlt
2. Hast, verkauft
3. haben, repariert
4. hat, erzählt
5. habe, studiert
6. haben, probiert
7. hat, zerstört
8. Hat, gehört
9. Hast, telefoniert
10. haben, bestellt

35.
1. Wir haben viel studiert.
2. Hast du Geld gebraucht?
3. Warum hat der Hund gebellt?
4. Er hat viel gearbeitet.
5. Man hat das Haus zerstört.
6. Haben Sie den Jungen gesucht?
7. Habt ihr oft geträumt?
8. Sie hat sehr laut geatmet.
9. Ich habe stark geblutet.
10. Die Kinder haben gerne gebadet.
11. Wo habt ihr gewohnt?

36.
1. Er hat meine Schwester gekannt.
2. Die Kinder haben die Antwort gewusst.
3. Ich habe Blumen gebracht.
4. Hast du daran gedacht?
5. Die Häuser haben gebrannt.
6. Wir haben das Paket gesandt.
7. Habt ihr den höchsten Berg genannt?
8. Ich habe das Blatt gewandt.

37.
1. sind, gerannt
2. seid, gereist
3. bin, geklettert
4. Ist, gereist
5. Seid, gewandert
6. bin, gerannt
7. sind, begegnet
8. ist, gereist
9. Bist, geklettert
10. bin, begegnet

38.
1. Hast, gelesen
2. hat, geschlagen
3. habe, gegeben
4. habt, gesehen
5. haben, gebacken
6. habe, gemessen
7. hat, gefressen
8. haben, gegraben
9. hat, getragen
10. habe, gewaschen
11. Habt, gefangen
12. hat, gegessen
13. Hast, gelassen
14. habt, geschlafen

39.
1. Mein Bruder ist schnell gefahren.
2. Bist du ins Haus getreten?
3. Wir sind schon wieder gewachsen.
4. Seid ihr nach Bremen gefahren?
5. Die Kinder sind immer gewachsen.
6. Ich bin gestern gefahren.
7. Seid ihr ins Haus gelaufen?
8. Wann bist du gekommen?
9. Die Leute sind schnell gelaufen.
10. Ich bin ins Wasser gefallen.

40.
1. Bist du oft geritten?
2. Wir haben laut geschrien.
3. Warum habt ihr nicht geschrieben?
4. Die Sonne hat geschienen.
5. Warum hat er gebissen?
6. Seid ihr lange geblieben?
7. Die Kranken haben gelitten.
8. Warum habt ihr geschwiegen?
9. Bist du auf die Leiter gestiegen?
10. Ich habe dir Geld geliehen.
11. Er hat dem Kind die Haare geschnitten.
12. Habt ihr nicht gelitten?
13. Ich habe nicht geschrien.
14. Hast du den Brief geschrieben?

41.
1. Hast, verloren
2. hat, gerochen
3. Seid, geflogen
4. hat, gewogen
5. hast, geschossen
6. hat, gezogen
7. ist, geflohen
8. ist, geflossen
9. hast, geschlossen
10. haben, gefroren
11. hat, gebogen
12. hat, gelegen
13. hat, gesoffen
14. habe, verloren

42.
1. Die Sonne ist ins Meer gesunken.
2. Die Vorlesung hat begonnen.
3. Seid ihr von der Brücke gesprungen?
4. Ich habe das Lied gesungen.
5. Bist du über die Nordsee geschwommen?
6. Er hat den Preis gewonnen.
7. Das Gas hat gestunken.
8. Hast du den Hund an den Baum gebunden?
9. Die Männer sind über die Hürde gesprungen.
10. Habt ihr oft gesungen?
11. Ich habe Wasser getrunken.
12. Wir haben gestern begonnen.
13. Er hat auf dem Sofa gesessen.
14. Habt ihr die Frau gebeten?
15. Wer hat den Schmuck gefunden?
16. Er hat kaltes Bier getrunken.

43.
1. Habt ihr sie getroffen?
2. Sie haben den Ball geworfen.
3. Warum hast du es in Stücke gebrochen?
4. Ich habe ihr geholfen.
5. Das Kind hat nichts genommen.
6. Der Verletzte ist gestorben.
7. Warum hast du gestohlen?
8. Frau Knauer, Sie haben zu schnell gesprochen.
9. Wir haben dem Kranken geholfen.
10. Hast du viel gesprochen?
11. Bist du ins Kino gegangen?
12. Ich habe hier gestanden.
13. Wir haben die Suppe empfohlen.
14. Der Kran hat das Auto gehoben.
15. Was hast du getan?

44.
1. Hast du Hunger gehabt?
2. Ich bin krank gewesen.
3. Wir haben Hunger gehabt.
4. Sie sind immer dicker geworden.
5. Er ist wieder gesund geworden.
6. Wann sind Sie dort gewesen?
7. Ich habe Kopfweh gehabt.
8. Wir sind nass geworden.
9. Bist du auch müde gewesen?
10. Ich bin böse geworden.
11. Habt ihr Geld gehabt?
12. Ich habe Sorgen gehabt.
13. Sie ist unglücklich gewesen.
14. Die Pferde sind unruhig gewesen.
15. Bist du nervös geworden?
16. Seid ihr krank gewesen?

45.
1. Haben, besichtigt
2. hat, gegeben
3. hast, gewohnt
4. hat, gekauft
5. haben, gekannt
6. hast, gebacken
7. Habt, gesehen
8. haben, geschrien
9. hat, telefoniert
10. habe, gearbeitet
11. Habt, bestellt
12. bist, begegnet
13. hat, geschwiegen
14. haben, verloren
15. hat, gefressen
16. bist, gewachsen
17. Seid, gesprungen
18. habe, geträumt
19. hat, zerstört
20. Hast, studiert
21. bist, gekommen
22. habe, erzählt
23. Habt, gegessen
24. Haben, gewartet
25. haben, getrunken
26. haben, verkauft
27. Hast, geblutet
28. bin, gestiegen
29. hat, gesagt
30. hat, repariert
31. Hast, empfohlen
32. ist, gesunken
33. habt, getroffen
34. hast, geschlafen
35. haben, geschlossen

46.
1. Wir hatten getanzt.
2. Hattest du gesungen?
3. Sie waren gefahren.
4. Hattet ihr gefragt?
5. Man hatte es genommen.
6. Sie hatten viel getrunken.
7. Hattest du studiert?
8. Ich hatte es repariert.
9. Wann war er gekommen?
10. Er hatte mich besucht.
11. Hattest du den Wagen gewaschen?
12. Konrad war dort geblieben.
13. Ich hatte die Jacke getragen.
14. Sie war in Rom gewesen.
15. Hatte er dem Kranken geholfen?
16. Wir hatten gearbeitet.

47.
1. Wir waren arm, denn wir hatten alles verloren.
2. Sie hatte Angst, denn sie war schon oft im Krankenhaus gewesen.
3. Ich wusste alles, denn ich hatte viel studiert.
4. Sie bestellten viel, denn sie hatten den ganzen Tag nichts gegessen.
5. Laura war traurig, denn ihr Freund hatte sie nicht besucht.
6. Sie waren schwach, denn sie waren krank gewesen.
7. Ich war müde, denn ich hatte schlecht geschlafen.
8. Wir hatten Durst, denn wir hatten nichts getrunken.
9. Es roch nach Wein, denn er hatte die Flasche zerbrochen.
10. Ich hatte kein Geld, denn ich hatte viel gekauft.

48.
1. Werdet, bleiben
2. Wirst, telefonieren
3. werden, glauben
4. werde, bezahlen
5. wird, lesen
6. werden, machen
7. Werdet, helfen
8. werden, schreiben
9. werde, öffnen
10. Wirst, kaufen
11. werdet, bestellen
12. wird, kommen
13. werde, vergessen
14. werden, biegen
15. werden, schreien
16. wirst, frieren

49.
1. Wir werden das Auto bringen.
2. Ich werde nach Berlin fahren.
3. Wirst du kommen?
4. Er wird das Gedicht schreiben.
5. Werdet ihr euren Eltern das Haus zeigen?
6. Sie werden arbeiten.
7. Ich werde bei Inge essen.
8. Wirst du es kaufen?

50.
1. Sie wird vielleicht krank sein.
2. Wir werden wohl kommen.
3. Sie werden vielleicht weinen.
4. Kinder, ihr werdet wohl Hunger haben.
5. Peter, du wirst es wohl wissen.
6. Ich werde wohl gehen.
7. Er wird wohl arbeiten.
8. Sie werden vielleicht helfen.

51.
1. Ihr werdet wohl getanzt haben.
2. Sie werden wohl gekommen sein.
3. Maria wird wohl geschlafen haben.
4. Wir werden es wohl nicht gesehen haben.
5. Du wirst wohl nicht gefragt haben.
6. Er wird wohl das Gedicht geschrieben haben.
7. Sie wird sich wohl gefreut haben.
8. Du wirst wohl lange gewartet haben.

52.
1. bekommt
2. zerbreche
3. verkauft
4. verstehen
5. empfange
6. bestellt
7. Gefällt
8. Besucht
9. erkläre
10. Erzählst
11. empfehlen
12. vergisst

53.
1. Wir haben das Wort verstanden.
2. Es hat mir nicht gefallen.
3. Sie haben die Wahrheit gestanden.
4. Warum ist es zerfallen?
5. Ich habe das Examen bestanden.
6. Wer hat dich besucht?
7. Habt ihr das Haus verkauft?
8. Er hat den Brief empfangen.
9. Warum hast du alles erzählt?
10. Was hat er entdeckt?

54.
1. steigt, ein
2. kommen, zusammen
3. fahre, mit
4. ziehst, an
5. Legt, nieder
6. lernen, kennen
7. kommst, zurück
8. gehe, hin
9. steht, auf
10. fahren, spazieren

55.
1. Er aß alles auf.
2. Ich schrieb das Lied ab.
3. Wir lernten ihn kennen.
4. Arnim sammelte für die Armen ein.
5. Die Kinder machten alles nach.
6. Wer machte das Fenster zu?
7. Wie nähte er das Leder zusammen?
8. Wann gingen die Studenten heim?

56.
1. Gisela, lauf nicht weg!
2. Frau Bayer, machen Sie schnell zu!
3. Konrad, fahr bitte mit!
4. Ursula und Theo, tretet leise ein!
5. Frau Breuer, stehen Sie langsam auf!
6. Helga, komm doch her!
7. Mutter, mach die Schachtel zu!
8. Arno, schau es nicht an!

57.
1. Wir werden fortgehen.
2. Ich werde hinausgehen.
3. Er wird es zurückbringen.
4. Sie werden nichts wegnehmen.
5. Wirst du ausgehen?
6. Ich werde das Album anschauen.

58.
1. Sie haben auch mitgelacht.
2. Wir haben bei ihr nachgeschaut.
3. Ich habe ihn kennengelernt.
4. Der Zug ist bald angekommen.
5. Wir sind spazierengegangen.
6. Ich bin mit ihm heimgefahren.
7. Gudrun ist dann aufgestanden.
8. Sie haben bald nachgeschaut.

59.
1. war, eingestiegen
2. hatte, ausgemacht
3. hatten, abgeschrieben
4. hatten, niedergelegt
5. Wart, zusammengekommen
6. hatte, kennengelernt
7. waren, fortgeblieben
8. hatte, zugehört

60.
1. Ich weiß, dass er fortgegangen ist.
2. Ich weiß, dass sie herkommen wird.
3. Ich weiß, dass wir morgen abfliegen.
4. Ich weiß, dass ihr Peter kennengelernt habt.
5. Ich weiß, dass der Zug angekommen war.
6. Ich weiß, dass ich nachkomme.
7. Ich weiß, dass er ausging.
8. Ich weiß, dass wir heimkommen werden.
9. Ich weiß, dass du mitfährst.
10. Ich weiß, dass er nachgeschaut hatte.

61.
1. Ich zeige dem Kind das Buch.
2. Er schickt deiner Mutter eine Karte.
3. Wir glauben dem Mann.
4. Ich bringe der Studentin den Roman.
5. Dankst du deinem Lehrer?
6. Wir helfen unserer Großmutter.
7. Das Haus gehört meinen Eltern.
8. Antwortet ihr der Lehrerin?
9. Maria kauft ihrer Freundin eine Kette.
10. Der Wagen gehört meinem Bruder.
11. Wer holt dem Kranken eine Pille?
12. Die Blumen gefallen unserer Tante.
13. Warum gratulierst du deiner Schwester?
14. Er schenkt dem Baby eine Puppe.
15. Wir schicken dem Präsidenten einen Protest.
16. Die Kinder folgen dem Großvater.

62.
1. er	10. em
2. em	11. er
3. ie	12. en
4. em, e	13. er
5. em	14. er
6. er	15. en
7. er	16. er, e
8. em	17. em
9. er	18. er

63.
1. interessiere mich
2. unterhalten uns
3. regst dich, auf
4. setzt, euch
5. erkälte mich
6. stellst, dich vor
7. ziehen sich um
8. freut sich
9. legt sich
10. freuen uns
11. rasiert sich
12. amüsiere mich
13. bewegt sich
14. Freust, dich
15. Wascht, euch
16. entscheidet sich
17. verspäte mich
18. Erinnern, sich
19. zieht sich, an
20. Entschuldigst, dich

64.
1. Er hat sich vor Pferden gefürchtet.
2. Wir haben uns für die Sammlung interessiert.
3. Sie haben sich ganz nett benommen.
4. Habt ihr euch über das Geschenk gefreut?
5. Ich habe mich schon umgezogen.
6. Wir haben uns heute vorgestellt.
7. Hast du dich oft erkältet?
8. Sie hat sich schon gewaschen.
9. Die Männer haben sich rasiert.
10. Habt ihr euch verspätet?

65.
1. Ich habe mich auf seine Ankunft gefreut.
2. Wir legen uns aufs Bett.
3. Ich habe mich am Freitag verletzt.
4. Ich interessiere mich für Briefmarken.
5. Ich habe mich schon an die Arbeit gewöhnt.
6. Er hat sich im Winter erkältet.
7. Ich wundere mich über die Explosion.
8. Die Kinder fürchten sich vor dem Gewitter.

66.
1. Reg dich nicht auf. OR Regen Sie sich nicht auf.
2. Kinder, verspätet euch nicht!
3. Peter, erkälte dich nicht!
4. Herr Ziegler, stellen Sie sich vor!
5. Setzen wir uns!
6. Gisela, wasch dich!
7. Mädchen, entschuldigt euch!
8. Frau Klein, beeilen Sie sich!
9. Ute, fürchte dich nicht vor dem Hund!
10. Vater, rasier dich!

67.
1. X	6. X
2. sich	7. uns
3. mich	8. X
4. sich	9. X
5. sich	10. sich

68.
1. tust dir, weh
2. putzen uns
3. kaufe mir
4. wascht, euch
5. bildet sich, ein
6. setzt sich, auf
7. bestellt sich
8. stelle mir, vor
9. kaufen uns
10. holt sich
11. Nehmt, euch

69.
1. Ich stelle mir das Haus vor.
2. Ich habe mir das Papier geholt.
3. Wir bestellen uns das Essen bald.
4. Ich habe mir am Fuß weh getan.
5. Die Gäste ziehen sich im Schlafzimmer an.
6. Gisela bildet sich etwas ein.

70.
1. Herr Müller, bestellen Sie sich das Buch!
2. Kinder, putzt euch die Zähne!
3. Peter und Heinz, kauft euch etwas!
4. Marlene, tu dir nicht weh!
5. Kinder, wascht euch die Hände!
6. Frau Wimmer, nehmen Sie sich etwas!

71.
1. dürfen
2. dürfen
3. darfst
4. Darf
5. darf
6. darfst
7. Dürft
8. darfst

72.
1. Er muss schwer arbeiten.
2. Sie müssen Brot holen.
3. Musst du studieren?
4. Müssen Sie heute singen?
5. Wir müssen aufstehen.
6. Wann müsst ihr im Büro sein?
7. Die Kinder müssen zu Hause bleiben.
8. Ich muss das Essen bestellen.

73.
1. Ich kann die Geschichte nicht glauben.
2. Könnt ihr morgen mitkommen?
3. Wir können unserem Freund nicht helfen.
4. Max kann gut tanzen.
5. Kannst du langsamer sprechen?
6. Ich kann alles hören.

74.
1. mag
2. mag
3. mögen
4. Magst
5. Mögt
6. mag
7. Mögen
8. mögen

75.
1. Wir wollen helfen.
2. Ich will es nicht sehen.
3. Er will kommen.
4. Wollen sie schlafen?
5. Ursel, willst du gehen?
6. Sie will studieren.
7. Erika und Franz, wollt ihr arbeiten?
8. Ich will das Museum besuchen.

76.
1. Ich soll dem Kind etwas kaufen.
2. Er soll schnell kommen.
3. Sollst du die Wahrheit sagen?
4. Die Studenten sollen lernen.
5. Man soll nicht stehlen.
6. Wir sollen nicht kommen.
7. Sollt ihr bleiben?
8. Ich soll das Auto reparieren.

77.
1. Wir können Englisch.
2. Ich mag keine Suppe.
3. Sie müssen nach Hause.
4. Kann er Deutsch?
5. Sie muss in die Stadt.
6. Er mag keine Milch.

78.
1. Wir wollten mitmachen.
2. Ich mochte keinen Reis.
3. Konntest du bleiben?
4. Durftet ihr denn rauchen?
5. Du konntest nicht heimgehen.
6. Luise wollte bezahlen.
7. Warum wollten Sie helfen?
8. Musstest du studieren?
9. Ich wollte es sehen.
10. Konntet ihr das machen?

79.
1. Konntet ihr ihm helfen?
2. Ich wollte etwas kaufen.
3. Sollte er auch mitmachen?
4. Wir mussten ihn anrufen.
5. Die Kinder mochten kein Gemüse.
6. Durftest du nicht gehen?

80.
1. Herr Maier, wollten Sie schlafen?
2. Durftet ihr rauchen?
3. Konntest du ausgehen?
4. Mochtet ihr Bananen?
5. Frau Lang, sollten Sie daran glauben?
6. Musstet ihr helfen?
7. Solltest du es kaufen?
8. Wolltet ihr fragen?
9. Durftest du mitmachen?
10. Konntet ihr es sehen?
11. Mussten Sie alles nehmen?
12. Solltet ihr Bier bestellen?
13. Mochtest du keine Milch?
14. Wollten Sie Konrad kennenlernen?

81.
1. Ich habe ihn nicht gemocht.
2. Sie hat nach Köln gewollt.
3. Hast du das gedurft?
4. Wir haben zur Schule gemusst.
5. Hat er das gekonnt?
6. Die Leute haben nicht gemocht.
7. Ihr habt doch Deutsch gekonnt.
8. Sie haben Englisch gekonnt.
9. Ich habe zur Arbeit gemusst.
10. Wir haben es gedurft.
11. Hast du keine Limonade gemocht?
12. Ich habe in die Stadt gesollt.

82.
1. Wir haben nicht mitfahren sollen.
2. Ich habe nicht schreiben können.
3. Habt ihr hier bleiben müssen?
4. Warum hat er anrufen wollen?
5. Ich habe es bringen dürfen.
6. Man hat Musik hören können.
7. Sie haben nicht aufstehen mögen.
8. Warum hast du es zerstören wollen?
9. Er hat es sehen dürfen.
10. Habt ihr dort parken wollen?
11. Ich habe heimgehen wollen.

12. Hast du zu Hause bleiben müssen?
13. Sie haben gut lesen können.
14. Hubert hat studieren müssen.

83.
1. Wir hatten es gekonnt.
2. Ich hatte abfahren müssen.
3. Er hatte es gewollt.
4. Sie hatten keinen Kuchen gemocht.
5. Sie hatte mich anrufen sollen.
6. Hattest du sie besuchen dürfen?
7. Ich hatte nicht davon sprechen wollen.
8. Ihr hattet es ja wissen dürfen.
9. Sie hatte das Fenster aufmachen können.
10. Ich hatte zur Schule gemusst.
11. Wir hatten Peter nicht gemocht.
12. Hattest du hinausgehen wollen?
13. Ich hatte Russisch gekonnt.
14. Er hatte den Wagen reparieren müssen.

84.
1. Sie werden nicht schlafen können.
2. Wir werden den ganzen Tag studieren müssen.
3. Er wird es sehen wollen.
4. Ich werde klingeln müssen.
5. Ihr werdet nichts kaufen dürfen.
6. Wirst du es schicken können?
7. Gudrun wird nicht mitmachen wollen.
8. Werdet ihr die Suppe probieren wollen?
9. Sie werden nicht schreien dürfen.
10. Wir werden nicht arbeiten können.

85.
1. Wir lassen das Bild in der Schule.
2. Ich helfe Rita den Hund suchen.
3. Siehst du deine Schwester arbeiten?
4. Hören Sie die Sonate?
5. Er hört seine Frau schreien.
6. Lasst ihr Hans gehen?
7. Die Leute hören uns sprechen.
8. Ich sehe die Kirche.
9. Frau Berger hilft heute.
10. Er lässt Gerda mitkommen.

86.
1. Ich habe es liegen lassen.
2. Wir haben sie lachen hören.
3. Er hat seinen Freund gesehen.
4. Sie haben Heinz das Auto reparieren helfen.
5. Er hat nichts gehört.
6. Ich habe Pia reiten sehen.
7. Sie haben Sonja weinen hören.
8. Wir haben die Zeitungen zu Hause gelassen.
9. Wir haben den Kindern geholfen.
10. Vater hat uns gehen lassen.

87.
1. Er wird Peter schreiben sehen.
2. Ich werde Otto kommen hören.
3. Wir werden den Kindern zeichnen helfen.
4. Wirst du Dieter lachen sehen?
5. Sie werden Rainer sprechen hören.

6. Werden Sie Anneliese lesen helfen?
7. Ich werde den Mantel hier liegen lassen.
8. Werdet ihr Großmutter rufen hören?

88.
1. Er sagt, dass du die Jacke hast liegen lassen.
2. Er sagt, dass wir Josef haben studieren helfen.
3. Er sagt, dass sie Franz haben singen hören.
4. Er sagt, dass ich es habe machen lassen.
5. Er sagt, dass sie das Geschenk hat öffnen dürfen.
6. Er sagt, dass du den Bleistift hast zurückgeben wollen.
7. Er sagt, dass wir Peter haben kommen lassen.
8. Er sagt, dass ihr das Auto habt bringen müssen.

89.
1. ohne Norma zu sehen
2. anstatt zur Schule zu gehen
3. um Gertrud zu helfen
4. ohne anzurufen
5. um mich umzuziehen
6. um die Kinder einzuladen
7. anstatt es Helga zu bringen
8. ohne einen Mantel anzuziehen
9. um zu fragen
10. ohne es zu lernen

90.
1. sich zu entschuldigen
2. uns zu fragen
3. den Kindern zu helfen
4. die Geschichte zu erzählen
5. sich zu rasieren
6. mitzukommen
7. es zu holen
8. Geld zu nehmen
9. den Hund zu füttern
10. den Kuchen zu essen

91.
1. anzurufen
2. zu schreiben
3. mitzugeben
4. einzuladen
5. zu schneiden
6. zu sein
7. zu lesen
8. zu besuchen
9. zu begleiten
10. mitzunehmen
11. zu sehen
12. zu glauben

92.
1. Er braucht nicht zu studieren.
2. Ich brauche nicht zu lesen.
3. Wir brauchen das Buch nicht zurückzugeben.
4. Sie braucht nicht zu arbeiten.
5. Ihr braucht es nicht zu machen.
6. Du brauchst Herbert nicht zu helfen.
7. Ich brauche Bert nicht zu besuchen.
8. Renate braucht nicht zu lesen.
9. Sie brauchen die Geschichte nicht zu erzählen.
10. Ich brauche es nicht zu bestellen.

93.
1. beim Gehen
2. beim Tanzen
3. beim Singen
4. beim Arbeiten
5. beim Malen
6. beim Reparieren
7. beim Studieren
8. beim Spielen
9. beim Telefonieren
10. beim Schwimmen

94.
1. leidend
2. lesende
3. fließendem
4. bellenden
5. Blutend
6. singende
7. weinenden
8. schlafende
9. lächelnde
10. Grüßend

95.
1. zerstörte
2. angebrannt
3. gestohlenen
4. geschriebene
5. gebackene
6. begonnene
7. gefangen
8. gefütterte
9. reparierte
10. geöffnete

96.
1. en
2. er
3. e
4. e
5. e
6. en
7. en
8. e
9. e
10. e

97.
1. Ja, schreiben Sie bitte!
2. Ja, schlafen Sie bitte!
3. Ja, gehen Sie bitte!
4. Ja, tanzen Sie bitte!
5. Ja, lächeln Sie bitte!
6. Ja, reden Sie bitte!
7. Ja, arbeiten Sie bitte!
8. Ja, erzählen Sie bitte!
9. Ja, singen Sie bitte!
10. Ja, fahren Sie bitte!

98.
1. Findet
2. Sprecht
3. Trinkt
4. Holt
5. Schlaft
6. Parkt
7. Studiert
8. Geht
9. Bleibt
10. Ruft
11. Esst
12. Nehmt
13. Reitet
14. Bestellt
15. Schreibt

99.
1. Sing lauter!
2. Komm jetzt!
3. Such das Geld!
4. Bleib hier!
5. Mach es!
6. Grüß Tante Ida!
7. Geh ins Haus!
8. Probier die Wurst!
9. Wein nicht!
10. Spring ins Wasser!
11. Schwimm schneller!
12. Sag die Wahrheit!
13. Ruf die Polizei!
14. Frag den Lehrer!
15. Rauch nicht!

100.
1. Ja, warte!
2. Ja, rede!
3. Ja, lächle!
4. Ja, füttere es!
5. Ja, behandle ihn!
6. Ja, öffne es!
7. Ja, antworte!
8. Ja, ändere es!
9. Ja, beobachte es!
10. Ja, rechne!
11. Ja, schneide es!
12. Ja, sammle es!
13. Ja, wandere!
14. Ja, arbeite!

101.
1. Hilf dem Kind!
2. Sprich lauter!
3. Gib es dem Lehrer!
4. Stiehl nicht!
5. Lies die Zeitung!
6. Brich es nicht!
7. Triff die Frau!
8. Stirb nicht!
9. Erschrick nicht!
10. Iss das Fleisch!
11. Nimm den Schmuck!
12. Vergiss nichts!

102.
1. habt
2. sei
3. werden Sie
4. wisst
5. seien Sie
6. werde
7. sei
8. hab
9. haben Sie
10. wissen Sie

103.
1. Kochen wir das Abendessen!
2. Fragen wir den Lehrer!
3. Trinken wir warme Milch!
4. Kaufen wir Wein!
5. Gehen wir jetzt!
6. Schreiben wir die Aufgaben!
7. Rufen wir den Hund!
8. Holen wir das Buch!
9. Arbeiten wir viel!
10. Ändern wir nichts!

104.
1. Wir würden nichts nehmen.
2. Würdest du bezahlen?
3. Ich würde den ganzen Tag schwimmen.
4. Sie würden viel arbeiten.
5. Er würde nicht studieren.
6. Würdet ihr nach Deutschland fahren?
7. Würden Sie laut singen?
8. Ich würde nicht ins Wasser springen.
9. Würdest du das Buch lesen?
10. Er würde den Wagen reparieren.
11. Würdet ihr kommen?
12. Sie würden das Geschenk bringen.
13. Würdet ihr mir helfen?

14. Ich würde auch gehen.
15. Würden Sie die Jacke tragen?
16. Würden die Kinder laufen?

105.
1. Würden Sie bitte kommen?
2. Würdest du das bitte nehmen?
3. Würdet ihr bitte hier bleiben?
4. Würden Sie bitte schneller fahren?
5. Würdest du mir bitte das Messer geben?
6. Würden Sie bitte langsamer sprechen?
7. Würden Sie bitte gehen?
8. Würdest du bitte das Auto parken?
9. Würdet ihr bitte das Essen bestellen?
10. Würden Sie es bitte den Kindern zeigen?
11. Würden Sie bitte Ihren Vater besuchen?
12. Würdest du bitte hier warten?

106.
1. Sie besuchten uns.
2. Wir machten viel.
3. Kauftet ihr es?
4. Ich erzählte es.
5. Zerstörtest du es?
6. Arbeiteten Sie dort?
7. Ich fragte ihn.
8. Wir zahlten.
9. Er glaubte es.
10. Ich sagte es.
11. Wohntest du dort?
12. Hörtet ihr es?
13. Sie lernten es.
14. Wir weinten nicht.
15. Ich bezahlte.
16. Er studierte.
17. Bautet ihr das Haus?
18. Spielten Sie dort?
19. Sie hörten alles.
20. Maltest du?

107.
1. Ich weinte.
2. Wir spielten.
3. Sie holten es.
4. Er glaubte es nicht.
5. Kinder, spieltet ihr?
6. Gerda, kauftest du Blumen?
7. Frau Treibl, wohnten Sie dort?
8. Sie arbeitete.
9. Wir lernten.
10. Sie probierten die Suppe.

108.
1. Das Haus brennte.
2. Dächtet ihr daran?
3. Ich brächte etwas.
4. Nenntest du es?
5. Sie rennten schnell.
6. Wir wüssten es.
7. Ich sendete den Brief.
8. Wir wendeten das Blatt.
9. Ich wüsste das.
10. Brächtest du das Buch?

109.
1. Ich schriebe das Gedicht.
2. Wir tränken nichts.
3. Ließest du ihn gehen?
4. Die Alten gingen zur Kirche.
5. Die Sonne schiene nicht.
6. Die Studenten lasen das Buch.
7. Er flöge auch.
8. Schliefest du lange?
9. Ich gäbe Anna alles.
10. Er liefe schnell.
11. Die Leute führen mit dem Auto.
12. Wir schrien laut.
13. Er schnitte das Haar.
14. Ich bliebe hier.
15. Wir kämen auch.
16. Nähmest du das Papier?
17. Ich äße Brot.
18. Das Pferd zöge den Schlitten.
19. Er verlöre das Geld.
20. Wir sprängen hoch.

110.
1. Er stürbe.
2. Sie hülfen.
3. Wir würfen den Ball.
4. Sie stünde hier.
5. Ich hülfe.
6. Sie stürben.
7. Wir stünden hier.
8. Helga, hülfest du?

111.
1. Wir hätten kein Auto.
2. Ich wäre reich.
3. Sie hätten keine Ferien.
4. Du wärest nicht glücklich.
5. Ich hätte keinen Hund.
6. Sie wäre böse.
7. Sie wären nicht intelligent.
8. Ihr hättet kein Geld.
9. Er hätte nichts.
10. Hättet ihr Geld?
11. Wir wären krank.
12. Hättest du Angst?
13. Wir hätten alles.
14. Wäret ihr müde?
15. Wärest du froh?
16. Ich wäre arm.

112.
1. Könnten Sie mir helfen?
2. Wolltest du auch zeichnen?
3. Müsstet ihr nicht studieren?
4. Dürfte er mitgehen?
5. Solltest du Marianne besuchen?
6. Könnte ich ein Stück nehmen?
7. Müsstest du nicht lernen?
8. Wolltet ihr den Film sehen?
9. Könnte sie es holen?
10. Dürfte ich bleiben?

113. 1. Möchtest   6. Möchtest
2. möchte   7. Möchten
3. möchten   8. möchte
4. möchten   9. Möchtet
5. Möchten   10. Möchtest

114. 1. Ich wollte, er bliebe nicht dort.
2. Ich wollte, sie könnten nicht abfahren.
3. Ich wollte, wir lebten in keinem Dorf.
4. Ich wollte, ich hätte kein Zahnweh.
5. Ich wollte, ihr arbeitetet nicht so viel.
6. Ich wollte, ich müsste nicht studieren.
7. Ich wollte, wir wären zu Hause.
8. Ich wollte, du kauftest dir etwas.
9. Ich wollte, sie weinte nicht.
10. Ich wollte, ich wäre nicht arm.
11. Ich wollte, wir hätten es nicht.
12. Ich wollte, er nähme es nicht.
13. Ich wollte, er sähe Paula nicht.
14. Ich wollte, sie besuchten Oma nicht.

115. 1. Wenn wir nur in München wären!
2. Wenn er nur das Fenster öffnete!
3. Wenn ihr doch ein Auto kauftet!
4. Wenn die Leute nur nicht so laut schrien!
5. Wenn ich nur alles wüsste!
6. Wenn er nur nicht krank wäre!
7. Wenn die Kinder nur zu Hause blieben!
8. Wenn ich nur Deutsch könnte!
9. Wenn ihr nur mehr hättet!
10. Wenn Georg nur nicht abführe!

116. 1. Sagte sie nur die Wahrheit!
2. Könnte ich doch schlafen!
3. Reparierte er nur das Auto!
4. Tränken sie nur nicht so viel!
5. Schwiege er doch!
6. Hätten wir nur keine Angst!
7. Wärest du nur hier!
8. Bliebe er nur hier!
9. Glaubte sie es nur!
10. Lerntet ihr nur mehr!

117. 1. würde ich arbeiten.
2. würde ich nicht hier wohnen.
3. würde ich dir nichts geben.
4. würde ich nicht nach Hamburg fliegen.
5. würde ich mir nichts bestellen.
6. würden wir Kaffee trinken.
7. würden wir uns unterhalten.
8. würde ich mich freuen.
9. würde ich mich umziehen.
10. würde ich mich nicht fürchten.

118. 1. hätte, hülfe
2. wäre, wäre
3. sähe, beschriebe
4. bliebest, besuchten

5. studiertet, wüsstet
6. bestellten, äßen
7. lerntest, könntest

119. 1. Hülfest du mir, dann wäre ich froh.
2. Käme er, dann bliebe ich dort.
3. Fragten wir ihn, dann würde er uns antworten.
4. Wollte sie es, dann gäbe ich es ihr.
5. Hätte ich Angst, dann würde ich schreien.

120. 1. Wäre ich krank, bliebe ich zu Hause.
2. Wüssten wir es, erzählten wir es Alexander.
3. Hätte sie Geld, kaufte sie den Mantel.
4. Arbeiteten sie, wären sie glücklicher.
5. Käme er an, holte ich ihn ab.

121. 1. hätten   6. könnte
2. liebtest   7. bliebe
3. ginge   8. arbeiteten
4. wären   9. sähe
5. wollte   10. nähmen

122. 1. Wenn wir nur in der Schule gewesen wären!
2. Wenn du nur angerufen hättest!
3. Wenn ich nur gebadet hätte!
4. Wenn er nur Angst gehabt hätte!
5. Wenn ihr nur gekommen wäret!

123. 1. Hättest du nur geschrien!
2. Wären wir ihr nur begegnet!
3. Wäre ich nur hingegangen!
4. Wäre er nur nicht gestorben!
5. Hätte sie nur geschrieben!

124. 1. gegessen hätte, hätte, gehabt
2. zurückgebracht hättest, hätte, geholt
3. zugemacht hättet, hättet, erkältet
4. angerufen hättest, hätte, gesagt
5. geblutet hätte, hätte, geschrien

125. 1. Hätte es geklingelt, hätten wir aufgemacht.
2. Hättest du angerufen, wäre ich gekommen.
3. Hätten wir es gefunden, hätten wir es wieder zurückgegeben.
4. Hättet ihr geschrieben, hätten wir euch dort getroffen.

126. 1. Er tut, als ob er es gekauft hätte.
2. Sie tun, als ob sie nicht geschlafen hätten.
3. Sie tut, als ob sie krank gewesen wäre.
4. Er tut, als ob er mitgekommen wäre.

127. 1. Hätte er nur bleiben dürfen!
2. Wenn ich doch nicht hätte gehen müssen!
3. Er tut, als ob er es hätte sehen können.
4. Du tust, als ob ich es hätte schreiben sollen.
5. Wenn ich hätte reiten wollen, hätte ich es dir gesagt.

6. Hätte er nur singen können!
7. Wenn du nur nichts hättest essen wollen!
8. Wenn wir hätten fragen dürfen, hätten wir die Antwort gewusst.
9. Hätte sie nur helfen können!
10. Sie tun, als ob sie auf mich hätten warten müssen.

128.
1. sei	9. schicke
2. bleibe	10. schenke
3. wohne	11. habe
4. studiere	12. wisse
5. arbeite	13. könne
6. gebe	14. wolle
7. kaufe	15. finde
8. bringe	16. trinke

129.
1. Er sagt, er habe schon geschrieben.
2. Er sagt, ich sei ins Kino gegangen.
3. Er sagt, sie sei im Krankenhaus gewesen.
4. Er sagt, er habe etwas geholt.
5. Er sagt, er habe nicht kommen dürfen.

130.
1. Sie sagte, Mutter wäre krank gewesen.
2. Sie sagte, Großvater hätte Geld gehabt.
3. Sie sagte, Peter hätte Angst.
4. Sie sagte, sie wäre allein gewesen.
5. Sie sagte, er hätte ihn gesehen.
6. Sie sagte, Christa wäre nach Köln gefahren.
7. Sie sagte, Onkel Werner wäre in Hamburg.
8. Sie sagte, sie hätte dich besucht.

131.
1. Er hat gesagt, Mutter sei krank gewesen.
2. Er hat gesagt, Großvater habe Geld gehabt.
3. Er hat gesagt, Peter habe Angst.
4. Er hat gesagt, sie sei allein gewesen.
5. Er hat gesagt, er habe ihn gesehen.
6. Er hat gesagt, Christa sei nach Köln gefahren.
7. Er hat gesagt, Onkel Werner sei in Hamburg.
8. Er hat gesagt, er habe dich besucht.

132.
1. wird vom, gebacken
2. wird durch, gerettet
3. wird, serviert
4. werden von, angeschaut
5. wird von, genommen
6. wird vom, geholfen
7. wird von, geschrieben
8. wird von, gewaschen
9. wird von, gegraben
10. wird durch, zerstört
11. werden von, gesehen
12. werde von, geschlagen
13. wird von, gehört
14. wird durch, zerstört
15. wird von, repariert

133.
1. Das Kind wird von dem (vom) Hund gebissen.
2. Das Haus wird durch das (durchs) Feuer zerstört.
3. Der Kaffee wird von meinen Freunden getrunken.
4. Das Pferd wird von ihm gefüttert.
5. Dem Kranken wird von dem (vom) Vater geholfen.

134.
1. Wir wurden abgeholt.
2. Die Rechnung wurde von Renate bezahlt.
3. Wurdest du beobachtet?
4. Das Auto wurde geparkt.
5. Es wurde schon von den Leuten gemacht.
6. Das Museum wurde von der Klasse besucht.
7. Das Wort wurde von dem Studenten buchstabiert.
8. Ich wurde gesehen.
9. Die Maschine wurde von dem Mechaniker repariert.

135.
1. Er wurde gesehen.
2. Das Fenster wurde von Marlene geöffnet.
3. Sie wurden von ihrem Vater gefragt.
4. Sie wurde gehört.
5. Es wurde von meiner Tante gewaschen.
6. Uns wurde von dem Jungen geholfen. OR Es wurde uns von dem Jungen geholfen.
7. Ich wurde beobachtet.
8. Die Stadt wurde durch eine Bombe zerstört.

136.
1. Das Museum ist 1911 erbaut worden.
2. Es ist ihr darüber erzählt worden.
3. Das Kleid ist rot gefärbt worden.
4. Es ist ihm gegeben worden.
5. Du bist überall gesucht worden.
6. Ich bin von ihm gesehen worden.
7. Er ist vom Arzt behandelt worden.

137.
1. Das Haus wird von meinen Freunden gebaut werden.
2. Die Geschichte wird erzählt werden.
3. Der Patient wird durch Medikamente geheilt werden.
4. Das Geschenk wird von den Kindern bewundert werden.
5. Die Rechnung wird von meinem Vater bezahlt werden.
6. Der Brief wird geholt werden.
7. Das Haus wird beobachtet werden.
8. Der Brief wird vom Lehrer geschrieben werden.
9. Rudi wird gefragt werden.
10. Franz wird abgeholt werden.

138. 1. Man zerstört die Ruine.
2. Man ruft uns an.
3. Man bestellt das Essen.
4. Man erzählte die Geschichte.
5. Man holte den Arzt.
6. Man schickte den Katalog.
7. Man hat das Bild verkauft.
8. Man hat den Mann angerufen.
9. Man hatte den Brief geschrieben.
10. Man hatte die Limonade getrunken.
11. Man wird wohl die Stadt aufbauen.

139. 1. Es wird gefunden.
2. Es wurde zerstört.
3. Es wurde gezeigt.
4. Es wurde gerettet.
5. Es wird repariert.
6. Es wird begonnen.
7. Es wird geschnitten werden.
8. Es war gebaut worden.
9. Es wurde bezahlt.
10. Es wird gesagt.

140. 1. Es ist gefunden.
2. Es war zerstört.
3. Es war gezeigt.
4. Es war gerettet.
5. Es ist repariert.
6. Es ist begonnen.
7. Es wird geschnitten.
8. Es war gebaut gewesen.
9. Es war bezahlt.
10. Es ist gesagt.

141.
1. kennst
2. kenne
3. können
4. Wisst
5. weiß
6. kennt
7. weiß
8. Kannst
9. Kennt
10. wissen

142. 1. Wir kennen den Präsidenten.
2. Sie können Französisch.
3. Inge, hast du meine Tante gekannt?
4. Ich weiß die Antwort.
5. Er weiß alles.

143.
1. liegt
2. liege
3. Liegt
4. legst
5. leg
6. liegen
7. legt
8. lege

144.
1. setzt
2. sitzt
3. setze
4. setzt
5. setzt
6. sitze
7. sitzt
8. Sitzt

145.
1. stehen
2. stellt
3. stelle
4. Stellst
5. stelle
6. steht
7. stellen
8. Stehst

146. 1. lassen
2. lässt, wohnen
3. lassen, gehen
4. lasse, singen
5. Lässt
6. lässt, rufen/anrufen
7. lass
8. lasse

147. 1. Wir haben die Kinder spielen lassen.
2. Er hat das Fahrrad dort gelassen.
3. Hast du die Jacke zu Hause gelassen?
4. Sie haben uns mitmachen lassen.
5. Rudi hat Inge mitmachen lassen.
6. Ich habe die Katze im Garten gelassen.

Chapter 8

1. 1. Er kennt den Herrn nicht.
2. Wir geben es den Leuten nicht.
3. Ich wasche mich nicht.
4. Heinz weiß es nicht.
5. Sie kamen vorgestern nicht.
6. Ich kaufe den Mantel nicht.
7. Sie nimmt es nicht.

2. 1. Sie haben nicht gespielt.
2. Ich wollte die Rechnung nicht bezahlen.
3. Wir haben sie nicht schreien hören.
4. Maria hat nicht neben dem Hotel gewartet.
5. Ich weiß, dass er nicht fliegen will.
6. Das ist nicht meine Tante.
7. Er sagt, dass er sie nicht gesucht hätte.
8. Das Mädchen fährt nicht heim.
9. Wir sind nicht zur Schule gegangen.
10. Ich bin nicht dort geblieben.
11. Wir sind nicht im Kino.
12. Ich sehe sie nicht kommen.
13. Er kommt nicht mit.
14. Ihr könnt es nicht sehen.
15. Sie sind nicht reich.
16. Er hat nicht hier gewartet.
17. Wir haben es nicht geholt.
18. Das sind nicht meine Bücher.
19. Ich hoffe, Inge nicht zu sehen.
20. Du hast sie nicht genommen.

3.
1. Sie ist nicht bei ihrer Tante geblieben
2. Er hat nicht das Auto repariert
3. Wir haben nicht das rote Buch gekauft
4. Ich brauche nicht den Löffel
5. Ihr habt das Radio nicht gewonnen
6. Ich lese nicht die Zeitung

4.
1. Habt ihr ihnen nicht geholfen?
2. Sind sie nicht abgefahren?
3. Holt sie es nicht?
4. Macht sie nicht mit?
5. Darfst du nicht bleiben?
6. Hast du ihn nicht gefragt?
7. Ist das nicht dein Freund?
8. Hast du nicht mitgesungen?
9. Rasiert er sich nicht?
10. Hat sie es nicht vergessen?
11. Willst du ihm nicht helfen?
12. War das nicht seine Frau?
13. Ist sie nicht schön?
14. Kaufst du die Blumen nicht?
15. Kann er sich nicht daran erinnern?

5.
1. Ja, er war krank.
2. Doch, er ist gestorben.
3. Ja, ich habe es gekonnt.
4. Doch, wir brauchen es.
5. Doch, er hat es gefressen.
6. Doch, sie ist intelligent.

6.
1. Sie braucht nicht zu kommen.
2. Hans braucht nicht zu schreiben.
3. Ihr braucht nicht abzufahren.
4. Wir brauchen nicht zu gehen.
5. Ich brauche nicht zu studieren.
6. Sie brauchen nicht zu arbeiten.
7. Wir brauchen nicht zu springen.
8. Du brauchst den Roman nicht zu lesen.

7.
1. Er fragt uns nie.
2. Wir sind gar nicht müde.
3. Sie wohnt nicht mehr in Bonn.
4. Ich kann noch nicht fahren.
5. Er hat sie noch nie gesehen.
6. Er hilft nie.
7. Sie geht nicht mehr ins Kino.
8. Er war noch nie in Deutschland.
9. Wir sind noch nicht nach Hause geflogen.
10. Sie sind gar nicht freundlich.
11. Ich habe Schnecken noch nie gegessen.
12. Er kennt mich nicht mehr.
13. Sie lernte den Präsidenten nie kennen.
14. Wir machen gar nicht mit.
15. Er hat die Sammlung noch nicht verkauft.

8.
1. Er erzählte kein Märchen.
2. Wir besuchten keine bekannte Stadt.
3. Er hat unser Kind nicht gesehen.
4. Hat sie keine Blumen gekauft?
5. Trinkt er kein Wasser?
6. Ich habe keinen warmen Mantel.
7. Das sind keine Haselnüsse.
8. Ich habe mich nicht auf die Ferien gefreut.
9. Wir essen keine Bananen.
10. Ich habe keinen Freund.
11. Ich kenne den Herrn nicht.
12. Sie singt das Lied nicht.
13. Er hat keine Kinder.
14. Dieser Ring ist nicht teuer.
15. Hier liegt kein Buch.
16. Wer isst kein Brot?
17. Das ist kein Tachometer.
18. Die Lehrerin schreibt nicht.
19. Ist die Milch nicht sauer?
20. Ich habe keine Zeit.

9.
1. Er kann nichts sehen.
2. Niemand hilft uns.
3. Ich habe nichts Altes.
4. Sie wissen nichts.
5. Er fragt niemand/niemanden.

Chapter 9

1.
1. Kommt er morgen?
2. Bringt Herbert es zurück?
3. Setzte er sich aufs Bett?
4. Weißt du alles?
5. Arbeiteten die Männer viel?
6. Braucht ihr es?
7. Amüsiert ihr euch?
8. Bestellte Petra auch Bier?
9. Besichtigen die Touristen das Schloss?
10. Will er nicht?
11. Hörst du nichts?
12. Muss sie in die Stadt?
13. Bleiben sie dort?
14. Rauchte er viel?
15. Schwimmst du nicht?

2.
1. Hat er schon geschrieben?
2. Haben sie sich gestern kennengelernt?
3. Habt ihr alles verloren?
4. Wird sie es aufmachen?
5. Darfst du es nehmen?
6. Hat er sich verletzt?
7. Werdet ihr euch umziehen?
8. Hättest du es gekauft?
9. Ist er gestorben?
10. Können sie nicht dort bleiben?
11. Lässt du Peter helfen?
12. Sieht sie die Kinder spielen?

3.
1. Ist er nicht hier?
2. Fährst du nicht mit?
3. Dürft ihr nicht nach Bonn fahren?
4. Kommst du nicht mit?
5. Hilft sie nicht den Kindern?

4.
1. Wann	8. Wie oft
2. Wie	9. Wie lange
3. Wie oft	10. Um wie viel Uhr
4. Wie	11. Wann
5. Wie lange	12. Wann
6. Wie viel	13. Warum
7. Wie	14. Um wie viel Uhr

5.
1. Wo	5. Wohin
2. Woher	6. Wo
3. Wohin	7. Woher
4. Woher	8. Wohin

6.
1. Wohin fährt sie?
2. Wann bringen sie es?
3. Wie oft besuchte uns Alexander?
4. Wie ist es heute?
5. Wo ist sie?
6. Woher kommt Ella?
7. Wie lange bleiben sie dort?
8. Wie viel kostet es?

7.
1. Was	11. Wem
2. Wem	12. Wen
3. Was	13. Wer
4. wem	14. Wem
5. Wer	15. Wessen
6. wem	16. wem
7. Wen	17. wen
8. Wessen	18. Wessen
9. wen	19. Was
10. wem	20. Was

8.
1. Wovon	9. Über wen
2. Was	10. Was
3. Womit	11. Mit wem
4. Wen	12. Wofür
5. Wonach	13. Worin
6. Wofür	14. Wozu
7. Worauf	15. Hinter wen
8. Für wen	

9.
1. Welche	7. welchem
2. welchen	8. Welches
3. welcher	9. welchem
4. Welchen	10. Welche
5. welcher	11. Welcher
6. welchen	12. Welche

10.
1. Welcher	4. Welche
2. welchem	5. Welchen
3. welche	

11.
1. Welche nimmst du?
2. Welche hat er gekauft?
3. Von welchen erzählt er?
4. Welche brauchst du?
5. Für welche kauft er es?

12.
1. Was für ein Auto ist das?
2. Was für ein Mädchen ist das?
3. Mit was für Leuten fährt er nach Deutschland?
4. In was für einem Haus wohnen sie?
5. Was für Bücher schreibt er?

Chapter 10

1.
1. Der Schnellzug ist vor einer Stunde angekommen.
2. Norma bleibt bei uns.
3. Der kleine Junge will mitmachen.
4. Die Goldkette wurde von ihm zurückgebracht.
5. Wir haben ihn sehen können.
6. Gerda geht mit Klaus spazieren.
7. Der Hund beißt den Jungen.
8. Ich habe es kaufen dürfen.
9. Er wird die Geschichte erzählen.
10. Er sieht mich kommen.

2.
1. Sie haben schneller laufen müssen.
2. Wir haben die Schachtel aufgemacht.
3. Er hat nicht heimgehen wollen.
4. Ich habe es ihm zeigen wollen.
5. Seine Großeltern haben es mitgebracht.
6. Mein Vater hat mich gehen lassen.
7. Er hat gut singen können.
8. Der Alte hat sich auf die Bank gesetzt.
9. Der Zug ist vor einer Stunde abgefahren.

3.
1. Das Auto wollten wir in Deutschland kaufen.
2. Heute kommen sie zurück.
3. Im Kino hat er es vergessen.
4. Meistens ist er am Abend müde.
5. Leider waren meine Eltern zu Hause.
6. Wegen meiner Erkältung konnte ich nicht kommen.
7. Gestern Abend haben wir es gemacht.
8. Mit dem Zug fahren sie in die Schweiz.
9. Im Zentrum ist das Museum.
10. Oft habe ich es hören müssen.

4.
1. Wann machst du das Fenster zu?
2. Was darf das Kind wissen?
3. Wie viel kostet die Kamera?
4. Wo wollen die Leute wohnen?
5. Warum setzt du dich nicht nieder?
6. Wohin fährst du mit dem Auto?
7. Worauf sollen die Bücher liegen?
8. Woher kommen die Kinder?

5. 1. Weil ich viel zu tun habe, kann ich nicht mit ins Kino.
2. Als ihre Mutter ins Zimmer kam, las sie ein Buch.
3. Wenn ich Zeit habe, werde ich meine Tante besuchen.
4. Während ich studierte, habe ich viel lernen müssen.
5. Bevor du abreist, sollst du deiner Großmutter helfen.

6. 1. X
2. Vor einer Woche hat uns Axel besucht.
3. Im Theater hat sich Konrad amüsiert.
4. Jeden Tag schickt ihr Mutter etwas.
5. Wo hat dich Ursel getroffen?
6. X
7. X
8. Gestern hat uns Vater etwas gebracht.
9. Um neun Uhr trifft sie ihr Freund.
10. X

7. 1. Hast du ihm den Brief geschrieben?
2. Kennt mich Peter?
3. Wollte Gerda das Museum besuchen?
4. Helft ihr ihm den Baum pflanzen?
5. Macht Herr Klein die Tür auf?
6. Kann er Deutsch?
7. Hat sich Erika bei ihr entschuldigt?
8. Hast du dir das schnelle Auto gekauft?
9. Habt ihr es ihm genommen?
10. Hat man dich gefragt?

8. 1. Zeig OR Zeigt
2. Öffne OR Öffnet
3. Frag OR Fragt
4. Komm, heim OR Kommt, heim
5. Mach, nach OR Macht, nach

9. 1. Ja, trinken Sie das Bier!
2. Ja, lachen Sie darüber!
3. Ja, schicken Sie es mir!
4. Ja, ziehen Sie den warmen Mantel an!

10. 1. Er ist arm, aber seine Eltern sind reich.
2. Ich freute mich, denn er wollte sofort mit der Arbeit anfangen.
3. Wir sind nicht dort geblieben, sondern wir sind ausgegangen.
4. Sei vorsichtig, oder es geht kaputt!
5. Ich spiele Golf, und er spielt Tennis.
6. Er ist glücklich, denn er hat Geld gewonnen.
7. Wir sind nicht in Deutschland, sondern wir sind in Spanien.
8. Du kannst zu Hause bleiben, aber ich muss zur Schule.
9. Er trinkt Milch, und ich trinke Limonade.

11. 1. Wann liest du das Buch?
2. Wenn sie krank ist, bleibt sie zu Hause.
3. Wenn er mich besuchte, brachte er mir etwas.
4. Weißt du, wann er ankommt?
5. Als es kalt wurde, ging ich ins Haus.
6. Wenn er mehr Geld hätte, führe er nach Deutschland (OR würde er nach Deutschland fahren).

12. 1. Sie hat Kopfweh, weil die Kinder viel Lärm gemacht haben.
2. Er ist in Berlin, während seine Frau noch hier ist.
3. Ich fragte ihn, ob sie wieder gesund sind.
4. Es war sehr kalt, als wir in Alaska waren.
5. Sie konnte gut Deutsch, nachdem sie in Deutschland studiert hatte.
6. Wir kauften alles, da wir viel Geld gewonnen hatten.
7. Wir blieben im Wald, bis es dunkel wurde.
8. Konrad musste mithelfen, bevor er ausgehen konnte.
9. Er trägt einen Pullover, damit er sich nicht erkältet.
10. Sie ist immer müde, seitdem sie nicht gut schlafen kann.

13. 1. dass   6. Seit(dem)
2. Obwohl   7. Je
3. bis   8. damit
4. als ob   9. da
5. ob   10. während

14. 1. Ich weiß nicht, wo er gewohnt hat.
2. Ich weiß nicht, wie viel sie noch machen muss.
3. Ich weiß nicht, wovon er lebt.
4. Ich weiß nicht, warum er es mitbringt.
5. Ich weiß nicht, worüber er erzählen wird.

15. 1. Wo ist der Mantel, den ich gekauft habe?
2. Die Kinder spielen mit der Puppe, die er mitgebracht hat.
3. Dort steht das Flugzeug, mit dem ich abfliege.
4. Hilfst du dem Mädchen, dessen Vater gestorben ist?
5. Wo sind die Karten, die er mir geschenkt hat?

16. 1. Er ist glücklich, weil er hat gehen dürfen.
2. Ich glaube, dass er hat fragen wollen.
3. Kennst du den Mann, den ich habe schreien hören?
4. Weißt du, ob er hat arbeiten müssen?
5. Ich weiß, was er hat machen sollen.

17. 1. Denke ich daran, bestelle ich es.
2. Hätte er es gewollt, hätte ich es ihm gekauft.
3. Wird es kalt, heizen wir das Haus.
4. Willst du mitmachen, musst du dich umziehen.
5. Nehme ich es ihr weg, weint sie.

18. 1. Da ich keine Zeit hatte, konnte ich es nicht machen.
2. Als er ins Zimmer kam, spielte sie Klavier.
3. Wenn ich das Auto habe, werde ich euch besuchen.
4. Während ich krank war, musste ich viel schlafen.
5. Bevor du gehst, musst du mir helfen.

19. 1. Wir zeigten ihr die Lampe.
2. Wann hat er ihm die Karotte gegeben?
3. Ich habe ihr eine Vase geschenkt.
4. Hat er ihm das Motorrad gekauft?
5. Wer hat ihnen das Geld genommen?
6. Weißt du, ob er ihnen die Schokolade gegeben hat?

20. 1. Wir zeigten sie der Dame.
2. Wann hat er sie dem Hasen gegeben?
3. Ich habe sie meiner Tante geschenkt.
4. Hat er es seinem Sohn gekauft?
5. Wer hat es den Leuten genommen?
6. Weißt du, ob er sie den Kindern gegeben hat?

21. 1. Willst du es ihr vorlesen?
2. Wann hat er ihn ihnen gebracht?
3. Weißt du, ob er sie ihm erzählt hat?
4. Wann hat er es ihnen gezeigt?
5. Ich habe sie ihr gegeben.

22. 1. Gibt dir Peter den Ring?
2. Warum kann uns Ursula nicht besuchen?
3. Kennt ihn der Professor?
4. Hat sich Frau Schafft schon umgezogen?
5. Sie weint, weil sie die Leute auslachten.

23. 1. Er sieht sie täglich.
2. Wir geben ihnen natürlich alles zurück.
3. Sie besucht sie abends.
4. Ich habe ihn wirklich getroffen.
5. Er kann sie leider nicht abholen.

24. 1. Ich bin am Nachmittag nach Hause gekommen.
2. Wir treffen sie um zehn Uhr im Hotel.
3. Ich war jeden Tag dort.
4. Ich gehe heute Abend mit Ursel spazieren.
5. Ich bin sehr schnell in die Stadt gefahren.
6. Wir sind gestern mit dem alten Wagen ins Kino gefahren.

25. 1. Ja, wir besuchen dich morgen um drei Uhr.
2. Ja, wir fahren diesen Sommer im Juli in die Berge.
3. Ja, ich gehe nächste Woche am Mittwoch ins Theater.
4. Ja, wir fliegen heute Abend um sechs Uhr ab.
5. Ja, ich bin morgen zwischen sieben und acht Uhr zu Hause.

Verb Chart

Principal Parts of Verbs

Following is a list of the most commonly used strong and irregular verbs.

Infinitive	Simple Past	Past Participle	Third-person Singular Present	English
backen	backte (OLD FORM: buk)	gebacken	bäckt	*to bake*
beginnen	begann	begonnen		*to begin*
beißen	biss	gebissen		*to bite*
biegen	bog	gebogen		*to bend*
binden	band	gebunden		*to bind*
bitten	bat	gebeten		*to ask*
bleiben	blieb	(ist) geblieben		*to stay*
brechen	brach	gebrochen	bricht	*to break*
brennen	brannte	gebrannt		*to burn*
bringen	brachte	gebracht		*to bring*
denken	dachte	gedacht		*to think*
dürfen	durfte	gedurft	darf	*to be allowed*
essen	aß	gegessen	isst	*to eat*
fahren	fuhr	(ist) gefahren	fährt	*to go, drive*
fallen	fiel	(ist) gefallen	fällt	*to fall*
fangen	fing	gefangen	fängt	*to catch*
finden	fand	gefunden		*to find*
fliegen	flog	(ist) geflogen		*to fly*
fliehen	floh	(ist) geflohen		*to flee*
fließen	floss	(ist) geflossen		*to flow*
fressen	fraß	gefressen	frisst	*to eat* (of animals)
frieren	fror	gefroren		*to freeze, be cold*
geben	gab	gegeben	gibt	*to give*
gehen	ging	(ist) gegangen		*to go*
gewinnen	gewann	gewonnen		*to win*
graben	grub	gegraben	gräbt	*to dig*
haben	hatte	gehabt	hat	*to have*
halten	hielt	gehalten	hält	*to hold, stop*
helfen	half	geholfen	hilft	*to help*
kennen	kannte	gekannt		*to know*
kommen	kam	(ist) gekommen		*to come*
können	konnte	gekonnt	kann	*can, to be able*
lassen	ließ	gelassen	lässt	*to let, leave*
laufen	lief	(ist) gelaufen	läuft	*to run, walk*
leiden	litt	gelitten		*to suffer*
leihen	lieh	geliehen		*to loan*
lesen	las	gelesen	liest	*to read*

Infinitive	Simple Past	Past Participle	Third-person Singular Present	English
liegen	lag	gelegen		to lie
messen	maß	gemessen	misst	to measure
mögen	mochte	gemocht	mag	to like
müssen	musste	gemusst	muss	must, to have to
nehmen	nahm	genommen	nimmt	to take
nennen	nannte	genannt		to name, call
reiten	ritt	(ist) geritten		to ride
rennen	rannte	(ist) gerannt		to run
riechen	roch	gerochen		to smell
saufen	soff	gesoffen	säuft	to drink (of animals)
scheinen	schien	geschienen		to shine, seem
schießen	schoss	geschossen		to shoot
schlafen	schlief	geschlafen	schläft	to sleep
schlagen	schlug	geschlagen	schlägt	to hit
schließen	schloss	geschlossen		to close
schneiden	schnitt	geschnitten		to cut
schreiben	schrieb	geschrieben		to write
schreien	schrie	geschrien		to scream
schweigen	schwieg	geschwiegen		to be silent
schwimmen	schwamm	(ist) geschwommen		to swim
sehen	sah	gesehen	sieht	to see
sein	war	(ist) gewesen	ist	to be
senden	sandte	gesandt		to send
singen	sang	gesungen		to sing
sinken	sank	(ist) gesunken		to sink
sitzen	saß	gesessen		to sit
sollen	sollte	gesollt	soll	ought, to be supposed to
sprechen	sprach	gesprochen	spricht	to talk, speak
springen	sprang	(ist) gesprungen		to jump
stehen	stand	gestanden		to stand
stehlen	stahl	gestohlen	stiehlt	to steal
steigen	stieg	(ist) gestiegen		to climb
sterben	starb	(ist) gestorben	stirbt	to die
stinken	stank	gestunken		to stink
tragen	trug	getragen	trägt	to wear, carry
treffen	traf	getroffen	trifft	to meet
treten	trat	(ist) getreten	tritt	to step
trinken	trank	getrunken		to drink
tun	tat	getan		to do
verlieren	verlor	verloren		to lose
wachsen	wuchs	(ist) gewachsen	wächst	to grow
waschen	wusch	gewaschen	wäscht	to wash
wenden	wandte	gewandt		to turn
werden	wurde	(ist) geworden	wird	to become
werfen	warf	geworfen	wirft	to throw
wiegen	wog	gewogen		to weigh
wissen	wusste	gewusst	weiß	to know
wollen	wollte	gewollt	will	to want to
ziehen	zog	gezogen		to pull

Index